THE LAW OF FREEDOM

The Supreme Court has been at the center of great upheavals in American democracy over the last seventy years. From the end of Jim Crow to the rise of wealth-dominated national campaigns, the Court has battled over if democracy is an egalitarian collaboration to serve the good of all citizens, or a competitive struggle by private interests. In *The Law of Freedom*, Jacob Eisler questions why the Court has the moral authority to shape democracy at all. Analyzing leading cases through the lens of philosophy and social science, Eisler demonstrates how the soul of election law is a battle between two philosophical understandings of democratic freedom and popular self-rule. This remarkable book reveals that the Court's battle over democracy has shaped how Americans rule themselves, marking election law as the most dramatic judicial intervention in constitutional history.

Jacob Eisler is Associate Professor at the University of Southampton Law School where he focuses on democratic theory, election law, and corruption law. In 2023, he will join Florida State University College of Law as the James Edmund and Margaret Elizabeth Corry Professor.

The Law of Freedom

THE SUPREME COURT AND DEMOCRACY

JACOB EISLER
University of Southampton
Florida State University

CAMBRIDGE
UNIVERSITY PRESS

Shaftesbury Road, Cambridge CB2 8EA, United Kingdom

One Liberty Plaza, 20th Floor, New York, NY 10006, USA

477 Williamstown Road, Port Melbourne, VIC 3207, Australia

314–321, 3rd Floor, Plot 3, Splendor Forum, Jasola District Centre, New Delhi – 110025, India

103 Penang Road, #05–06/07, Visioncrest Commercial, Singapore 238467

Cambridge University Press is part of Cambridge University Press & Assessment, a department of the University of Cambridge.

We share the University's mission to contribute to society through the pursuit of education, learning and research at the highest international levels of excellence.

www.cambridge.org
Information on this title: www.cambridge.org/9781108419826

DOI: 10.1017/9781108304269

© Jacob Eisler 2023

This publication is in copyright. Subject to statutory exception and to the provisions of relevant collective licensing agreements, no reproduction of any part may take place without the written permission of Cambridge University Press & Assessment.

First published 2023

A catalogue record for this publication is available from the British Library

A Cataloging-in-Publication data record for this book is available from the Library of Congress

ISBN 978-1-108-41982-6 Hardback
ISBN 978-1-108-41224-7 Paperback

Cambridge University Press & Assessment has no responsibility for the persistence or accuracy of URLs for external or third-party internet websites referred to in this publication and does not guarantee that any content on such websites is, or will remain, accurate or appropriate.

For Darel, John, and George

* * *

In memory and to the honor of David C. Eisler, 1956–2023

Opposition is true Friendship.
—WB

Man errs as long as he strives.
—JWvG

All is not lost; the unconquerable Will…
—JM

Contents

Preface		*page* ix
Acknowledgments		xi
	Introduction	1
1	The Counterpopular Dilemma	29
2	Constitutionalism and the Counterpopular Dilemma	51
3	Traversing the Dilemma: Normative Struggle over Freedom	90
4	One Person, One Vote: The Triumph of Minimal Procedural Equality	117
5	Campaign Finance: Contesting Voters' Cognitive Capacities	158
6	Parties in Democracy: Facilitators or Usurpers of Popular Self-Rule?	200
7	Race and Elections: Equity of Access or Equity of Power?	244
	Conclusion: The Battle over Liberalism, the Trap of Partisanship, and the Future of Election Law	291
Selected Bibliography		313
Index		321

Preface

This book addresses a puzzle about liberal democracy and rule of law: If democracy's legitimating value is the autonomy of the people, how can an impartial court transform the terms of that autonomy?

To address that puzzle, this book does two things. First, it frames and answers the question in philosophical terms. The dignity of democratic autonomy and the justice of rule of law neutrality are both essential for legitimate liberal democracy where the people rule but individual rights are respected. But in the context of electoral process, it creates a *counterpopular dilemma*: if courts dictate terms of elections, they intrude upon the extent of democratic autonomy. The best answer cannot solve this dilemma. It can only ameliorate it. The best approach is for courts to engage in ongoing contestation over the nature of freedom, directed toward what electoral procedures will best serve popular self-rule.

Second, this book evaluates the American election law doctrine in light of this dilemma, and this answer. It shows how the Supreme Court's transformation of democratic process has consisted of a long-running, fiercely contested debate over the ideal of popular autonomy. Moreover, this debate has settled into two opposed sides: a conservative view that advances a libertarian understanding of just elections and a progressive view that advances an egalitarian understanding. Conservative libertarians see elections as a means for converting private power and position into political representation. They wish to maintain elections as a zone of private power and reject both state action and judicial interpretation that intrudes upon private power. Progressive egalitarians see elections as an expression of the mutualist aspects of a democracy that aspires toward civic equality. They wish to use the bench to advance a vision of democracy as a shared space of rule by equals.

This struggle over the meaning of freedom on the Supreme Court has shaped American democracy, and American life. The struggle reflects partisan allegiances, but it shows that deeper than the partisan divide is a philosophical dispute over the meaning of liberty. The Supreme Court's battle shows a shared commitment to the ideal of liberty, as well as how deeply the different justices understand liberty, and how much these divergent understandings mean for American democracy.

***

This book should be of interest to lawyers, social scientists, and anyone who wishes to deepen their understanding of how the Supreme Court has shaped American politics. The argument as a whole may be of the most interest to scholars of the Constitution, of elections, and of American democracy, but the individual chapters are meant to be accessible for any reader with an interest in a particular topic.

This book makes a unified argument, but it is also meant as an introduction to both the theory and doctrine of elections. It sets forth background that provides an overview that is both accessible and penetrating on questions of democracy, judicial review, and constitutionalism, as well as the four main areas of American election law doctrine: one person, one vote; campaign finance; parties in elections; and race in elections. Readers should feel comfortable dipping into single chapters – particularly those on substantive areas of election law – as they find useful.

***

The book is divided into two main parts. The first three chapters lay out the problem and answer of judicial review of elections: outlining the counterpopular dilemma of judicial review of democratic process (Chapter 1); discussing the inadequacy of existing scholarly accounts to reconcile judicial review with constituent democratic autonomy (Chapter 2); and explaining why a normative dispute over freedom on the bench is the best way through the dilemma (Chapter 3).

The next four chapters address the Supreme Court doctrine on elections through this lens: one person, one vote (Chapter 4), campaign finance (Chapter 5), parties in elections (Chapter 6), and race in elections (Chapter 7). Each describes how the given area of law is best framed as contestation over popular self-determination and the status of each in the egalitarian–libertarian debate. The Conclusion synthesizes the doctrinal dispute and its redemptive potential in election law and more broadly while noting the threats to this potential from partisan overdetermination and the increasing use of summary procedures.

***

This book is meant to answer a question and show a remarkable pattern, but also inspire and show paths for new understandings of democracy, the courts, and just liberal constitutionalism. I hope you find it useful.

Acknowledgments

The Law of Freedom was written during my time at Jesus College, University of Cambridge and Southampton Law School, University of Southampton. I am grateful to these institutions for their support, as well as to the Centre for Research in the Arts, Humanities, and Social Sciences at the University of Cambridge where early steps for developing this book were taken.

Furthermore, this book was presented at multiple conferences during its development, which were invaluable for its refinement. Ideas and a chapter draft were shared at the Roundtable on Systems Theory and Human Rights at Lancaster University (organized by Steven Wheatley and invited by Eric Heinze) and at the Southeastern Associate of Law Schools Conference in 2017 (organized by Atiba Ellis) and 2019 (organized by Josh Douglas and Franita Tolson). An entire early draft was presented at a conference at Southampton Law School in July 2019, attended by Greg Conti, Chris Macleod, Hayley Hooper, Adam Lebovitz, Sam Zeitlin, David Gurnham, Uta Kohl, Alun Gibbs, Haris Psarras, and Jonathan Havercroft, where I received invaluable advice and feedback that shaped the rest of the book. Further iterations of portions of the book were presented at the University of Georgia Law School in 2019 (facilitated by Lori Ringhand) and at the AALS Election Law Section in January 2021 (organized by Gene Mazo). A near-final version of the book was presented at the Southeastern Associate of Law Schools Conference in the summer of 2022 at a dedicated workshop, attended by Richard Briffault, Michael Kang, Jim Gardner, Benji Cover, Lori Ringhand, Pedro Gerson, Atiba Ellis, Anthony Gaughan, Josh Douglas, and Gene Mazo, who provided exceptional advice and thoughts on the book's completion, and at Southampton Law School in the fall of 2022. Certain persons, moreover, read multiple drafts of this book independently as well as at these events and provided thoughtful feedback that improved the book immensely. Exceptional thanks to Richard Briffault, Michael Kang, Jim Gardner, Eric Beerbohm, Adam Lebovitz, Jonathan Havercroft, Sam Zeitlin, and Samuli Seppänen. Thanks are also due to those who engaged at various points with particular chapters within or outside any formal context or engaged in vibrant discussion related to its ideas – thanks to

Adriaan Lanni, Uta Kohl, Helen Carr, Nick Stephanopoulos, Rick Pildes, Derek Muller, Bertrall Ross, Mike Parsons, Peter Turner, Justin DuRivage, Evan Miller, Billy Magnuson, Michael da Silva, and Joel Fleming.

As a first major project, moreover, this book reflects long-standing investment and generosity by colleagues, mentors, and teachers, whose brief mention here can only be a gesture toward my gratitude and thankfulness. During my undergraduate years at Williams College, Darel Paul, William Dudley, Michael MacDonald, Alan De Gooyer, Nicole Mellow, Philip Weinstein, David Bullwinkle, Peter Grudin, Lynn Chick, Steven Tifft, and Stephanie Solum were more generous than could be asked and helped my intellectual and personal growth immensely. John Dunn, Quentin Skinner, and Harald Wydra were monumental presences in my time as an MPhil student at Emmanuel College, Cambridge. In my time at Harvard as a law student, Adriaan Lanni, Bruce Mann, Carol Steiker, Lawrence Lessig, and Michael Klarman were mentors as well as great teachers in the law school and have continued to be so into my career. Eric Beerbohm, Eric Nelson, Nancy Rosenblum, and Richard Tuck were extraordinarily supportive during my time as a Harvard political science PhD student and into my career as an academic. My time as a clerk with the Honorable Judge Gerard Lynch was both an apex of my time in practice and forged my skills as a lawyer, with a fantastic community of fellow clerks Ana Muñoz, Antonio Haynes, and Lena Hughes. As I joined the scholarly community, Michael Kang, Richard Briffault, George Brown, Jim Gardner, Lori Ringhand, David Landau, Luis Fuentes-Rohwer, Jo Shaw, and Atiba Ellis have been particularly welcoming colleagues and mentors. During my time at Jesus College, Findlay Stark, Claire Fenton-Glynn, Michael Waibel, Geoff Parks, Ian White, Simon Deakin, Jeremy Green, Grego Conti, David Howarth, Jon Morgan, Antje du Bois-Pedain, Francois Du Bois, Jodi Gardner, Alison Young, Duncan Kelly, and Peter Turner provided the finest possible support network to begin one's scholarly career. At Southampton Law School, Uta Kohl, Brenda Hannigan, Werner Scholtz, Harry Annison, Nina Jorgensen, Helen Carr, Jan Steele, Jonathan Havercroft, and Alun Gibbs have been particularly valued colleagues.

At Cambridge University Press, Matt Gallaway's wisdom has been matched only by his patience, and Jadyn Fauconier-Herry has provided excellent support through the publishing process. Kelley Friel provided an exceptionally thoughtful, timely, and helpful close edit of the text for which I am profoundly grateful, and Mabel Newton provided a heroic effort in tracking down and updating references.

None of this would have been possible without the support of a network of friends (some of whom have also been colleagues) who have provided support, intellectual and emotional, through the writing of this text. A mention here is only a glinting reflection of the gratitude I owe to Michael Eros, Michael Stern, Alexis Medina, Billy Magnuson, Evan Miller, Tom Wolf, Teddy McGehee, Eileen Bevis, Richard Rodriguez, Chris Douglas, Alexis Saba, Emily Bryk, Gabe Katsh, Si Rutherford, Peter Leek, Tim Taylor, Vanessa Badino, Pete Deutsch, Jeff

Garland, Adam Kinon, Tommy Hutton, Joel Fleming, Meg Krench, Ben Weiner, Scott Caplan, John Playforth, Ani Ravi, Sam Flaks, Lior Ziv, Julian Feldman, Chad Priest, Rob Glass, Samuli Seppänen, Elaine and Arie Hochberg, Cesar and Luann Medina, Vanessa Maire, Serene Hung, Adam Lebovitz, Graham Clure and Maddy Dungy, Tae-Yeoun Keum, Jen Page, Aidan Finley, Yaron Peleg, Thiago Uehara, Miriam Wagner, Nita Felizardo, Edmund Gazeley, Jeff Hendrickson, and Peter Turner.

Finally, wherever I have gone, I have had a home with Sue, Dave, and Jon. Thank you, and I love you.

Introduction

The Supreme Court has transformed American democracy in the last century. It has mandated numerical equality in the process of allocating voters to districts, heralding the "reapportionment revolution." It has strictly curtailed campaign finance regulation, allowing private wealth to dominate political discourse. It has influenced the processes by which increasingly polarized parties select their candidates. It has defined the constitutional bounds within which legislatures may seek racial justice. When constituents engage in self-governance, they now do so in the shadow of a judiciary that – by institutional design and the moral requirements of the rule of law – can act with impunity, insulated from political pressure.

The federal judiciary's influence over the democratic process has created a fundamental difficulty. Democracy has unique moral legitimacy as a mode of governance because it directly allocates power over governance to its constituent members. Yet to realize legitimate self-rule, constituents must not only be able to express their will through democratic procedures (typically elections); they must also have the authority to construct and validate these procedures. When politically neutral (i.e. non-accountable) courts make decisions that impact democratic procedure, this directly challenges the foundation of democracy as autonomous constituent self-rule.

The central question – *how can non-accountable judicial authority over democratic process be legitimate?* – has been strangely neglected in academic research. The last major analysis is John Hart Ely's influential but controversial *Democracy and Distrust*, now almost half a century old.[1] Subsequent scholarly debates over constitutional interpretation have generally overlooked the unique challenges posed by this transformation of democratic process. While the rapid growth of election law studies echoes the Court's impact on democratic process, research in this field has predominantly deployed a structural lens, interrogating what electoral features and practical designs the Court should advance as a matter of policy. Mostly recently, election law scholars have described the judiciary as another player in

---

[1] Both Ely and his critics are discussed extensively in Chapter 2.

the game of power politics, asserting that election law is now overdetermined by partisan conflict on the bench.[2]

This book addresses this gap in the research in two parts. First, in Chapters 1 to 3, it presents a theoretically rigorous, philosophically informed account of the challenge posed by judicial oversight of democratic process. This challenge, which I call the *counterpopular dilemma*, is based on the confrontation between the competing normative implications of judicial oversight of electoral process. The first implication is that democracy is a uniquely legitimate mode of governance because it allocates power over governance to the constituent members of the polity. Constituent autonomy requires both (1) the authority to establish the procedures that realize that autonomy and (2) participating in those procedures. Allocating this authority to a non-accountable judiciary limits constituent autonomy and subordinates the moral role of constituent freedom to some other value. This undermines the constituency's autonomy – and with it, democracy's moral value.

However, the value of impartial and institutionally insulated review of electoral process evokes the second normative implication of judicial oversight of democracy. Without judicial review, representatives and elites can manipulate the integrity of democratic procedures for their own political gain. Leading scholars in election law have observed that political actors tend to adopt self-serving democratic procedures to entrench themselves and their allies. This practice taints the imprimatur of democratic autonomy in subsequent elections. These scholars have argued that the judiciary is uniquely positioned outside typical political struggles, and thus especially well-suited to guarantee fair elections.

No prior account of judicial review can reconcile these competing values. I argue in this book that this dilemma is intractable, but that its intractability can be crafted into a virtue. The best judicial approach is to focus on the highest value of democracy, constituent freedom, and to recognize the two conflicting mandates that the judiciary faces in serving it: recognizing the importance of constituent authority over terms of self-rule, and preventing the self-interested manipulation of processes that advance such self-rule. The tension that emerges from these two conflicting mandates cannot be eliminated. Therefore, *judicial review of election law is most legitimate when it engages in continual and unsettled struggle and debate over the principles of constituent self-rule*.

The second part of the book (Chapters 4–7) demonstrates that the Supreme Court election law doctrine is such *a philosophical struggle between egalitarian and libertarian conceptions of constituent self-rule*. Each chapter offers a coherent, theoretically rich analysis of the doctrine to illuminate this debate over constituent liberty. Chapter 4 outlines the debate surrounding the notion of one person, one vote, which consisted

---

[2] See, e.g., Nicholas O. Stephanopoulos, "The Anti-Carolene Court" (2019) 2019 *Supreme Court Review* 111, 177–180; Richard L. Hasen, "The Supreme Court's Pro-Partisanship Turn" (2020) 109 *Georgetown Law Journal* 50. As discussed in the Conclusion, while some trends in modern election law support this claim, a comprehensive analysis of the doctrine reveals that a far more nuanced philosophical conflict.

of a disagreement and then consensus regarding the principle that liberal democracy demands minimal procedural equality for constituents. Chapter 5 describes how campaign finance regulation has interrogated whether state intervention or the unequal deployment of private wealth constitutes a greater threat to individuals' ability to reason freely about politics. Chapter 6 explores how parties' constitutional status has queried whether parties, as extra-constitutional organizations including both elites and rank-and-file members, enhance or threaten constituents' capacity to achieve self-rule. Chapter 7 investigates whether the constitutional command for racial equity requires the state and the courts to advance only minimal procedural equality that disregards past racial injustices, or whether racial equity demands enhancing the representative power of groups that have suffered discrimination.

These debates highlight a singular battle over the meaning of self-rule on the bench. This struggle is between (1) an "egalitarian" understanding of liberal self-governance that prioritizes establishing a shared baseline for all constituents and (2) a "libertarian" understanding that prioritizes protecting individuals' pre-political identities from state overreach. This struggle between egalitarianism and libertarianism calls into question whether election law should aim to ensure that all constituents have a shared baseline of political influence, or whether it should protect individuals' pre-electoral endowments from being nullified in electoral competition. While this struggle crystallizes along progressive–conservative lines, it also demonstrates that a shared commitment to constituent self-rule is the foundational value of American democracy. It thereby suggests a way forward for dialogue instead of conflict even in the face of judicial polarization. Yet, as the Conclusion describes, the doctrine's long-running emphasis on freedom is threatened by a loss of a philosophical focus on freedom from both pure tribal partisanship (a risk exemplified by *Bush v. Gore*) and from an increasing reliance on summary disposition of election law questions.

That philosophical struggle offers a coherent account of election law confirms the centrality of constituent autonomy to judicial decision-making. It also offers evidence that the framing of debate over constituent autonomy best ameliorates the counterpopular dilemma. Thus, this book synthesizes the philosophical problem of judicial review of rules of democratic self-governance with a descriptive account of election law. It represents a transformative starting point for understanding election law and offers a new understanding of how the mandate of judicial constitutionalism can inform the role of courts.

STARTING PRINCIPLES: POPULAR AUTONOMY, THE COUNTERPOPULAR DILEMMA, AND RECONCILIATION THROUGH PHILOSOPHICAL DISPUTE

Democracy is a uniquely legitimate regime type – likely the *only* legitimate regime type – because it operates through self-rule by the polity's constituent members. The rulers and the ruled are the same. Such self-determination enables a normatively acceptable and politically accountable system because it satisfies the requirement that moral evaluation be attributable to free will. While this book focuses on philosophical accounts of democracy as legitimated by freedom, more popular and applied accounts also accept this as a premise.[3] Without this freedom, just conduct and the idea of the good are imposed upon individuals, crowding out the space for moral value. The relationship between morality and freedom is the root of Immanuel Kant's statement that free will is, morally, the "jewel that shines with its own light."[4] Free will is the self-justifying (or reflexive) foundation of morality. The most influential contemporary manifestation in political theory is John Rawls's lexical ordering of liberty as the highest priority.[5] This ideal is now interwoven throughout political and legal thinking on democracy.[6]

The claims that (1) free self-determination of the constituency is the essential prerequisite for democratic legitimacy, and (2) that such freedom gives democracy its unique moral standing, are polestars of the liberal democratic tradition. This root commitment to freedom stands as a starting point of consensus even where subsequent debates lead to foundational disagreements regarding liberal democracy. This is strikingly demonstrated by Barbara Fried, who quotes a statement that mirrors Rawls's lexical prioritization of liberty – and then reveals that the quote is not from Rawls or an egalitarian working in the Rawlsian tradition, but from libertarian stalwart Loren Lomasky.[7] It is this point of consensus regarding the priority of liberty that is the foundation for this book's treatment of the doctrine as a debate over the meaning of this liberalism. Even those who are not wholly committed to the premise that freedom is the foundation of legitimate democracy but are interested

---

[3] See, e.g., Francis Fukuyama, *The End of History and the Last Man* (New York: Free Press, 1992), p. 45.
[4] Immanuel Kant, *Groundwork for the Metaphysics of Morals*, Mary Gregor (trans.), ed. 4 (Cambridge: Cambridge University Press, 1998), p. 394. Chapter 3 sketches the relevant Kantian understanding of freedom, and touches upon the extensively researched relationship between morality, free will, and political justice.
[5] John Rawls, *A Theory of Justice* (Cambridge, MA: Harvard University Press, 1999).
[6] For example, according to James Fleming, "Securing Deliberative Democracy" (2004), 72 *Fordham Law Review* 1435, 1437, the *"free* exercise of [citizens'] capacity for a conception of the good" undergirds democracy (emphasis added). Richard Bellamy asserts that "we value democracy as giving effect to the status of individuals as autonomous rights-bearers." Richard Bellamy, *Political Constitutionalism: A Republican Defence of the Constitutionality of Democracy* (Cambridge: Cambridge University Press, 2009), p. 90. There are challenges to these views from a variety of perspectives. Some challenge the foundational relationship between morality and freedom. P. F. Strawson, "Freedom and Resentment" (1962) 48 *Proceedings of the British Academy* 1. More relevant to the book's legal argument, the relationship between democracy and constituent freedom has also faced a challenge from descriptive political scientists who query whether democratic governance is, as an empirical matter, a response to reasoned will. Christopher Achen and Lawrence Bartels, *Democracy for Realists* (Oxford: Princeton University Press, 2017); Martin Gilens and Benjamin I. Page, "Testing Theories of American Politics: Elites, Interest Groups, and Average Citizens" (2014) 12 *Perspectives on Politics* 564.
[7] Barbara H. Fried, "The Unwritten Theory of Justice," in Jon Mandle and David A. Reidy (eds.), *A Companion to Rawls* (Chichester: Wiley-Blackwell, 2014), p. 436.

in (and committed to) American democracy should be moved by the observation that sustained dispute over liberal freedom offers the most compelling and unified understanding of the Supreme Court doctrine.

However, political self-determination requires that the procedures that actualize it are legitimate and effective. The judiciary plays an essential role in ensuring this, particularly by advancing fair and equal implementation of process. The judiciary has an institutional obligation to protect constitutional rights, and the moral authority to advance the equal position of persons as mandated by impartial rule of law. But if the judiciary curates democratic process in fulfilling this role, it comes at the cost of constituent authority over self-governance. The anti-democratic potential of judicial review is familiar, but the problem for democratic procedure is unique.

Liberal democratic self-rule therefore faces an intrinsic tension: it must simultaneously realize and discipline the freedom of the constituency. According to Samuel Issacharoff, "successful liberal democracies…must enable majority rule while also institutionally limiting it."[8] This Janus-faced quality reflects the intrinsic tension in collective freedom: state governance must be beholden to the will of its constituent members, yet for their will to be free, even in a popularly governed state individuals must enjoy some protection from state overreach so that they may continue to make free choices (including in their contributions to collective governance).[9] Therefore, the practice of liberal democratic rule does not involve the unadulterated conversion of free will into state action. Instead, it relies on institutions and embedded practices that aggregate, channel, and modulate such will.

THE COUNTERPOPULAR DILEMMA: CRITIQUES OF JUDICIAL REVIEW AND COURTS AS GUARDIANS OF PROCESS

Some institutions and practices that contribute to democratic self-rule can be readily attributed to popular will. Some structures are established by mechanisms that are directly democratically accountable (e.g. statutes that set terms of electoral

---

[8] Samuel Issacharoff, *Fragile Democracies: Contested Power in the Era of Constitutional Courts* (Cambridge: Cambridge University Press, 2015), p. 2.
[9] Tom Ginsberg and Aziz Huq capture this weighing of the collective freedom of self-governance and the individual freedom of rights in their account of the three features of successful liberal democracies. Tom Ginsberg and Aziz Z. Huq, *How to Save a Constitutional Democracy* (Chicago: University of Chicago Press, 2019), pp. 8–14. In addition to holding sound majoritarian elections, such democracies must vigorously protect rights essential to individual political freedom (such as speech and political association) and respect the rule of law. Although I do not take a technical perspective on it, there is a fierce debate over whether the rule of law and rights protection can be considered singular and entwined – i.e. whether neutral rule-of-law adjudication *entails* certain rights protection. This debate pitches HLA Hart and his student Joseph Raz against Lon Fuller. Since neutral rule of law is necessary for the effective realization of both majority rule and the protection of individual rights, I posit that liberal democracies that realize the moral freedom of their constituents adhere to a "thicker" conception of the rule of law. However, seeking to inform how the judiciary should address intervention in democratic process by reverting to principles of legality faces the evergreen difficulty of imposing

administration), or that can be allocated at least in principle to the constituency itself, such as the widely held value of democracy within civil society. Yet the rule of law's centrality to democracy points to an institution that cannot be as neatly reconciled with the primacy of constituent self-rule – the judiciary. By advancing rule of law and protecting rights, the judiciary plays a central role in safeguarding the equal freedom of individuals whose collective will empowers democratic governance.[10] It is thus a pivotal institution for successful democracies.

The judiciary has taken on an increasingly central role in shaping American electoral process. Over the past 60 years, there has been an efflorescence of federal case law that directly impacts elections. The result – which Richard Pildes calls "the constitutionalization of democratic politics"[11] – has been a restructuring of multiple aspects of electoral practice. The Supreme Court has set in motion the reapportionment revolution of one person, one vote, innovated anti-corruption law to regulate campaign finance, and revolutionized the constitutional mandate of racial equality in voting. These interventions have structurally transformed how Americans rule themselves. Furthermore, the Court's intervention into election law has uniquely wide-ranging implications for fair governance. Decisions that identify and delineate substantive individual rights can transform specific relationships between persons and the state (e.g. *Roe v. Wade* or *Gideon v. Wainwright*). Yet in exerting constitutional authority over the conditions of collective self-rule, the Court has impacted the content and legitimacy of all other lawmaking.[12]

The judiciary's centrality to successful democracy poses a dilemma for the primacy of self-determination. A defining feature of sound judicial decision-making is judges' neutrality and independence – i.e. political non-accountability.[13] If a democracy is morally vindicated by the self-determination of its constituent members, how can the democratic processes that realize constituents' autonomy be subject to an institution that is politically non-accountable? Meaningful freedom requires that an outside entity does not overdetermine constituent power over politics (here, the

substantive values upon a free electorate, and thus constricting freedom in a context that is meant to enable it; this parallels the difficulties facing general accounts of constitutional review.

[10] This role is seminally articulated in Tom Bingham, *The Rule of Law* (London: Allen Lane, 2010). There is debate over how extensively rule of law advances substantive justice. See, e.g., Joseph Raz, "The Rule of Law and Its Virtue" in *The Authority of Law: Essays on Law and Morality* (ed. 2) (Oxford: Oxford University Press, 2009).

[11] Richard H. Pildes, "The Constitutionalization of Democratic Politics" (2004) 118 *Harvard Law Review* 29, at 42.

[12] Scholars have typically been critical of the rights-based understanding of judicial oversight of electoral practice. For a seminal example, see Pamela S. Karlan and Daryl J. Levinson, "Why Voting is Different" (1996) 84 *California Law Review* 1201.

[13] The nature of this independence is widely debated, but its presence as a quality of sound judging is incontrovertible. See, e.g., Lon L. Fuller, *The Morality of Law* (New Haven: Yale University Press, 1964); Irving R. Kaufman, "The Essence of Judicial Independence" (1980) 80 *Columbia Law Review* 671; Cass R. Sunstein, "Neutrality in Constitutional Law" (1992) 92 *Columbia Law Review* 1; Paul Gowder, "The Rule of Law and Equality" (2013) 32 *Law and Philosophy* 565.

processes by which constituents make political choices).[14] Just as a person who votes under physical threat would not be said to act freely, a polity that has processes of decision-making exogenously imposed upon it cannot be considered wholly free.

The role of judicial review in shaping elections therefore poses what I call the *counterpopular dilemma*: the integrity of self-rule requires sound (i.e. neutral) judicial advancement of equal constituent right in the democratic process; yet such intervention (at least when it assumes the structurally transformative forms of modern American election law) contravenes the principle that authority over processes of self-rule must come from the constituents rather than an external, non-accountable source. While some have argued that action initiated by the judiciary is not necessarily less democratic than activities undertaken by accountable institutions (such as legislatures), Alexander Bickel's classical formulation still resonates: "nothing can finally deprecate the central function that is assigned ... to the electoral process; nor can it be denied that the policymaking power of representative institutions, born of the electoral process, is the distinguishing characteristic of the system. Judicial review works counter to this characteristic."[15]

Judicial restructuring of electoral process poses this problem in two linked ways. First, the purpose of elections is to convert constituent will into governance and thereby attribute state power to constituents. While in many contexts judicial intervention can be vindicated as preventing majoritarian mistreatment of vulnerable individuals or marginal groups, this is insufficient to justify judicial intervention in elections. *Democracy has moral power because it realizes the collective will; interdicting that will cannot be a guiding principle of democratic procedure.* Second, as a structural corollary to this normative problem, where the judiciary redefines democratic process, it redefines the baseline of the collective will. Any subsequent expression of popular will – including future electoral rules – following judicial reworking of electoral process reflects this judicially curated version of popular will. Since this

---

[14] Jeremy Waldron calls this general capacity, "on which large numbers of right-bearers act together to control and govern their common affairs" "the right of rights." Jeremy Waldron, *Law and Disagreement* (Oxford: Oxford University Press, 1999), pp. 232–3. He notes on p. 283 that the principle of democratic self-determination demands that when "a common decision is needed, every man and woman in the society has the right to participate on equal terms in the resolution of that disagreement," thus showing the continued expression of equality as a facet of freedom. This book focuses on the unique demands of democratic process as such a type of common decision. Waldron's analysis captures the political–philosophical basis of the problem of non-accountable authoritative determination, which Chapter 2 of this book invokes through Isaiah Berlin's description of a "temple of Sarastro" where a concept of freedom is imposed upon others. *Two Concepts of Liberty* in Henry Hardy (ed.), *Liberty* (Oxford: Oxford University Press, 2002). In the most metaphysical sense, this generates a deep debate regarding the nature of free will, particularly the question of compatibilism. See R. Jay Wallace, *Responsibility and the Moral Sentiments* (Cambridge: Harvard University Press, 1994).

[15] Alexander M. Bickel, *The Least Dangerous Branch* (New Haven: Yale University Press, 1986), p. 19. Some prominent responses to Bickel have sought to minimize the tension posed by of rule of law rights enforcement by denigrating the significant of elections generally. In Chapter 2 I revisit this issue in my discussion of Dworkin and Eisgruber.

externally determined version influences any later expressions of popular autonomy, this recursively disrupts the foundation of democracy as legitimated by (and expressing) such autonomy.

As discussed in Chapter 1, the counterpopular dilemma operates at the intersection of two contemporary bodies of scholarship. This book is one of the first scholarly accounts to bring these bodies of literature into meaningful dialogue. On the one hand, scholars skeptical of judicial review – led by Jeremy Waldron, Samuel Moyn, Ran Hirschl, and Richard Bellamy – have argued that assertive judicial review of legislation intrudes upon constituent freedom and fails to generate superior outcomes in governance. On the other hand, American election law scholars – led by Samuel Issacharoff, Richard Pildes, and Pamela Karlan – identify judicial review, and specifically its non-accountable nature, as essential to prevent self-serving legislative manipulation of democratic process. These scholars observe that legislators often exploit electoral legislation to consolidate power, with the result that democratic process no longer accurately expresses popular will. This approach posits that courts should robustly intervene to benefit the moral integrity and representative efficacy of democracy.

The counterpopular dilemma emerges from the cogency of each position: judicial review of electoral process simultaneously contravenes and sustains constituent autonomy. It contravenes this autonomy by empowering an institution defined by the characteristic (according to its advocates as well as its critics) of lacking political accountability. This implies that popular autonomy is only legitimate if it is subordinated to conditions imposed by an external entity thereby undermining the primacy of popular self-determination. Yet without such non-accountable oversight, the integrity of democratic process is vulnerable to manipulation by political elites. Judges' non-accountability insulates them from such manipulation, and thereby sustains constituent autonomy.

BETWEEN CONSTITUENT SELF-RULE AND DEMOCRATIC INTEGRITY

The lack of engagement between election law scholarship and criticism of judicial review exposes a gap in the literature. Since the normative difficulty of non-accountable authority is heightened in the context of electoral process, the casual willingness of election law scholars to treat robust, substantive judicial intervention as acceptable is especially puzzling. Prior election law research has presumed that robust judicial intervention is valid, rather than adequately investigating who has moral authority to guarantee constituent autonomy.

There are three immediate and decisive answers to this dilemma. The first is that some existing account vindicates judicial intervention in democratic process. However, as Chapter 2 shows, none of the three leading candidates – interpretivism–deliberativism; originalism–contractarianism; and structuralist instrumentalism – offers a satisfactory explanation. All three accounts contravene democratic autonomy by suggesting that judges have the moral knowledge or political authority to impose conditions of self-rule, and can define democracy in a manner lexically prior to constituent freedom. Examining these accounts highlights the unique onus of justifying authority over democratic process. Even if these scholarly explanations can vindicate robust judicial review of "typical" substantive policymaking, such explanations are insufficient to justify courts' oversight of constituent self-rule. This is because democratic process is the functional incarnation of the foundational value of democracy, autonomy of the constituents who make up the polity. Non-accountable authority over such autonomy cannot be vindicated by referencing some other value or feature of the constitutional order, because this suggests there is a higher priority than autonomy. Such an account would contravene popular autonomy as the legitimizing principle of democracy. The normativity of such a claim collapses in on itself.

The second possibility would be that the virtues of judicial intervention in electoral process reveal a strict limit to popular authority over democratic self-rule. Yet this runs contrary to the principle that democracy is legitimized by constituent self-determination (the premise of this book). It, would suggest a "hard" juristocratic limit to Waldron's wry claim that "everything is up for grabs in a democracy."[16] While some defenders of robust constitutional review accept the proposition that democratic autonomy has such limitations,[17] it contradicts the bedrock principle that democratic procedure is morally redeemed by self-determination of the people.

This might suggest the third possibility, that judicial review skeptics have identified a profound reason to condemn judicial intervention in electoral process. Yet skepticism of judicial review of election law faces two complexities of its own. The first is that the doctrinal legacy of judicial intervention has been, by any reasonable assessment, thoroughly mixed (discussed further in Chapters 4–7, which examine the substantive law). Some judicial interventions into democratic process seem, by both popular acclaim and according to any reasonable account of legitimate democratic process, desirable. The interdiction of legislative malapportionment by *Baker v. Carr* and the prohibition of gross racial discrimination in *Gomillion v. Lightfoot* and the White Primaries cases would likely be the most widely accepted examples. Some non-interventions, particularly those related to failures to prevent racial discrimination – *Giles v. Harris* and *Lassiter v. Northampton* – illustrate the Court's unequivocal failure to make democratic process available to all. Other interventions have mixed (*Buckley v. Valeo*) or fiercely disputed (*Shelby County v. Holder*) reputations, as do some non-interventions (*Rucho v. Common Cause*). Still, others lack a clear basis in sound judicial reasoning (*Bush v. Gore*). Thus, it is difficult to

---

[16] Waldron, "Law and Disagreement," p. 303.
[17] See Theunis Roux, "In Defence of Empirical Entanglement: The Methodological Flaw in Waldron's Case against Judicial Review," in Ron Levy, Hoi Kong, Graeme Orr, and Jeff King (eds.), *Cambridge Handbook of Deliberative Constitutionalism* (Cambridge: Cambridge University Press, 2018), pp. 210–211 (invoking Issacharoff's empirical observations about the value of constitutional courts in challenging Waldron's implicit radical view of political constitutionalism).

conclude that judicial intervention in electoral process leads to juristocracy and non-intervention to more autonomous democracy. Rather, and in line with the instrumental focus of election law scholarship, the impact of judicial intervention depends on its substance and legacy. The second is that understanding (and seeking to limit) judicial review by understanding politics purely as a matter of power faces a problem of moral justification. If the judicial review critique is fully accepted and the judiciary excluded from shaping democracy, it leaves the structures of political process wholly subject to political outcomes themselves (a condition critics might well accept as a desirable). However, this means that democracy is wholly determined by power itself – which, when unconstrained, can impair the legitimacy of a democracy, from malapportionment to racial oppression.[18] Such an account neglects to explain how the characteristic moral legitimacy of democracy can be sustained over time.

Thus, the counterpopular dilemma is profoundly sharpened by simultaneously recognizing (1) that the moral premise of democracy, autonomy of the constituent members of the society, should be realized as directly as possible; and (2) that the abuse of power can undermine the legitimacy of democratic process, creating at a plausible argument for expansive judicial review, and clearly vindicating some specific instances of it. Many attempts to vindicate judicial review based on democratic autonomy only do so by ultimately claiming autonomy-displacing moral authority or eroding the rule of law neutrality that makes judicial review an effective check on power.[19] In this book, I explore whether there is an account that retains the legitimizing primacy of democratic autonomy *and* the normative virtues (neutrality, rule of law) and practical inevitably of judicial review.

RECONCILING THE COUNTERPOPULAR DILEMMA: PHILOSOPHICAL DISPUTE OVER FREEDOM

This dilemma seems insoluble. Democratic procedure must be self-determined to be morally valid, yet aspects of it must be exogenously determined to preserve democratic integrity. Any solution to this conflict must balance or sustain, rather than

---

[18] The instrumental scholarship is of course directed toward such power-based understandings of elections, and part of its own rich tradition traceable to Schumpeter. Samuel Issacharoff and Richard H. Pildes, "Politics as Markets: Partisan Lockups of the Democratic Process" (1998) 50 *Stanford Law Review* 643, 649–650 (discussing Anthony Downs and public choice theory).

[19] Eisgruber advances a variation of this by arguing that federal courts are to some degree accountable and thus democratically legitimate. Christopher L. Eisgruber, *Constitutional Self-Government* (Cambridge: Harvard University Press, 2001) p. 60. Lafont maintains that citizen participation in litigation makes judicial review valid. Christine Lafont, *Democracy without Shortcuts: A Participatory Conception of Deliberative Democracy* (Oxford: Oxford University Press, 2020) p. 225. Yet even if describing constituents (who have political attributes such as power and self-interest) as involved in litigation makes judicial review more procedurally democratic, introducing this democratic procedure based on citizen participation erodes the 'strong' neutrality that makes judicial review an effective check on the deployment of democratic power over process.

eliminate, the tension between the moral primacy of constituent self-determination and the structural necessity of judicial review.

The incontrovertible guiding principle is that if the touchstone of democratic process is free constituent self-rule, judicial oversight of democratic process must advance this self-rule. Judicial reasoning must aspire to return power over self-rule to constituents, rather than impose settled values on them. *Legitimate judicial decision-making regarding democratic process consists of ongoing, unsettled struggle over the principles of freedom that best advance autonomous constituent self-rule.*

The three central features of this account – its philosophical nature, its substantive focus on freedom, and its tendency toward unsettlement – are necessary to balance the primacy of constituent self-rule and the benefits of neutral judicial adjudication of election law. By continuously wrestling with the appropriate terms of constituent self-rule – within individual cases, across cases within doctrinal domains, and across the field through the grand debate between egalitarianism and libertarianism – judges protect freedom without imposing terms of autonomy.[20]

As analysis of substantive law demonstrates, the established domains of election law doctrine can be characterized as disputes over appropriate terms of popular self-rule. Furthermore, these domain-level debates can be consolidated into a field-unifying account. This unified account has two distinct facets. The normative facet observes that struggle over principles of popular autonomy is the best way to reconcile judicial review of electoral process with democratic self-rule. The descriptive facet queries, does the case law reflect such a struggle? Reviewing the substantive law precisely reveals such a debate. Thus, at the level of abstraction that explores the *aspiration* of judicial reasoning, the case law on electoral procedure is vindicated. This does not speak to the practical wisdom of the judges' substantive positions. These are questions of policy, the subject of most election law scholarship. Nor does it suggest that the bench has set out to philosophically interrogate freedom in the development of election law. Rather, in their interrogation of electoral process, the justices have inevitably engaged in philosophical debates about the nature of self-rule. Recognizing that the Court has converged on a mode of analysis that explicates the nature of constituent freedom best redeems judicial review of democratic process.

If judicial review of election law consists of ongoing struggle over autonomy, it weakens the moral authority of any specific account that courts might advance.

---

[20] While this book remains agnostic regarding this question, various theorists have proposed substantive bounds on the views that judges advance in this contestation. For example, Pildes synthesizes and contextualizes Robert Dahl's view that organic political realities will ensure the Supreme Court never deviates too far from the views of the electorate as a whole. Richard H. Pildes, "Is the Supreme Court a 'Majoritarian' Institution?" (2011) 2010 *The Supreme Court Review* 103, 104. Eisgruber characterizes judges as actors who are still in some sense accountable to a broader political order. Eisgruber, "Constitutional Self-Government," p. 60. Lafont observes how judges judge in response to citizen appeals for justice Lafont, "Democracy without Shortcuts," p. 225.

However, this less decisive understanding of the authority of judicial decisions is a virtue in the context of democratic process for two reasons. First, it offers an account of judicial review that is more capacious, because it incorporates multiple conceptions of freedom and legal decision-making (e.g. interpretivism or originalism). Since the legitimating quality of judicial review is service to constituent autonomy, sound judicial reasoning will include the possibility that different legal decision-making methods could effectively serve this autonomy.

The second reason is that this contestatory approach lends itself to perpetual unsettlement in legal debates, rather than the march toward resolution that typically characterizes common law.[21] A debate over election law is not settled until there is unequivocal consensus over the question at issue, and the relevant feature is considered a necessary precondition of self-rule. The only domain of election law that has reached such status is the minimum procedural egalitarianism of one person, one vote; all others are marked by prolonged dispute. Chapters 4–7 unpack this quality, but pairings from each area reveal the instability of election law: *Austin v. Michigan Chamber of Commerce* and *Citizens United v. Federal Election Commission*; *Davis v. Bandemer* and *Rucho v. Common Cause*; *South Carolina v. Katzenbach* and *Shelby County v. Holder*.[22] According to this interpretation, judges are merely debating what the norms *might* be, and making a weaker claim regarding how a society should be ordered. The traditional decisiveness of legal reasoning is sacrificed to maintain the priority of democratic autonomy.

The nature of such morally laden judicial decision-making bears some initial resemblance to other prevalent accounts of judicial reasoning, especially the interpretivist–deliberativist approach championed by Ronald Dworkin and Rawls. However, it is worth noting the difference. Rawls famously calls judges "exemplars of public reason."[23] Dworkin echoes this in his characterization of the ideal judge as a "Hercules" who coherently integrates a society's values. Normative contestation over freedom does not ascribe to judges the same special moral power. In this sense, it is somewhat closer to the participatory view of constitutionalism described by Christine Lafont and Larry Kramer. Yet unlike the participatory view, normative debate emphasizes the structural position of judges as insulated from normal political competition (the very feature emphasized by election law scholars). This

---

[21] The nature of such lawmaking is itself the subject of prolonged debate, but typical accounts that treat it as a substantively meaningful endeavor rather than fundamentally arbitrary or overdetermined (eg, critical realist or postmodern accounts) identify some degree of resolution in distinctly legal reasoning. Consider, for example, H. L. A Hart's account in *The Concept of Law*, 2nd ed. (Oxford: Oxford University Press, 1997) and Ronald Dworkin's in *Law's Empire* (Cambridge: Harvard University Press, 1986).

[22] In this regard, the level of moral authority asserted by decisions as a debate over freedom is weaker than interpretivist–deliberativist understandings, because the bench is not assumed to synthesize all of the community's moral norms. Dworkin, "Law's Empire," p. 225.

[23] John Rawls, *Political Liberalism* (New York: Columbia University Press, 1996).

insulation does not give them any special moral authority of reasoning; it is only a structural feature that enables rule of law neutrality. The reasoning that judges (albeit professionalized by training and position) undertake is closer in character to the reasoning of rank-and-file constituents (at least in accounts of democracy that look to constituent rationality to legitimize democracy).[24]

That judges' philosophical engagement is not especially sharply differentiated from that of other constituent members of the polity may seem to lean into the teeth of the anti-judicial review critique. After all, if their reasoning has no special claim to moral insight, why should judges have authority if they are non-accountable? One aspect of the answer is the institutionalist explanation, which is largely based on the courts' position relative to representative manipulation and majoritarian abuses. Federal judges stand outside this electoral process, so they have both the disinterest towards and the insulation from direct political effects to opine on it. Yet this feature highlights the difficulty described in Chapter 1 of simply thwarting popular will and defying freedom. Therefore, if non-accountable judges who lack special moral insight are to have legitimate authority, their decision-making must have two further features: it must be characterized by ongoing philosophical reflection (rather than decisive resolution based on a claim of moral authority) and a continual focus on realizing constituent freedom. Ongoing philosophical engagement destabilizes the imposition of judicial views, and a focus on freedom ensures that the institutional role remains focused on empowering the constituency. As the Conclusion demonstrates through an analysis of *Bush v. Gore*, when these features are lost, the result is dire: the Court becomes a locus of a pure partisan power struggle, and its institutional claim to authority is lost.

PHILOSOPHICAL CONTESTATION IN THE DOCTRINE

Most of this book is dedicated to analyzing election law doctrine. Synthesizing the substance of contestation across the doctrine yields a remarkable insight: the case law comprises a grand debate over liberalism. Rawls most prominently advanced the *egalitarian* view of liberalism, which seeks to afford all constituents equal opportunity to freely participate in self-rule *as members of a public collective*. That is, the crux of constituent autonomy is freedom *within* shared political life. In this egalitarian view, the law should advance rules and structures that achieve parity among constituents. The *libertarian* alternative, put forward by Robert Nozick, is derived from the principle that the highest priority is protecting individuals from state intrusion. According to libertarians, freedom is best served by ensuring constituent autonomy *outside* political life. The libertarian view advances rules and structures

---

[24] Such constituent reasoning is pervasive in deliberative democracy; a feature of entry in contractarianism (seminally captured by Hobbes's rationality-based account of entry into the state); and a critical part of the argument that support the design of public institutions in Rawlsian contractualism.

that insulate constituents' *private endowments* from state interference. Libertarians wish to prevent rules that would "smooth" differences between members by reallocating or redistributing resources. It is therefore focused on safeguarding persons' extra-political identities and capabilities.

Despite the divergence between these views, they share some essential features. Both prioritize autonomy as the moral linchpin of politics, even if they profoundly disagree about what this means or how it should be achieved. Further, both claim analytic validity by grounding themselves in the commitments that freely reasoning – that is to say, morally rational – constituents of a polity would make when organizing a society. As such, both approaches harmonize with the commitments of this book and the value of democratic process.

The egalitarian–libertarian debate offers a redemptive account of the election law doctrine. Academics widely treat election law as brutally partisan, pitting progressives against conservatives. Yet this philosophical framing shows that the Supreme Court's modern election law doctrine can be described as a prolonged interrogation of constituent freedom. The debate tracks the partisan divide: progressives are egalitarian, and conservatives are libertarian. But rather than being a simplistic battle overdetermined by partisanship (except when sound legal reasoning is deficient, as in *Bush v. Gore*), the doctrine reflects the Court's legitimate role as a locus of debate over the nature of freedom.

EGALITARIANISM VERSUS LIBERTARIANISM IN ELECTORAL PROCEDURE

The egalitarian–libertarian struggle applies to justice generally, and manifests most familiarly in the debate over the distribution of economic resources. Yet it can also be applied to conceptualize competing approaches and values related to electoral design. Which approach to liberalism is considered morally legitimate will affect what conclusions the Court reaches when adjudicating election law disputes. From the egalitarian perspective, all constituents must have *a shared baseline of electoral power* to satisfy legitimate collective self-governance. To achieve this shared baseline, state intervention in the practices and conditions of elections is permissible (or obligatory). According to the egalitarian view, electoral self-rule demands some "levelling" of inequities that influence electoral access and outcomes. This resonates with various progressive understandings of democracy, such as Dworkin's claim that liberty and equality can be reconciled by redefining political liberty to require some measure of participant equality.[25] The legislature may advance this baseline, in which case the Court should be restrained in striking down legislation that might otherwise be constitutionally suspect because the legislation's impact upon

---

[25] Ronald Dworkin, *Sovereign Virtue: The Theory and Practice of Equality* (Cambridge: Harvard University Press, 2002), pp. 126–7.

self-governance is valid.[26] Examples of such reasoning include the views that campaign finance legislation should be treated leniently, and that racial categorizations that aid oppressed minorities should pass constitutional muster. The judiciary can also advance the baseline through robust and innovative constitutional interpretation, such as the one person, one vote rule and prohibiting partisan gerrymandering.

The other (typically conservative) position is that constituent autonomy demands minimal interference with the *pre-existing endowments and allocations of power* that constituents bring to electoral competition. According to this view, the legitimate outcome of democratic process converts pre-existing allocations of power into electoral outcomes. The legitimacy of the political process derives from its ability to translate individuals' pre-electoral identities into governance, even if these identities seem arbitrary or unequal. This typically expresses suspicion of state overreach. More fundamentally, libertarianism holds that individuals should be able to bring whatever resources they have prior to politics *into* politics, echoing the Nozickean view of the minimal state. Subsequently, the judiciary should protect (or avoid upsetting) the "natural" outcomes of political power struggles. The Court should avoid interfering with legislative action that instantiates such struggle, such as when a victorious group aggrandizes itself through partisan districting as a "victory bonus."[27] Such outcomes are a function of pre-existing private power (here, the coordinating capacity of the successful coalition) that is the legitimate driver of democratic struggle. The Court is also obligated to protect pre-existing endowments when legislative action seeks to "neutralize" existing private power allocations. Prior to the decontestation of one person, one vote, this view resisted judicial correction of malapportionment. The libertarian position also considers state regulation of campaign finance to interfere with personal liberty, even though unregulated campaign finance introduces economic inequality into the political ecosystem. Perhaps most controversially, this view prohibits legislatures from seeking to correct entrenched racial oppression by favoring minorities. Instead it demands formalist race blindness in legislation, which leaves intact existing inequities of power that stem from racial discrimination.

This conflict between egalitarianism and liberalism resonates with established competing accounts of democracy. A complete account would comprehensively and decisively integrate constituent freedom and democratic process (a project beyond the scope of this book). The most obvious approach would be contractarian in nature. Yet even without exhaustively tracing the path of consent from personal freedom to collective governance, the contractarian account points to the salient feature of the debate: entry into state governance transmutes, rather than destroys,

---

[26] This ideal is already present in American constitutional thinking, albeit typically partitioned by traditional doctrinal understandings. For one compelling instance oriented around the First Amendment, see Cass R. Sunstein, *Democracy and the Problem of Free Speech* (New York: The Free Press, 1995), p. 37.
[27] Peter H. Schuck, "The Thickest Thicket: Partisan Gerrymandering and Judicial Regulation of Politics" (1987) 87 *Columbia Law Review* 1325, 1350.

the individual's moral autonomy. The seminal issue is the legitimate character of this transmutation when people participate in collective self-governance, and accept the constraints of collective life in exchange for a share in setting those constraints. The egalitarian view emphasizes that entry into the state, if legitimate and fair, must guarantee all participants some minimum of recognition and power in public governance. This view can be linked to several strands of political thought,[28] but its most direct analog is the Rawlsian view that individuals should, when conceiving of the ideal state, seek fair terms of cooperation for *all* constituents rather than pursue their own self-interest.[29] The mutualist aspect of collective self-government, and the regard that each participant should have for others, is given normative priority. While participation in a shared project necessarily involves some restraint of individual conduct, the determinative question is how the shared quality of the project can be emancipatory, and how the public character of collective governance can enhance the autonomy of all participants.

The libertarian view emphasizes what is sacrificed by participation in collective governance and seeks to insulate individuals from collective domination when they participate in public life. In this view, democracy is a means of coordinating individuals' pre-political capacities. Its legitimate scope must intrude on these capacities no more than is necessary to achieve group coordination. This idea that legitimate self-rule does no more than serve and protect the private interests of the participants in politics resonates most strongly with the Nozickean ideal of a minimally intrusive state. The corresponding approach to democratic practice defines the process as an agonistic struggle over constituent interests,[30] in which any mandated equal standing

---

[28] Influential examples include Dworkin's defense of "partnership democracy" in *Freedom's Law: The Moral Reading of the American Constitution* (Cambridge: Harvard University Press, 1997), Pettit's conception of republicanism in his eponymous volume, and G. A. Cohen's ideal of deliberation as rationally motivated consensus. See Joshua Cohen, "Deliberation and Democratic Legitimacy," in Alan Hamlin and Philip Pettit (eds.), *The Good Polity: Normative Analysis of the State* (New York: Blackwell, 1989), pp. 17, 23. Practical manifestations of such public-minded governance are described by, inter alia, Bruce Ackerman and James S. Fishkin, "Deliberation Day," in James S. Fishkin and Peter Laslett (eds.), *Debating Deliberative Democracy* (New Jersey: Wiley-Blackwell, 2003); James Fishkin and Cynthia Farrar, "Deliberative Polling: From Experiment to Community Resource," in John Gastil and Peter Levine (eds.), *The Deliberative Democracy Handbook* (San Francisco: Jossey Bass, 2005), pp. 68–79; Robert E. Goodin and John S. Dryzek, "Deliberative Impacts: The Macro-Political Uptake of Mini-Publics" (2006) 94 *Politics & Society* 219; and Archon Fung and Erik Olin Wright, "Deepening Democracy: Innovations in Empowered Participatory Governance" (2001) 29 *Politics & Society* 5, 25–9. However, since the Court is not engaging in whole cloth democratic design but resolving particular disputes, even the progressive justices do not advance conceptions with this level of particularity.

[29] Rawls conceives of this in different ways – through the veil of ignorance, but more broadly through the concept of public reason. See Rawls, "Political Liberalism," pp. 77–80.

[30] Ian Shapiro, *The State of Democratic Theory* (Princeton: Princeton University Press, 2003), p. 51 (discussing Joseph Schumpeter's account of elite-led democracy). More recent competitive-democratic theorists are less dismissive of non-elite political participation. See, e.g., Robert A. Dahl, *Preface to Democratic Theory* (Chicago: The University of Chicago Press, 2006), pp. 67–71 (defining democracy as a competitive preference-realizing infrastructure); Adam Przeworski, "Minimalist Conception of Democracy: A Defense," in Ian Shapiro and Casiano Hacker-Cordon (eds.),

of participants is instrumental. The purpose of equality in the libertarian view is to ensure that governance remains fair enough so that constituents retain sufficient self-interested incentive to continue participating. The defining moral commitment of this view is private liberty, and state legitimacy is primarily defined by its minimal intrusiveness upon this liberty. Considering the realities of the issues in election law, however, reveals a quite devastating foundational, Marxist-flavored critique of this view. Many of the existing inequities that adherents of this view would argue are personal and pre-political to justify their insulation from the state only exist because of a past unjust application of state power. This ranges from the role of the state in enforcing (and, through some policies, exacerbating) economic inequality to the legacy of state-endorsed slavery and other discriminatory policies in generating racial inequities. However, the libertarian view still elevates the status of the pre-electoral individual at a given moment, despite the problematic origins of such endowments.

THE DOCTRINE AS A STRUGGLE OVER LIBERALISM

The individual disputes that comprise the election law doctrine do not address lofty theories of liberalism and democracy; the bench resolves specific questions. Yet synthesized across domains, the doctrine reveals a long-standing debate over what practices best advance constituent autonomy. This debate is best framed as an expression of the egalitarian–libertarian divide. The following table provides an overview of this pattern; Chapters 4–7 establish the pattern in detail.

Domain of Law	Egalitarian Position	Libertarian Position
One person, one vote	Procedural egalitarianism limits legislative malapportionment	No judicial authority to correct malapportionment
Campaign finance	Wealth in campaigns threatens popular autonomy	The state has no authority to limit the use of private wealth in campaigns
Parties in elections	Parties must be constrained as a prospective usurper of constituent political power	Parties are facultative intermediaries that should not be subject to judicial constraint
Race in elections	Racial equity requires affording minorities substantive representative power	Racial equity only requires formally equivalent access to political process
Synthesis	*Constituent autonomy requires the constitutional advancement of the egalitarian status of each participant in politics*	*Constituent autonomy is best advanced by ensuring each participant can unrestrictedly deploy existing resources and endowments*

Democracy's Value (Cambridge: Cambridge University Press, 1999), pp. 23, 31. The same limit regarding the judicial application of the philosophical conception applies here.

The characteristic questions in each domain inform this framework. The watershed topic of modern election law, whether malapportionment is justiciable, raises the threshold issue: are elections, the gateway between private life and public power, subject to norms of public justice (specifically, a norm of minimum procedural equality)? As Chapter 4 shows, contrary to prevalent scholarly views, *Baker v. Carr* was not an unheralded novelty. Rather it was the culmination of a fierce debate that occurred in the first half of the twentieth century over if constitutional justice mandated minimum political equality in voting power. Justices debated whether fair electoral procedure requires basic equality in constituent power, or if it simply translates existing power allocations – expressed in malapportionment through the drawing of district lines – into governance. The ultimately triumphant egalitarian view identifies citizenship as a locus of mutualism and equal participation; the latter libertarian view considers elections as no more than a mechanism for expressing private allocations of power. One person, one vote exemplifies the philosophical struggle over the nature of self-rule that marks modern election law.

The campaign finance jurisprudence has struggled over this question in the context of preference formation. The Court has debated whether the private power of wealth or the public power of state regulation comprises a greater threat to the capacity of voters to reason freely. Wealth is distributed unequally in a capitalist system, creating a fundamental tension with norms of democratic equality. The egalitarian view is that the infiltration of unequal private power into reasoning about governance is a form of coercion, and that regulatory efforts to limit such infiltration benefit constituent freedom. Libertarians, however, believe the state and its capacity to limit speech is the great threat to free reasoning. The underlying question speaks to the nature of moral autonomy at the core of the egalitarian-libertarian divide: is the essence of legitimate democracy participation in shared governance of equals, or is it advancement of private interests through the arena of politics? *Buckley v. Valeo* sought to dodge this question by using the anti-corruption rationale to assess the legality of campaign finance regulation. Ever since, the nature of corruption has served as an oblique battlefield for contrasting egalitarian and libertarian views of the impact of wealth on constituent decision-making.

The appropriate legal treatment of parties in elections requires interrogating an aspect of democratic governance that sits on the public–private divide. Parties act as an intermediary coordinating mechanism, serving as a conduit for constituents' interests and formalizing the coalitions that constituents form. As such, they are structurally extra-constitutional, yet intimately intertwined with the apparatus of the state. The doctrine is driven by the question of whether parties and their influence are subject to the mutualist norms of egalitarianism, or if they can unabashedly deploy private power to coordinate governance. The White Primaries cases prohibited blatantly racist party practice and established that the Court will subject even private organizations to certain minimal normative standards. Yet the still-contentious issue of partisan gerrymandering demonstrates that it remains unsettled whether party influence in its pure form is beholden to norms of public-mindedness. The egalitarian view is that the influence of partisanship must conform to values of mutualist other-regardingness, whereas the libertarian view sees the impact of partisanship as a private matter, beyond the scope of judicial monitoring. Since partisan gerrymandering reinforces private power via state action, this raises the question of whether private actors may exploit the levers of governance itself to enhance their own power.

The status of race in elections seems to present the easiest legal question. The Fifteenth Amendment declares the right to vote may not be denied on the basis of race, and the equal protection clause of the Fourteenth Amendment prohibits discrimination. Yet race has elicited exceptionally complex struggles regarding the minimum the Constitution requires and the maximum the Constitution permits to achieve racial equity. The question of the minimum is posed by how the Court should interpret these constitutional amendments to require electoral process to satisfy racial equity. The question of the maximum emerges from Congress's efforts to end Jim Crow laws with the Voting Rights Act, which has forced the Court to assess how far legislation may go in seeking substantive political equality. In struggling with this nexus of questions, egalitarians aspire to ensure all constituents, including disadvantaged minorities, have an equitable opportunity to attain political power. Conversely libertarians limit the legitimate scope of racial justice to be formal race-blindness, and nothing more. The question is most directly presented by enforcement of equal protection clause. Its mandate for equality can be interpreted as requiring only formal equality of political access, which prohibits state action that aims to benefit disadvantaged minorities. In the alternate, the equal protection clause can also be interpreted as a substantive command to empower minorities to give them an equitable political status. The former, formalist view is libertarian in nature, for it identifies the legitimate extent of the constitutional mandate as ensuring that all constituents have bare access to process. The latter, substantive position is egalitarian, requiring equitable power in governance for disadvantaged racial groups. Underlying the debate on race is a fundamental expression of the egalitarian–libertarian divide: may (or must) constituents' power be "levelled" to ensure free self-rule, or should the expression of private power-holding in politics be insulated from state rebalancing? Racial discrimination has been the source of grave injustice in American history, giving the debate particular exigency.

In each of these areas, the decisive question is whether elections should robustly guarantee political engagement on equal terms, or if elections should just mirror private power. The arc of the doctrine reveals a struggle between two competing conceptions of the moral aim of democracy, and how the modulation of personal freedom through elections can preserve that freedom. This confirms that the Court is undertaking a philosophical endeavor, rather than merely technical lawmaking. Furthermore, the doctrine itself reveals novel features of these two competing approaches to liberal democracy, specifically how they inform the aspects of substantive democratic procedure that the Court has addressed. This analytic move reverses the typical direction of analysis (using a theory to make sense of doctrine) by looking to the doctrine to provide guidance regarding the best theory.

This unifying account of the Supreme Court's engagement with processes of democratic governance can be incorporated into a rich tradition of debating norms of liberal self-rule. Since judicial influence over democratic self-governance is best validated as a struggle over the terms of liberal self-rule, this account legitimizes the Court's modern foray into elections. While the Court's holdings may often be controversial and their policy effects subject to harsh critique, as a philosophical matter it is undertaking its appropriate role as a participant in the development of reasoned public values.

CONTEXT AND BACKGROUND ASSUMPTIONS

The book applies an analytically novel method to the conventional topics of election law: one person, one vote, campaign finance, parties in elections, and race in elections. This topical compartmentalization tracks the Supreme Court's own use of precedent as well as other discipline-spanning accounts.[31] I choose not to recategorize conceptual problems or constitutional rights (such as describing vote dilution as a problem that spans partisan gerrymandering and some race-in-elections topics)[32] or to use new higher-order principles to reframe the field.[33]

This project also makes two other commitments about the nature of the law. First, I take the content and reasoning of judicial opinions at face value. I accept opinions as justices' sincere attempts to resolve legal problems, rather than a (deliberate or unconscious) smokescreen for some ulterior goal. Many prominent methods in US legal scholarship, most notably critical legal studies and related approaches, treat judicial lawmaking as a raw exercise of power.[34] Such a cynical view of judging may find this project's philosophical treatment of doctrine naïve (though the tension that drives this book – judges' power to impact political freedom – is broadly sympathetic

---

[31] Leading election law casebooks provide the clearest scholarly indication that this division is conventional. Samuel Issacharoff, Pamela Karlan, Richard H. Pildes, Nathan Persily, and Franita Tolson, *The Law of Democracy: Legal Structure of the Political Process*, 6th ed. (New York: Foundation Press, 2022); Daniel Hays Lowenstein, Richard L. Hasen, Daniel P. Tokaji, and Nicholas Stephanopoulos, *Election Law: Cases and Materials*, 7th ed. (Durham: Carolina Academic Press, 2022); and James Gardner and Guy-Uriel Charles, *Election Law in the American Political System*, 2nd ed. (Springfield, Mo: Aspen Publishing, 2018).

[32] See, e.g., Issacharoff et al., "The Law of Democracy," p. 609 (grouping racial and partisan vote dilution).

[33] Examples include Daryl J. Levinson, "Rights and Votes" (2012) 121 *Yale Law Journal* 1286 (approaching the problem of majoritarianism through the competing ideas of rights and votes) and Bertrall L. Ross, "Democracy and Renewed Distrust: Equal Protection and the Evolving Judicial Conception of Politics" (2013) 101 *California Law Review* 1565 (tracking the change in election law to a switch from pluralism to public choice theory).

[34] For an exhaustive summary of critical legal studies, see Amna A. Akbar, Sameer M. Ashar, and Jocelyn Simonson, "Movement Law" (2021) 73 *Stanford Law Review* 821, 833.

to critical legal studies). Yet there is value in establishing the philosophical unity of the doctrinal narrative even for those who find earnest treatment of the case law unconvincing. If nothing else, it demonstrates cohesion in judges' instrumental manipulation of the concept of freedom.

In a second commitment, this book brackets the broadest debates over how constitutional interpretation could potentially transform democratic process. Instead it focuses on the decisions the Supreme Court has made, and the major lines of precedent that have emerged. This allows me to treat the established doctrine of election law as a comprehensive corpus of law. In one sense, this is the methodological commitment of a legal scholar: I analyze the case law that exists, not the case law that could exist. But insofar as this book is a *philosophical* treatment of election law, it is necessary to consider how the Constitution could plausibly, even defensibly, be applied to alter democracy in other, perhaps far more radical ways. Why should the prospective capability of the judicial constitutional review to transform other aspects of democratic process not also be part of such a philosophical account, even where the Court has declined to do so or not even considered to do so? In other words, why not address the roads neither taken nor considered by the Court in a philosophical account of judge-made election law, if constitutional interpretation could potentially enable going down such roads?

In one sense I accept some level of settled linguistic communication as fixed, and identify philosophical contestation as emerging from constitutional instructions where the core provision could plausibly have open or unsettled linguistic meaning (the meaning of "equal" in the equal protection clause, the meaning of "free speech" in the First Amendment). Michael Perry characterizes some constitutional clauses as "initially intelligible."[35] If language can perform even the minimum expected communicative function, there is no dispute over such clauses' meaning. For example, the semantic and practical meaning of lowering the voting age from 21 to 18 in the 26th Amendment is "initially intelligible," as there appears to be no "space" in which there can be rational (let alone reasonable) disagreement. Some seemingly "initially intelligible" provisions are quite controversial, such as the procedure of selecting a president through the Electoral College (which Kate Shaw describes as "a profoundly dangerous institution"),[36] but their unequivocally clear expression in the Constitution has prevented them from being the basis for judicial disagreement. If, however, as Richard Fallon notes, in "hard cases, the meaning of statutory and constitutional provisions does not exist as a matter of prelegal linguistic fact... [when] standards are indeterminate – as they typically are in disputed

---

[35] Michael J. Perry, *The Constitution in the Courts: Law or Politics?* (Oxford: Oxford University Press, 1994), p. 38. Perry is no apologist for originalism – he spends much of the rest of the text explaining why the determinacy that originalists attribute to history is, in fact, absent. His criticisms share much with those brought by Fallon.

[36] Kate Shaw, "'A Mystifying and Distorting Factor': The Electoral College and American Democracy" (2022) 120 *Michigan Law Review* 1285.

cases – legal interpreters must make constrained normative choices."[37] Whether Fallon and those sympathetic to him are correct is a general problem of jurisprudence, and scholars have offered a number of responses.[38] But if Fallon is correct, there is no reason why the 26th Amendment or the status of the Electoral College could not hypothetically also be ripe, legitimate grounds for judicial contestation (and intervention), if there was a normative case for contesting their meaning. In sum, the intrinsic ambiguity in the legal meaning of words could make every decision a prospective matter of moral struggle – the very quality that this book attributes to the election law doctrine.

The universal potential for normative struggle in constitutional interpretation could subsume this book's specific claim that election law doctrine is best framed as a philosophical dispute over freedom. Such a broader theory would conveniently explain why Supreme Court's election law jurisprudence has been marked by dramatic shifts in constitutional interpretation that cannot be fully informed by textual interpretation (e.g. the ramifications of the equal protection clause, the implications of federalism for the preclearance requirement, and the definition of speech in campaign finance).

Yet there are reasons that I can only brief sketch to be somewhat more constrained in approaching election law, and deal only with the existing doctrine as the locus of normative contestation. The first is that judicial intervention differentiates between reasonable interpretation of the constitutional command and pure normative reasoning. The most relevant manifestation of this are the limits of the doctrine. If every act of constitutional interpretation is wholly normative, why have some "initially intelligible" constitutional instructions (such as the Electoral College) not become grounds for judicial contestation? A comprehensive account of election law as unconstrained normativity would explain what is contested (e.g. the ramifications

---

[37] Richard H. Fallon, Jr., "The Meaning of Legal 'Meaning' and its Implications for Theories of Legal Interpretation" (2015) 82 *The University of Chicago Law Review* 1236, 1307. Dworkin raises a similar problem with his attack on "plain fact" legal interpretation, "Law's Empire", pp. 7–8. In a form more particularized to originalism-textualism, Eisgruber does the same, with his observation regarding the ambiguity of language, "Constitutional Self-Government", pp. 31–2.

[38] William Baude and Stephen Sachs, "The Law of Interpretation" (2017) 130 *Harvard Law Review* 1079 have challenged Fallon's conclusion by arguing that lawyers have their own tools, internal to the practice of law, for resolving unclear meaning. More particular to the challenges leveraged against originalism such as those raised by Eisgruber and Dworkin, Michael McConnell has argued that a principle of "interpretive fidelity" is enough to allow original meaning (in the sense of original understanding) to guide judges in applying the constitution. See Ronald Dworkin, "Fidelity as Integrity" (1997) 65 *Fordham Law Review* 1269, 1285. See also Michael W. McConnell, "Originalism and the Desegregation Decisions" (1995) 81 *Virginia Law Review* 947, 1101. ("It is widely agreed among originalists that the intentions or understandings of the framers regarding a specific issue, while informative, are not ultimately authoritative, for it is their understanding of the constitutional principles embodied in the constitutional provision – not their analysis of a particular legal phenomenon – that is controlling.") Others have suggested that original meaning of the constitution has an initial power that decays and is supplanted over time. David A. Strauss, "Does the Constitution Mean What it Says?" (2015) 129 *Harvard Law Review* 1, 57.

of the equal protection clause) and what is not (e.g., the legal status of the Electoral College). Yet, in the absence of any constraint or guidance from constitutional text or the boundary between interpretation and normative reasoning, such an approach to judging would rapidly become a general enquiry into the appropriate arrangement of liberal constitutional democracy. This is a project of a very different scope from what the Court has done and such a project does not, at least in the same way as this book, recognize the unique position that judges have in shaping democracy. That the Court has declined to intervene on such broad terms may be the most dramatic, albeit subtle, expression of the bench's awareness of the counterpopular dilemma. In short, the boundaries of the doctrine suggests that the Court operates under some institutional interpretive constraint.

In its approach, particularly its emphasis on existing doctrine, this book declines (as has the Court, apparently) to pursue such a general democratic architecture. Instead, the Court has addressed a narrower range of questions ostensibly elicited by its constitutional remit. Likewise, this book focuses on the constitutional questions that the Supreme Court treats, in the doctrine itself, as constitutionally debatable. This limitation does not reject the value of integrating a comprehensive theory of constitutional interpretation into a theory of liberal democracy. Rather, it expresses a methodological commitment to a close analysis of the actual doctrine, and the idea that the highest-level boundaries of that doctrine are not arbitrary. This accepts, implicitly, that there is some logic in the topics that have become of normative debate on the bench. I do not reject of the importance of topics that have not so become a matter of judicial interest. But I do posit that the array of topics the Court has addressed is not so random or arbitrary as to render the patterns in the case law meaningless. Such a postulation makes is arguably supported by the fact that a coherent normative debate can be extracted from the narrower range of topics of democratic design that have been of interest to the Court.

Accordingly, this book does not advance a complete theory of democratic organization. This would be a vastly broader project even in terms of pure politics and require engaging with a dizzying array of normative and descriptive questions. This is a book about the judge-made law of democratic process.[39] Two examples at different levels of abstraction illustrate the types of issues this book brackets, except as elicited by the case law. A high-level example is the threat of majoritarian tyranny, a concern that has existed as long as America itself,[40] and has continued to animate constitutional and political analysis.[41] To take a much more granular example, the Senate has come under increasing criticism that it lacks democratic legitimacy,

---

[39] It thus can be differentiated from a general account of voting rights, exemplified by Alexander Keyssar's *The Right to Vote* (New York: Basic Books, 2009).

[40] James Madison, "The Federalist No. 51," *Independent Journal*, June 2, 1788.

[41] This is most extensively addressed in contemporary scholarship by the structuralists described in Chapter 2. Majority tyranny has also inspired an interest in alternative voting methods such as ranked-choice voting, Borda counting, and so forth, most visible in Maine. See, e.g., Jack

despite being a bedrock of the constitutional structure.[42] How to address majority tyranny and the validity of the Senate are both fundamental to assessing legitimate democratic structure in America, yet are beyond the scope of this book except insofar as the questions are activated by doctrine. Thus, the question of majoritarian tyranny – which is often invoked to explain constitutional reasoning – at times becomes relevant to the book. Yet the question of the Senate's validity – which lies beyond the Court's attention – does not.

More broadly, democracy is rooted in social and cultural practices as much as in political and constitutional institutions. By focusing on judicial review of electoral rules advanced by the legislature, this text operates within the tradition of what Pippa Norris calls "rational choice institutionalism," which emphasizes the importance of formal electoral rules to a democracy's functioning and success.[43] Rational choice institutionalism assigns direct and independent significance to electoral rules for the behavior of actors (voters, elites, parties) and the operation of the democratic system as a whole, and predicts "major consequences" from formal changes to the rules.[44] However, this does not mean that I overlook the fact that a host of cultural and social factors are a prerequisite of functional democratic society. It would be, as Ernest Gellner notes, "naïve" to suggest that the successful realization of democracy can be detached from "institutional and cultural" conditions.[45] Yet the book focuses on what Nicholas Stephanopoulos calls one aspect of "law's domain"[46] – the legally established (by legislature, judiciary, and constitution) aspects of democracy.

BOOK OUTLINE

The book is divided into two main parts. In the first part, three chapters lay out the theoretical problem by outlining the counterpopular dilemma of judicial review of democratic process (Chapter 1), discussing the inability of existing scholarly accounts to reconcile judicial review with constituent democratic autonomy (Chapter 2), and explaining why a normative dispute over freedom on the bench is the best way out of the dilemma (Chapter 3). In the second part, four chapters examine how normative struggle offers the best description of election case law: one

---

Santucci, "Maine Ranked-Choice Voting as a Case of Electoral-System Change" (2018) 54 *Representation* 297.

[42] See, e.g., Aaron-Andrew P. Bruhl, "The Senate: Out of Order?" (2011) 43 *Connecticut Law Review* 1041.

[43] Pippa Norris, *Electoral Engineering: Voting Rules and Political Behaviour* (Cambridge: Cambridge University Press, 2012).

[44] *Ibid.*, p. 8. Norris calls the alternative understanding "cultural modernization theory," which asserts that embedded social norms and habits are decisive. *Ibid.*, p. 16.

[45] Ernest Gellner, *Civil Society and its Discontents* (London: Hamish Hamilton, 1994), p. 186.

[46] Nicholas O. Stephanopoulos, "Elections and Alignment," (2014) 114 *Columbia Law Review* 283, 360.

person, one vote (Chapter 4), campaign finance (Chapter 5), parties in elections (Chapter 6), and race in elections (Chapter 7). Each describes how the given area of law is best framed as contestation over popular self-determination and expresses the egalitarian–libertarian debate. The Conclusion synthesizes the doctrinal dispute and its redemptive potential in election law while noting the threats to this potential from partisan overdetermination and the increasing use of summary procedures.

Chapter 1: The Counterpopular Dilemma

The first chapter defines the counterpopular dilemma that the judiciary faces when, as an rights-protecting, state-limiting institution, it opines on the collective expression of political freedom. Through such decisions, politically non-accountable courts constrain the realization of democratic will. This creates a fundamental tension between the democracy as constituent self-determination and judicial authority. Prevalent scholarly accounts have observed either harm or the benefit of judicial review for popular self-rule, but few have sought to reconcile them as this chapter proposes to do.

Chapter 2: Constitutionalism and the Counterpopular Dilemma

This chapter evaluates whether scholarly accounts of constitutionalism can reconcile judicial review with popular autonomy. It evaluates three prevalent approaches: the Constitution as a fixed contract among the people (originalism) that includes judicial review; the Constitution as a fluid, dynamic instrument (living constitutionalism); and instrumental institutionalist understandings of the judiciary as an intercessor in power politics. Despite their insights and merits, none of these accounts can explain how the power to shape democratic process can be legitimately allocated to a non-accountable, apolitical actor.

Chapter 3: Traversing the Dilemma: Normative Struggle over Freedom

Even if the tension between democratic autonomy and judicial authority over democratic process cannot be wholly resolved, courts must adopt a coherent approach to election law. The best way to balance this dilemma incorporates, rather than resolves or eliminates, an unsettling reality about democratic self-rule: the values and realization of freedom are necessarily subject to intractable struggle over freedom's moral realization. Conceiving of judicial review of election law as a dispute over self-rule answers the challenge at three levels: it (1) explains how nonaccountable courts can play a legitimate role in democratic self-determination; (2) allows courts to opine on self-rule without overdetermining the meaning of freedom, and undermining its moral value; and (3) offers the best account of the doctrine as a battle over the meaning of liberalism.

Chapter 4: One Person, One Vote: The Triumph of Minimal Procedural Equality

Chapter 4 examines the most stable point in election law – one person, one vote – to establish that judicial contestation over freedom has been present since the inception of modern election law. While one person, one vote is now a settled and widely accepted principle, its reception has been far more varied. Jurists and activists have celebrated it as advancing democratic fairness and breaking the rural stranglehold over state legislatures. Yet scholars have criticized it as lacking a clear or logical foundation. This chapter challenges that orthodox critique by reconstructing the legal development and moral significance of one person, one vote. The idea that malapportionment is unconstitutional, far from being woven from whole cloth in *Baker v. Carr*, was fiercely debated in the first half of the twentieth century. The further development of the one person, one vote doctrine demonstrates how a requirement of equipopulous districting advances minimum standards of legitimate democratic self-rule. As a normative innovation, one person, one vote represents the culmination of a hard-fought debate, the conclusion of which established that minimal procedural egalitarianism is morally obligatory in a liberal democracy.

Chapter 5: Campaign Finance: Contesting Voters' Cognitive Capacities

Since *Buckley v. Valeo*, campaign finance jurisprudence has been riven by the constitutional limits on the regulation of funded campaign speech. The Court's enduring but unpopular compromise that contributions can be limited to prevent corruption but that limiting expenditures infringes the right to free speech has been assailed as both too restrictive and insufficiently robust. The debate is typically cast as a straightforward question of which source of power is the greater threat: plutocratic wealth that can corrupt leaders, or a state that can oppress its members? However, this intractable conflict can be unified by considering democratic governance as a matter of constituent self-rule. Both private and state influence over campaign media operate to influence voters. The critical question is what poses the greater threat to voter cognition and preference development. This observation, framed by a Kantian understanding of free will, captures the true core of the judicial debates – contestation over what circumstances pose the greatest threat to the autonomy of voter preference formation.

Chapter 6: Parties in Democracy: Facilitators or Usurpers of Popular Self-Rule?

Political parties serve as intermediaries in converting individual political will into collective state governance. When they do so, are they servants or usurpers of constituent self-governance? While the White Primaries cases established that parties are prohibited from effecting unequivocally illegitimate (i.e. racially exclusionary) democratic practice, when party affiliation activates constitutional scrutiny generally remains unsettled. In areas such as state control over primary design and ballot access, the Court has struggled with parties' dual status as public utilities and private organizations. This dual character has led to fierce debate regarding when the Court should police parties, and when they should be protected. The partisan gerrymandering litigation, despite its unhelpful framing as a matter of justiciability, epitomizes the debate over whether party coordination's centrality to American governance facilitates or threatens popular self-rule.

Chapter 7: Race and Elections: Equity of Access or Equity of Power?

Given America's history of racial oppression, addressing racial discrimination has been the Court's most sustained and transformative engagement with democratic governance. The Reconstruction Amendments' explicit prohibition of racial discrimination explicitly legitimizes judicial advancement of racial equity in elections. Relying on this mandate during the Civil Rights era, the Court struck down explicitly discriminatory laws (and permitted robust congressional action) with little controversy. However, in recent decades, the Court has been fiercely divided over the substance of racial equity. Conservatives have argued that racial equity requires only ensuring formal equality in terms of race, a view that prohibits legislation that benefits minorities to correct past injustice and interprets the Reconstruction Amendments to advance a minimalist conception of equality. Progressives, conversely, have argued for a substantive constitutional conception of racial equity that would permit laws and rulings that benefit disadvantaged minorities and afford them substantive political power. The chapter first observes the unity of this debate across doctrinal topics – applying the equal protection clause to districting, Section 2 of the Voting Rights Act, and the preclearance requirement of the Voting Rights Act. It then explores which philosophical conception of racial equity (as formally equal access or as equitable substantive power) better sustains the legitimacy of collective self-rule by analogizing it to Rawls's and Nozick's famous debate over the fair allocation of resources.

Conclusion: The Battle over Liberalism, the Trap of Partisanship, and the Future of Election Law

This chapter unifies the doctrinal domains by mapping each onto the egalitarian–libertarian conflict. Does autonomous constituent self-rule require that all constituents enjoy a baseline substantive opportunity to contribute to public governance? Or does it require non-interference with the application of private power and constituent preferences (including by powerful or privileged constituents who exert disproportionate influence over politics)? This debate, while often fiercely partisan, falls within a liberal tradition that prizes autonomy of both the person and the body politic.

The Conclusion also describes the threats to normative engagement with democracy that could delegitimize the coexistence of judicial review and constituent autonomy. First, there is the threat, most clearly apparent in *Bush v. Gore*, that purely tribal partisanship will dictate election law outcomes, and displace rather than frame the debate over freedom. Second, increasing judicial reliance on summary modes of disposition in election law disputes further erodes the opportunities for philosophical engagement. These two trends could compound each other, threatening to turn the Court into an institution that illegitimately overdetermines electoral outcomes on the basis of the justices' partisan allegiances without even the pretense of adequate moral reflection.

The book ends on twinned notes of hope and caution. Despite the political nature of election law, the doctrine has shown the potential to serve as a forum where the appropriate terms of democratic freedom are assayed. The Court has, with this legacy, avoided the unitary, concerted displacement of popular will. Philosophizing on the bench, while often disdained, is the preferable mode of intervention in democratic governance. The Conclusion ends by observing how such moral engagement, while most immediately exigent and relevant in judicial review of democracy governance, could structure analysis of constitutional law and judicial review more generally.

1

The Counterpopular Dilemma

This chapter considers the fundamental challenge facing judicial review of election law, which I call the *counterpopular dilemma*. Election law serves the fundamental democratic principle of constituent *control over governance*, while judicial review seeks to ensure that all constituents enjoy fundamental rights that offer *protection from governance*. The tension between state-legitimating elections and state-limiting rights assumes a paradoxical form when rights protection shapes electoral procedure. As judicial constitutional review of electoral procedure becomes increasingly robust, constituent autonomy can only be realized on terms acceptable to an institution with authority that is not directly accountable to the people. This raises a basic dilemma for democratic legitimacy: Free self-rule is the defining characteristic of democracy, but if a non-accountable entity oversees the terms of democratic process, how can this requirement be satisfied?

1.1 THE UNIQUE QUALITIES OF ELECTORAL PROCESS AS A SUBJECT OF JUDICIAL REVIEW: THE COUNTERPOPULAR DILEMMA

How can popular will be identified as coming from a particular source without a preexisting theory of democratic legitimacy that intrudes upon popular self-determination? Elections are held precisely to convert constituent will into political action. The structural core of the law of electoral procedure cannot entail thwarting popular will, nor can counterpopular judicial review be justified by adverting to some higher norm.

1.1.1 *The Uniqueness of Election Law: Reflexively Shaping Democratic Autonomy*

If democracy is a valid mode of governance because it expresses constituents' free will, constituents must have control over state decision-making processes. Imposing the government's coercive power on constituents is morally acceptable only because it can be attributed to the collective will of the polity, and is legitimate only to the extent that it incorporates the will (i.e., the consent) of the individuals subject to its coercion. How members of a polity legitimize state action to which they might object as individuals is a great puzzle of democracy. Explanations frequently advance contractarian postulations of a higher order or lexically prior authorization of collective self-governance. This tradition is deep, and its legacy stretches from Thomas Hobbes to Jean-Jacques Rousseau to John Rawls; its technical features lie beyond the scope of this project.

The moral legitimacy of state action derives from the ability of the democratic process to translate constituent will into collective decisions. Personal freedom alone can ultimately vindicate state coercion. But state action necessarily intrudes upon personal freedom; thus state action must be legitimated by being traced back to personal freedom. Democratic process must therefore convert individual will into collective choices, and then into state action. Rawls's seminal description of liberal democracy identifies the root of this challenge as expressing "the power of free *and equal* citizens as a collective body."[1] For constituents of a democracy to rule themselves freely, their liberty to act – whether in a personal capacity or to control the state – must be balanced against and limited by other individuals' capacity to act freely.[2] Because such constraint serves the ultimate shared freedom of the members of a state (all of whom must accept the terms of political rule), it can, in principle, be made compatible with freedom as the highest value of democracy.

Elections are pivotal to realize and balance these two bedrock values of freedom and equality. They are the dominant mechanism by which constituents of an established democratic polity realize their capacity for political autonomy as equal members.[3] By converting individual preferences into unified governance, elections legitimate democracy as collective self-rule. They are also the mechanism via which government is responsive to popular preferences, and those who deploy coercive state power are held accountable. While a significant body of scholarship attacks the efficacy of electoral control[4] and offers alternative modes of

---

[1] John Rawls, *Political Liberalism* (New York: Columbia University Press, 1996), p. 136 (emphasis added).

[2] According to the Rawlsian tradition, basic liberties extend until they intrude upon others' liberties. John Rawls, *A Theory of Justice* (Cambridge: Harvard University Press, 1999), p. 266; Frank I. Michelman, "Justice as Fairness, Legitimacy, and the Question of Judicial Review: A Comment" (2004) 72 *Fordham Law Review* 1407, 1410.

[3] As seminal a source as the Universal Declaration of Human Rights states: "The will of the people shall be the basis of the authority of government; this will shall be expressed in periodic and genuine elections," Article 21, Section 3. As John Hart Ely notes in *Democracy and Distrust: A Theory of Judicial Review* (Cambridge: Harvard University Press, 1980), pp. 5–6, "We have as a society from the beginning, and now almost instinctively, accepted the notion that a representative democracy must be our form of government."

[4] This tradition can be traced back to Joseph Schumpeter and, in a slightly less cynical mold, Anthony Downs, with a recent and particularly cutting incarnation being Christopher H. Achen and Larry M. Bartels, *Democracy for Realists: Why Elections Do Not Produce Responsive Government* (Princeton: Princeton University Press, 2017).

social organization,[5] these challenges are notable because they challenge the near-axiomatic orthodoxy that elections legitimate and manifest popular self-rule.

The significance of elections to democratic governance shifts attention to the rules and laws by which such self-rule is achieved. The law of elections is a unique domain of law because it acts as a gateway to most substantive policymaking: coercive state power is presumably deployed with constituents' consent. In this regard, the law of democratic process infiltrates all other areas of substantive governance. Lawmaking by accountable government actors will only have been undertaken because democratic process authorized them to do so. The law of democratic process not only speaks to its own substantive content, it also shapes all later substantive government action. An electoral law that appears to be marginal or trivial can have vastly magnified effects because of how it inflects the authorization of representatives, and what substantive lawmaking they undertake.

Furthermore, the law of elections is uniquely recursive. Pathological, autonomy-infringing rules potentially act as rachets that will yield future pathologies. The governmental authority to determine policy includes the power to set the conditions of later elections. Election law not only shapes the terms of all substantive policymaking undertaken by those authorized by an election; it also has the capacity to shape the terms of later elections.[6] Given how central elections are to the realization of democratic autonomy, power over election law is, in effect, the ability to determine the contours of democratic autonomy.

The example of a voter ID law (requiring formal photographic identification in order to vote) illustrates the subtle yet tectonic force of election law.[7] Such laws impose a relatively trivial administrative requirement on individual voters and have less immediate impact on those affected than, for instance, a law that dictates whether a person receives state-provided health care or racially segregated education. But since voter ID laws can modulate which groups participate in elections (and have disproportionate effects on vulnerable groups such as the poor)[8] and the results of these elections determine substantive policy, such laws will indirectly

---

[5] The most prevalent such approaches are those associated with empowered deliberative democratic approaches that advocate for deliberative polling, mini-publics, and the like.

[6] In this respect, the governmental control of elections' significance may be analogized to the boundary problem, which describes how the capacity to determine who is a member of a democracy gives the state the capacity to define the substantial identity of a democracy. Frederick G. Whelan, "Prologue: Democratic Theory and the Boundary Problem" (1983) 25 *Liberal Democracy* 13. Many thanks to Eric Beerbohm for this observation.

[7] See Spencer Overton, "Voter Identification" (2007) 105 *Michigan Law Review* 631; Benjamin Highton, "Voter Identification Laws and Turnout in the United States" (2017) 20 *Annual Review of Political Science* 149 (executing a study broadly in line with Overton's suggestion). For the older version of such suppression, see Richard L. Hasen, *The Supreme Court and Election Law: Judging Equality from Baker v. Carr to Bush v. Gore* (New York: New York University Press, 2003), pp. 21–31 (discussing *Lassiter* and similar cases).

[8] Bertrall L. Ross II and Douglas M. Spencer, "Voter Suppression: Campaign Mobilization and the Effective Disenfranchisement of the Poor" (2019) 114 *Northwestern University Law Review* 633.

determine these substantive policies. Moreover, representatives elected with unjust voter ID laws in place will not only have the opportunity to pass substantive policy that does not accurately reflect the legitimate will of the constituency; they can also reshape future electoral processes (e.g., by further modifying ballot access or redrawing district lines). This can create a vicious (or, in the case of legitimate and just election law, virtuous) spiral. A just voter ID policy (as part of just electoral process generally) is therefore a necessary precondition for ensuring such substantive policies are just (insofar as legitimately reflecting the franchise's will is a requirement of justice) and protecting democracy in the future.

Those who have done the most to shape election law have recognized its significance. Chief Justice Earl Warren celebrated *Baker v. Carr* as the finest achievement of his time leading the Court, preferring it even to the explicitly anti-discriminatory landmark of *Brown v. Board of Education*. Underlying Warren's reasoning was the identification of a virtuous spiral that would follow from ensuring that every person in a polity has equal power in voting by eliminating malapportionment in districting. It seems difficult to deny that *Brown* had greater first-order policy effects: it transformed the daily lives of millions in perpetuity. *Baker* merely demanded a set of seemingly quotidian administrative changes in how voters are allocated to districts. Yet Warren speculated that this shift in voter allocation might have made citizen control over policy more just and accountable and might have yielded a political solution to school segregation that would have made *Brown* unnecessary.[9] He recognized the transformative potential of election law not only to shift substantive policy but also to alter the very terms of democracy. Where the baseline terms of electoral process are made to conform to the conditions of democratic legitimacy, sound policy will follow. And in the wake of such sound policy and legitimate electoral process, further legitimate electoral process will follow.

1.2 JUDICIAL REVIEW OF DEMOCRATIC PROCESS: CONTRASTING THE PRIMACY OF AUTONOMY WITH THE VALUE OF PRACTICAL EFFICACY

Legal scholars recognize the significance of authority over electoral process, and the power of courts to shape democracy. This has manifested in two contrasting ways in the scholarship. One scholarly approach emphasizes the practical ramifications of sound electoral procedure. Focused on the possibility that the functioning of democratic practice can substantively go awry due to either deep-rooted social factors or manipulation by elites, these scholars have queried how the judiciary can ensure the structural integrity of electoral process. As the field has matured, this instrumentalism has become increasingly hard-edged.

---

[9] Luis Fuentes-Rohwer and Charles Guy-Uriel, "Reynolds Reconsidered" (2015) 67 *Alabama Law Review* 485.

Yet the judiciary's capacity to robustly intervene in electoral process is distinguished by lying *outside* democratic accountability. Because judges (or at least federal judges) need not worry about their own electoral fates, they are safely insulated from political pressure and can advance what they identify as sound or legitimate democratic process without fear of reprisal. Yet this very insulation of judges from democratic accountability has inspired another body of scholarship. Democracy is defined by constituent autonomy. Given the recursive character of electoral process, this constituent autonomy is nowhere more crucial than in having the power to shape elections. If a constituency has the terms of its own self-rule dictated to it, this suggests that autonomy is not the driving feature of democracy. This observation has led some critics to suggest judicial review is itself undemocratic.

These two approaches diverge in the normative priority they afford to democratic process and, correspondingly, the appropriate means of curating it. Election law scholars have expressed little normative concern that the Court might reshape popular autonomy, so long as the Court proposes sound democratic procedures. Critics of judicial review are first and foremost concerned that the meaning of democratic autonomy will be imposed from outside accountable political process and lose its moral primacy. The contrast between these two approaches highlights the fundamental dilemma facing the judiciary's role in shaping election law.

1.2.1 *American Election Law Scholarship: From Rights toward a Substantive Democratic Theory*

The emergence of the field of election law has been marked by three features: (1) recognition of the pathologies that can afflict democratic structures from social and political circumstances, and courts' ability to address them; (2) the need to move beyond a rights-based understanding to achieve this; and (3) the proposal that the next logical step is for the judiciary to adopt substantive understandings of democratic process.

This pattern frequently recurs in the field's founding scholarship. Samuel Issacharoff and Richard Pildes argue that a major threat to the integrity of democratic process is the capacity of representatives and elites to entrench themselves through self-aggrandizing processes.[10] They maintain that courts are uniquely positioned outside the political process to break up such entrenchment, but to do so effectively, courts must move beyond an individual rights-based understanding to a substantive conception of democracy as forged in competition. Pildes has written further about the worldwide transformation of democracy effected by the judiciary and of the potential of such interventions to address the pathologies of mature

---

[10] Samuel Issacharoff and Richard H. Pildes, "Politics as Markets: Partisan Lockups of the Democratic Process" (1998) 50 *Stanford Law Review* 643.

democracy, such as "disaffection, distrust, and disillusionment."[11] Yet he argues that rigidly traditional rights enforcement, instead of more systemic consideration of sound democratic practice, can impair rather than encourage innovation and adaptation in democratic design.[12] Issacharoff and Pamela Karlan have argued that the rights-based approach to campaign finance advanced by *Buckley v. Valeo* has had perverse impacts on the dynamics of political fundraising. Identifying equality through neutralization of money in politics as an unrealistic option, they advocate for institutionally sensitive disclosure-based reforms, rather than a rigidly rights-bound approach.[13] Heather Gerken takes a more theoretical approach. She has examined a diverse array of topics and argued that the Supreme Court's election law jurisprudence lacks sufficiently clear normative vision or commitments, even though its rights-based enforcement has had clear structural effects. She has urged the Court to develop "mid-level intermediary theories" to achieve moral and structural coherence.[14]

The most recent development in the field has been even more unabashedly instrumental: empirical and quantitative outcomes have become a touchstone of legal analysis.[15] Nicholas Stephanopoulos advocated for – and led the litigation to apply – a quantitative measure he calls the efficiency gap to assess the egregiousness of partisan gerrymanders.[16] He also has offered a system-wide analysis that concludes the aim of election law is to correct "misalignment between the preferences of voters and the preferences of their elected representatives."[17] Stephanopoulos's focus on achieving particular outcomes and offering a mid-level theory to support them exemplifies the dominant trends in election law scholarship.

Prevalent scholarly approaches have accurately exposed the odd fit in the framing of judicial review of elections through rights (though, as this book's thesis shows, the

---

[11] Richard H. Pildes, "The Supreme Court, 2003 Term: The Constitutionalization of Democratic Politics" (2004) 118 *Harvard Law Review* 25, 37.

[12] Pildes, "Constitutionalization of Democratic Politics," 97 gives a specific example regarding the interpretation of Section 5 (*Georgia v. Ashcroft*) of the VRA discussed in Chapter 7.

[13] Samuel Issacharoff and Pamela S. Karlan, "The Hydraulics of Campaign Finance Reform" (1999) 77 *Texas Law Review* 1705, 1711, 1734.

[14] Heather K. Gerken, "The Costs and Causes of Minimalism in Voting Cases: *Baker v. Carr* and Its Progeny" (2002) 80 *North Carolina Law Review* 1411, 1417. For the parallel argument in the racial vote dilution context, see Heather K. Gerken, "Understanding the Right to an Undiluted Vote" (2001) 114 *Harvard Law Review* 1663, 1717, and in the partisan gerrymandering context, Heather K. Gerken, "Lost in the Political Thicket: The Court, Election Law, and the Doctrinal Interregnum" (2004) 153 *University of Pennsylvania Law Review* 503, 507.

[15] For a general critique of this trend, see Jacob Eisler, "Partisan Gerrymandering and the Illusion of Unfairness" (2018) 67 *Catholic University Law Review* 229; Jacob Eisler, "Partisan Gerrymandering and the Constitutionalization of Statistics" (2019) 68 *Emory Law Journal* 979.

[16] Nicholas O. Stephanopoulos and Eric M. McGhee, "Partisan Gerrymandering and the Efficiency Gap" (2015) 82 *University of Chicago Law Review* 831.

[17] Nicholas O. Stephanopoulos, "Elections and Alignment" (2014) 114 *Columbia Law Review* 283, 286; Nicholas O. Stephanopoulos "Aligning Campaign Finance Law" (2015) 101 *Virginia Law Review* 1425, 1499.

odd fit is only a matter of *framing* – the Supreme Court's election law jurisprudence is driven by a normative debate). Popular elections and rights protection (the typical judicial point of entry) serve different goals. Elections consolidate and express popular will, making a government capable of legitimately acting on behalf of the polity. Rights protect individuals from such state action, shielding isolated persons from the coercive apparatus backed by centralized power. Justice Black's concurrence in the Pentagon Papers case illustrates this general principle: rights operate to protect the liberties of individuals against the central government.[18]

In American constitutional scholarship, the judiciary has long been considered to be affiliated with both rights protection and the advancement of equality (including in its general form as rule of law neutrality). The concern regarding majority tyranny has animated not only constitutional thinking about explicitly state-constraining (and minority-protecting) enumerated rights but also the structural logic of federalism and the separation of powers.[19] This applies even to general theories of constitutional governance, demonstrated by Daniel Ortiz's claim that in order to "get anywhere interesting," even Ely's theory of representation–reinforcement (discussed below) must be based on minoritarian protection.[20] Yet having entered the political thicket, the judiciary has been compelled to grapple not only with how the rights of vulnerable individuals should be protected but also with how the franchise should self-govern generally. Conceptualizing how the dominant will within a polity can legitimately exert its power as a general matter is orthogonal to the traditional role of majority-constraining rights protection, which may explain why the Court has struggled to translate some typical doctrines of constitutional law into the election law context.[21] Phrased in terms of the basic values of democracy, judges must not only ask how rights can be applied to protect the vulnerable members of a polity, as scholarship in this area tends to return to the more comfortable question of minoritarian protection.[22] They must also ask how successful individuals and coalitions can legitimately realize their freedom.

That the judiciary must engage with both rights and structures expresses a mid-level tension; its highest incarnation is the complex coexistence of freedom and equality as the foundations of democracy. Electoral procedure is legitimate if it effectively translates the will of the franchise into corresponding political outcomes, thus advancing the cause of collective freedom. This requires assessing not only how electoral rules affect *individuals* as they engage in politics, but also whether

---

[18] *New York Times v. US*, 403 US 713, 716 (1971).
[19] David Landau, Hannah J. Wiseman, and Samuel R. Wiseman, "Federalism for the Worst Case" (2020) 105 *Iowa Law Review* 1187.
[20] Daniel R. Ortiz, "Pursuing a Perfect Politics: The Allure and Failure of Process Theory" (1991) 77 *Virginia Law Review* 721, 728–9.
[21] See Franita Tolson, "Election Law 'Federalism' and the Limits of the Antidiscrimination Framework" (2018) 59 *William & Mary Law Review* 2211.
[22] Daryl J. Levinson, "Rights and Votes" (2012) 121 *Yale Law Journal* 1286.

such rules succeed as *systems* that convert collective political will into governance. According to Richard Tuck, if a polity is seeking to undertake collective self-rule but is large and diverse enough that consensus among its members is unrealistic, majoritarianism is "the only principle that offers both equality and agency."[23] A minority group would have to assert a morally legitimate authority to dominate others based only on a claim to intrinsic superiority. Thus, groups that wish to autonomously rule themselves need both equality and freedom, as each member of the group must be identified as equal in the relevant way if their political ability to contribute to group decision-making is to be realized. Equality is not a competitor or limiter of autonomous self-rule, but a prerequisite to its legitimate realization.[24] From this high-level perspective, the courts must ask a unitary query about elections. What constitutional principles (whether framed directly as necessary for freedom or as equality-serving rights that are facultative of freedom) would do the most to generate the conditions under which persons can rule themselves? Thus the thrust of election law scholarship – a turn toward institutions, structures, and the values that should undergird them – is analytically valid.

The challenge of campaign finance jurisprudence illustrates this point. The conservative justifications for an anti-regulatory posture are presented as protecting individuals from government oppression (i.e., equality to speak freely), with the fear that regulating speech will lead to tyranny.[25] The core of the progressive riposte is that this view disregards the vast and disproportionate *economic* power of many who influence campaign speech.[26] Progressives justify equalizing regulation by arguing the wealthy have superior social power and that unconstrained use of this wealth threatens the liberty of the poorer members of society (and the polity as a whole).[27] Both wings seek to frame regulating speech as defending the vulnerable (the classic understanding of rights protection). Yet the underlying issue highlighted in the case law and judicial opinions touches on the universal question of the necessary social conditions for collective political self-determination in a society rife with economic inequality. The core question of campaign finance is how the polity as a whole should regulate money in the context of campaign speech to facilitate legitimate self-rule, rather than the state's capacity to harm a threatened subgroup.

---

[23] Richard Tuck, *The Sleeping Sovereign: The Invention of Modern Democracy* (Cambridge: Cambridge University Press, 2016), p. 261.
[24] Phillip Pettit describes the unity of these two values, as described in Chapter 3.
[25] *McConnell v. Federal Election Commission*, 540 US 93, 283 (2003) (the logical endpoint of the progressive view of campaign finance is "outright regulation of the press").
[26] Sabeel Rahman, *Democracy against Domination* (Oxford: Oxford University Press, 2017); Joseph Fishkin and William E. Forbath, "The Anti-Oligarchy Constitution" (2014) 94 *Boston University Law Review* 671; Timothy K. Kuhner, *Capitalism v. Democracy: Money in Politics and the Free Market Constitution* (Stanford: Stanford University Press, 2014).
[27] *McCutcheon v. Federal Election Commission*, 572 US 185, 241 (2014).

1.2.2 Democratic Self-Determination and Skepticism of Judicial Review

The major takeaway from election law scholarship is that judges must undertake a new – and, for the judiciary, novel – type of query: what structural arrangements advance legitimate democracy? This proposition gives courts the power to dictate the meaning of freedom to the constituent polity. On the surface, this suggests that autonomy is not a preeminent value of democracy, but rather should be beholden to some other structural value – such as competitiveness or preference alignment. Even if the electorate has the opportunity to express its preferences, the broader context in which it may do so is externally dictated by an institution basing its authority on a claim to elite moral knowledge. Curiously, election law scholarship has neglected to explore why courts are well positioned to dictate the terms of this autonomy.

This critique has driven the major scholarly challenge to the legitimacy of judicial review. Doubts regarding courts' capacity to uphold democratic process have a long legacy in American constitutional thinking. In his description of the countermajoritarian difficulty, Alexander Bickel notes a fundamental challenge to the innovative, highly structural type of judicial review that has characterized modern election law. He observes that of the plausible alternatives, elections are the most democratic means of dictating government action. Courts are unaccountable to the people, which raises a threshold challenge to any judicial negation of action undertaken by the people's elected representatives.[28] Bickel identifies elections as the primary engine of democratic self-governance, which gives them a particular claim to legitimacy that judicial review lacks. He does not, broadly speaking, ascribe special standing to judicial review of the law of electoral procedure. He notes how the Court's entry into the political thicket raises questions regarding who determines democratic norms, though he wrongly predicted that, following *Baker v. Carr*, the Supreme Court would be cautious and reserved in its engagement with electoral procedure.[29]

Distinguishing my approach from Bickel's, I favor the term *counterpopular* since a given decision reached via democratic procedures may not necessarily be majoritarian. The US constitutional arrangement accommodates both legislative (in the Senate) and executive (through the Electoral College) deviation from per-voter majoritarianism. These practices remain *popular* mechanisms for representation, reflecting the will of the people (albeit filtered through the constitutional commitment to federalism). By contrast, rule-of-law neutrality prohibits judges from basing their opinions on political will and accountability.

The inheritors of Bickel's skepticism have highlighted the morally problematic nature of the judiciary displacing political autonomy. Some of these critiques have

---

[28] The general form of this proposition is contained in Alexander M. Bickel, *The Least Dangerous Branch* (Connecticut: Yale University Press, 1986), p. 19.
[29] Ibid., pp. 192, 196.

noted the increasing importance of judicial intervention and judicially defined rights across liberal democratic regimes, often in ways that displace popular democratic decision-making or claim normative priority.[30] This book focuses less on these observational accounts and more on the normative problem posed by judicial review. I examine two leading critics of judicial review in democratic regimes, Jeremy Waldron and Richard Bellamy. Their accounts advance two fundamental challenges to judicial review:[31] it is both morally wrongful (because it displaces democratic constituent autonomy) and practically ineffective (at least at achieving the ends that are offered to justify the unique and non-accountable role of a strong judiciary).[32] Waldron describes these as "process related" and "outcome related," respectively, while Bellamy calls an even more fundamental understanding of this problem "input" and "output" considerations.[33] The former argument is normative in character, as it identifies the failure of judicial review to conform to the legitimating principle of democratic self-rule: constituent self-determination. The latter is functional in character, as it argues that the judiciary is ineffective (or at least not uniquely effective) at sustaining democratic viability by, for example, checking the excesses of representatives and powerful cliques or protecting the rights of vulnerable groups. The election law scholarship has at least meaningfully engaged with, if not decisively answered, these descriptive arguments.

The normative argument, however, has been oddly neglected. When judges (functionally) make policy, the people do not determine the substance of their own governance and do not steer the coercive power of the state. Thus constituent members of the polity are coerced by an authority whose will cannot be clearly attributed back to those constituents. Jeremy Waldron is the best-known critic of the legitimacy of judicial review of democratic structure on these terms.[34] He argues that since the foundation of democracy is autonomous self-determination, any claim that this autonomy is conditioned on external curation undermines this foundation. This theme runs throughout Waldron's argument, but is most purely captured in his description of participation in democracy as "the right of rights"[35] and his

---

[30] Leading examples of this trend include Samuel Moyn, *Not Enough: Human Rights in an Unequal World* (Cambridge: Harvard University Press, 2018) and Ran Hirschl, *Towards Juristocracy: The Origins and Consequences of New Constitutionalism* (Cambridge: Harvard University Press, 2009).

[31] Richard Bellamy, *Political Constitutionalism: A Republican Defence of the Constitutionality of Democracy* (Cambridge: Cambridge University Press, 2009), p. 27, cites Jeremy Waldron, "The Core of the Case Against Judicial Review" (2006) 115 *Yale Law Journal* 1346, 1372–75 to draw both parallels and differentiations for the two main features this account notes.

[32] Waldron notes that this criticism is directed against "strong judicial review," that is, review in which a judiciary can override decisions of democratically accountable representatives, rather than ordinary conflict resolution and interpretative actions required to resolve any legal dispute. Waldron, "The Core of the Case against Judicial Review," 1354.

[33] Bellamy, "Political Constitutionalism," p. 27.

[34] Bellamy is Waldron's most sympathetic ally, although Bellamy is focused on rights constitutionalism rather than the role of the courts specifically. *Ibid.*, Chapter 3.

[35] Jeremy Waldron, *Law and Disagreement* (Oxford: Oxford University Press, 1993), Chapter 11.

argument that democratic autonomy must allow citizens to freely assert the meaning of democracy and autonomy themselves.[36] Bellamy advances a parallel claim in his critique that using legal constitutionalism to "depoliticize" conflict over the substance of rights is a type of domination.[37] It is perhaps telling that accounts that confront Waldron directly tend to undermine the non-representative character of judicial review or attack it as a matter of practical impact.[38]

Electoral process poses this problem with particular incisiveness. The purpose of elections is to convert constituent will into political action and thereby validate state power by attributing it back to constituents. Even if there are moral limits to what popular political action may authorize (classically framed as preventing the tyranny of the majority, but the procedures for allocating constituent political power, and the problem of limiting political decision-making, need not be so narrow),[39] the normative facet of this problem is uniquely sharp in the context of democratic procedure. Elections are morally valid because they express political will and are the practical engine via which the principle of democratic autonomy is realized. Their characteristic, redeeming feature is that they instantiate the free moral capacity of the constituent members of the polity. To fully realize this attribute, their realization must therefore be determined by this same constituent autonomy – and likewise be politically determined. If the terms of elections are subject to some higher authority, this implies that individual moral freedom must be conditioned and thus that it is not the highest value. It is therefore much harder to offer a normative justification for externally imposing terms of elections upon the polity compared to, say, imposing a rights-based rule that even popular will cannot authorize torture.

If substantive judicial curation of the conditions of electoral process is defended on instrumental grounds as necessary to maintain democratic durability, it deepens rather than resolves the dilemma. What is the legitimate source of the value that justifies non-accountable curation? Since it does not come from the electorate itself (in which case it would be an expression of autonomy), it must suggest that even free persons in a democracy are beholden to some authoritative moral values. The moral untenability of imposing terms of self-governance on a liberal system with self-determination as a guiding principle is epitomized by Isaiah Berlin's rejection of positive freedom. Berlin declines to adopt an ideal of freedom that mandates particular

---

[36] Waldron, "Law and Disagreement," Chapter 13 (especially at p. 296).
[37] Bellamy, "Political Constitutionalism," p. 147.
[38] Cristina Lafont, *Democracy without Shortcuts* (Oxford: Oxford University Press, 2019), Chapter 8; Theunis Roux, "In Defense of Empirical Entanglement: The Methodological Flaw in Waldron's Case against Judicial Review," in Ron Levy, Hoi Kong, Graeme Orr, and Jeff King (eds.), *Cambridge Handbook of Deliberative Constitutionalism* (Cambridge: Cambridge University Press, 2018).
[39] More recent versions of this article emphasize democratic theory based on values other than the self-determination of the polity. See, for example, Christopher L. Eisgruber, *Constitutional Self-Government* (Cambridge: Harvard University Press, 2001) (discussed extensively in Chapter 1), and Corey Brettschneider, *Democratic Rights: The Substance of Self-Government* (Princeton: Princeton University Press, 2007).

conduct (even appealingly framed as obedience to "rational self-direction") because it "leads to despotism, albeit by the best or the wisest."[40]

Empowering judges to dictate the terms of individuals' own political freedom would introduce such a claim of elite moral knowledge into procedures of democratic governance. The solution cannot be to simply adopt a "thin" conception of liberalism, akin to Berlin's idea of negative freedom, and instruct the Court to advance this interpretation, as opposed to the "thicker" concept of liberalism that has been prominent in the more didactic scholarship. This is because judicial interpretation and advancement of a specific idea of freedom, even a negative one, is still contrary to ultimate terms of self-rule residing with the constituency.[41] This is not mere judicial activism,[42] but a direct contravention of the foundations of democracy in constituent freedom. In short, substantive judicial review of the terms or circumstances of elections implies that some feature of democracy other than the autonomy of the electorate is the defining moral value of democracy.

The positive edge of the argument of Waldron and his kin is that standard channels of politics (such as elections) should – and do – perform the function of rights protection typically assigned to courts and can do so without sacrificing constituent autonomy.[43] Forms of democratic process can perform the same substantive function of judicial review and be led by the very people they affect. This answers Bickel's countermajoritarian difficulty by returning power to the constituency. Democratic participation can substitute for magisterial judicial authority. John Hart Ely's scholarship, discussed extensively in Chapter 2, is largely a reply to Bickel's countermajoritarian difficulty, yet it is typically seen as a general (albeit highly influential) constitutional argument rather than a specific work on election law. Surprisingly, his attempt to justify judicial review has not become a thematic touchstone in the field.[44]

1.2.3 Implicit Tolerance of Instrumental Judicial Intervention in the Election Law Scholarship

These critiques of judicial intervention into democracy have been strangely absent from American election law scholarship. Judicial review is often portrayed as

---

[40] Isaiah Berlin, *Two Concepts of Liberty in Liberty*, ed. Henry Hardy (Oxford: Oxford University Press, 2002), p. 200.
[41] I owe this point to extremely thoughtful discussions with Samuli Seppänen.
[42] This is a familiar concept, from Bickel's concept of the countermajoritarian difficulty to Ran Hirschl's concern articulated in "Towards Juristocracy" to Jeremy Waldron's broader skepticism of judicial review.
[43] Waldron, "Law and Disagreement," pp. 244, 305; Waldron, "The Core of the Case against Judicial Review," 1378; Bellamy, "Political Constitutionalism," p. 152.
[44] Intriguingly, there has been a resurgent interest in Ely's approach in a comparative context, though this approach does not center the tension of counterpopularism. See, for example, Stephen Gardbaum, "Comparative Political Process Theory" (2020) 18 *International Journal of Constitutional Law* 1429.

beneficial for, if not essential to, the viability of democracy, even if the seminal virtue of democracy is popular self-rule. Chapter 2 discusses a stronger, normative form of this objection – advanced by constitutional law scholars such as Eisgruber and arguably Dworkin – which identifies constitutional rights protection as the defining value rather than a facultative feature of democracy. The generalized, weaker form of this approach is an institutional understanding that considers courts and values such as the rule of law to be practical necessities. Critics of judicial review challenge the weaker practical case descriptively through the outcome-/output-based argument that judicial review is *not* uniquely effective at achieving justice or at least is not worth the cost to democratic legitimacy.[45]

This descriptive critique of judicial review – that its benefits do not justify the normative onus – would seem to cut especially hard in the context of election law, for the reason described above. Since elections are the typically decisive instantiations of democratic autonomy, the side of the scale in favor of popular self-rule would seem heavily weighted. Yet strangely, the focus of election law scholarship has been almost exclusively instrumental in nature, focused on how judges can bring about the "best" democratic practice. Contemporary scholarship has neglected the paradoxically autonomy-infringing effects of judicial intervention in the sphere of elections.

Prior studies in this area have instead treated judicial intervention as a policymaking problem. The prevalent question is always which legal interventions would yield a good electoral design. Scholars, in other words, have concentrated almost exclusively on one side of the counterpopular dilemma, courts' capacity to benefit democratic process through their institutional position. The difficulties posed by the judiciary's political insulation and non-accountability have been neglected. If anything, prior studies have noted non-accountability in passing as an institutional virtue that enables judicial oversight of democratic process.[46] This is particularly salient in one leading account, Issacharoff and Pildes's "Politics as Markets: Partisan Lockups of the Democratic Process."[47] Issacharoff and Pildes assert that the Supreme Court has failed to articulate "any underlying vision of democratic politics that is normatively robust or realistically sophisticated about actual political practices."[48] They advocate for competition-generating, entrenchment-policing judicial intervention, modeled on judicial intervention in corporate governance that seeks to protect shareholders from executive mismanagement. Their argument is unabashedly institutionalist and structuralist, treating

---

[45] See Jeremy Waldron, "The Rule of Law and the Role of Courts" (2021) 10 *Global Constitutionalism* 91, 94.
[46] See Issacharoff and Pildes, "Politics as Markets."
[47] Heather Gerken describes this work as "the finest article written in the field." Heather K. Gerken, "Playing Cards in a Hurricane: Party Reform in an Age of Polarization" (2017) 54 *Houston Law Review* 911, 912.
[48] Issacharoff and Pildes, "Politics as Markets," 646.

the Court's defining feature as its capacity to deploy power insulated from political reprisal or accountability.[49]

The normatively extraordinary feature of Issacharoff and Pildes's account is implicit. If adopted, their approach would transform the Court into a nonaccountable yet broadly empowered regulator of democratic process. Insofar as the Court's authority derives from a normative or constitutional remit, the article circumvents such difficulties by seeking "to read into the Constitution an indispensable commitment to the preservation of an appropriately competitive political order."[50] This argument parallels that of Dworkin and Eisgruber, who are willing to subordinate constituent autonomy to other values. Indeed, in the first sentence, Issacharoff and Pildes dismiss the "autonom[y]" of democratic self-governance. They barely acknowledge that the unique features of the Court that should limit or discipline such an ambitious judicial role in shaping politics. The seemingly sympathetic work of Ely is brushed aside as excessively concerned with, inter alia, individual rights.[51] However, Ely's work is defined by trying to justify judicial review as a normative matter. Insofar as Issacharoff and Pildes's account includes a moral justification, it is reverse engineered from justifying judicial involvement to achieve a particular vision of democracy. The rights-based approach that Issacharoff and Pildes reject in favor of this structuralist turn, for all its analytic inadequacies (including its inability to explain dramatic interventions such as one person, one vote), has a readier explanation for the Court's authority to intervene in elections: it is merely fulfilling its constitutional mandate.

Paralleling the turn away from rights-based understandings, subsequent election law scholarship typically followed the tradition of enquiring *what should democracy look like?* and advocating judicial intervention to achieve it. This has neglected the question *why are the courts the appropriate mechanism to do so?* This implicit instrumental justification for judicial review has been reflected in multiple ways. Following from Gerken's critique of rights-based approaches to elections as inadequacy is her claim that the Court *must* advance a structural theory of legitimate democratic process to answer the legal questions posed by topics such as the racial protections afforded by the equal protection clause, one person, one vote, and the permissibility of partisan gerrymandering. Yet Gerken notes that advancing such a structural theory, as opposed to relying on the more traditional rights-based approach, imposes a clear normative vision of democracy.[52] Insofar as she concedes that the Court has been hesitant to explicitly impose such visions, she describes it as an institutional blind spot and tends to suggest that even if the Court tries to avoid imposing such theories, in resolving cases it will inevitably do so. The underlying normative

---

[49] Ibid., 648.
[50] Ibid., 716.
[51] Ibid., 710.
[52] Gerken, "The Costs and Causes of Minimalism," 1463; Gerken, "Lost in the Political Thicket," 521.

tension elicited by the counterpopular dilemma tends not to play a significant role in Gerken's analysis. The goal, even philosophically, is to advance the right democratic theory through the available institutional channels, despite the fundamental features of those institutions that might prove to be normatively problematic (that is, the non-accountable nature of the judiciary). Stephanopoulos's descriptions of what he thinks democracy should look like largely overlook the Court's unique normative remit. In his influential advocacy to adopt the efficiency gap to address partisan gerrymandering, other than analogizing the proposed quantitative standard to the one person, one vote rule in terms of its descriptive efficacy, he does little to explain why the judiciary is the appropriate institution to advance districting standards. Likewise, his field-encompassing argument that judicial adoption of the alignment interest would "launch a doctrinal revolution"[53] does not consider the unique normative weight the Court must bear to advance a "particular vision of democracy."[54]

1.3 SHARPENING THE MORAL ONUS OF THE COUNTERPOPULAR DILEMMA

Critics of judicial review would unequivocally reject the conclusion that courts should develop a robust freestanding theory of democracy to guide structural interventions in democracy. Asserting that courts should undertake baldly structural intervention is an even more direct affront to popular autonomy, because (unlike rights protection) it cannot be vindicated by the risk of majority tyranny. Advocates for such intervention can only revert to the claim that the constituency itself lacks the competence to generate structures with soundness and integrity. Because they find this premise untenable, skeptics of judicial review would reject the legitimacy of courts policing democratic structures. They would instead prefer governance by whatever structures emerged from accountable political processes.[55]

Despite being an affront to the principle of autonomy championed by judicial review skeptics, positing the institutional incompetence (or at least the tendency toward pathology) of democratic process is present in much of the election law scholarship. Issacharoff and Pildes explicitly declare that the Supreme Court should address what they identify as the recursive failures of democracy (i.e., entrenchment); Pildes identifies the intersection of constitutionalization of democracy and structural challenges to democratic self-rule as the defining quality of the election law as a field.[56] Critics of Waldron have invoked Issacharoff's description of the role

---

[53] Stephanopoulos, "Aligning Campaign Finance Law," 1454.
[54] Ibid., 1449.
[55] Waldron, "Law and Disagreement," p. 303 openly grasps (grabs?) the nettle that this would make all substance in democratic process "up for grabs"; Bellamy notes "ordinary legislation within the legislature has to be the sphere of constitutional politics" if ultimate constitutional authority is to rest with the people, "Political Constitutionalism," p. 139.
[56] Pildes, "The Constitutionalization of Democratic Politics," 39.

of the judiciary in preserving democracy in times of crisis to counter Waldron's anti-judicial review stance.[57] These views are unspoken but implied in recent scholarship that advocates for theoretical or technocratic judicial intervention. Underlying these approaches is the proposition that the Court's neutrality – essential to sound rule of law – also gives it a uniquely disinterested position from which to curate democratic process.

This belief seems to refer back to the second aspect of the criticism of judicial review. Bellamy describes how political process is "overwhelmingly stronger than courts with regard to 'input' criteria, with courts doing better on 'outputs'."[58] This output question is empirical: is judicial review ineffective or superfluous for ensuring the integrity of democratic process? One form of anti-judicial review attack is essentially a repackaging of the prominent critique of political process theory that it has insufficient content to guide judicial review. Any assertion that the judiciary can more effectively advance legitimate democratic process requires an authoritative consensus on what democratic process *is*; if popular mechanisms are ineffective, this consensus cannot come from the constituency itself.[59] I discuss below how this can be developed into a problematic paradox for judicial review, but the more practical critique of judicial review is not process-based. This practical claim is that "[r]eal change only comes with legislation, and judicial review may hinder as much it promotes that process."[60] Bellamy points to *Brown v. Board* and *Roe v. Wade* to exemplify how judicial intervention often fails to achieve the social benefits that champions of judicial review claim.

The difficulty is that making such a descriptive, substance-based assessment of which measures advance legitimate democratic procedure introduces a further seemingly insoluble question. With no obvious descriptive baseline regarding legitimate terms of democratic process, such a query necessarily becomes circular. The legitimacy of a democratic procedure can ultimately only be assessed against what the constituents themselves would authorize – which in turn requires a reliable way to evaluate the content of popular will. This poses a problem for both advocates of structural judicial intervention and for critics of judicial review. The former cannot offer a truly foundational explanation of the efficacy of judicial review without referring to an authoritative norm. The latter cannot decisively assert that judicial review is ineffective at promoting democracy without citing an authoritative vision of their own of what democracy should be (which is, of course, the very trap they accuse advocates for robust judicial review of falling into).

It is worth noting that judicial intervention in election law has achieved some great victories in interdicting democratic pathologies. This gives the prevalent

---

[57] Roux, "In Defence of Empirical Entanglement," 210 (citing Issacharoff's *Fragile Democracies*).
[58] Bellamy, "Political Constitutionalism," p. 27.
[59] This is developed from Waldron, "Law and Disagreement," p. 243.
[60] Bellamy, "Political Constitutionalism," p. 44.

structural approach to election law ammunition to use against critics of judicial review. The most successful interventions appear to be the early moves against racist electoral procedure (the White Primary cases and the striking down of illicit districting in *Gomillion*) and one person, one vote. These interventions assailed entrenched cliques whose electoral power was enhanced unjustly; yet they cannot be explained wholly in rights-based terms. The White Primary cases prohibited even a wholly private organization from effecting exclusionary electoral policies.[61] The attacks on malapportionment in one person, one vote, which has an uncertain constitutional footing, increased popular control over electoral outcomes by breaking up practices of rural entrenchment (see Chapter 4). As the election law scholarship has noted, these cases are noteworthy precisely because they do not easily fit into a rights-based framework.[62] Furthermore, insofar as they involve breaking up cliques, they vindicate the underlying feature of judicial review – political neutrality based on lying outside the political process – that defines the courts' role in the rule of law and justifies counterpopular judicial review.

These interventions have incontrovertible normative appeal. Yet the appeal of these rules (what Waldron or Bellamy might call outputs) does not explain why the Court has the institutional authority to legitimately impose electoral rules in the first place. Beyond highlighting the struggle between election law scholarship and skepticism of judicial review, this tension elicits the deeper normative onus associated with judicial review of election law.

The counterpopular dilemma emerges from this intersection of (1) the foundational problem of authority over freedom and (2) the practical realities of democratic process. Election law scholars have focused on the latter. The inevitable concentration of power in the hands of representatives and elites creates opportunities for them to redesign electoral rules for their own benefit. Regardless of who (independent judges or accountable politicians) has "deep" moral authority to dictate the terms of autonomy, the practical reality is that the electoral processes that legitimately serve constituent autonomy are under constant threat. This problem is exacerbated by the fact that "pathologized" election law can be a self-reinforcing rachet: subsequent elections may legitimize increasingly abusive electoral rules. Election law scholars favor judicial power because federal judges are well positioned to interdict representatives who engage in such abuses because they are not representatives themselves. They are, by constitutional design, insulated from the pressures and processes of direct political accountability. They can therefore intervene as morally and structurally appropriate when representatives who *are* subject to such political pressures seek to enact self-aggrandizing election law.

---

[61] See the discussion of *Terry v. Adams* 345 US 461 (1953) in Chapter 6.
[62] Issacharoff and Pildes, "Politics as Markets," 653 (discussing the White Primary cases); Gerken, "The Costs and Causes of Minimalism" (discussing one person, one vote).

Yet this justification for judicial review glides over the foundational countervailing argument: if electoral procedure does have the unique capacity to dictate the terms of constituent autonomy, it is especially crucial that it be under (or close to) the constituents' control. Mid-level structural innovation by an outside, unaccountable actor is especially problematic in the domain of election law because it compromises the moral principle that vindicates democracy in the first place. Proposing that a rule is valid in a democracy even though it does not derive from constituent self-determination suggests that democracy ought to be guided by some external authority. This in turn implies that some external principle can dominate self-determination in democratic organization – a normative commitment that, regardless of how it is packaged, eventually requires moral authoritarianism. Given that electoral rules are the dominant means by which popular freedom is realized and democracy is legitimized, it is especially (and recursively) important that these rules are attributable to constituent will. Even if this creates circularity in trying to identify and shape electoral rules because constituent will cannot be identified without some initial valid mechanism, Bickel's core critique that elections and representatives are closer to the people than the judiciary remains compelling. Conversely arguing that courts are the direct agents of that will is implausible. The closer courts are to being accountable, the more they lose the practical benefit of neutrality and detachment from political pressure that election law scholars consider to be a virtue.

The problem elicited by judicial review of election law resonates with and extrapolates from Waldron's general critique. Elections are valuable *because* they serve as a conduit for the popular will. A counterpopular approach to judicial rights enforcement can be justified in the context of substantive policymaking by observing that the popular will can abuse the fundamental integrity or functionality in those domains and that advancing their basic values may require restraining outputs of the political process. When a court protects free speech rights from illicit restriction or prohibits a law that illicitly uses racial classifications, it does so because First Amendment and equal protection rights, respectively, prevent the majority (acting through representatives) from oppressing minorities. While the higher authorization that justifies such countermajoritarianism needs to be attributed to a deeper shared commitment (discussed further in Chapter 2), if the right is identified as having freestanding status in the broader constitutional order, judicial intervention against popular decisions can be vindicated. Thwarting the expression of popular will is not a defect in such types of rights enforcement; it is an essential feature – an idea that can be traced back to James Madison.[63]

Such a standard defense of judicial review, however, cannot legitimize judicial oversight of electoral process. Since elections are meant to convert constituents' autonomous choices into governance, the law of electoral procedure cannot seek

---

[63] Jesse H. Choper, *Judicial Review and the National Political Process: A Functional Reconsideration of the Role of the Supreme Court* (New Orleans: Quid Pro Quo Books, 2013), Chapter 2.

to thwart constituent will, because this would assert a principle of higher priority than autonomy. If electoral procedure is legitimized by a principle other than the realization of constituent autonomy, it contradicts its own normative foundations, and there is no way of advancing it in a coherent manner. This difficulty is the core of the counterpopular dilemma. Despite the practical benefits of judicial review of electoral process and its potential to interdict the pathologies of democracy, it can only be authorized through a principle higher than constituent autonomy, which contradicts democracy's foundational, legitimizing principle.

The ramifications of such interventions are reinforced by the recursive implications of allocating authority over electoral process to a source other than the constituents. Such rules embed externally imposed values in subsequent electoral rules that reflect such non-autonomously imposed decision-making procedures. Thus externally imposing electoral rules can influence the polity's processes indefinitely. Even if these democratic processes are authorized by later electoral decisions, they were not truly legitimate expressions of constituent will when they were introduced.

Ironically, this "stickiness" of electoral pathologies, when effected by representatives and elites, is what motivates election law scholars to look to the courts to intervene. Representatives' adoption of self-entrenching electoral procedures is the most classic example. The judiciary is a prospectively appealing mechanism for addressing "stickiness" that comes from within the accountable democratic process because judges are outside this process, but this calls into question the judiciary's authority to legitimately shape the terms of freedom. The potential benefits of having the judiciary structurally address electoral problems can only be realized by contravening the legitimizing principle of democracy.

1.4 THE DURABILITY OF THE COUNTERPOPULAR DILEMMA

It is worth addressing some preemptive challenges (perhaps better termed "easy solutions") to this problem. Some easy solutions question the centrality of elections to autonomy and instead emphasize features of the liberal constitutional order that fit more comfortably with robust judicial review, such as rights and the rule of law. Dworkin and Eisgruber have gone so far as to openly denigrate elections as the characteristic property of democracy, preferring a substantive rights-favoring conception. Eisgruber maintains that "we must first put aside the idea that free elections are constitutive of democracy."[64] Rebecca Brown epitomizes how this substantively rights-favoring view of democracy undermines Bickel's countermajoritarian difficulty: she asserts that Bickel reduces democracy "to its most elemental populist foundations" of majoritarian will and thereby ignores the "collection of interacting mechanisms"

---

[64] Eisgruber, "Constitutional Self-Government," pp. 50, 83. See also Ronald Dworkin, *Freedom's Law: The Moral Reading of the American Constitution* (Cambridge: Harvard University Press, 1997), p. 17.

that protect it.⁶⁵ This position is a hard-edged extrapolation of the account of democracy articulated by Ginsberg and Huq (in which electoral self-rule is only one feature, along with rights protection and the rule of law). This more extreme critique suggests that Bickel's argument relies upon a problematically minimalist conception of democracy.

What are the implications of this skepticism toward electoral primacy? Since elections require certain background conditions (some of which are directly related to electoral rules and others to establishing socio-political circumstances that are conducive to self-rule more broadly), it logically follows that elections are a necessary but not sufficient condition for liberal democracy. Yet if a polity's elections do not always realize constituent autonomy, is it truly a liberal democracy? This leads naturally enough to the thesis that elections – as a form of majority rule – may not, in fact, be a necessary trait of liberal democracy. Legal scholars typically identify an alternative foundation of democracy as defined by rights, rather than autonomy over governmental decision-making.

This line of reasoning entails an alarming leap – from the observation that electoral representation is an imperfect realization of self-rule (both because elections do not realize constituent will perfectly and because elections require other conditions to function) to the conclusion that political self-determination is not, in fact, the central feature of democracy. If this jump is considered compelling and decisive, then the premise of this book – that self-rule achieved through elections must be reconciled with judicial transformation of electoral procedure – may be of little interest (though the coherent descriptive account of election law may be of interest as a hermeneutic exercise). However, this jump entails far more; its logical conclusion is that democracy is not a system of autonomous constituent self-determination of governance. Rather, democracy is defined by a characteristic other than autonomy, presumably a set of social conditions such as equal application of the law and citizens' ability to exercise rights. Elections may have a key role to play in protecting these features, but if self-rule is not a first-order value, then giving judges the power of electoral design will not cause problems as long as doing so yields a social order that protects these conditions. The significance of de-prioritizing citizen autonomy should not be diminished. It does not merely attempt to address majority tyranny. Rather, it rejects self-rule as the legitimating quality of politics. It thus rejects the basic premise that the power of a person (or collective) over its own political fate is decisive. This in turn goes against this book's premise regarding the link between morality and freedom.

Thus, if constituents' political autonomy is accepted as the core value of democracy, the substantive weight of the counterpopular dilemma cannot be so easily

---

⁶⁵ Rebecca Brown, "How Constitutional Theory Found its Soul: The Contributions of Ronald Dworkin," in Scott Hershovitz (ed.), *Exploring Law's Empire: The Jurisprudence of Ronald Dworkin* (Oxford: Oxford University Press, 2008), p. 46.

1.4 The Durability of the Counterpopular Dilemma

brushed away. As Ely describes it (in a way Michael Klarman describes as "unanswerable"),[66] even if election-based representation is an imperfect expression of constituent autonomy – that is, it is procedurally imperfect – judicial intervention has a lexically weaker claim to articulate the will of the franchise because it does not even aspire to accountably express constituent autonomy.[67] Even if one recognizes the virtues of robust judicial review and the flaws and risks of representation, there is no question that elections are a *more* direct expression of constituent autonomy. Judicial intervention in electoral process can only be justified by asserting that there is some higher substantive value than constituent self-determination that can grant democratic legitimacy and that the right authorities can advance as settled moral fact (which is precisely what Eisgruber and Dworkin come to assert). Taken to its logical extreme, such a view could vindicate purely technocratic rule (rule by philosophers, one might quip). If the technocrats advanced the normatively "correct" views and operated within a properly arranged institutional framework, this would justify minimizing the role of constituent determination of the terms of self-rule altogether. While those who recognize rule of law and independent rights protection are unlikely to take such an extreme view, the problematic *principle* remains apparent. Empowering those who are *less* (rather than more) accountable to the franchise to set the terms of electoral procedure requires a substantive vision of good governance that necessarily undermines the primacy of autonomous constituent self-determination.

There is a further problem facing any ultimate force given to judicial review of election law that activates another aspect of its recursive character. If judges' substantive conclusions are fixedly authoritative, this confirms that the terms of democratic self-determination are closed to debate.[68] It is possible to make experiential observations about what types of electoral arrangements and circumstances are more or less desirable according to a posited set of criteria. But considering this to be decisive begs the question of who has the authority to posit the criteria. The character of legitimate democracy can only be defined by the constituents who rule (and are ruled by) it. The ongoing process of disputing its meaning is a reflexive aspect of democratic process, which is necessary to retain the legitimacy of self-rule, even as it destabilizes the fixity of its definition. When the judiciary dictates what democracy means from a position of non-accountable technocratic authority, this undermines this reflexive aspect of democratic self-determination.

Another argument that brushes away the counterpopular dilemma fails due to the unique characteristic of election law. Some have argued that judicial review

---

[66] Michael J. Klarman, "The Puzzling Resistance to Political Process Theory" (1991) 77 *Virginia Law Review* 747, 777.
[67] Ely, "Democracy and Distrust," p. 206 n.9.
[68] See Waldron, "Law and Disagreement," p. 303.

of legislative action is generally unproblematic because judges, who lack direct control over coercive levers of the state, will always be sensitive to voters' interests and preferences.[69] Lafont articulates a version of this argument by emphasizing the role of litigants in shaping legal outcomes.[70] According to this perspective, even if judges are not directly accountable, they will avoid taking action that is so at odds with popular preference that it deprives the judiciary of normative legitimacy due to fears of being institutionally circumvented or disempowered. Yet where judges transform the very terms by which popular will is collectively synthesized into representative state action, the soft restraints of public opinion offer far less comfort. This is because judges are not merely shaping policy that constituents may react to via expressions of political will; they are determining what that political will looks like in the first place. If judges favor (or take away) a particular group's power through the democratic process, that group, which now has control of the state (or not), will be able to act (or be hindered from acting) to reinforce and incentivize (or be prevented from disincentivizing) such non-accountable overdetermination of political power. The judiciary, since it is an initial gatekeeper, is insulated from retaliation by those who are excluded from power unless the situation becomes so dire that the entire constitutional order is threatened. In short, where the judiciary curates the universe of manifest constituent will that makes up the political process, that constituent will cannot be relied upon to police the judiciary. This problem is especially salient where the judiciary condones or accelerates a moment of majoritarian domination that may become entrenched, including long-condemned examples of racial oppression and still-contested instances of partisan gerrymandering.

The counterpopular dilemma cuts deep. Judicial review has the potential to prevent the pathological domination of the democratic process by those in power. But for such judicial review to be effective, it must be able to make some claim to moral knowledge of good democracy that does not undermine the very popular autonomy that elections are meant to vindicate. Addressing this problem requires not merely describing what judges should do when they police elections, but stipulating precisely how an anti-majoritarian structuring of electoral process can be vindicated and what its content should be, given that it acts against the most direct expression of popular will, accountable representation.

---

[69] Eisgruber, "Constitutional Self-Government," p. 3.
[70] Lafont, "Democracy without Shortcuts," Chapter 8.

2

Constitutionalism and the Counterpopular Dilemma

This chapter considers three main accounts of the *general* problem of the legitimacy of judicial review, which may be the most extensively interrogated topic in legal scholarship. The chapter shows that each account – originalism, interpretivism, and instrumentalism – fails to adequately address the counterpopular dilemma. Despite their diverse ways of making sense of how courts should engage in judicial review, all threes accounts encounter the same problem. They resolve the counterpopular dilemma by intruding upon constituent autonomy, and imposing, from some alternate source of authority, the conditions of self-rule.

2.1 RECONCILING POPULAR SELF-GOVERNANCE AND JUDICIAL CONSTITUTIONAL REVIEW: THE CONSTITUTION AS CONTRACT?

If judicial review can be accurately characterized as protecting the popular will regarding electoral procedure from *less* directly authorized changes made by the legislature, the tension vanishes. Courts transition from a counterpopular institution to an agent of the people, defending the popularly authorized higher law of the Constitution. This justification has roots in social contract theory and adherents among progressive and conservative thinkers. Both the conservative originalist account and the progressive living constitutionalist account treat the Constitution as a foundational contract among constituents and thus the pre-eminent political commitment. The judiciary merely ensures that any subsequent, lower-priority legislation (including electoral rules) adheres to this contract.

2.1.1 *The Contractarian Account, Constitutional Validity, and the Originalist Solution*

The notion that treating the constitution as a contract can reconcile judicial review and constituent autonomy hangs on the assertion that constitutional formation is an authoritative expression of constituent autonomy. Richard Tuck has offered a magisterial account in *The Sleeping Sovereign*, where he describes the role of direct citizen approval in the founding of the United States. Since the Constitution was legitimized by the people as a sovereign body, it serves as the decisive expression of autonomous popular will. This decisiveness is tempered by any flaws in the actual social practice of the plebiscite at the moment of framing (see the discussion of Levy below). Tuck's account of why the Constitution is the pre-eminent expression of popular will is couched in a social contractarian tradition that provides the dominant account of (1) why the state is legitimate and (2) how this legitimacy flows from the will of the persons involved in state formation.[1] He draws on Hobbes's interpretation of state legitimacy, which entails individuals allocating decision-making authority to a state.[2] Tuck contrasts this approach with Rousseau's assertion that since the sovereign will of the people cannot be alienated from itself, a democratic form of governance legitimately expresses sovereignty.[3]

Tuck's account offers a tempting vindication of judicial review of electoral procedure. If the Constitution is an authoritative expression of citizen autonomy, the normatively valid project becomes the Constitution's implementation. This does not diminish the role of representation *per se* – in the Constitution, representative structures have the central lawmaking role[4] – but it does explain why constitutional commitments can dominate contrary legislative action. The legislature's lawmaking authority and the courts' power and duty to protect rights flow from the same source – direct popular autonomy manifested by the Constitution. Interpretive work may be necessary to determine the precise meaning of these constitutional commitments, yet this parsing does not evoke the troubling competition between judicial moral authority and popular autonomy through representation. Rather, it is a technical exercise with clear popular legitimation.

In American constitutional law, the originalist–textualist approach is the most explicit attempt to make sense of judicial review as such a technical exercise. Originalism exists in so many forms that leading scholars have made independent projects of mapping its variations.[5] Yet – and this allows originalism to be treated with more unity than the varieties of living constitutionalism – originalism has a

---

[1] Richard Tuck, *The Sleeping Sovereign: The Invention of Modern Democracy* (Cambridge: Cambridge University Press, 2016).

[2] *Ibid.*, pp. 100–3.

[3] *Ibid.*, p. 140. While Tuck closely unpacks the relationship between European contractarian thought and the ideals of American civic figures during the Framing, others such as Anita Allen have observed the impact of social contractarian thinking during this period. Anita L. Allen. "Social Contract Theory in American Case Law" (1999) 51 *Florida Law Review* 1, 4–5.

[4] John Hart Ely, *Democracy and Distrust: A Theory of Judicial Review* (Cambridge: Harvard University Press, 1981), p. 5.

[5] See Lawrence B. Solum, "Originalism versus Living Constitutionalism: The Conceptual Structure of the Great Debate" (2019) 113 *Northwestern University Law Review* 1243. This diversity is further complicated by hybrid understandings such as Jack M. Balkin's *Living Originalism* (Cambridge: Harvard University Press, 2014).

meaningful shared core. As Keith Whittington synthesizes, "At its most basic, originalism argues that the discoverable public meaning of the Constitution at the time of its initial adoption should be regarded as authoritative for purposes of later constitutional interpretation. The text of the Constitution itself ... is a primary source of that meaning."[6] The diversity of originalism largely emerges from the need to patch in where that meaning is incomplete or unclear. The aspiration of originalism as a coherent school is best captured by its most famous advocate, Justice Antonin Scalia, who explained that the Constitution is "an enactment that has a fixed meaning."[7] Once a theory deviates from this project of establishing the fixed meaning of the Constitution at the time of its adoption, it is better classified as another type of theory (living originalism, if it claims to continue to operate as a theory of pure constitutional enforcement).

Treating the Constitution as a document with fixed meaning makes originalism ostensibly capable of resolving the dilemma of judicial review of election law. If constituents have freely contracted into a set of overriding commitments whose meaning can be definitely settled by the terms of the initial commitment, there is no inconsistency in holding them to these commitments through judicial review. When the judiciary enforces a certain set of electoral procedures in line with these commitments, including preventing later legislators from adopting electoral procedures that deviate from them, it only holds champions constituents' own choices. There is a pleasing symmetry in this view with Hobbes's idea of the power of the sovereign as derived from the covenant of persons to leave the state of nature by allocating their power to that sovereign.[8] The sovereign's legitimate capacity to command – and even harm – subjects comes from the original free covenant that subjects enter.

2.1.2 The First Challenge to Originalism: The Legitimacy of Constitutional Authorization

If originalism is successful, judicial review does not suffer from the defect attributed to it by Alexander Bickel and John Hart Ely. Instead, the Court is policing constituents' freely made higher-priority constitutional commitment. This view has prominent adherents on the bench. Judge Frank Easterbrook, for example, has argued that "the fundamental theory of political legitimacy in the United States is contractarian," and that judges should enforce this contract.[9]

---

[6] Keith E. Whittington, "Originalism: A Critical Introduction" (2013) 82 *Fordham Law Review* 375, 377; William Baude, "Is Originalism Our Law?" 115 *Columbia Law Review* 2345, 2357.
[7] Antonin Scalia, "Originalism: The Lesser Evil" (1989) 57 *University of Cincinnati Law Review* 849, 854.
[8] Thomas Hobbes, *Leviathan: Or the Matter, Forme and Power of a Commonwealth, Ecclesiasticall and Civil (1650)*, ed. Michael Oakeshott (New York: Simon and Schuster, 1997).
[9] Frank H. Easterbrook, "Textualism and the Dead Hand" (1998) 66 *George Washington Law Review* 1119, 1120–2. See Richard A. Posner, *Law, Pragmatism, and Democracy* (Cambridge: Harvard University Press, 2005) pp. 268–72 for critiques of Easterbrook's view with some resonance to the analysis that follows.

However, to legitimately dominate subsequent expressions of constituent autonomy, any such authoritative contracting must initially be valid and persist over time. Tuck recognizes that a constitution is only an expression of popular will at the moment it is passed, and that to give it continued dominance allows an abstract historical concept of "the people" to override true self-rule.[10] He subsequently advocates for living constitutionalism, and asserts that the sovereignty of the people is "asleep." This solution is not entirely satisfactory for guiding legal interpretation. It disregards that (1) even as the direct will of the people "sleeps", popular will *is* through representation and (2) an institution (i.e. the courts) must enforce the text of the Constitution that the "sleeping" sovereign approved of while "awake." Thus, Tuck's analysis explains why the Constitution is a general expression of popular autonomy, but does not resolve the tension between representation and judicial enforcement.

However, the problem runs deeper than the change in the composition of the franchise over time. Contractarian accounts are often framed as hypothetical to resolve this problem: they are arrangements that persons *would* make if they were contracting into politics.[11] Yet, whether treated as real (with some mechanism for circumventing the passage of time and the change in constituent persons, as proposed by Akhil Amar)[12] or hypothetical, there are serious challenges to the legitimacy of the American founding as a meaningful expression of constituent autonomy. Amar proposes treating the Constitution as ratified at the date of its most recent amendment. Yet the problem with this approach as a means of autonomy is that it gives an enormous amount of weight to recent actions taken by state legislatures on relatively marginal matters (congressional pay raises, a slight drop in the voting age) to vindicate the entire document.

Even a hypothetical contractarian account derives its power from the claim that the political order is one that individuals would choose to enter if they were constructing the foundations of the political order from some pre-political condition. But whether actual or hypothetical, the attempt to justify the Constitution as a contract runs into the problem that the circumstances of its formation cannot reflect some idealized neutral position. As Jacob Levy observes, "[e]nacted constitutions do not come into being against the background of a state of nature of isolated individuals."[13] They instead reflect the features and norms of the society at the time the Constitution was drafted. Some of the problematic features of the founding reflect what are now recognized as blatant injustices, such as the exclusion of women, racial

---

[10] Tuck, "The Sleeping Sovereign," pp. 279–80.
[11] This view has adherents from both sides of the political spectrum. James Buchanan, *Reason of Rules: Constitutional Political Economy* (Cambridge: Cambridge University Press, 1986), p. 27; cf. John Rawls, *Political Liberalism* (New York: Columbia University Press, 1996), p. 224 (the constitutional regime should be based on what persons would agree to recognizing as free and equal).
[12] Tuck, "The Sleeping Sovereign," p. 280.
[13] Jacob T. Levy, "Not So Novus an Ordo" (2009) 37 *Political Theory* 191, 192.

minorities, and the poor.[14] Others reflect a more subtle internalization of the values at the time the Constitution was drafted – what Levy refers to as the "pre-contractarian social fact[s]"[15] – which entail their own social and normative commitments. Insofar as the Constitution is enforced as a fixed document as the basis for judicial review (the seminal principle of originalism), these commitments are advanced whenever judges enforce the Constitution. Yet there is no reason to presume these values are normatively superior. Since the Constitution was not contracted at a moment of intrinsic normative purity or validity, it is unclear why it should be able to determine later modes of normative self-realization (i.e. self-governance) by the polity. In the American legal tradition writ large, this is expressed as the "dead hand" problem.[16] Why should we still adhere to values adopted by those who are long gone (and who held many specific normative commitments that contemporary persons would wholeheartedly reject)?

Because a contractarian understanding of the Constitution requires adhering to a distant moment of social context and value, it impairs the capacity of originalist judicial review to resolve the counterpopular dilemma. If the original meaning of the constitutional contract is to be prioritized over the determination of election law procedure through the normal political process, the commitment contained in the Constitution must reflect a more normatively legitimate commitment by the people than their later expressions of political will through ongoing elections. This is especially urgent if the Constitution is taken to do more than advance "initially intelligible"[17] rules (e.g. that the House of Representatives should be 435 members) that are the minimum necessary to sustain the mechanics of governance.[18] If the Constitution goes beyond such a minimum, it enables a broader reworking of the political process based on the Court's interpretation of provisions with multiple plausible meanings.

This upends the originalist claim that judges can simply enforce the polity's political commitments from the time of the framing as a descriptive exercise, and thereby avoid making their own normative judgments. This claim that they are undertaking a neutral process of pure description fails if, even when they do no more than try to advance the meaning of the Constitution at the time it was entered, judges must enforce normatively contestable commitments (i.e. norms derived from social facts

---

[14] Louis Henkin, "The United States Constitution as Social Compact" (1987) 131 *Proceedings of the American Philosophical Society* 261, 263.

[15] Levy, "Not so Novus an Ordo," 210.

[16] Michael J. Klarman, "Majoritarian Judicial Review: The Entrenchment Problem" (1997) 85 *Georgetown Law Journal* 491–554 at 494. For a dissolution of the problem, see Michael W. McConnell, "Textualism and the Dead Hand of the Past" (1997) 66 *George Washington Law Review* 1127.

[17] Michael J. Perry, *The Constitution in the Courts: Law or Politics?* (Oxford: Oxford University Press, 1994), p. 38.

[18] McConnell, "Textualism," 1130 (rules "do not merely *constrain* those who wish to play the game, but also make the game possible"). Cf. Baude, "Is Originalism Our Law?," 2367.

at the time of the founding). This problem of advancing contestable commitments is, for the reasons described above, particularly salient if courts rely on constitutional interpretation to rework electoral rules. Why should these past commitments (which may have been made under thoroughly imperfect conditions for contracting, and have incorporated undesirable values) be prioritized over the electorate's present capacity to rule itself through democracy? Although imperfect, representation at least has a plausible claim to direct accountability. If both the moment of contracting and contemporary representation could be flawed, why favor the older, less accountable form which has rigidly internalized a set of prospectively unjust social norms to guide the terms of current self-rule?

Many of the arguments that advocate for originalism as a form of constitutional interpretation exacerbate, rather than resolve, this tension. Whittington observes that the various justifications for originalism as the preferred mode of constitutional interpretation are ultimately based on "normative theory."[19] That is, originalist treatment of the Constitution is justified by claims that it leads to better normative outcomes than alternative forms of constitutional interpretation. But this reinvokes the problem of simply imposing values on the electorate in a context (in this case, elections) in which the goal is to maximize popular self-determination. If democracy is justified as a procedure because it empowers constituents' autonomy, and electoral rules are designed to facilitate that end, then giving force to less accountable procedures (such as an imperfectly authorized constitution, enforced by unaccountable judges) contravenes this value. To argue that originalism as determined by judges yields normatively more attractive outcomes than alternate modes of constitutional enforcement is simply to assert that some norms are *ex ante* correct – and to suggest that a higher set of normative values in democracy exists than self-determination.

Such a purely norm-based justification for the Constitution as a contract thus cannot justify constitutional policing of electoral procedure. The answer must lie in a theory that explains not why the Constitution is *better* by some objective claim of efficacy, but why it is a *superior expression of popular autonomy*. A compelling answer offered by Michael McConnell seems to bridge originalist analysis and popular self-determination. As social beings who live in a historical context, the "concept of 'self-government over time' does not refer to an ideal of governance at each successive moment by the will of the governed at that moment, nor to the imposition of one moment's democratic will on the rest of the nation's future, but rather to the nation's struggle to lay down temporally extended commitments and to honor those commitments over time."[20] If judges apply this principle, this means the Constitution is taken to have its original meaning and that this commitment dominates later political acts that are not constitutional in nature. This account may

---

[19] Whittington, "Originalism," 396–400.
[20] McConnell, "Textualism," 1134–5.

offer a compelling justification for why the Constitution's substantive commitments can legitimately override later legislative action.

This historicity must face a particular challenge if it is to be used to justify structural intervention in electoral procedure because such procedure is the very means by which a polity rules itself in the present. For past commitments to dictate ongoing self-rule, these obligations should unequivocally reflect the will of the electorate (because only these unequivocal commitments appear to be the free expression of the people). Invoking history uses the continuity of the polity's identity to describe the constitutional commitments as freely entered.

Yet the solution of the durability of the polity's identity raises the problem that Tuck notes regarding the right of a people to rule *itself*, not to be ruled by others (including those from the past). Originalism must therefore determine which is the more autonomous expression of the electorate's will: the constitutional commitment, or representative action. When judges advance constitutional commitments, if they serve as the vessel of the weightiest free commitment of the people, this poses no problem. But if they begin to make normative judgments about what this commitment means in pursuit of this originalist task, they are less able to claim to better reflect autonomy than the more current and accountable practices of democracy. Judges' own normative considerations intrude upon their ability to act as mere agents of the highest commitments of the popular will. As McConnell concedes, when originalists apply the constitutional text, they "mediate[] between past and present."[21] Such mediation suggests that the cognitive labor of the judges, rather than the will of the people, does much of the work – which the diversity of theories advanced to make sense of originalism seems to support. When judges advance an originalist understanding of the Constitution, they do not merely advance the will of the electorate. They interpret and adapt it.

This softens the asserted flaws in the initial social contract, but it also demonstrates that originalist judicial review does more than enforce popular commitments. Originalist judges make independent decisions regarding norms and politics. In the context of electoral procedure, they intrude upon the autonomy of self-rule at the core of the counterpopular dilemma. In its implementation by judges, then, originalism cannot cleave to its original promise to be the uncomplicated expression of a direct and superior political commitment by the people. It does not resolve the tension that judicial review of election law elevates judges over representatives in the shaping of popular autonomy.

2.1.3 Normative and Linguistic Interpretation in the Originalist Mold

Even if the Constitution does not perfectly reflect the autonomy of the franchise, originalists might defend their approach as the best among imperfect alternatives.

---

[21] Ibid., 1136.

In this view, originalism most strictly obliges judges to adhere to a framework of self-governance that constituents consented to, and which articulates the mode of self-governance these constituents selected. Originalism thus limits the excursions judges may undertake that infringe upon the autonomously made commitments of the constituency.[22]

However, the originalist promise that it preserves constituent autonomy faces more intrinsic challenges as a mode of judicial reasoning. The first question is if text alone contains sufficient clarity to resolve legal disputes, at least with the high level of fixedness that makes originalism attractive. The second is whether, when resolving hard cases (the type that tend to be contentiously litigated, such as election law doctrine), applying the Constitution requires adverting to a normative framework or value set that is in fact not contained within the Constitution as originally understood. These two critiques are conceptually linked. The text's inability to fully determine the legal ramifications of applying the Constitution forces judges to advance novel norms to resolve disputes. According to Posner, a strictly contractarian approach to the Constitution would yield "less law."[23] Yet the battles over the implementation of originalism as well as the significant legal implications of originalist lawmaking make it unclear this is the case.

Whether this challenge defeats originalism is a seminal struggle of contemporary American constitutional scholarship. Critics of originalism argue that (1) the meaning of the text is not sufficiently determinate to be the touchstone of legal interpretation[24] and therefore that (2) originalist judges engage in creatively normative, rather than historical or linguistic analysis.[25] As David Strauss observes, "We routinely read principles we have developed for other reasons back into the text."[26] As Christopher Eisgruber notes, this leads (and should lead) judges to introduce normativity into constitutional interpretation, informed by their moral commitments rather than textual limitations.[27] Proponents of originalism respond that there are consistent ways to assign legal meaning to text (such as what Baude and Sachs call "canons of interpretation" that resolve such ambiguities)[28] and that originalism can

---

[22] Solum calls the principles that articulate this constraint the Fixation Thesis and Constraint Principle. Solum, "Originalism Versus Living Constitutionalism," 1265.
[23] Posner, "Law, Pragmatism, and Democracy," p. 272.
[24] Christopher L. Eisgruber, *Constitutional Self-Government* (Cambridge: Harvard University Press, 2001), pp. 28–30.
[25] For the general form of the theory, see Richard H. Fallon, "The Meaning of Legal 'Meaning' and its Implications for Theories of Legal Interpretation" (2015) 82 *The University of Chicago Law Review* 1235.
[26] David A. Strauss, "Does the Constitution Mean What It Says?" (2015) 129 *Harvard Law Review* 1, 17. For a more extensive discussion of why such normative analysis is necessary, see Curtis A. Bradley and Neil S. Siegel, "Constructed Constraint and the Constitutional Text" (2015) 64 *Duke Law Journal* 1213, 1217.
[27] Eisgruber, "Constitutional Self-Government," 30–1.
[28] William Baude and Stephen Sachs, "The Law of Interpretation" (2017) 130 *Harvard Law Review* 1079.

adequately inform legal meaning so as to dictate legal reasoning.[29] Originalists need not demonstrate that plain language reading or identifying the framers' decisive intent is a trivial task. They only need to show that it is the best way to make sense of the Constitution. Scalia refers to originalism as the lesser evil because he believes that, compared to alternative forms of constitutional interpretation, it provides the steadiest guide.[30]

If the originalist defense is satisfactory, it is especially compelling in the context of election law. If judges are "democratically authorized to create fundamental law," as Whittington maintains,[31] the claim that judicial review contravenes popular autonomy evaporates. This notion strikingly parallels Rawls' invocation of "higher law," though they yield very different outcomes.[32] The fragility of the initial moment of popular consent discussed above might raise concerns about the integrity of the constitutional foundations, but this lies outside the judiciary's remit. If the judiciary is to advance the Constitution at all, it should do so on terms that are most readily accommodated by the democratic commitment to self-rule among equal constituents. If the courts can undertake judicial review in the manner that most closely tracks the most authoritative expression of popular will, then interventions into elections elicit as little tension as possible. Originalists can claim this virtue if they can establish that their interpretation of constitutional text generally conform to the Constitution's original intent.

However, if the Constitution does not communicate enough information to represent the genuine will of the electorate, originalism only gives judges a deceptively firm pretext to impose their own normative judgments. Originalist judicial review is thus arguably more dangerous than other modalities, as judges can interfere with the procedures of popular self-determination, but claim that such interference is based on authoritative popular will. For originalist judicial review to truly advance the will of the people, judges must not engage in moral or creative reasoning, but instead in restrained conceptual and linguistic transplantation. The Constitution must have a clear enough meaning that judges are intermediaries of the popular will that it expresses.

It is difficult to accept that originalist analysis can operate without normative reasoning by judges that exceeds the document's bare linguistic commitments. This is illustrated by the diversity of theories and the vibrancy of the debate within the originalist community. If the application of constitutional text were sufficiently mechanical such that judges were simply giving voice to popular will, there should be less debate over how this mechanical application could occur. These debates introduce extra-constitutional value in deducing the popular will the Constitution is meant to express.

---

[29] Baude, "Is Originalism Our Law?" For a critical account see Whittington, "Originalism," 403–4.
[30] Scalia, "Originalism," 863.
[31] Whittington, "Originalism," 399.
[32] Rawls, "Political Liberalism," 234.

Underlying this discussion is a theoretical problem associated with claiming to mechanically apply the text – what Ronald Dworkin calls the "semantic sting." Judges' conclusions about the meaning of language are not purely mechanical.[33] Rather, the nature of legal decision-making requires seeking consistency of substantive morality, a philosophical quality of judging that becomes increasingly salient when the text is open-ended (as it tends to be in election law cases). Cases thus become "hard." For example, in *Buckley v. Valeo*,[34] which explored the issue of campaign finance, the Court asked a question related to the nature of campaigns that could not be resolved by mechanically parsing the First Amendment. The question required determining whether the use of private funding to appeal to voters comprised a type of social practice that fits with the broader picture of American political and constitutional practice. This point can be derived from Judge J. Skelly Wright's compelling analysis of the question of if money is speech. While he initially frames the question as assessing whether money is core speech or one of many possible mechanisms by which speech may be affected,[35] it evolves into a query about whether American politics is better imagined as a pluralist battle between special interests or as a holistic process of self-governance.[36]

The doctrinal question not only requires going beyond the text (the question "is money speech" is unanswerable without further context). It also necessitates considering competing visions of political organization (both of which are consistent with the text, but neither of which the text favors). The question is what moral theory best enables constituent autonomy with regard to the treatment of private campaign finance. Dworkin would be pleased with this development because it reveals that reaching adequate legal conclusions requires evaluating the community's moral values.[37] An originalist might argue that Wright did not adequately limit himself to consider the constitutional text and associated original intent. But this critique misses the fact that the theoretical richness of his analysis is not an optional excursion, but is necessary to determine if money is speech with any descriptive social accuracy. A more explicit attempt to conform to originalist optics would simply overlook certain issues that are central to determining whether money is speech *in the relevant socio-political context*.

But in undertaking this normative weaving, judges perform a task that is far from mechanical: It is laden with moral evaluation as well as linguistic analysis. Judges are not only faithful to the constitutional commitments of the text, but they also take into account, for example, the moral theories that the bare text suggests, as well as previous decisions and the coherence between these competing interests. The

---

[33] Ronald Dworkin, *Law's Empire* (Cambridge: Harvard University Press, 1986), p. 43.
[34] The doctrinally definitive account is given in *Buckley v. Valeo*, 424 US 1, 16 (1976).
[35] J. Skelly Wright, "Politics and the Constitution: Is Money Speech" (1976) 85 *Yale Law Journal* 1001, 1005.
[36] *Ibid.*, 1018.
[37] Dworkin, "Law's Empire," p. 225.

central role of judicial reasoning in the application of the Constitution undermines any conclusion that judges directly realize constituent freedom by directly applying their consent to a written contract. When evaluating electoral law, judges may be seeking to *serve* popular autonomy, but constitutional interpretation itself cannot be characterized as the direct *expression* of popular autonomy. Insofar as it is, what judges do is closer to the action undertaken by representatives – i.e. acting on behalf of the polity.

Originalists might reply that if nothing else, an originalist approach is more likely to generate fidelity to the Constitution, and therefore to conform *more* closely to the Constitution as an expression of popular will. This is in effect the question of what moral theory best enables the autonomy of the constituency, which then must be specifically applied to a given regulation.[38] According to Michael McConnell, originalists generally agree that "the intentions or understandings of the framers regarding a specific issue, while informative, are not ultimately authoritative, for it is their understanding of the constitutional principles embodied in the constitutional provision – not their analysis of a particular legal phenomenon – that is controlling."[39] But this argument is simply an attempt to make a strength out of a concession. It ignores the depth of the interpretive analysis that judges undertake when the constitutional text is vague and "hard" cases would turn on precise or deeply informed meanings – as it is in every area of election law, typically involving indeterminate concepts such as free speech and equal protection of the law.

The originalist approach runs at least two risks if it is taken to be satisfactory to resolve the dilemma of judicial review of election law. The first is that it will generate excessive confidence in terms of the legitimacy of judicial review, given its cost to popular autonomy. If judges believe they are only expressing the will of the electorate, they may fail to recognize the normative character and consequences of their reasoning. If judging is necessarily a philosophical task, it can override other expressions of democratic autonomy even if it is undertaken with fidelity to the Constitution. This possibility may be valid by certain philosophical lights, but a theory of judging that denies the possibility that such overriding may occur is likely to be less sensitive to the full ramifications of judicial review. The second risk points to the fact that a narrow focus on giving effect to original intent through text may prevent judges from directly considering the material norms at issue. In particular, it might preclude them from intervening to perform the type of autonomy-benefiting action to which they are uniquely well suited: correcting entrenching pathologies in representation. Originalism does little to incentivize judges to evaluate what types of decisions may benefit constituent self-governance, even if not contained in the initial text.

---

[38] Michael W. McConnell, "The Importance of Humility in Judicial Review: A Comment on Ronald Dworkin's Moral Reading of the Constitution" (1997) 65 *Fordham Law Review* 1269, 1285.

[39] Michael W. McConnell, "Originalism and the Desegregation Decisions" (1995) 81 *Virginia Law Review* 947, 1101.

Originalism thus cannot adequately justify judges dictating to the population how it ought to rule itself. Its claim to turn judges into mere agents of a higher, popularly authorized law is appealing, but the practice of judging does not sufficiently express the direct popular will to deliver on this promise. The original grant of authority it claims is too controversial and unsettled to resolve whether it is decisively representative of popular will, or what popular will should be. Even if it is taken to be authoritative, the open-ended provisions of the Constitution require too much independent moral reasoning to be put into legal action to be characterized as the direct will of the electorate.

2.2 THE INTERPRETIVIST–DELIBERATIVIST ACCOUNT: "LIVING" CONSTITUTIONALISM AND THE PROBLEM OF JUDICIAL NORM IMPOSITION

If normative decision-making lies at the center of judicial review, might judges' moral reasoning be independently legitimate, even where it contravenes the expressions of constituent autonomy? This is the shared claim of the diverse array of "living constitutionalist" theories. These theories propose that judicial lawmaking may reach moral conclusions that extends beyond the Constitution as framed or written. The array of these theories is diverse; Lawrence Solum identifies eleven types of living constitutionalism (twenty-one including subfamilies).[40]

The living constitutionalist approach still can be characterized as protecting the social contract among constituents. However, this contract is fluid and adaptable, defined by a shared moral and political vision rather than the fixed text of a document. To be reconciled with personal autonomy, living constitutionalism must be characterized as a contractualist endeavor as John Rawls describes in *Political Liberalism*: a contract entered by persons who accept one another as equals engaged in a shared project of governance on terms each participant respects (and would reasonably expect others to respect).[41] The reasonableness (as defensible to each participant) of the terms of ongoing governance, even if constituents have not acceded to particular policies, is the legitimating touchstone of such an account. Rawls calls this mutual reasonableness "public reason."

Solum suggests that living constitutionalist theories share two features: (1) they reject originalism's assertion that constitutional meaning stays static and (2) they maintain that the meaning of the Constitution can change due to new circumstances.[42] In the context of election law, these diverse theories must all give judges the authority to creatively and independently make sense of democratic process. This might seem to classify some theories, such as those of Bruce Ackerman and

---

[40] Solum, "Originalism versus Living Constitutionalism," 1271.
[41] Rawls, "Political Liberalism," p. 234.
[42] Solum, "Originalism versus Living Constitutionalism," 276.

Larry Kramer, as a distinct sub-branch of popular constitutionalist theory. Their theories point to the franchise (or at least some members of the franchise) as the source of change.[43] However, giving judges the authority to interpret popular will requires asserting that judges have a capacity for moral reasoning to settle the meaning of the Constitution as a socio-political arrangement rather than a settled contract.

Such an approach generates an initial tension in the authority to set the terms of self-governance. If judges are not bound by the constitutional text, they cannot justify counterpopular political structures by asserting that they are giving effect to the visibly articulated will of the people. Of course, the critique of originalism summarized above is that it also ultimately relies on trust in unconstrained judicial reasoning. One could say – and living constitutionalists likely would – that all constitutional enforcement depends on discretionary judicial reasoning. But as living constitutionalists do not even claim that judges are merely enforcing articulated constituent will, they must explicitly legitimate judicial authority over self-rule.

How this tension manifests, and how scholars try to resolve it, varies according to the variety of living constitutionalism. There are two broad forms of living constitutionalism. The first, *moderate* living constitutionalism, describes what lawmaking under a Constitution looks like, given that judges (and other actors) must adapt their understanding of the Constitution as social circumstances change. This form does not necessarily suggest that judges should answer a given constitutional question in a particular way. Rather, it identifies the types of influences that act upon constitutional lawmaking, how judges should sift through these influences, and what the subsequent aggregated legal edifice looks like. David Strauss and Jack Balkin have advanced core theories of this type. Richard Posner's pragmatism is slightly further afield but still falls into this category.

The second form asserts that the living constitution has a specific content that judges should seek to advance. The underlying characteristic of this *decisive* living constitutionalism is that it rests on a coherent moral framework that, if properly realized, indicates to judges the substance of the political order. The exemplar of this type is Ronald Dworkin and his woven conception of legal interpretation, which unifies the granular process of legal reasoning with a specific moral vision. Similarly, Christopher Eisgruber derives the moral content of American constitutionalism from its specific history.

For the purposes of the counterpopular dilemma, the critical distinction between moderate and decisive living constitutionalism is if constitutional analysis specifies normative content. This clarifies the challenge that a given living constitutionalist account faces in legitimating judicial authority over electoral procedure. Moderate living constitutionalism ultimately describes the influences and general type of

---

[43] Bruce Ackerman, *We the People* (Cambridge: Harvard University Press, 1993); Larry Kramer, *The People Themselves: Popular Constitutionalism and Judicial Review* (Oxford: Oxford University Press, 2004).

reasoning that judges should undertake, and thereby lacks the specific normative justification necessary to sustain coherent structural intervention. The assertiveness of decisive living constitutionalism offers a coherent and ontologically grounded vision of liberal democratic process, including elections – but can only do so by subordinating self-determination to a substantive moral vision.

2.2.1 Moderate Living Constitutionalism and Recourse to Judicial Discretion

If originalism is faulted for rigidly seeking meaning only from the Constitution as framed, one solution is to retain constitutional primacy but expand the range of sources to which judges can turn for guidance. David Strauss has advocated common law constitutionalism, which adapts the principles of common law precedential analysis.[44] Interpreting the Constitution should incorporate (1) the linguistic meaning of the constitutional text treated as a standalone document and (2) the meaning that has been assigned to it through past legal interpretation. The result is an "evolutionary process"[45] driven by the incorporation of "later opinions"[46] as well as judges' assessments "about fairness or good policy."[47] Strauss has also described common law constitutionalism as relying on both aggregated history ("traditionalism") and the status of provisions as providing clear resolutions to some problems ("conventionalism") to answer constitutional questions.[48]

Jack Balkin proposes an arguably more open-ended means of filling in constitutional meaning with "living originalism." He differentiates between the text of the Constitution – which may provide decisive guidance for a small proportion of questions – and the principles the Constitution reflects.[49] Giving effect to constitutional principles is informed by contemporary practices and requires "construction" rather than "interpretation."[50] "Fidelity to the Constitution means applying its text and principles to our present circumstances"[51] through a variety "modalities" that recognize and accommodate shifting social circumstances. Strauss and Balkin recognize the primacy of the Constitution, but explicitly look further afield to make sense of much of it. The similarity between their accounts is the critical feature for the current analysis, but the two theories use different types of material and process to accomplish this end. Strauss critiques Balkin for suggesting that judges may

---

[44] Strauss, "Does the Constitution Mean What It Says?," 13.
[45] David A. Strauss, *The Living Constitution* (Oxford: Oxford University Press, 2010), p. 53.
[46] Ibid., p. 64.
[47] Ibid., p. 33.
[48] David A. Strauss, "Common Law Constitutional Interpretation" (1996), 63 *University of Chicago Law Review* 877.
[49] Balkin, "Living Originalism," p. 5.
[50] Ibid., 4; Jack M. Balkin, "The Construction of Original Public Meaning" (2016) 31 *Constitutional Commentary* 71, 81.
[51] Balkin, "Living Originalism," p. 19.

2.2 The Interpretivist–Deliberativist Account

rely on many "modalities" to make sense of the constitution; Strauss takes a more streamlined and jurisprudence-focused common law approach. This critique may reflect their different priorities. Strauss emphasizes the role of judges to fill in constitutional meaning, whereas Balkin champions the perspective of citizens.[52]

These moderated approaches possess a practical sensitivity, and enable more accurate descriptions of what judges do and the substance of contemporary constitutional law. As Strauss observes, according to a truly originalist understanding, many "settled and important principles of constitutional law"[53] would need to be jettisoned. Strauss and Balkin maintain that the law can have updated substance and remain faithful to the Constitution. Furthermore, many prominent constitutional cases receive little, if any, guidance from the text itself (Strauss cites *Obergefell v. Hodge*'s recognition of same-sex equality as a particularly salient example);[54] Balkin would observe that they might be informed by underlying constitutional principles. The racial gerrymandering jurisprudence is a good example. The grossly discriminatory line drawing raised in *Gomillion* may be an easy equal protection case, but recent jurisprudence demands a subtle inquiry into the purpose of districting that cannot be answered by the bare meaning of the Fourteenth Amendment (as Chapter 7 demonstrates). Under living constitutionalism, judges can determine whether a given districting is discriminatory by looking at the text of the constitutional provision, how precedent handled past instances of racial discrimination, and the broader social context of districting in a society rife with racial oppression and wedge block voting. At one level, this is precisely what the equal protection districting cases do.

Moderate living constitutionalism softens any conflict between popular self-rule and judicial decision-making. The accounts reconcile how judges can reach decisions regarding electoral structure with norms of self-rule. Because of their flexibility, they do not dictate to judges what those outcomes are, but only the character of the general reasoning. Yet the balanced and flexible character of moderate living constitutionalism undermines its ability to resolve the counterpopular dilemma. Both Strauss and Balkin try to locate the locus of constitutional change beyond judges. Balkin emphasizes the citizens' perspective and suggests (with some echoes of Ackerman and Kramer) that citizens drive constitutional change through popular politics.[55] Strauss attributes change in the meaning of the Constitution to the jurisprudence itself. He describes the evolution of constitutional common law as curiously devoid of agency, noting that it unfolds of its own accord. Yet these accounts obscure the actors who make the decisions (balanced and prudent

---

[52] David Strauss, "Book Review (reviewing Jack M. Balkin, "Living Originalism (2011))," (2013) 23 *Law and Philosophy* 369, 374; Balkin, "Living Originalism," p. 17.
[53] Strauss, "Does the Constitution Mean What It Says?," 20.
[54] Ibid., 16.
[55] Balkin, "Living Originalism," pp. 18–9.

as they may be) about how constitutional text, past law, social circumstances and norms, and good policy ought to be weighed in a particular dispute: the judges themselves. By concluding that a particular electoral law arrangement is desirable or undesirable and restructuring the processes of politics, judges intervene in the exercise of self-governance. Even if they do so through a process that is respectful of past law, judicial intervention into the arrangement of electoral process still intrudes upon the mechanisms and decisions of popular autonomy effected by representation.

This is not to say that the engines of constitutional change identified by Strauss and Balkin do not alleviate one side of the counterpopular dilemma. The aggregative, adaptive nature of Strauss's account of constitutional development, and the practical, citizen-focused nature of Balkin's, suggest that their understandings should limit the judiciary's ability to seize outright control of democratic process. Moderate living constitutionalism thus seems to have the potential to mitigate the counterpopular character of judicial review. Yet two features of election case law contraindicate this claim with regard to election law. The first is the degree to which the election law jurisprudence has reflected extraordinary judicial innovation – from one person, one vote, to the foray into partisan gerrymandering, to the development of the anti-corruption rationale in campaign finance. None of these pillars of contemporary election law could be plausibly based on common law precedent (and, in the case of one person, one vote, they directly contradicted past case law). Balkin offers a solution. He argues that the Constitution can be interpreted as containing an anti-entrenchment mandate, particularly if representatives cease to stand for the majority.[56] Yet he does not explain how judges can construct the Constitution to realize this anti-entrenchment mandate without advancing their own substantive vision of democracy. The difficulty that moderate living constitutionalism faces with such an anti-entrenchment mandate is exacerbated by the structural quality of election case law, which it must have to play a robust role in defending democracy. Balkin could argue that the structure is implicit in the Constitution, but it is judges who must fill out constitutional principles with specific structures – and risk counterpopularism. Likewise, Strauss could assert that this structural quality is a function of the judiciary's role in maintaining sovereignty by ensuring fair elections.[57] Yet this gives judicial protection of election law a character akin to representation reinforcement, which introduces its own set of problems, as discussed below.

Without guidance from a clear normative commitment (a commitment originalists assert should be the contractarian plain meaning of the constitution), moderate living constitutionalism simply permits judges to impose their own values. Where this not only shapes points of policy but also imposes a normative vision

---

[56] Ibid., pp. 252–4.
[57] Strauss, "Does the Constitution Mean What It Says?," 54.

upon constituent self-governance, it faces the very teeth of counterpopularism. Indeed, Strauss implicitly concedes that the election law case he treats in the most detail, *Arizona State Legislature v. Arizona Independent Redistricting Commission*, imposed a constitutional meaning that fit its policy preferences.[58] The conclusion reached by the majority in this case (that a state referendum can set the terms of congressional districting) is, as a pure normative matter, eminently reasonable; but it openly conflicts with the text of the Constitution. Yet originalists have made the point that the Constitution is at least plausibly an expression of popular will; it is a harder argument for the other contributors to legal reasoning Strauss weighs, purely legal precedent and intuitions regarding good policy. Strauss vindicates *Arizona* as reflecting legitimate "general principles" about the nature of the legislature that have emerged through common law over time. But the priority assigned to these general principles, and the subsequent shaping of self-rule, derives from the Court, not the people.

Is moderate living constitutionalism, with its balanced approach and *general* ability to explain the diverse and evolving influences upon judicial reasoning, the most promising way to make sense of election law? It certainly avoids theoretical commitments that lead it into unabashed conflict with the core principles of constituent autonomy (as do the other theories discussed in this chapter). But it only does so insofar as it gives judges a sort of discretion that necessarily prizes some value above constituent self-rule. Richard Posner's theory of judicial pragmatism (which Solum classifies as a variety of living constitutionalism)[59] directly addresses this problem.[60] Challenging the notion that judges have some special interpretive skill,[61] Posner urges reasonableness in judicial resolution of problems, rather than invoking principle (based in the Constitution or otherwise). Yet urging judges to be pragmatically outcome-focused in resolving questions of how elections should be structured concedes to technocratic authoritarianism. This view pushes Posner into some strange corners, such as arguing that *Bush v. Gore* is as constitutionally reasonable a decision as *Reynolds v. Sims*.[62] While this view diminishes the value of constituent autonomy, it is conceptually consistent with Posner's preference for an admittedly "elitist" conception of democracy.[63] He advocates a political arrangement that achieves certain outcomes, and is willing to allocate power, and define the nature of judicial review, as necessary to get it. But this is simply the rejection of the animating interest in constituent self-governance as the prime virtue of democracy.

---

[58] Ibid., 11.
[59] Solum, "Originalism Versus Living Constitutionalism," 1274.
[60] Posner, "Law, Pragmatism, and Democracy"; Richard A. Posner, *The Federal Judiciary: Strengths and Weaknesses* (Cambridge: Harvard University Press, 2017).
[61] Posner, "Law, Pragmatism, and Democracy," p. 351.
[62] Ibid., p. 242.
[63] Ibid., p. 187.

2.2.2 Decisive Living Constitutionalism: Judges as Weavers of the Moral Order

Compared to originalism, the distinguishing feature of moderate living constitutionalism is the claim that judges can incorporate changed social circumstances and norms of justice during constitutional interpretation. Yet this approach still recognizes the Constitution as authoritative where it speaks clearly. An alternative view is that the Constitution has no such claim to dominance in judicial review. Rather, it is subordinate to some other moral goal.

This approach prizes unitary moral vision over other forms of political – and legal – decision-making. It asserts that American democratic constitutionalism entails specific substantive political values. When capable judges advance this substantive vision, constitutional lawmaking has the purity of moral philosophy. This moral advancement of democratic values can contradict even popular self-rule. Jürgen Habermas offers a philosophical justification for an approach like decisive living constitutionalism with the "discourse principle."[64] He argues communicative acts such as legal decision-making necessarily advance normative ends. Constitutional reasoning, regardless of whether or not it claims to consist of interpretation of some authoritative text, is an eminently moral pursuit. In a democracy the normative end judges should advance is freedom. However, given that the authoritative reasoning by judges necessarily binds constituents with the coercive power of the state, this philosophical account faces the same problem as Dworkin and Eisgruber: it requires at a minimum accepting a posited view of communicative freedom. As a *political* act, such normative reasoning imposes values upon those affected by such judging. In the context of democratic procedure, such authoritative imposition of norms evokes the counterpopular dilemma with especial sharpness.

Ronald Dworkin's work exemplifies decisive living constitutionalism within the common law constitutional tradition. He offers an account that weaves together the entire lawmaking process, from the granular application of legal principle to specific cases;[65] to the appropriate treatment of the written constitution;[66] to a theory of judicial interpretation ("law as integrity");[67] to the substantive values that this theory of judicial interpretation should advance.[68] His theory of constitutional decision-making has a seamless unity rather than building up from a dedicated single value

---

[64] Jürgen Habermas, *Between Facts and Norms: Contributions to a Discourse Theory of Law and Democracy*, William Rehg (trans.), (Malden, MA: Polity Press, 1996), p. 128.
[65] Dworkin, "Law's Empire," p. 30.
[66] Ibid., pp. 379–80.
[67] Ibid., p. 225.
[68] This account is distributed across multiple texts. Dworkin's theory of legal interpretation is most extensively recounted in *Law's Empire* (which argues for a view of law as informed by moral readings that seek integrity in law), his theory of democracy in the introduction to *Freedom's Law*, and his account of specific democratic value in *Sovereign Virtue*.

(a quality that Arthur Ripstein calls "anti-Archimedean").[69] Some have criticized the seamlessness of Dworkin's approach, particularly when he indicates appropriate policy positions. Thomas Eisele has suggested that Dworkin's substantive vision of the Constitution (as expressed in *Freedom's Law*) hangs together only because "Dworkin seems to think that he knows how the constitution works" and has a particular capacity to pick out its "moral connotations or overtones."[70] This criticism is based on Dworkin's underlying view of morality as "a distinct, independent dimension of our experience."[71] This requires judges to be able to identify the principles that animate the constitutional infrastructure to resolve cases (rather than resort to their own intuitions). As Michael McConnell sharply observed, it is difficult to disentangle when a judge is correctly identifying and precipitating the moral character of the Constitution, and when they are simply imposing their own moral intuitions onto the law.[72] However, Dworkin would deny this, and instead argue that judges should advance moral principles derived from social context in a manner that flows from interpretation.[73]

Yet Dworkin's theory boldly activates the counterpopular dilemma. He argues that judges (ideally) resolve legal disputes by fitting each outcome into a single "coherent conception of justice and fairness."[74] Judicial review ought to yield an aggregation of rights and duties that is harmoniously integrated such that it could be the hypothetical product of a "single author"[75] who synthesizes the moral posture of the polity. This quality of unifying moral synthesis applies just as much to disputes over constitutional interpretation as it does to resolving any competing claim to legal right. Dworkin argues that, if anything, the philosophical quality of judging is more explicit in constitutional judicial review because such questions are based on the core principles of social organization.[76] Echoing Habermas, judges always act as philosophers, particularly when opining on the political order articulated in the Constitution.

---

[69] Arthur Ripstein, "Introduction: Anti-Archimedianism" in Arthur Ripstein (ed.), *Ronald Dworkin* (Cambridge: Cambridge University Press, 2007).

[70] Thomas D. Eisele, "Taking Our Actual Constitution Seriously" (1997) 95 *Michigan Law Review* 1799, 1819–20.

[71] Ronald Dworkin, "Objectivity and Truth" (1996) 25 *Philosophy and Public Affairs* 87–139 at 99; Richard A Posner, "The Problematics of Moral and Legal Theory" (1998) 111 *Harvard Law Review* 1637, 1656.

[72] McConnell, "The Importance of Humility in Judicial Review," 1270; see also T.B. McAffee "The Constitution as Based on the Consent of the Governed – or Should We Have an Unwritten Constitution?" (2001) 80 *Oregon Law Review* 1245, 1259.

[73] Ronald Dworkin, *Freedom's Law: The Moral Reading of the American Constitution* (Cambridge: Harvard University Press, 1997), p. 11; Edward J. McCaffery, "Ronald Dworkin, Inside-Out" (1997) 85 *California Law Review* 1043, 1050.

[74] Dworkin, "Law's Empire," p. 225.

[75] Ibid.

[76] Ibid., p. 380.

Turning judges into philosophers with the (hypothetical)[77] moral authority to fully understand law (and the just coercive potential of government) as a "coherent and structured whole,"[78] Dworkin diminishes the legitimacy of constituent citizen self-governance. Constituents, particularly in a diverse large-scale democracy, do not self-govern like Dworkin's ideal Hercules. Democracy is conflictual, rife with compromise and bargaining, and frequently inconsistent at particular points in time – and *especially* over time. Dworkin argues that the *sine qua non* of democracy should not be popular self-rule, but rather "government subject to conditions...of equal status for all citizens."[79] Some scholars embrace the antipopular potential of Dworkin's theory of judicial review even more explicitly than Dworkin himself; Rebecca Brown indicates that the reinvigorating power of Dworkin's account is not that it answered the "simplification" of Bickel's countermajoritarian difficulty, but rather that it demonstrated Bickel's formulation was "flat and self-contained."[80] Justice inheres in conformity between policies achieved by law and the coherent moral commitments of the community. Judges may counter popular will if coherent moral commitments of the polity (in the abstract) demand it.

Dworkin's theory is unusually unified. He maintains that the ideal judge resolves any systemic tension as they engage in constitutional reasoning. Eisgruber has adapted a similar (but less totalizing) theory for American constitutionalism. Like Dworkin, he characterizes judicial review as a philosophical enterprise.[81] Yet Eisgruber includes the caveat that judges only resort to moral principle when deciding hard cases, which reveals a distinction from Dworkin's totalizing approach. Dworkin would argue that judges *always* rely on a moral theory when deciding *any* case; in an easy case, the theory explains why the case is decisively resolved by legal principles that reflect a coherent moral view.[82] In the constitutional domain, the subject of this philosophical analysis is "the institutional structure of the United States,"[83] a capacity where judges should advance the American people's conception of justice.[84] Yet Eisgruber is adamant that judges may permissibly make constitutional judgments that contravene popular will, and may even contravene the broader drift of the democratic structure.[85] Judges thereby have a role that enables

---

[77] Dworkin's (fictional) ideal judge is, after all, called Hercules.
[78] Dworkin, "Law's Empire," p. 400.
[79] Dworkin, "Freedom's Law," p. 17.
[80] Rebecca Brown, "How Constitutional Theory Found its Soul: The Contributions of Ronald Dworkin," in Scott Hershovitz (ed.), *Exploring Law's Empire: The Jurisprudence of Ronald Dworkin* (Oxford: Oxford University Press, 2008), pp. 46–47
[81] Eisgruber, "Constitutional Self-Government," p. 40.
[82] Ibid., p. 162.
[83] Ibid., p. 206.
[84] Ibid., p. 126.
[85] Ibid., p. 134.

them to both act in an agential capacity *for* the people,[86] and, if justice requires, *against* the will of the people.

The open turn to judicial review as *authoritative* and *conclusive* moral philosophizing directly challenges popular autonomy. Judges acting so have no real popular mandate, either in the form of ongoing expressions of popular will (i.e. elections) or a historically authorized constitution. Neither Dworkin nor Eisgruber would deny this. They simply redefine constitutional democracy as morally substantive rather than politically procedural. Democracy consists of a set of moral features in political practice rather than direct constituent power over policymaking.[87] Dworkin calls this "constitutional democracy" or "partnership democracy,"[88] and it possesses the woven substantive quality characteristic of his method. Eisgruber identifies four characteristics of just governance that give judges the authority and guidance to shape constitutional democracy: impartiality, effective choice, participation, and public deliberation.[89] Concomitantly Dworkin and Eisgruber openly reject the primacy of popular, collective self-rule and diminish the importance of elections.[90]

This resolves the counterpopular dilemma by fiat. Both Dworkin and Eisgruber identify freedom as the moral fulcrum of democracy, but reconcile this claim with the power they grant to judges only by imposing a specific substantive conception of freedom. As Chapters 4–7 demonstrate, such decisiveness in the arrangement of electoral matters should be a cause for unease. The array of electoral arrangements that Eisgruber argues maximize citizens' freedom to rule themselves should undercut any confidence that such substantive conclusions can be presumed. One of Eisgruber's claims – that judges should be more cautious in striking down legislation that requires comprehensive and strategic assessments of the political system – seems to return power to the legislature.[91] But this simply moves the ball. Judges must still differentiate between "discrete" and "comprehensive" political principles, and will simply legitimate their decisions to intervene (or not) on these terms. Indeed, comprehensive claims may often be more compelling from the structuralist anti-lockup perspective discussed below. Furthermore, Eisgruber's treatment is inconsistent, given that he celebrates one person, one vote, one of the most comprehensively structural (and textually and precedentially innovative) decisions in the history of the Supreme Court.[92] As is seen in Chapter 4, it is precisely the type of issue that for critics of its justiciability, requires a "comprehensive" assessment, but for

---

[86] Ibid., p. 78. Eisgruber takes care to delineate the features of judges that make them suited to such an agential role, and which soften concerns about judicial tyranny.
[87] Dworkin, "Freedom's Law," p. 17.
[88] Ronald Dworkin, *Sovereign Virtue: The Theory and Practice of Equality* (Cambridge: Harvard University Press, 2002).
[89] Eisgruber, "Constitutional Self-Government," pp. 83–5.
[90] Dworkin, "Freedom's Law," p. 17; Eisgruber, "Constitutional Self-Government," p. 83.
[91] Eisgruber, "Constitutional Self-Government," p. 169.
[92] Ibid., p. 73.

those who find it unabashedly offensive, is a "discrete" violation of voting equality. The power to decide returns to judges.

This challenge becomes more complicated in a comprehensive consideration of judge-asserted living constitutionalism. Such an analysis requires an ontology of democratic constitutionalism that derives its legitimacy from some characteristic beyond expressed constituent will. It further demands that judges have moral knowledge to understand, and subsequent moral authority to enforce, such a vision. Assigning such unique moral knowledge to judges can be reasonably criticized as technocratic when applied to the mechanism by which constituents realize their political freedom (i.e. elections). Dworkin and Eisgruber vindicate their accounts of judicial moral authority by asserting that these visions operate in the service of freedom. Yet ironically, they justify imposing a concept of democratic constitutionalism because it fits their substantive conclusions of what legal and political arrangements characterize a free society rather than because constituents were responsible for determining these arrangements. Giving judges the power to determine these procedures requires a highly specified substantive vision of what constitutes good governance. The underlying concept of freedom – at least vis-à-vis electoral procedure – obliges society to deliver certain conditions or policy outcomes rather than give constituents the power *to set those conditions themselves*. This is reminiscent of the concept of positive freedom, in which being free consists of achieving certain goals rather than ensuring autonomous self-determination. But, as Isaiah Berlin observes in his critique of positive freedom, this is simply a euphemism for asserting that individuals do not have the moral authority to set their own path. This concept of freedom uses judicial authority to interpret the Constitution in order to create an interpretive temple of Sarastro, imposing a view of ideal self-governance on the polity.

This view contrasts sharply with the initial promise of the Constitution as a resolution to the counterpopular dilemma. The Constitution offers a plausible means by which judicial shaping of electoral procedure can be authorized by the very people whose capacity to self-rule is affected. Under decisive living constitutionalism, this authorization has meaning only in a metaphorical or paternalistic sense. It does not mean the result of an election, the passing of a referendum, or even the framing of a constitution, but rather moral knowledge of just political organization to which persons ought to adhere because of the rectitude of this account. By giving the judiciary the power to identify this knowledge, the decisive living constitutionalist account suggests it is most readily available to intellectual and professional elites. These judicial elites are thought to somehow be able to access the moral principles undergirding a political community better than constituents themselves.

Championing judicial power in this way jeopardizes the moral primacy of popular self-rule. An independent, majority-checking institution such as the judiciary plays an incontrovertibly valuable role in liberal democracy by protecting rights and interdicting state coercion by partisan forces. But this account does not adequately explain why judicial elites can set the terms by which the franchise realizes its own capacity to self-govern. It is telling that Dworkin and Eisgruber denigrate the role of elections in a democracy – because their concept of judicial review cannot be felicitously reconciled with a vision of democracy that derives its legitimacy from functional practices of self-rule.

2.3 INSTRUMENTALIST INSTITUTIONALISM

These varieties of constitutionalism treat judicial review as a normative problem: how can the role of courts be vindicated in a democracy? Focusing on outcomes rather than principled justifications casts the query differently: how should courts intervene to most benefit representative governance? This approach emphasizes the distinctive institutional features of courts, their rule of law independence from political accountability.

This institutionalist approach elegantly informs one side of the counterpopular dilemma: when are the courts the right institution to police electoral procedures? The answer is, whenever the power to set electoral rules lies with those who would benefit from a certain arrangement, such as incumbent representatives or blocs of voters who currently hold power. As Ely snappily phrases it, "We cannot trust the ins to decide who stays out."[93] Courts' independence from politics allows them to successfully identify and condemn self-serving misfeasance in the design of election law.

The problem comes from the other side of the equation – the normative validity of judicial intervention. Self-dealing in the design of electoral procedures might be incontrovertibly condemnable, but determining when a particular design qualifies as undesirable self-dealing (as opposed to political business as usual), and then deciding when self-dealing crosses into illegality, requires a substantive theory of democratic representation.

The question of when state action crosses from a political practice to a violation of the constitutional arrangements of representation has been most prominent in the context of partisan gerrymandering. Supreme Court justices agree on the undesirability of the practice, but there has been a fierce divide over whether judges are equipped to assess when it is sufficiently oppressive so as to be illegal. A classic example that presaged much of the fierce debate is *Gaffney v. Cummings*, in which the Supreme Court approved a bipartisan gerrymandering that maintained the balance of power between the two major parties.[94] A bipartisan gerrymander may be entrenching, but the nature of the wrong is slipperier than in typical one-sided partisan gerrymanders that harm the minority party. Bipartisan gerrymanders have also been also part and parcel of politics in a two-party system where it is desirable to reach agreements regarding continued (and at least somewhat stabilized) terms of representation.

---

[93] Ely, "Democracy and Distrust," p. 120.
[94] *Gaffney v. Cummings*, 412 US 735 (1973).

This is characteristic of the general problem for any wide-scale shaping of political process already identified in originalism and living constitutionalism, and which the instrumental account cannot evade. Any judicial declaration of illegality rests not only upon a descriptive evidentiary judgment (has a given practice occurred?), but upon a normative one (is the practice wrongful, and if it is wrongful does it cross the line into illegality?). While in some cases the normative account is trivial given both explicit constitutional commitments and the norms of a polity – instances of blatant racial discrimination, such as *Gomillion* and *Smith v. Allwright* are exemplary from a modern perspective – the battles typically take place over the hard cases and reasonably contested values. In *Gomillion*, Alabama argued *not* that its conduct was not discriminatory, but that the Court had no authority to regulate districting. One can construct an elaborate counterfactual normative argument regarding the preferability of even noxious political preferences being worked out purely politically, and support extraordinary judicial passivity. But this counterfactual is beyond the scope of this book, which concentrates on contemporary doctrine. The law of race now focuses on much more subtle questions of what comprises discrimination. In the racial gerrymandering domain, for example, the question has become when racial classifications of voters for a racially neutral or even progressive purpose are nevertheless illicit. As Chapter 7 demonstrates, this turns to the question of what form of equality voters can demand as members of a bloc in the pursuit of self-rule, which can only be resolved by adverting to a theory of democracy.

The institutional justification for judicial review intensifies rather than resolves the counterpopular dilemma. It explicitly accommodates the benefits of judges overseeing the electoral process and uses this to justify the counterpopular quality of judicial review. In doing so, however, it reveals the complexity, and ultimately the insolubility, of the questions of democratic design.

2.3.1 The Classical Institutional Account: Ely's Process-based Representation Reinforcement

Ely's *Democracy and Distrust* provides the seminal institutional account. Ely introduces representation reinforcement to justify the Warren Court's interventionism against Bickel's countermajoritarian challenge. The theory hangs on a distinction between substantive and procedural intervention. Ely asserts that "the original Constitution was principally, I would say overwhelmingly, dedicated to concerns of process and structure and not to the identification and preservation of specific substantive values."[95] This informs what "activist" judicial review should seek to accomplish: "unblocking stoppages in the democratic process."[96]

The influence and appeal of Ely's argument are unequivocal. His approach resonates strongly with the influential anti-lockup view discussed below. Even those who

---

[95] Ely, "Democracy and Distrust," p. 92.
[96] Ibid., p. 117.

do not identify themselves as direct heirs of the Ely tradition can often be understood as working within the backdrop he set, such as the suggestions by Bertrall Ross and Douglas Spencer as well as Ganesh Sitaraman that poverty or economic power should receive judicial attention, or Nicholas Stephanopoulos's call to look to power in politics to guide election law.[97]

Accountable representation is the fundamental mechanism of large-scale democracy,[98] and, in Ely's account, a central theme of the Constitution.[99] Courts, as defenders of the Constitution, have a strong justification to step in when representatives are unresponsive to the voters' preferences. But the core principle guiding judicial review is that it should not impose substantive values, but only ensure the political process is fair.

Ely's theory is a general one, meant to vindicate *Brown* as much as *Baker*. It is particularly tricky to apply it to election law.[100] His explanation of how representation reinforcement justifies striking down illicit classifications *generally* (as opposed to specifically protecting "discrete and insular minorities") requires a much more elaborate bridge between democratic representation and discriminatory policy. It is justified by the concept of power-based self-dealing generally rather than a specific idea of representation.

Representatives have an "obvious vested interest" in maintaining an electoral setup that will allow them to remain in office.[101] Where they promulgate electoral rules that contravene effective representation, the courts are justified in intervening to stop them. Malapportionment is a straightforward example: If those in power can decide how much proportional power those who will select them in the future will have, they obviously have a strong incentive to diminish the power of their opponents as much as possible. *Baker* and *Reynolds* are examples of the Court intervening to restore representation to its rightful condition in accordance with good democratic practice. Rural cliques were obstructing majority rule in an urbanizing America, and the one person, one vote rule addressed this pathology.

Yet Ely's account of judicial review as wholly procedural and thus substantively agnostic does not hold. A claim of good process is itself laden with values, "hidden within [Ely's] view of democracy."[102] That is, *any claim about what comprises good*

---

[97] Bertrall L. Ross II and Douglas M. Spencer, "Voter Suppression: Campaign Mobilization and the Effective Disenfranchisement of the Poor" (2019) 114 *Northwestern University Law Review* 633; Ganesh Sitaraman, *The Crisis of the Middle-Class Constitution: Why Economic Inequality Threatens Our Republic* (New York: Alfred A. Knopf, 2017); Nicholas O. Stephanopoulos "Political Powerlessness" (2015) 90 *New York University Law Review* 1527. For an insightful discussion of how contemporary election law can be traced back to Ely, see Luke P. McLoughlin, *The Elysian Foundations of Election Law*, 82 *Temple Law Review* 89 (2009). Many thanks to Nick Stephanopoulos for bringing this article to my attention.
[98] Ely, "Democracy and Distrust," p. 78.
[99] Ibid., p. 87.
[100] Ibid., p. 158.
[101] Ibid., p. 117.
[102] Pamela S. Karlan, "Democracy and Disdain" (2012) 126 *Harvard Law Review* 1, 15.

or fair process contains substantive norms. Ely executes an elegant sleight of hand to bury the problem he seeks to solve. Lawrence Tribe successfully captures this when he states "The process theme by itself determines almost nothing unless its presuppositions are specified, and its content supplemented, by a full theory of substantive rights and values – the very sort of theory the process-perfecters are at such pains to avoid."[103] As William Eskridge explains, process theory's dependence on substantive value in this way "deepen[s] rather than solve[s] the problem of unguided judicial activism," characterizing the approach as "indeterminate" for guiding judicial decision.[104] Ely concedes that "elaboration of representation-reinforcing theory of judicial review could go many ways."[105] Yet the consequences of rulings cannot be indeterminate, particularly where they do not merely resolve single disputes but establish structures of governance. The Supreme Court has reached several conclusions on good electoral arrangements, and these must redound upon values as morally substantive as the moralizing Lochnerism from which Ely distances himself. An electoral procedure imposed externally – by a judge or a Solomonic lawgiver – necessarily asserts that there is some value above or beyond the autonomy of the electorate and its capacity to rule itself that can legitimately shape democratic procedure. Such a claim demands unique or special wisdom regarding the ontology of citizens as politically free beings that political self-organization cannot sustain. Ely seeks to derive this knowledge from the Constitution,[106] but if this is the foundation of his claim, it transforms him into a type of living constitutionalist who assigns judges the power to make determinations about American political culture.

Ely's process-based argument for representation reinforcement illuminates, rather than solves, the core problem of judicial review. It demonstrates that any claim to neutrally enhance democratic process is really a substantive claim regarding legitimate self-rule. Such a substantive imposition of value explicitly confronts, but does not resolve, the counterpopular dilemma. I develop this point with regards to one person, one vote and racial gerrymandering later in the book, but in general, all political practices – such as deviation from per-person voting power equality that one person, one vote seeks to correct – must have emerged from prior political conditions. These conditions have their own social history and moral logic with some level of legitimacy and desirability. The originalist account seeks to rest upon such features, which complicates its reliance on pre-contractual social facts.

---

[103] Lawrence H. Tribe, "The Puzzling Persistence of Process-Based Constitutional Theories" (1980) 89 *Yale Law Journal*, 1063, 1063. For other seminal critics, see Mark Tushnet, "Darkness on the Edge of Town: The Contributions of John Hart Ely to Constitutional Theory" (1980) 89 *Yale Law Journal* 1037; Daniel R. Ortiz, "Pursuing a Perfect Politics: The Allure and Failure of Process Theory" (1991) 77 *Virginia Law Review* 721, 728; William N. Eskridge, Jr., "Pluralism and Distrust: How Courts Can Support Democracy by Lowering the Stakes of Politics" (2005) 114 *Yale Law Journal* 1279, 1282.

[104] Eskridge, "Pluralism and Distrust," 1282.

[105] Ely, "Democracy and Distrust," p. 181.

[106] *Ibid.*, p. 87.

These prior conditions determine electoral procedure. Since reshaping such procedure by means other than the political process requires an external touchstone, this requires the conclusion that at some point political practice deviated from the polity's "true" or "higher" will. The originalist account characterizes this "higher" will as historical, while the living constitutionalist account classifies it as moral. The problem of identifying this "true" or "higher" foundation is a political version of what Robert Nozick defends as "historic" as opposed to "patterned" distributions.[107] Even if such external judgments are made to serve those constituents – e.g. redrawing district lines to comport with some measure of fairness or racial equality – it still negates law that derives directly from some historical process of democratic representation. Such negation of popular will, taken without a popular mandate, leaves itself open to criticism that it is authoritarian.

2.3.2 Anti-lockup: Issacharoff, Pildes, Karlan, and Their Successors

Does this require courts to "stay out of the area [of electoral design] altogether"?[108] If interference with constituent self-determination is deemed to be too damning, courts could rely on passive virtues to avoid opining on election law matters.[109] Alternatively, they could frame responses to election law queries in the narrowest possible form to avoid the structuralism that has characterized election law.[110] Samuel Issacharoff, Richard Pildes, Heather Gerken, and others implicitly critique such a minimalist approach by arguing that the individual rights framework is not applicable to election law.[111]

Yet this minimalist approach ignores that courts are central to the broader democratic constitutional order. The tension between fair adjudication and the nature of elections does not absolve the courts of their constitutional duty to advance justice, but rather gives the counterpopular dilemma its unique force. The question is how courts can make counterpopular decisions that together contribute to, rather than infringe upon, the electorate's capacity to rule itself.

Issacharoff, Pildes, and Pamela Karlan have developed such an account. They argue that judicial review of election law should interdict practices that allow representatives to entrench themselves and impair electoral competition. This anti-lockup theory refines Ely's general focus on representation reinforcement[112] into a realist,

---

[107] Robert Nozick, *Anarchy State and Utopia* (Malden, MA: Basic Books, 1974), p. 156.
[108] Ely, "Democracy and Distrust," p. 124.
[109] Alexander M. Bickel, "Passive Virtues" (1961) 75 *Harvard Law Review* 40.
[110] Cass R. Sunstein, *One Case at a Time: Judicial Minimalism on the Supreme Court* (Cambridge: Harvard University Press, 2001).
[111] See, for example, Gerken, "Lost in the Political Thicket," 507.
[112] Samuel Issacharoff, "Political Judgments" (2001) 68 *University of Chicago Law Review* 637, 654; Issacharoff and Pildes, "Politics as Markets," 709–10 identify this, though it is curious that the relationship with Ely does not play a more central role in the anti-lockup theory. Issacharoff, "Political Judgements" in particular describes Ely as only affiliated with minoritarian protection, when as demonstrated above Ely articulated a far more general theory of process review.

institution-centric understanding of democratic constitutionalism. Its advocates argue that democratic constitutionalism should focus not on individual rights or democratic ideals, but on the realities of power.[113]

The anti-lockup view asserts that judicial intervention is justified when legal rules "protect established powers from the risk of successful challenge"[114] because "groups in power have barricaded themselves into place or have permanently excluded a class of citizens from participating fully in civic life."[115] Under such conditions, "the political process has become immune to competitive challenge to the status quo," creating "incapacity for repair from within."[116] The defining characteristic of these pathologies is that electoral procedures cease to ensure that representatives remain responsive to their constituents and instead allow them to retain power *in defiance* of the popular will. Underlying this is the structural reality that accountability is lost when citizens cannot credibly threaten to vote politicians out of office. The role of the courts – and specifically the Supreme Court – is to "destabilize these lockups."[117] Courts are perhaps the *only* institution that can perform this function in this account due to the governing coalition's unresponsiveness to "the claims of injustice by those on the outs politically"[118] – the very rule-of-law judicial independence celebrated in general accounts of liberal constitutional democracy. The anti-lockup account is compelling because it justifies counterpopular judicial action in response to a particular structural pathology in electoral politics. Counterpopular judicial review is legitimized as part of the general architecture of liberal democracy. Courts only act to address threats to the foundational relationship of representative democracy – constituent self-rule.

One person, one vote is a seminal example of appropriate intervention for breaking up self-serving behavior by those in power.[119] So is the prohibition of White primaries. Beyond ending a discriminatory practice, it broke down an ossified political alliance perpetuated by exclusionary legal rules. As Issacharoff and Pildes explain, "the Democrats' use of state authority to bar black participation was a classic political lockup."[120] Conversely, Issacharoff and Pildes criticize the Supreme Court for condoning anti-fusion laws, which weaken third parties and therefore make it easier for dominant parties to freeze out political competitors.[121] Yet the Court should

---

[113] Richard H. Pildes, "The Constitutionalization of Democratic Politics" (2004) 118 *Harvard Law Review* 29, 40.
[114] Issacharoff and Pildes, "Politics as Markets," 646.
[115] Karlan, "Democracy and Disdain," 11.
[116] Issacharoff, "Political Judgements," 654.
[117] Issacharoff and Pildes, "Politics as Markets," 644.
[118] Issacharoff, "Political Judgements," 655.
[119] Samuel Issacharoff, "Judging Politics: The Elusive Quest for Judicial Review of Political Fairness" (1993) 71 *Texas Law Review* 1643, 1650; Karlan, "Democracy and Disdain," 4.
[120] Issacharoff and Pildes, "Politics as Markets," 664.
[121] *Ibid.*

only act where representatives are advancing electoral practice that has such an anti-competitive effect. Issacharoff and Karlan have noted that the judiciary should not intervene to advance majoritarian aims when the representative branches are effectively facilitating citizen self-rule.[122] Karlan argues that courts should defer to legislation when they advance inclusive and functional democratic structures (as the Warren Court often did, most notably in the Voting Rights Act of 1965).[123]

The anti-lockup approach identifies the structural conflict between representatives and their constituents to vindicate judicial intervention. Lockups occur when representatives cease to act as faithful agents of their constituents and instead exploit their role as agents for their own benefit. Underlying this account are two assumptions about politics. The first is that representative democracy is best modeled as a competitive market, with constituents and representatives in cutthroat power relationships marked by instrumentalism, distrust, and opportunism. Voters want representatives who will execute their will; representatives are desperate to maintain their grip on power. This is apparent in the anti-lockup theorists' affinity for public choice theory. The second, complementary assumption is that for the purposes of judicial review, mass democracy is best conceived as dominated by an elite managerial class.[124] Together, these features suggest a grimly Schumpeterian understanding of politics as elite battles for the approval of the masses.

The obvious critique is that such a specified conception of politics itself comprises a normative commitment and that the judiciary imposes such a vision if it relies on it to legitimize counterpopular judicial review. Yet on its own, this critique is less cogent than might be expected. Nothing in anti-lockup theory specifies that democracy *must* be organized along such lines (though it appears to be more accurate than many other models of contemporary, highly polarized mass democracy), and adherents recognize the diversity of democratic theories.[125] Rather, anti-lockup theory indicates a condition when courts *should* intervene: When democratic representation takes on a certain feature that can be helpfully identified through a particular theory. Anti-lockup does *not* specify how democracy should look; it merely identifies a non-exclusive condition when judicial oversight of elections is justified. Asserting that a loss of accountability due to entrenchment justifies judicial intervention is a hard argument to reject. By definition, it ties judicial contravention of legislation to a very *loss* of popular control, circumventing the claim that judicial review is counterpopular.

The real critique of anti-lockup theory is more subtle: Its key ideas – competition and entrenchment – do not, in and of themselves, have intrinsic substance. Instead,

---

[122] Issacharoff, "Political Judgements," 655.
[123] Karlan, "Democracy and Disdain," 12–8.
[124] Issacharoff and Pildes, "Politics as Markets," 646.
[125] Pildes, "The Constitutionalization of Democratic Politics," 43; Issacharoff and Karlan, "The Hydraulics of Campaign Finance Reform," 1723–4.

they require specifying what good democracy looks like. That is, identifying when leaders are entrenched (and competition is absent from a political system) is not merely a descriptive exercise. It involves making a set of judgments about how democratic process should work if it helps leaders stay in office rather than ensure the stability of governance or a fair opportunity to realize policy by a victorious bloc, and so forth. The problem is not that preserving electoral competition is the counterpopular imposition of a value, but rather that it is underinformed. Like Ely's theory of representation-reinforcement, it passes along the ball of normative judgment.

Campaign finance case law offers several illustrations of this point. The anti-lockup theorists, for example, have suggested that public funding of campaigns does not help reduce campaign finance corruption by reducing reliance on private money, but rather that it entrenches established major parties that can claim a greater share of public funds.[126] Issacharoff and Pildes maintain that courts should be willing to strike down public financing measures that favor successful parties for the structural reason that they impair competition.[127] The effects of the public financing regime can be descriptively assessed; some research has shown that public financing *increases* the likelihood of competitive elections, at least between the two major parties.[128] Anti-lockup theorists could argue that such studies focus on two-party competition, thus enhancing rather than diminishing lockups. However, even if the descriptive effects of public financing could be exhaustively parsed, this would not answer the question of if, as a *normative* matter, it was more or less desirable for courts to take the counterpopular step of striking down legislation that supported public financing. This is because a legal decision based on such descriptive evidence must come to a normative conclusion that electoral arrangements are better off if such legislation is nullified by an extra-democratic actor.

Public financing that favors major parties could (1) increase the amount of communication constituents receive about candidates who received funding, (2) decrease the amount of private money that flows to candidates who receive private funding, and (3) reduce the number of successful minor party challenges to major parties. Each of these effects can be described as either beneficial or harmful. Increased communication could be deemed beneficial to informed constituent decision-making, but if it generates an "information overload" (e.g. due to large amounts of issue advertising), it could also increase voter numbness to further information.[129] A reduction in private money could not only reduce corruption but also decrease responsiveness; and a reduction in third-party challenges could not only

---

[126] Issacharoff and Pildes, "Politics as Markets," 696; Issacharoff and Karlan, "The Hydraulics of Campaign Finance Reform," 1735.
[127] Issacharoff and Pildes, "Politics as Markets," 697.
[128] Neil Malhotra, "The Impact of Public Financing on Electoral Competition: Evidence from Arizona and Maine" (2008) 8 *State and Politics Policy Quarterly* 263.
[129] See G. Michael Parsons, "Fighting for Attention: Democracy, Free Speech, and the Marketplace of Ideas" (2020) 104 *Minnesota Law Review* 2157.

channel effective mid-point competition around major parties but also consolidate major parties' control.

A judicial conclusion that public financing should be typically deemed unconstitutional if it favors major parties and facilitates lockups could reverse these effects. Yet whether it is normatively acceptable to adopt such a position depends *not* on exhaustively identifying the effects, but on (1) the values of electoral procedures (i.e. is it worth impairing third-party viability to reduce private money influence on major party candidates, a major concern of scholars such as Larry Lessig, Sabeel Rahman, and Timothy Kuhner) and (2) determining whether, even if nullifying such legislation is desirable, it is worth the cost of sacrificing self-rule through representation in favor of counterpopular judicial action. No descriptive evidence can resolve such a question.

The issue of partisan gerrymandering further illustrates this point. Parties may use this practice to entrench their control. Judicial prohibition of gerrymanders benefits competition by preventing parties from reinforcing their dominance. An anti-lockup view should inspire courts to strike down partisan gerrymanders, at least when they are intentional egregious.

Yet judicial nullification of district lines drawn by representatives requires at least three presumptions. The first is that a partisan "victory bonus"[130] beyond proportional success is not a desirable aspect of democracy, and that courts, rather than the electorate, should evaluate the concept of such a bonus. The second assumption is that partisan gerrymandering does not induce parties and voters to adapt to changed district lines, perhaps inducing a sort of broad realignment of party bases.[131] Third, partisan gerrymandering will not necessarily spread the gerrymandered party thinner than it might be otherwise, potentially leaving as demographics change.[132]

Each of these claims can be evaluated as a descriptive matter (e.g. does a victory bonus produce more responsive governance? Do voters and parties adapt their partisan affiliation after redistricting?). Yet regardless of how much evidence is gathered, the ultimate evaluation is normative. One cannot determine, for example, whether governance after a victory bonus is more or less accountable without some vision of what accountable representation looks like. Notably, each of these mechanisms provides levers by which constituents might come to autonomously react to partisan gerrymandering in a manner that *harms* the gerrymandering party. A party that has enjoyed a victory bonus and still rules incompetently, for example, might expect to be defeated; if it does not, perhaps the failure should be laid at the feet of the constituents. The normative implications of it failing to harm the gerrymandering

---

[130] Peter H. Schuck, "The Thickest Thicket: Partisan Gerrymandering and Judicial Regulation of Politics" (1987) 87 *Columbia Law Review* 1325, 1350.
[131] This thesis is developed extensively in Jacob Eisler, "Partisan Gerrymandering and the Illusion of Unfairness" (2018) 67 *Catholic University Law Review* 229.
[132] Bruce Cain, *The Reapportionment Puzzle* (Berkeley: University of California Press, 1984).

party can be further debated. If parties and constituents do not react to new district lines to return to competitive equilibrium, for example, it can be deemed either a violation of constitutional legality or simply constituents' failure to engage politically. Determining which is the case requires articulating principles of fair political competition. Justifying counterpopular review requires a deeper explanation of why such a practice is illicit beyond merely the descriptive observation that it reduces competition.

Neither of these examples nullifies the appeal of the anti-lockup approach. They highlight the most egregious examples of undesirable election law legislation. A law that makes it illegal for a defeated party to engage in political advertising, for example, is a bald-faced attempt to suppress fair competition and should produce an immediate backlash from the courts and beyond. From a Waldronian perspective, this "beyond" would suggest that by the time judicial intervention is unequivocally necessary, it may also be redundant, because the popular backlash against such legislation would comprise the real policing mechanism. Rather, this analysis demonstrates that any appeal to competitiveness as a virtue of elections, and entrenchment as the attendant evil, turns on normative claims about how democracy should be organized. This analysis can occur within or outside of these concepts of competition and entrenchment, but ultimately requires a principled account.

Recognizing that any assessment of democratic practice depends on terms of legitimate self-rule, moreover, shows the risks that could occur if a court comes to rely on an anti-lockup framework. One risk is that the judiciary will fail to carefully interrogate the underlying qualities of a given electoral arrangement. Racial majority-minority districts, for example, could be seen as reducing competitiveness by "locking up" districts for identity-based wedge groups. Yet they can also provide otherwise marginal groups with at least a minimal level of representation (a dilemma addressed extensively in Chapter 7). An approach that is too focused on competition threatens to undermine careful consideration of competing values. Of course, advocates of a given theory of competition could always argue their way around this critique. But if this can be done, the most dangerous risk is that anti-lockup theory could serve as a cloak for substantive political interests. As discussed above, a set of assertions about the nature of democracy underlies anti-lockup theory. The seemingly value-neutral claim that courts should use the framework of competition to evaluate legislation can alternately be interpreted as advancing a normative understanding of democracy that accedes to public-choice competition and managerial control of politics by a Schumpeterian elite. This view of democracy can beneficially induce courts to act at times when, under a traditional individual rights view, they might fail to act. But simply asserting that courts act legitimately when they do so, without further interrogation, simply allows the judiciary to surreptitiously add its own value judgments. Thus, anti-lockup theory runs straight into the other horn of the counterpopular dilemma: Why are courts the appropriate institution to set the basic norms of democratic self-rule?

2.4 ACKNOWLEDGING AND ACCOMMODATING THE ROLE OF PARTISANSHIP

Since the goal of this project is to provide a unified theoretical account of modern election law, it is necessary to address a less theoretical alternative – that judges decide election law cases based on their partisan inclinations. Recent election law disputes have highlighted the fierce partisan divide on the Supreme Court bench. *Citizens United* and *McCutcheon* exposed this trend in campaign finance; *Shelby County* and *Brnovich* made it painfully clear in the context of race and elections; and the partisan gerrymandering cases of *Vieth* and *Rucho* have illustrated how long running it is in the party and elections context. This book might be critiqued as using an analytic scalpel where a sledgehammer that exposes tawdry political loyalties would do.

It is easy enough to offer a straightforward description of the partisan divide in recent years. It pits the progressives – Sotomayor, Kagan, and most recently Jackson (and, until recently, Breyer, Ginsburg, Souter, and Stevens) – against the conservatives – Roberts, Thomas, Alito, Gorsuch, Kavanaugh, and Barrett (and, until recently, Scalia, Rehnquist, and, most tentatively, Kennedy). While the fractures can be traced further back, with Marshall, Brennan, and Blackmun belonging to an older generation of progressives, and Burger an earlier conservative, the further back one traces the more diffuse this divide becomes. O'Connor is arguably the last justice whose allegiance cannot be reliably modeled using partisanship, even if she leaned conservative in her readings. She consistently sided with the conservative wing in the context of racial districting, the Voting Rights Act, and partisan gerrymandering, and wrote opinions that encapsulated essential conservative principles in each of these areas. Seminal examples include *Shaw v Reno, Georgia v. Ashcroft*, and *Davis v. Bandemer*. As discussed in Chapter 6, O'Connor's opinion in *Bandemer* encapsulates the main argument for rejecting judicial defense of parties – that parties are an organic expression of political will. However, after rejecting the progressive high-water mark in campaign finance law in *Austin v. Michigan*, she joined the progressives in the later pivotal campaign finance case of *McConnell v. FEC*. O'Connor's retirement likely marked the beginning of the transformation of campaign finance law by the conservative Court.

The bluntest account of the partisanship identifies a brute struggle between two ideologies. The progressives (appointed, with the exception of Souter, by Democrats)[133] wish to expand the power of the government (particularly the federal government), protect disadvantaged classes (particularly minorities and the poor), and advance robust and multifarious substantive egalitarianism – even if, in the eyes

---

[133] For an account of Souter's defiance of partisan expectation, see Jeff Greenfield, "The Justice Who Built the Trump Court" (July 9, 2018) *Politico*, www.politico.com/magazine/story/2018/07/09/david-souter-the-supreme-court-justice-who-built-the-trump-court-218953.

of their critics, this equality comes at a cost to personal liberty and the autonomy of state governments. The conservatives (typically appointed by Republicans) advance a libertarian vision of politics and identify an intrusion when the government acts to constrain the freedom of constituents, markets, or state governments.

Thus, the progressives want the government to take a forceful role in preventing private wealth from dominating campaigns; to police and prevent racial discrimination, expansively construed; and to require egalitarian voting procedures. They aspire to use constitutional judicial review to advance the substantive equality of constituent power across characteristics, such as race and party identity, that might be grounds for majoritarian oppression, even if this imposes some constraints on individual and collective action.[134] In doing so, they contribute more broadly to the agenda of post-Roosevelt New Deal Democrats, such as an expansive state, social liberalism, and robust redistribution. Conversely, the conservatives wish to constrain the government – specifically the federal government – from taking such action and leave the unfolding of social organization to economic and political struggle free from paternalistic interference. The conservatives view the prospective costs – systemic inequality and that exacerbation of disadvantaged social positions, in the eyes of critics – as categorically less problematic than the risk of excessive government intervention.[135] They employ judicial review to prohibit state action that runs the risk of infringing on liberty, both as free individual action and the free unfolding of the system of politics at lower levels. In doing so, they advance the views of the contemporary Republican Party, such as rejection of state oversight (particularly for progressive programs such as affirmative action) and economic libertarianism. These two competing visions represent the most politicized facets – perhaps caricatures – of intellectual traditions. Though the judges would not admit it so explicitly, progressives might want to give force to Dworkin's *Sovereign Virtue*, while the conservatives wish to implement F. A. Hayek's *Road to Serfdom*. This ideological divide is reinforced by a thoroughly practical facet of election law: ideologically conservative policies (such as minimalist campaign finance regulation) tend to help elect Republicans, whereas progressive policies (such as aggressive defense of minority voting rights) help elect Democrats.

The general claim (not specific to election law) that judges do not undertake any sort of reasoned process but rather just advance their own beliefs has been the subject of extensive scholarly analysis.[136] Jeffrey Segal and Harold Spaeth provide the seminal social science account of the attitudinal model.[137] They claim that

---

[134] The scholarly exemplar of this is Dworkin, "Sovereign Virtue."
[135] The corresponding conservative account might be F.A. Hayek, *The Road to Serfdom*, ed. Bruce Caldwell (Chicago: University of Chicago Press, 2007).
[136] For a description of the problem and a review of the scholarship, see Michael S. Kang and Joanna M. Shepherd, "The Long Shadow of *Bush v. Gore*: Judicial Partisanship in Election Cases" (2016) 68 *Stanford Law Review* 1411, 1413–27.
[137] Jeffrey A. Segal and Harold J. Spaeth, *The Supreme Court and the Attitudinal Model Revisited* (Cambridge: Cambridge University Press, 2002).

specific judicial decisions are not made by a process of reasoned, neutral, or morally informed analysis, but by judges advancing their personal predilections, which are influenced by the same factors that shape any personal value or preference set. Judges, according to this view, are little more than voters who happen to sit on the bench. A significant amount of empirical scholarship has evaluated this model, and the broadly held view suggests that "ideology is a significant factor in judicial decision-making."[138] Others have observed that while ideology may be influential, its explanatory power is not comprehensive, for both methodological reasons (particularly sampling problems) and because some cases defy ideological trends.[139]

If taken as the authoritative account of judicial review, the attitudinal model would vindicate the critique that judging is merely politics with an institutional cloak.[140] Some accounts add a layer of analytic sophistication to this idea, suggesting that the shift is not purely political, but rather a deeper ideological one that tracks political affiliation.[141] If true, such a determination would, as Frank Cross phrased it, "obliterate[e] the foundations of much current and past legal scholarship" as well as the traditional understanding of the neutrality at the core of the rule of law.[142] More specifically, it would undermine any attempt to make sense of adjudication as a unique part of the constitutional order. It would instead indicate that the legal system simply provides another forum for the politics of power and preference. Having argued for the politicized nature of judicial decision-making, Segal and Spaeth conclude that the only logical course is greater judicial deference to the democratic process[143] (a normative claim with strong sympathies to the postulated weight that this book affords to franchise autonomy, as described in general in Chapter 3 below).

If the attitudinal model is a comprehensive account of adjudication, it renders the claim that there is a coherent battle over freedom in election law (or any other meaningful form of constitutional adjudication or interpretation) superfluous. The doctrine reflects no such internal normative or practical coherence, at least as a

---

[138] Allison P. Harris and Maya Sen, "Bias and Judging" (2019) 22 *Annual Review of Political Science* 241, 246. See also Jeffrey J. Rachlinksi and Andrew J. Wistrich, "Judging the Judiciary by the Numbers: Empirical Research on Judges" (2017) 13 *Annual Review of Law and Social Science* 203, 205–6. Pinello provides a compelling meta-study of the topic in Daniel R. Pinello, "Linking Party to Judicial Ideology in American Courts: A Meta-analysis" (1999) 20 *The Justice System Journal* 219. Adam B. Cox and Thomas J. Miles, "Judicial Ideology and the Transformation of Voting Rights Jurisprudence" (2008) 75 *University of Chicago Law Review* 1493 explore this in the context of Section 2 of the Voting Rights Act. Finally, as noted in note 1 to the Introduction, election law scholars generally have come to describe the Supreme Court's decision-making as driven by ideological polarization.

[139] Robert A. Carp, Kenneth L. Manning, Lisa M. Holmes, and Ronald Stidham, *Judicial Process in America* (Washington DC: CQ Press, 2020), pp. 373–4.

[140] Barry Friedman, "The Politics of Judicial Review" (2005) 84 *Texas Law Review* 257.

[141] See Bertrall L. Ross II, "Democracy and Renewed Distrust: Equal Protection and the Evolving Judicial Conception of Politics" (2013) 101 *California Law Review* 1565.

[142] Frank B. Cross, "Political Science and the New Legal Realism: A Case of Unfortunate Interdisciplinary Ignorance" (1997) 92 *Northwestern University Law Review* 251, 253, 263.

[143] Segal and Spaeth, "Attitudinal Model," p. 406.

description of how cases are actually decided. Judges just impose their ideology-informed beliefs, and dress up these (legally arbitrary) convictions with rhetoric (in the guise of reasoning in opinions). If this is the case, the constitutional and normative reasoning over structure and values that judges advance to debate their beliefs is empty. Any coherent debates over freedom that can be gleaned from the doctrine are incidental to the partisan battle. This narrows the responses to the counterpopular dilemma to the possibility that institutional architecture can constrain warring factions in politics. If the Supreme Court is merely another venue for blunt partisan conflict, the only justification that it, instead of some more accountable group of representatives, should set the terms of self-rule is that perhaps there is an instrumental benefit to having a particular partisan institution that is less directly accountable or enjoys a "lag" between the selection and enactment of its partisan views.

Yet for the attitudinal model to exclude theories of adjudication, it must be both correct (in terms of describing what judges do) and exhaustive (in terms of capturing all that can be reasonably asked of judging from a moral and institutional perspective, as opposed to merely identifying a defect in judicial reasoning). These two requirements illustrate why it is worth thinking about judicial review at all. Theories of judicial review presumably perform two functions: (1) they explain why adjudication is part of a legitimate constitutional order to offer some account of what judges *should* do and (2) they describe what judges actually *do* in making decisions and shaping the state and society through law. An account that performs the first function but has no bearing on the second is an interesting exercise in political philosophy but has little practical value. An account that does the inverse might provide insight into the state of legal practice, but does little to indicate whether judges are doing the *right* thing. The attitudinal model largely speaks to the second function, but various academic perspectives regarding its significance suggest that if it is exhaustively accurate, it upends, and perhaps makes the case for minimizing, the extent of judicial review.[144] If the model is correct and exhaustive, it means that judicial review can only be vindicated on realist-institutionalist terms. This might be compatible with a grimly minimalist account of constitutional liberal democracy, but it would invalidate any thinking about adjudication as morally distinctive.

Yet even in the politicized realm of election law, it is unclear that the attitudinal model has predominant explanatory power. Separately, it is worth querying if the attitudinal model analytically extinguishes any claim that judicial reasoning should have a special normative character. The two points are linked because the best explanation for why ideology does not totally determine the development of the law points to the unique moral quality of legal reasoning.

The descriptive question of whether the attitudinal model is the best account of election law can be straightforwardly addressed. While the justices have clear partisan leanings, boiling down the jurisprudence to ideology faces so many exceptions

---

[144] See generally Cross, "New Legal Realism"; Segal and Spaeth, "Attitudinal Model," Conclusion.

and caveats that it cannot be the predominant explanation. For instance, a key exception is that modern election law reflects some points of consensus that cross any partisan divide. The most prominent of these is one person, one vote, which, despite some initial objections led by Frankfurter and Harlan, quickly became a shared value. Yet it is at odds with much of the ideology and instrumental aims of conservative Republicans since it prevents Republican-dominated rural areas from exercising disproportionate power in state legislatures and contravenes the typical minimalism of federal intervention that shapes much of conservative judicial ideology. One might concede that one person, one vote is now entrenched as an ideal within the law, but that such a consensus itself reveals the presence of some modality of legal reasoning that cuts against pure ideological domination. The same could be said for certain bulwarks of race. The basic principle of advancing racial equity in districting articulated in *Gomillion* seems firmly entrenched in the case law, even though its rejection would benefit Republicans politically. A similar quality is present in the survival of the *Buckley* expenditure–contribution divide, and the fact that the contestation occurs over a (relatively) narrow range of legality. Even in the progressive high-water mark of *McConnell v. FEC*, the progressives agreed that there were some provisions so burdensome on speech that they were unconstitutional.[145] While it might be possible to attribute such partial consensus to bartering on the bench, this is an unnecessarily elaborate conclusion. The *McConnell* opinion explains the conclusion as a matter of respect for precedent and a shared belief across the ideological spectrum that parties have *some* independent speech rights that must not be interfered with.

This analysis suggests that justices' personal ideology determines the outcomes of a narrow range of election law questions. Precisely where should the line of regulatory authority be drawn in *Buckley*? What, exactly, does equality mean in districting when it is clearly activated? How extensively does the equal protection clause protect features such as party identity? One possibility is that most of the justices do share ideological views on these matters. However, this contravenes the narrative of sharp partisan contention and suggests that most justices are substantively content with most of the law in the first instance (an implausible proposition, given the values discussed throughout this book). Another, far more plausible possibility is that justices accept the status of law for reasons other than pure partisan ideology. For example, they may accept well-entrenched principles due to legal principles such as *stare decisis*, or they may internalize shared conceptual or linguistic meanings that operate through diverse mechanisms[146] that are not beneficial for their "side" (such as the idea that the equal protection clause prevents certain types of bald racial discrimination, even if such discrimination would benefit their partisan wing). One can, of course, assert that *any* shared meaning then forms part of the

---

[145] *McConnell v. Federal Election Commission*, 540 US 93, 213–4 (2003).
[146] See Fallon, "The Meaning of Legal Meaning," 1297–1306.

corpus of that given ideology. But this is conceptually circular. It simply defines any point of consensus of part of each ideology, and any point of disagreement as a matter of ideology.

In other words, a birds-eye view of election law suggests that justices commit to certain shared principles in a way that other aspects of the judging process (e.g. neutrality and consideration of interpretive principle) play a significant role – and that these aspects suggest that judging in practice includes types of reasoning that contradict, and can dominate, ideological affiliation. In other words, even if the attitudinal model helps explain election law decisions, other interpretations or rule-of-law models do a great deal of work as well. The attitudinal model operates within a narrow zone of disagreement that is determined by these other types of commitments.

This suggests that the role of partisanship in election law is constrained to a range of questions over which there is reasonable disagreement regarding the substantive issue at hand. *Yet this role for attitudinal influence is wholly compatible with, and even provides evidence for, the idea that judges agree that freedom is the core value of election law, and are undertaking a series of focused debates over its realization in particular domains.* If judges' ideological inclinations constitute one part (but not the exclusive or dominant part) of decision-making, then ideology might well vindicate contestation over freedom as a more accurate account than other interpretive theories. Theories of adjudication that vindicate the judicial role by requiring judges to advance principled positions might struggle to incorporate attitudinal realities because attitudinal decision-making would conflict with judges' ostensible normative obligations. Conversely, by allowing adjudication to serve as a context for contesting differing views, contestation over freedom can fully accommodate the presence of ideology in judicial decision-making. Judges, within the range of questions not settled by shared conceptual-linguistic meaning, advance values that are informed by their own ideological commitments. They then engage with the defensibility of these commitments through a type of social, normative, and political theorizing in the case law. In short, at most the attitudinal model informs the positions that justices take on particular aspects of freedom, but within a broader consensus over the value of freedom.

The first section of this book's Conclusion provides the most robust evidence to support this claim: Synthesizing the debates that occur across the four domains of law described in Chapters 4–7, it shows that even if the lines of disagreement in the case law correlate with judges' partisan beliefs, the best *substantive* description of the debates is as a confrontation between two well-established strands of liberalism. Progressives advance a view of liberalism (captured by Rawlsianism and sympathetic approaches, such as civic republicanism) that identifies free collective self-rule as requiring a high level of structural egalitarianism in a society. This view explains why progressives want to smooth out or bind the inequities of wealth, party influence, and race that can shape politics. Conversely, conservatives (most prominently Nozick) advance a view of liberalism that identifies the protection of pre-political

2.4 Acknowledging and Accommodating the Role of Partisanship

endowments as the foundation of free self-rule. These are hoary and foundational philosophical understandings – and they undergird the doctrinal disputes. Even if partisanship provides a useful roadmap for the contestation over freedom that guides election law doctrine (which this book makes use of as appropriate), the substance of the disputes is eminently philosophical. And most saliently, it occurs within the context of a rich philosophical position and reflects two positions. Each of these positions, even if controversial in its premises and applications, should be recognized as at least hypothetically legitimate.

However, there are some prominent instances of election law in which judicial ideology seems to be the only plausible explanation of the outcome. Appropriately enough, Segal and Spaeth begin their seminal book by discussing *Bush v. Gore* as an example of attitudinal determination of judicial decision-making. They observe that not only does the case reflect an unmistakable expression of partisan loyalty by the justices and have shaky jurisprudential foundations,[147] but it also involved a peculiar flip of the typical ideological treatment of the equal protection doctrine: The conservatives advocated a *more* expansive understanding of a principle typically invoked by progressives, while progressives argued for a *less* expansive interpretation.

This book identifies *Bush v. Gore* (which I revisit in the Conclusion) as a multiple outlier, which largely agrees with the critical analysis of the case presented by Segall and Spaeth. It is difficult to reconcile the case with an understanding of how best to realize franchise autonomy – or for that matter any understanding of law as institutionally or normatively coherent. Yet the fact that it exemplifies attitudinal domination of judicial decision-making does not vitiate framing election law as generally oriented around freedom. Rather, it suggests that a case that cannot be understood as good faith judicial interpretation is not good law. Contestation over freedom can make sense of many domains of election law, including those typically understood as highly partisan, such as campaign finance and partisan gerrymandering. Michael Kang and Joanna Shepherd *exclude* such cases from their analysis of the role of partisanship in state-level Supreme Court decision-making as "too ideologically valenced."[148] Yet even if partisanship shapes judges' initial views, a robust and realistic understanding of judicial review is not thwarted by the presence of ideological commitments in judging, but manages and incorporates it.

That *Bush v. Gore* resists any such attempt to manage or incorporate the role of partisanship into a coherent theory of judging instead suggests that adjudication is expected to possess some normatively meaningful quality. The broad condemnation of its reasoning suggests that it is the particular case, rather than coherent theories of judging as a whole, that should be viewed with suspicion. If the attitudinal model were exhaustive and complete, *Bush v. Gore* would be exemplary, rather than exceptional.

---

[147] Segal and Spaeth, "Attitudinal Model," pp. 1–3, 171–4.
[148] Kang and Shepherd, "Long Shadow," 1431.

3

Traversing the Dilemma

Normative Struggle over Freedom

Can robust judicial review and legitimate electoral procedures be reconciled? To respect the primacy of democratic autonomy, constituents must have authority over the circumstances of freedom. Authority over democratic autonomy must always be open to interrogation and reformulation by the constituents; otherwise an external source imposes terms of autonomy and erodes its moral value.

Conceiving of judicial review of election law as a perpetual and unsettled normative struggle over popular autonomy can reconcile courts' intervention in democratic process and the primacy of constituent autonomy. Such an understanding enables judges to make decisions designed to empower the electorate while recognizing that judicial authority cannot decisively dictate the terms of such autonomy.

Judicial review of election law as contestation over freedom also offers the best high-level account of election law doctrine. It explains why this doctrine has been uniquely unsettled. The best procedural realization of democratic freedom is fundamentally contestable, and a ready source of normative disagreement. Considering freedom as the bedrock of democratic process explains why this account of judicial review is preferable to alternatives (e.g., election law is primarily about equality or overdetermined by partisan affiliation).

3.1 REFRAMING JUDICIAL REVIEW OF ELECTION LAW: STRUGGLE OVER THE TERMS OF AUTONOMY

Evaluating the approaches to judicial review discussed in the previous Chapter reinforces the counterpopular dilemma. None of the theories can satisfactorily explain how courts have the authority to reshape election law – at least not without materially intruding upon constituent self-determination by imposing substantive values. However, examining the substance that both scholars and judges have struggled over reveals that all the theories share a familiar touchstone – the conditions that generate constituent self-rule. This shared value points toward the best way to reconcile the institutional benefits of judicial review and respect for constituent autonomy.

3.1.1 *The Whipsaw of Judicial Review of Election Law*

The anti-lockup theory starkly illustrates the tension posed by judicial review of electoral procedure. This theory is appealing because it specifies which features of democratic self-rule courts should advance. It thus advocates for a substantively defined, structural view of election law jurisprudence. Because of this practical bent, anti-lockup theory must more clearly justify its choice of democratic norms than a less substantive account of judicial review. It must explain not only why courts have the general authority to evaluate the legality of legislation but also why the substantive theory that the courts advance comprises a decisively legitimate conception of self-rule. If the justification for the theory of election law is weaker than this – if, for example, it is based on only one of many potentially valid theories of democracy – it cannot vindicate imposing an electoral structure except by authoritatively imposing norms of autonomous self-rule, and thus contradicting the very value it is ostensibly meant to protect.

Furthermore, the tradeoff between claimed authority in judicially imposing democratic process and intruding on the principle of constituent autonomy is hydraulic. The more decisively and extensively the terms of democratic process are imposed, the greater the intrusion upon constituent self-rule – and thus upon the very principle the intervention is meant to serve. Any argument that the courts have the authority to restructure electoral procedure to impose a particular configuration of electoral rules faces this heavy onus. An originalist explanation of election law decisions, for example, must explain why the Court's account of original popular will and pre-social fact is decisive. This returns to the distinctive feature of election law – its purpose is to serve as a conduit for popular political will, and any material transformation of it also transforms the political will. It seems that counterpopular restructuring of electoral procedure can only be vindicated by a specific vision of what democratic politics should look like and what it should aim to achieve. Such restructuring therefore requires a vision of politics that has a higher normative priority than self-determination by the franchise itself.

Judicial intervention in other areas does not activate this tension as sharply. For example, while judicial intervention to protect the right to abortion or free speech must face a general *countermajoritarian* difficulty, it does not directly place the nature of the right or freedom and the subject matter of the decision in conflict. For example, when a court declares that constitutional democracy protects an individual's right to choose to have an abortion, it creates a prospective conflict between democratic process (through which political actors may wish to restrict this right) and individuals' presumptively higher-priority right to enjoy non-interference with the freedom. A judicial declaration that there is a higher-than-political-process right to abortion may involve limiting political authority that would restrict abortion rights, but the tension is between two separate values – the right at issue and democratic authority. The conflict is over competing priorities – the priority of the rights-based freedom and the priority of outputs of the political process. Conversely, in the context of election law, the matter upon which the court opines *is congruent with* that which it limits – the capacity of the political process. The issue – the constituency's capacity to rule itself – is unitary between judicial review and political decisions. The question is, who has the authority to dictate the substance of this matter?

Robust and coherent judicial intervention to protect democracy can only be justified by a conception of judicial review that itself intrudes upon constituent autonomy. Ronald Dworkin articulates this dilemma most directly in *Freedom's Law* by arguing that the courts should advance a substantively rights-protecting political order even if doing so comes at the cost of constituent self-determination.

Without such a robust substantive vision of the values that electoral procedure should realize, judicial intervention would likely have to be minimalist, cautious, and incremental. Any approach that merely sought to give effect to the bare expressed constitutional will of the people would be unable to sustain the extensive structural entry into the political thicket, including the sort that has characterized modern election law. Even to achieve the current condition of the doctrine (let alone a more highly structured vision as articulated by anti-lockup theorists), the Court has had to radically reimagine core constitutional concepts. As Rachel Barkow has demonstrated, the development of contemporary election law has coincided with the diminishment of the political question doctrine (which, in its classic conception, would have excluded judicial review of electoral structure).[1] Heather Gerken points out that this is apparent from the need to move beyond the traditional rights framework to make sense of the systemic nature of contemporary electoral jurisprudence.[2] Yet a minimalist and deferential approach to election law would be ineffective against the systemic pathologies of representation, such as entrenchment, that the Court seems institutionally well positioned to address.

Trying to solve the counterpopular dilemma by decisively explaining the authority of judicial review thereby yields a deeper whipsaw. The more robustly and coherently a theory informs the type of action that courts should undertake to advance democratic norms, the more it must intrude upon constituent self-determination. But the purpose of such judicial intervention is, of course, to benefit constituent self-governance (as the anti-lockup theorists most vividly demonstrate). Thus, the *more decisively* a theory of judicial review of election law allows courts to advance just structures of politics, the *greater the procedure's cost* to constituent self-determination.

---

[1] Rachel E. Barkow, "More Supreme than Court? The Fall of the Political Question Doctrine and the Rise of Judicial Supremacy" (2002) 102 *Columbia Law Review* 237.

[2] Heather K. Gerken, "Understanding the Right to an Undiluted Vote" (2001) 114 *Harvard Law Review* 1663; Heather K. Gerken, "Lost in the Political Thicket: The Court, Election Law, and the Doctrinal Interregnum" (2004) 153 *University of Pennsylvania Law Review* 503.

If this tradeoff is the end of the story, it is damning, because it elicits a fundamental conflict between competing constitutional values. Effective judicial review is central to the constitutional order, most generically conceived as the presence of the rule of law. Structurally, it prevents abuses ranging from majoritarian diminishment of minority political values to entrenchment by self-interested representatives. If – as scholars such as Gerken and Pildes have convincingly argued – effective judicial review of election law requires systemic and structural intervention, it seems as though the rule of law can only come at the cost of popular self-determination on constituents' own terms.

Judicial review of election law, in this view, will either be either impotent or authoritarian. An aggressive judiciary can preserve the rule of law and cogent, structurally effective rights at the cost of imposing a set of values upon the electorate. Alternatively, the electorate can set its own terms of governance, at the risk that such self-governance will develop pathological features. Any attempt by courts to undertake ostensibly neutral identification and cure of such pathologies requires a value judgment about democratic self-rule that itself is anti-democratic.

3.1.2 *A Return to the Shared Core: The Value of Freedom*

Before conceding the insolubility of the counterpopular dilemma, it is worth returning to the one high-level point of consensus. The vindications of judicial review, the critiques of judicial review, and election law scholarship share a single bedrock commitment: to self-rule by the constituency. For critics of judicial review, this is best achieved by minimal judicial intervention. For originalists, this prioritizes the original expression of freedom by which individuals committed to the higher law of the constitutional contract. For living constitutionalists, the conditions of just rule allow individuals to live with appropriate protections for (and facilitation of) their liberty. For the representation reinforcement and anti-lockup theorists, it is voters' freedom over policy when representatives are accountable to effective electoral control.

Despite the diversity of these theories, freedom of the ruled is the purpose of judicial intervention; this focus on freedom vindicates judicial review. Indeed, the dispute among the theories can, at a philosophical level, be cast as being about how constitutional law can legitimately serve as a conduit for constituent freedom. Some theorists – Bruce Ackerman[3] and Larry Kramer[4] most conspicuously – have identified how non-judicial entities can invoke the Constitution to advance their autonomy. But even (in keeping with the case law focus of this project) looking solely at what courts have done and *should* do – freedom emerges as the shared bedrock goal of judicial intervention.

---

[3] Bruce Ackerman, *We the People: Volume 1: Foundations* (Cambridge: Harvard University Press, 1993).
[4] Larry Kramer, *The People Themselves: Popular Constitutionalism and Judicial Review* (Oxford: Oxford University Press, 2004).

Yet within this consensus that constituent autonomy is the goal of judicial review, there is tremendous breadth and intensity of contention, both about the substantive meaning of freedom and courts' appropriate role in parsing it. Living constitutionalism, particularly in its more hardline Dworkinian and Eisgruberian forms, arguably has the more perspicuous explanation of the judiciary's role: courts should resolve cases by simply advancing the substantively right conception of freedom at a granular policy level. The originalists take a more procedural approach: courts have an obligation to advance the commitments that the franchise has freely taken on; the higher law is the explicit constitutional commitments decided through plain textual meaning or original intent (or some form thereof). From a different angle, anti-lockup theorists characterize freedom as a practical problem that emerges from the role of institutional intermediaries. According to this view, individuals must delegate their political freedom to representatives, and the role of law is to protect the initial grant of freedom by preventing opportunistic abuse by representatives of the institutions that sustain this delegation.

Due to the fierce struggle over the meaning of freedom, its status as the unifying concept of judicial review of election law involves a level of abstraction. The following subsection uses the highly partisan dispute over campaign finance to illustrate the characteristic contestation over freedom. But first, I emphasize how neatly freedom as the defining shared concept of judicial review of election law fits with the purpose of elections generally. As elections' role in the political structure is legitimated as a conduit for constituent autonomy, it is congruent that judicial review of election law should prioritize political freedom. It thereby addresses the counterpopular dilemma, perhaps in the only way it can. Any other final goal by courts would comprise the interpolation of an unjustifiably distinct policy goal, using elections as an opportunity to insert technocratic values.

Chapters 4–7 establish the precise aspects of freedom with which each area of case law wrestles, and the Conclusion synthesizes the substance of these debates through prevalent understandings of liberalism. But even a cursory glance at some of the areas reveals the plausibility of the proposition that the realization of constituent freedom is the subject of election law – though, as discussed below, its terms are often fiercely disputed. Campaign finance, for example, is typically described as balancing anti-corruption (or, more systemically, socio-economic equality) with speech rights. Scholars from the progressive–living constitutionalist wing (such as David Strauss, Zephyr Teachout, Larry Lessig, and Timothy Kuhner) tend to identify the dominant concern in campaign finance regulation as socio-economic equality.[5] The concern that campaign finance should focus on in addressing such inequality manifests in the progressive *Citizens United* and *McCutcheon* dissents.

---

[5] While Strauss identifies equality as the issue at stake underlying regulation, he does so primarily to challenge the dominant anti-corruption narrative. Teachout, Kuhner, and Lessig directly identify vast infusions of unequal wealth as morally problematic. This idea is discussed more extensively in Chapter 5.

The progressive justices plaintively argue that the First Amendment speech rights are conceptually expansive enough to incorporate terms of justly egalitarian social engagement.[6] Conversely, the conservative wing emphasizes the prohibition on state speech restrictions as the sole constitutional instruction, and the pathological consequences of such restrictions.[7]

Conservatives and progressives appear to not merely prize different values, but to have vastly different conceptions of the problem. Egalitarian progressives see a society-wide malady in social inequality that infiltrates campaigns through campaign funding, through both the direct corruption of leaders and subtle poisoning of the political discourse, while libertarian conservatives see a looming state that threatens to restrict free expression. Yet as I describe in detail in Chapter 5, the underlying issues are singular conditions: what do the epistemic traits of political actors indicate is necessary for free self-rule? The progressives see a vulnerable society that requires collective management of social and economic inequality to achieve freedom – a wide-ranging approach that fits well with the comprehensive mandate of living constitutionalism. The conservatives (guided by originalist emphasis on the Constitution's explicit mandate on limiting state action) perceive the Court's sole remit as protecting individual freedom from the state. Both wings seek to ensure free self-rule, but are separated by differing normative commitments as well as divergent methodological priors. These differences should not distract from the unity of the question at issue: free self-rule in a capitalist liberal democracy.

The other domains of election law reflect this debate over how best to advance free self-rule by the electorate. Indeed, compared to campaign finance, these other domains tend to question the freedom issue more explicitly. What does it mean to vote freely in the context of racialized and politicized districting? How should entrenched inequality be corrected to ensure that voters are free? But even in campaign finance, which is as much concerned with the seemingly distinct aims of discouraging representative corruption and managing political equality, judicial review is oriented toward the question of what law will best facilitate constituent self-rule.

3.2 CONSTITUENT SELF-RULE AS CONTESTATION OVER THE NATURE OF FREEDOM

If there is consensus on the bench and among scholars that the autonomy of the franchise is the linchpin of democracy, why are election law cases so fiercely debated? The answer is that the substantive realization of constituent autonomy is deeply

---

[6] This is exemplified in Breyer's dissent in *McCutcheon v. Federal Election Commission*, 572 US 185, 236 (2014).
[7] In the case law, these are epitomized by Justices Scalia and Thomas's dissents in *McConnell v. Federal Election Commission*, 540 US 93, 262–4, 284–6 (2003). The most influential scholarly account is Bradley A. Smith, "Faulty Assumptions and Undemocratic Consequences of Campaign Finance Reform" (1996) 105 *Yale Law Journal* 1049.

disputed. The dispute is internal to the consensus regarding the value of autonomy; the question is its best conception and implementation. The counterpopular dilemma and the primacy of constituent autonomy further indicate why legitimate electoral procedure must be contestable, including on the bench. In the absence of overarching social and political consensus,[8] the terms of self-rule (i.e., the substance of autonomy) can only be respected if they remain subject to debate, reformulation, and challenge by these constituents.

If the Court adopts decisive views of how electoral process should be structured in areas in which constituents debate the terms of autonomy, this would intrude upon constituents' authority to establish their own terms of self-rule. If, however, the Court engages in continual struggle with (and disagreement over) the meaning of autonomy when opining on election law, it can intervene without decisively imposing electoral process – thereby respecting the primacy of constituent autonomy.

Such an approach to judicial decision-making about democratic process also incorporates both sides of the counterpopular dilemma as a practical matter. There will be circumstances in which judicial intervention, even if in accordance with typical modalities of constitutional interpretation or judicial reasoning, would deprive the electorate of the capacity to set its own terms of self-rule. Such circumstances would suggest that decisions should hew to the normative concern of displacing constituent autonomy advanced by judicial review critics such as Jeremy Waldron. In other circumstances, democratic procedures may be adopted that intrude upon the electorate's practical capacity to rule itself, justifying judicial intervention on structural terms even where the intervention does not cleanly fit in or follow from standard modes of judicial interpretation. This is precisely the foundations of the approach of US election law scholars, and their rejection of standard rights interpretation.

Philosophical struggle over constituent autonomy accommodates both sides of the dilemma, which reflects their shared commitment. Critics and advocates of judicial review in the electoral context both promote the best possible realization of constituent self-rule. Describing decision-making over democratic process as a struggle over freedom places the shared starting foundation at the center of the debate.

The remainder of this section offers three arguments. The first two vindicate contestation over freedom as a principled matter from a philosophical perspective. The

---

[8] As Bickel notes in his discussion of "the passive virtues," the Court will "avoid adjudication" when judicial intrusion would prove excessively damaging or costly at an institutional level. Alexander Bickel, "The Passive Virtues" (1961) 75 *Harvard Law Review* 40, 128. The Court's willingness to assert principles of democracy rather than engage in contestation where institutional-social consensus is present may be analogized to avoiding contestation. One such example of consensus would be the recognition in *Gomillion v. Lightfoot*, 364 US 339 (1960) that egregious fencing out of minorities is a violation of equal protection. As discussed in Chapter 7, in defending itself from litigation the state of Alabama did not even argue that the conduct at issue was not racially oppressive, but could only claim that such conduct was beyond the constitutional remit.

third unpacks the case law to argue why ongoing contestation of the nature of freedom is the best approach. The examination of the case law then comprises most of the rest of this book.

3.2.1 Deontological Foundations and the Moral Objection to Decisively Defining Democratic Process

The deepest explanation of why contesting constituent self-rule offers the best approach to lawmaking derives from the philosophical nature of freedom itself. Since the law of democratic process shapes the capacity of free constituents to self-determine their own political fate, the characteristics of freedom bear directly upon it. The nature of freedom is among the most studied topic in philosophy, and freedom is indisputably central to prevalent liberal understandings of democracy.[9] It also lies at the center of understandings of individual moral worth; as Immanuel Kant poetically phrases it, free will is "the jewel that shines with its own light."[10] Various aspects of this scholarship inform this book, from the discussion of the philosophical discussions of counterpopularism elaborated in Chapters 1 and 2 to the debate over liberalism.

This book does not address bases for morality that are founded on an ideal other than freedom, or alternative understandings of the significance of self-determination to morality, such as soft compatibilist views of the relationship between self-determination and moral responsibility. However, this philosophical discursion is not essential to the practical implications of the book's argument that describing the debate over freedom offers the best functional account of the doctrine. This book commits to the following position as rigorous and defensible: any account of politics or elections that assigns moral significance to any condition that cannot be derived from freedom is fundamentally objectionable, because such an objectionable account holds individuals responsible or culpable for that which is beyond their control. Some traditions adopt a more elaborate or constrained approach to structuring or adding content to this idea of freedom – such as natural law theories – but a Kantian model of free will is a broad tent that allows for debate over the proper direction of freedom, while insisting upon its necessarily central role.

One particular feature of the deontological nature of freedom explains why ongoing contestation on the bench is the best solution. In a Kantian vein, moral significance can only emerge from human freedom – the only aspect of personal identity that is non-contingent. The core principle is that moral judgment can only be legitimately based upon non-contingent features of human existence,

---

[9] For a summary of some of the contemporary philosophical debates that have emerged from the Kantian account of freedom relied upon below, see Uygar Abaci, "Noumenal Freedom and Kant's Modal Antinomy" (2022) 27 *Kantian Review* 175.
[10] Immanuel Kant, *Groundwork for the Metaphysics of Morals*, Mary Gregor (trans.), 4th ed. (Cambridge: Cambridge University Press, 1998), p. 394.

action, and identity. The alternative is to assign moral weight to aspects of the world that individuals did not freely choose, and to morally judge them for aspects of their lives over which they had no control. This is anathema, contrary to any principle of justice. Moral judgment can only spring from that to which responsibility may be legitimately assigned, and responsibility may only be legitimately assigned where the feature or outcome was not contingent upon an arbitrary feature of the phenomenal world. The concept that denotes features or outcomes that are not arbitrary phenomenal assignments is freedom – a condition in which persons have elected to take on a circumstance, rather than had it assigned to them. Alternately stated, any condition that is not freely chosen is a function of the lottery of the contingent world – and there is no morality in the outcomes of this lottery. If a feature has moral weight, it is because it was freely chosen, rather than arbitrarily assigned.

However, the non-contingency of freedom comes with a challenging ramification: It cannot be exhaustively delineated or described, because to do so would remove the non-determined primacy that makes it morally important. In lay terms, freedom is "mysterious" because it provides a causal "mover" within individual will that cannot be further explained without making it, paradoxically, unfree.[11] In formal philosophical terms, the essence of freedom must be "noumenal" or "transcendental" – that is, it lies beyond the standard causal accounts of the natural world in order to avoid falling into determinism. Such determinism would itself remove the moral nature of freedom of that which is under the control of personal will and legitimately the subject of moral significance.[12] Its mysterious quality is a necessary attribute of it.

Yet judges *must* make decisions that bear on freedom when they resolve questions of democratic process. They cannot avoid it. Relying on the "passive virtues" to avoid opining on matters that relate to constituent autonomy would allow legislative decisions, including those that are abusive or entrenching, to stand. Judges thereby necessarily assert norms of freedom. The best accommodation – which, given the nature of freedom, *cannot* be a decisive resolution – is continual debate about freedom's nature. This is a terse defense of why ongoing contestation over freedom is the best solution. Future research should more exhaustively integrate the philosophical literature.

The compelling nature of the philosophical observation is illuminated by the alternative. The most obvious and decisive solution to the counterpopular dilemma is for judges to apply social science and moral philosophy to ascertain

---

[11] Timothy Chappell, *Knowing What To Do: Imagination, Virtue, and Platonism in Ethics* (Oxford: Oxford University Press, 2014), pp. 74–5.
[12] For a more in-depth explanation and defenses of Kant's view, see Derk Pereboom, "Kant on Transcendental Freedom" (2006) 73 *Philosophy and Phenomenological Research* 537. For a technical analysis of the type of problems that arise from the intersection between transcendental freedom and the material world, see Abaci, "Kant's Modal Antinomy," 180 (identifying the problem of linking modal and non-modal properties).

the "right" procedures to enable legitimate constituent self-determination. This conclusion is self-contradictory. If a "right" configuration of democratic rules can be legitimately externally determined and imposed on a polity, thus negating the need for the polity to have the authority to set its own terms of self-rule, one of two conditions must apply. The first is that democratic rules do not need to conform to requirements of constituent self-determination and democratic justice. But if this is the case, and electoral rules do not need to conform to the demands of justice, then presumably they do not have any normative weight, and are morally and politically insignificant. The second condition is that electoral rules *are* significant, but that the right answer can be reached through technocratic moral philosophy rather than constituent self-determination. But if this is the case, the basic premise of democracy – constituent self-rule – does not apply. If the terms of democratic procedure can be externally imposed rather than self-determined by constituent, either the animating value of democracy (constituent self-determination) is irrelevant and the entire debate devoid of significance, *or* the rules do not matter because they do not affect democratic determination. If democratic procedure is morally relevant as a fulcrum of constituent self-determination, constituents must exert control over it with the same (indeed, arguably even more) urgency that they do over first-order political decisions.

3.2.2 Constituent Autonomy as an Essentially Contested Concept

Another philosophical concept offers a less foundational, less abstract justification for contestation over freedom. W.B. Gallie introduced the idea of "essentially contested concepts" over which there are "apparently endless disputes"[13] that appear to reflect genuine, significant, and meaningful disagreement, and where both sides have "a definite logical force."[14] Waldron helpfully consolidates these qualities into two features: "only normative concepts with a certain internal complexity are capable of being essentially contested."[15] When concepts are essentially contestable, it implies "recognition of rival uses of it (such as oneself repudiates) as not only logically possible and humanly 'likely', but as of permanent potential critical value to one's own use or interpretation of the concept in question."[16] Thus contestable concepts are subject *not* to analytic resolution, but to continual, unsettled debate over their meaning.

---

[13] W.B. Gallie, "Essentially Contested Concepts" (1956) 56 *Proceedings of the Aristotelian Society* 167, 169. See David Collier, Fernando Daniel Hidalgo, and Andra Olivia Maciuceanu, "Essentially Contested Concepts: Debates and Applications" (2006) 11 *Journal of Political Ideologies* 211 for an overview of the scholarship.
[14] Gallie, "Essentially Contested Concepts," 190.
[15] Jeremy Waldron, "Is the Rule of Law an Essentially Contested Concept (in Florida)?" (2002) 21 *Law and Philosophy* 137, 150.
[16] Gallie, "Essentially Contested Concepts," 193.

For example, the definition of democracy seems endlessly contestable.[17] Some would argue that selecting leaders by election is sufficient;[18] others maintain that democracy requires, at a minimum, other features such as rights protection,[19] while still others would argue that democracy demands a rich set of social conditions.[20] Some, such as John Rawls and Kuhner, would likely argue that a democracy requires features such as certain levels of economic and social equality. Others, such as F.A. Hayek, would argue the opposite – that enforced economic equality *impairs* democracy. This seems to establish that democracy is a contested concept.

These types of disputes are separate from the descriptive features of a system. Those contesting the concept can agree that the leader is the one who receives the most votes, and that the voting system had certain other descriptive features (such as first past the post or proportional representation). However, such descriptive agreement does not resolve the fundamental question of *what a democracy is*, because the moral features that characterize it are so complex as to resist easy definition. A contrast can be drawn with a simpler concept such as partisan gerrymandering. While the margins of when gerrymandering occurs can be debated, and its moral and legal status contested, its essence can be simply defined without dispute: drawing lines to favor the party with the power to draw them.

Freedom is an eminently contestable concept – and its quality as "mysterious," "noumenal," or "transcendental" explains why it must be so. It cannot be subject to reduction in the way that entities in the natural world can be. Consequently, as John Gray observes, freedom is an essentially contested concept in any liberal society where individuals have the opportunity to debate just political organization.[21]

3.2.3 *Sustained Contestation of Freedom as the Soul of the Doctrine*

These philosophical arguments explain why contestation over freedom is a fitting and plausible framework for judicial review of a topic that is focused on political freedom itself. However, this is a book about the doctrine of election law, and the most compelling argument for adopting this framework is that it *works*. The remainder of this book is dedicated to showing how contestation over freedom offers the best explanation of the Supreme Court doctrine. Furthermore, this doctrine demonstrates the development of coherent, longstanding, and foundational theories of liberalism on the bench (which explains why discrete case-by-case minimalism is not a satisfactory account). It also explains why judicial minimalism does not

---

[17] Ibid., 168; Waldron, "Is the Rule of Law an Essentially Contested Concept," 150.
[18] Joseph A. Schumpeter, *Capitalism, Socialism and Democracy* (Oxford: Routledge, 2010).
[19] Tom Ginsberg and Aziz Huq, "How to Lose a Constitutional Democracy" (2018) 65 UCLA Law Review 78.
[20] F.A. Hayek, *The Road to Serfdom*, ed. Bruce Caldwell (Chicago: University of Chicago Press, 2007).
[21] John Gray, "On Liberty, Liberalism, and Essential Contestability" (1978) 8 *British Journal of Political Science* 385.

adequately describe election law.²² It is worth noting at the outset that the idea of liberalism and the specific forms of egalitarianism and libertarianism are, like the higher-order concepts of democracy and democratic process, directed toward ensuring freedom.

3.3 REMAPPING AND REIMAGINING THE ELECTION LAW DEBATE

I first briefly describe how contestation over appropriate terms of constituent self-rule clarifies the central themes and problems of this project in three ways. First, contestation over freedom coordinates and synthesizes the differing scholarly approaches to election law discussed in the previous chapter. It shows both their high-level point of similarity – an effort to ensure that the courts serve as a conduit for, rather than an obstacle to, constituent self-determination – and their contestation over the specific meaning and practical realization of this principle. Second, as the rest of this book explores, contestation over freedom can be understood as the organizing axis of most domains of case law. Finally, describing the judicial role in election law as engaging in ongoing dispute over freedom ameliorates the counterpopular dilemma of judicial review.

3.3.1 Scholarly Disagreement as Contestation over Constituent Self-rule

While the scholarly debate has taken on politicized vehemence – particularly in the struggle between originalism and living constitutionalism – a detached perspective reveals that freedom is the driving interest of both sides. They disagree, however, about how judicial review should be reconciled with democratic self-governance.

Originalists assert that the defining feature of free self-rule is the identifiable expression of constituent intent (or some analogue), and that only when it can plausibly claim to identify such intent can the Court engage in lawmaking. The higher law is present only when concretized in the Constitution. Originalists show little interest in the content of such lawmaking as long as the judicial review procedure tracks such ostensible constituent will. Living constitutionalism, by contrast, is concerned with the substance that emerges from such lawmaking, and if it meaningfully advances the ideals of constituent freedom. Judicial review is valid when it harmonizes with the values of contemporary self-rule. The representation reinforcement account, meanwhile, looks to the future. A given legal decision must ensure that the electorate can make free choices going forward. The scholarship thus splits over the central value of legitimate constituent self-rule – procedure versus substance versus institutional design. The case law depicts the perpetual struggle among these claims.

---

²² For a prominent defense of judicial minimalism, see Cass Sunstein, *One Case at a Time: Judicial Minimalism on the Supreme Court* (Cambridge, MA: Harvard University Press, 2001).

3.3.2 *Contestation over Freedom in the Doctrine, and Its Anomalous Character*

The case law provides definitive evidence of the Supreme Court's treatment of election law as fundamental contestation over freedom. Each domain of law is shaped by its constitutional and historical details, and contains a procedure versus substance divide that mirrors the originalism versus living constitutionalism debate. The conservative–libertarian view, with its focus on the explicit articulation of constituent will, is generally skeptical of efforts by the legislature or judiciary to richly cultivate the viable conditions of constituent self-rule. The progressive–egalitarian view is both more tolerant of legislative efforts to craft such conditions and assertively interprets the Constitution to produce these conditions through case law.

In campaign finance, the contested question is whether the electorate is freer if it makes judgments regarding politics in an unregulated, free-wheeling, even anarchic environment, or if substantive regulatory enforcement of the integrity and equality of speech opportunities creates better governance. The former position, advanced by conservatives through a highly literal reading of the First Amendment, places an enormous amount of trust in voters' capacity to evaluate information and sees the only threat to their freedom as government constraint of this freedom. The latter, advanced by progressives, identifies political freedom as contingent on social and legal circumstances that facilitate cultivated reflection. Both conservatives and progressives portray themselves as champions of freedom, but fundamentally disagree on the circumstances that facilitate it in campaign finance.

With regard to racial justice in elections, it is uncontestable that electoral freedom requires recognition of equality. However, conservatives and progressives diverge on the issue of whether constitutional protection should be defined as pure procedural formalism, or incorporate equality of substantive outcomes. Conservative proceduralism interprets equal freedom as requiring process "inputs" that do not recognize race and challenges legislation that aspires to achieve specific outcomes of racial equity. Conservatives reject the proposition that the Constitution instructs the judiciary to creatively and substantively produce practical racial equity in political influence. Conversely, progressives evaluate pursuit of racial equity by its effects. Does a given set of rules yield effective political power for disadvantaged racial groups, as opposed to the nominal *opportunity* to equally realize their political power? The contestation over "freedom" in this context is between formalism and substantive effect.

The role of parties similarly turns on whether the processes of party politics are self-regulating, or if the potential threat from elite party domination justifies judicial counterbalancing. The conservative view, by requiring an explicit constitutional mandate to moderate politics, has rejected judicial intervention, even where state conduct seems to manipulate or exploit the advantages of party organization. This perspective trusts the broader political ecosystem to ensure responsive parties. Freedom is non-interference. Progressives, conversely, require non-domination by elites for constituents to truly rule themselves and identify a constitutional mandate to limit some practices that benefit elite party leadership. This has been most recently apparent in the partisan gerrymandering debate. Conservatives have been unwilling to identify an actionable intrusion upon political freedom, whereas progressives asserted that a just theory of politics would identify such practices as diminishing the legitimacy of self-rule.

The final line of doctrine, one, person, one vote, has been well established in the case law, though only following a period of fierce contestation that mirrors this procedure–substance divide. Led by Justice Frankfurter, initial opponents of one person, one vote rejected the principle that the constitutional mandate for equality applies to legislative districting. Yet with *Baker v. Carr*, *Wesberry v. Sanders*, and *Reynolds v. Simms*, the principle that free self-rule requires a minimum of procedural equality in districting has become established in the case law. It is the sole domain of election law that has undergone (at least in the courts, as described in Chapter 4) what Michael Freeden calls "decontestation."[23] Yet this idea – that the terrain of an essentially contested concept may evolve – is contained in Gallie's conception of contested concepts. Here it is used more generally to describe the acceptance of a principle or premise within the socio-legal context and beyond dispute on the bench.

The development of one person, one vote as the frontier of modern election law, and the judicial willingness to reflect on what conditions are necessary for freedom, answers one of the major scholarly critiques: why is one person, one vote, although it seems to lack a clear constitutional remit, so thoroughly respected on the bench? The answer is that constituent self-rule in a liberal democracy requires a *minimum* of equal constituent power. One person, one vote thereby comprises a minimum procedural commitment to constituents' functional capacity to rule themselves, even if it lacks a particularly compelling constitutional foundation. This bears some similarities to Richard Hasen's idea of social consensus described below, but operates at a much higher level: one person, one vote was decontested as a general principle that settled a broad concept. As the examination of the other three doctrinal areas shows, decontestation does not describe them as effectively as the core moral understanding of freedom. Even where single issues may be resolved, freedom remains the driver of judicial reasoning.

These various areas of election law share a common feature. Each is (or, in the case of one person, one vote, has been) undergirded by judges evaluating what constituent freedom *means*. In line with Gallie's conception, this is a complex debate: Freedom relies upon the intersection of the structures of the original constitutional commitment, ongoing and dynamic representative self-governance, and the social circumstances in which this self-governance is situated.

---

[23] Collier et al., "Essentially Contested Concepts," 218 (summarizing Michael Freeden, *Ideologies and Political Theory: A Conceptual Approach* (Oxford: Oxford University Press, 1998)).

3.3.3 *Judicial Contestation and Confronting the Counterpopular Dilemma*

The normative implications of conceiving of judicial review as a contestation over freedom may be even more compelling. This understanding softens the counterpopular dilemma by establishing that courts will not impose a decisive theory of democratic self-rule upon the polity. If the judiciary is engaged in continual hard-fought debates over the meaning of political freedom, it prevents the rigid imposition of a specific type of electoral design and creates space for continual responsive adaptation.

It is perhaps ironic to characterize such instability as a benefit. Final, decisive judgments are typically thought to be a virtue of lawmaking. Therefore, justifications for robust substantive judicial intervention (such as those provided by Christopher Eisgruber and Dworkin constitutionally, and Rawls and Jürgen Habermas philosophically) emphasize that judges operate under institutional constraints that impose accountability (even if less direct than that of elected representatives) and expect objectivity and moral integrity. These scholars therefore argue that the key to addressing the countermajoritarian difficulty is not the nature of judicial review, but judges' institutional characteristics. In effect, they maintain that judges' capacity to engage in substantive deliberation on democracy and rights explains why courts can opine on electoral process. However, these institutional characteristics are themselves contested. Originalists would assert that when judges go beyond the specific remit to enforce a higher constitutional law, they act without legitimacy. In effect, there is no consensus on whether institutional characteristics and the moral character of judging can give judges adequate legitimacy to widely opine on democracy. This also explains why contestation is not simply "thin" interpretivism–deliberativism. While it recognizes the plausibility of this account of the process of judging, it includes it as one prospective mode of reasoning regarding constituent autonomy, rather than the sole legitimate one. In particular, the assertion that the Court engages in normative contestation does not have the same aspirations that Rawls attributes to the Supreme Court as an "institutional exemplar" of public reason.

Normative contestation is a more conceptually expansive, and less normatively authoritative, understanding of the relationship between the judicial role and democratic structure.[24] Compared to the obligation that Rawls attributes to the justices of articulating "the best interpretation of the constitution they can," normative contestation is much less demanding; the justices must merely advance views of freedom that are plausible given the value of constituent autonomy. It *might* be argued that judges should engage in idealized interpretivism on Rawlsian or Dworkinian terms, but they need not do so to engage in legitimate normative debate; they might offer other modes or bases for reaching decisions. More specifically, they might advance their own moral interpretations of the nature of constituent autonomy in a manner that Rawls would characterize as illegitimate.[25]

---

[24] Rawls, *Political Liberalism* (New York: Columbia University Press, 1996), p. 235.
[25] *Ibid.*, p. 236.

Conceptualizing freedom as fundamentally contested obviates this dispute over the institutional role of judges by identifying the solution to the counterpopular dilemma within the character of the dispute itself, regardless of – and, indeed, incorporating – differing views of judges' institutional role. Since judges do not reach, and cannot claim the authority to reach, settled conclusions regarding appropriate terms of democratic process, they do not risk rigidly dominating self-rule. This feature can be seen as related to HLA Hart's observation that interpretations of law have an open texture, though with regards to election law this openness derives from the philosophical quality inherent to autonomy, rather than the prospectively non-exhaustive nature of legislation and the nature of linguistic command.[26] As such, the judicial approach to election law reflects the same continual debate and contestation over self-rule that characterizes democracy itself. Admittedly, this problem does not completely eliminate the tension of unelected judges making decisions about constituent self-rule, but it ameliorates its anti-democratic potential. The tension between neutral rule of law and democratic self-determination (which necessarily favors certain interests and victors in a given political dispute) may not be wholly soluble or subject to a single final conclusion. Characterizing judicial review of elections as contested provides the best way to accommodate the tension between these values.

Judicial contestation over freedom confers one other significant benefit. It transforms the judiciary into a locus of considering different forms of democratic arrangement.[27] By serving as a testbed for how a polity should rule itself, the courts become a venue for discussing differing types of democratic arrangements. This is partly a property of essentially contested concepts. Such contestation elicits compelling arguments from each side, and at least creates the opportunity for mutual recognition.[28] Another aspect is that courts as an institution are uniquely validated by judges' use of reason. When judges articulate their positions on election law questions, they are required to provide reasoned accounts of why they are advancing the most compelling account. This makes courts a forum in which reason, rather than interest, is the basis for assessing democratic organization, and where the conclusions must be explicitly articulated. Furthermore, given past courts'

---

[26] H. L. A. Hart, *The Concept of Law* (Oxford: Oxford University Press, 2012), pp. 128–36. For a discussion of law as necessarily discretionary and the difference in its openness from the openness of language, see Brian Bix, "H. L. A. Hart and the 'Open Texture' of Language" (1991) 10 *Law and Philosophy* 51, 67 and Frederick Schauer, "On the Open Texture of Law" (2013) 87 *Grazer Philosophische Studien* 197. The nature of freedom I advance here is fundamentally derived from its moral–philosophical qualities rather than its relational–political qualities.

[27] Prior research has established that democratic arrangement is a core example of a contested concept. See, e.g., Collier et al., "Essentially Contested Concepts," 222. Leading election law scholars have observed a range of democratic theories, identifying one area of space over which the debate can operate. See, e.g., Richard H. Pildes, "The Constitutionalization of Democratic Politics" (2004) 118 *Harvard Law Review* 29, 43.

[28] Gallie, "Essentially Contested Concepts," 193.

continuous revisions of reasoning, there will always be an opportunity to revisit a given decision, despite the typical closed nature of *stare decisis* – as reflected (to conservatives' delight and progressives' chagrin) in *Citizens United* overturning of *Austin v. Michigan* and the functional rejection of *Davis v. Bandemer* by *Rucho v. Common Cause*. While this ongoing contestation means courts cannot decisively "solve" problems of democratic organization, as a corollary it means they do not threaten to impose a fixed view of democracy. Rather, they explore and debate different approaches to particular contestable issues within the democratic-constitutional order.

Of course, in the heat of contestation, judges and litigants perceive themselves as ardently advancing the right view, rather than contributing to some long-run democratic equilibrium. The redemption of election law as contestation stands outside the specific commitments of any given litigation or dispute. It reconciles the dispute through a unifying theoretical frame that provides a unified account and minimizes the long-run counterpopular effects of judicial opining on democratic structure.

3.4 CURATING THE TERRAIN OF CONTESTATION OVER FREEDOM

The claim that the case law on elections is best framed as contestation over constituent freedom faces a major straightforward obstacle: much of the time judges appear to be debating topics other than freedom. Election law cases are frequently decided based on constitutional principles, such as equal protection, or prudential doctrines, such as the political question doctrine. Framing the corpus of election law disputes as being about freedom seems to distort the legal issues at stake.

At one level of abstraction, this claim has some merit. As with any analysis that hopes to bring order to a complex and multifaceted phenomenon, framing judicial disputes over election law as fundamentally about freedom requires reading certain content into case law beyond the obvious blackletter issues, and selectively identifying some as election law cases and others as involving other areas of law (such as civil procedure). This classificatory and critical analysis is precisely what social science is meant to do: show new patterns and orders.

Much of the evidence to support understanding election law as a matter of freedom is discussed in the domain-specific chapters, but there are general framing points as well. The first involves a contingent concession. Election law disputes, like all domains of law and policy, are elicited and resolved in a broader legal–constitutional context. Some ostensible election law disputes are resolved *not* through contestation over freedom, but via other decisive elements of legal constitutionalism. This claim carves away less substantive content from the unifying gloss of freedom than might be expected. It is clearly beyond the scope of the current project to incorporate all law that touches on self-governance, not least because it would require an exegesis of how each area of law expresses political will, and how the subsequent jurisprudence is a judicial assessment of the legitimate form of that will.

This section considers this challenge to the framing of freedom. It first considers the common-sense observation that so much of election law litigation appears to fall outside the issue of contestation over freedom. While as a matter of practice this may be true – courts do not resolve freedom when they dismiss a claim of voting fraud for failing a simple ripeness or jurisdictional test – as a matter of principle such disputes return to constituent self-rule. The second half of this section considers the most serious alternative framing to freedom: equality. While constituent equality may seem to be in the central theme of election law, a rigorous interpretation of the matters at issue shows that judicial consideration of equality is inevitably a subsidiary enquiry into legitimate constituent self-rule.

3.4.1 *The Diversity of Doctrinal Substance and the Pre-eminence of Freedom*

The thematic diversity of significant disputes in contemporary election law threatens to undermine any effort to create a unified theoretical account – at least one that does not require distortive or unrealistic analysis of the case law. An initial response to this challenge is that in a democratic polity, and likely in any polity that makes a claim to just rule, any legitimate claim to legal authority must derive from the autonomy of those it affects. Where a polity does not exert direct power over lawmaking, this takes the form that the people are being "made free" (in the sense of being made to live in accordance with virtue or a natural order) through coercive rule. In pre-modern times, this took the form of claims to divine knowledge or the moral supremacy of the collective. In the contemporary world, claims regarding the authority of some wise vanguard class in a Marxist mold are more typical. Almost every polity legitimizes itself by making a claim to "freedom," but outside of democracy this tends to operate through a claim to elite knowledge of goodness.

The fact that appropriate constitutional oversight of electoral procedure can countermand legislation illustrates the complexity of implementing self-determination in mass democracy. However, such complexity in the balancing of the sources of authority is a general quality of legal interpretation. This generality calls the utility of the framework into question. In other words, interpreting all legal analysis of election law as a substantive dispute over political self-determination perhaps operates at too high a level of abstraction to provide much content. Indeed, the intersecting complexities of legislative authority, constitutional "higher law," and the judiciary as the entity that makes sense of it are not unique to election law. Any legitimate state action can be traced back to popular authorization (either through representation or constitutional will), limited by the assessment of legality performed by courts that ensure the rule of law. Legislation that limits gun ownership, or restricts abortion, has initial legitimacy because it reflects the democratic will of the constituents through their representatives; the review of the law (and its possibility illegality) under the Second Amendment or the Due Process Clause, respectively, reflects the higher-law authorization of the Constitution by constituents, as interpreted by the judiciary. At a very high level, these laws might be said to be about freedom. Yet addressed with any level of useful specificity, the laws are about the right to bear arms and the extent of due process rights as applied to abortions, privacy, and medical operations. To speak of freedom in the abstract as the decisive principle offers little guidance.

However, the subject of election law is precisely the realization of freedom in the course of self-rule. When judges opine on election law, they engage with constituent autonomy in mind not as a distant ideal but as the practical subject matter that must be considered. Substantive reasoning should be directed to facilitating self-rule; this is why judicial intervention has legitimacy in such cases. This is the undergirding normative argument for the contestation over freedom as the unifying theme of election law.

Chapters 4–7 examine this claim with a detailed assessment of the doctrine. Here I note superficial challenges to the claim. Some of the most significant contemporary areas of election law have apparently been resolved by questions that, as a matter of blackletter classification, seem to be beyond direct consideration of electoral procedure, or are not easily linked to principles that evoke autonomy. The partisan gerrymandering debate was recently (and controversially) laid to rest *not* by considering any explicit principle of self-rule but by asserting the non-justiciability of the issue under the political question doctrine (*Rucho v. Common Cause*). Likewise, one person, one vote was elevated to the realm of election law by a reconceptualization of justiciability under the political question doctrine (*Baker v. Carr*). And the case that immediately preceded *Rucho* in the partisan gerrymandering debate, *Gill v. Whitford*, was resolved through a tense consensus that the plaintiffs lacked standing. These questions of justiciability and standing are matters of civil procedure, not constituent self-rule. Yet calling *any* dispute over justiciability or standing a matter of political self-determination seems to threaten to rise to the level of abstraction that makes the analytic category of "law that contests freedom" unhelpful. That said, it is plausible to propose expanding the idea of debate over freedom to necessarily include these legal principles as well. Antonin Scalia, for example, argued that standing is an essential component of the separation of powers, echoing a tradition that can be traced back to Montesquieu.[29] Such a capacious expansion need not be established for the sake of this project, because the usefulness of the framing concept of freedom is particularly urgent with regard to the landmark cases on elections. If these decisions

---

[29] Antonin Scalia, "The Doctrine of Standing as an Essential Element of the Separation of Powers" (1983) 17 *Suffolk University Law Review* 881.

3.4 Curating the Terrain of Contestation over Freedom

cannot be reasonably understood as bearing on the nature freedom, this threatens the usefulness of the category (and the viability of this project).

Examining each of these cases in detail demonstrates that the critical question is how constituents should rule themselves. The doctrine at issue turns on who has the authority to determine electoral procedures (the core of election law), and when legitimate self-rule is bettered structured by representatives as opposed to the judiciary giving force to higher constitutional law. These topics are thus central to the counterpopular dilemma.

In *Baker*, a majority of the Warren Court rejected precedent[30] to rule that malapportionment comprised a justiciable constitutional wrong. On its face, the tectonic shift of *Baker* does not involve constituent autonomy, but the procedural availability of a type of constitutional claim. By framing its analysis through the political question doctrine, which speaks to the judiciary's availability to hear the claim as a matter of procedure, the majority does not address any explicit question related to the substance of political organization (i.e., if malapportioned districts make constituents less capable of self-rule). Underneath this procedural façade, the substance of the question explicitly relates to the terms of legitimate self-rule: what underlying conditions must a democratic procedure have to be considered advancing self-rule, even where those procedures are themselves selected by representative democratic process? Stated more generally, to achieve franchise autonomy, what is the appropriate balance between constitutionally and judicially imposed requirements of self-rule and those imposed by the legislature? In this regard, the political question doctrine illuminates, rather than conceals, the question. It hangs upon when the legislation is the best expression of the tendency to self-rule, as opposed to the principles of judicially enforced constitutionalism. Thus, the dispute in *Baker* reveals not only that the substance at issue are the terms of legitimate constituent autonomy in the institutional context. It also illustrates the disputed nature of constituent autonomy in the context of the counterpopular dilemma. Justice Frankfurter's exhortations to avoid entering the political thicket[31] are at root an assertion that constituents rule themselves more freely when the institutional power to set the terms of democracy lies with the legislature rather than the courts as constitutional guardians. The majority in *Baker*, conversely, adapts the political question doctrine to reject this claim, and argues that equality of per-vote power is, in fact, mandated by the higher law of the Constitution. Chapter 4 extensively evaluates this question, but in brief the procedural question contains issues that cut to the core of contestation over how constituents can best rule themselves in an institutionally complex constitutional democracy.

---

[30] *Colegrove v. Green*, 328 US 549 (1946) and *MacDougall v. Green*, 335 US 281 (1948). See Chapter 4 for an extensive discussion of the nature of the relationship between the cases.
[31] Colegrove, 328 US at 556.

Rucho (the decisive case of partisan gerrymandering)[32] reflects a similar dynamic. Like one person, one vote, it is ostensibly decided by the political question doctrine. The five-judge conservative majority rejected the justiciability of partisan gerrymandering claims even as it conceded the wrongfulness of the practice.[33] The four dissenting progressive judges asserted that where a practice is wrongful, it is better to identify a constitutional claim and work out the standard as it proceeds.[34] Thus, the issue appears to be procedural on the surface of the dispute, regarding the mere availability of a viable legal standard. But the underlying question is what institutional arrangement best enables self-rule. The conservative opinion is founded on the assumption that partisan distortion of electoral arrangements is better managed by the political process itself. As Chapter 6 elaborates, this exposes the fundamental issue at stake: whether parties should be conceived of as organic expressions of popular will such that their influence is directed by their constituents, or whether they are elite intermediaries that threaten to impair popular autonomy. The formal doctrinal shell of justiciability, and even the more substantive institutional question of if politics or the judiciary is the correct forum for debating partisan gerrymandering, revolves upon a fundamental question of democratic organization. Is free self-rule naturally self-perpetuating (including in the capacity to manage partisanship), or does parties' elite influence legitimize countervailing elite intervention by the judiciary? Stated in terms of self-determination, the question is if partisan influence in districting renders the franchise heteronomously guided by party elites, or if parties are controlled by voters such that partisan influence is an expression of autonomy.

The indirect nature of these foundational debates reflects the constitutional limits of the judiciary's authority. If the judicial approach to election law interrogates and situates popular autonomy, why has the case law not reflected a more explicit and systematic examination of self-rule? The answer is that, as in all areas, the Court's competence is contextualized by the extent of its institutional remit. Courts resolve disputes where there are plausible claims. For federal courts addressing public law, this means where there is a constitutional question, typically in the form of a prospectively infringed constitutional right. This limit reflects the constitutional arrangement itself. One aspect of the contestation over freedom in election law involves how broadly courts may identify such rights, as the one person, one vote and partisan gerrymandering examples establish. Progressives/ living constitutionalists tend to broaden the range of structural features of elections that the Court can enforce to protect constitutional legitimacy. Conservatives/

---

[32] As Michael Parsons has observed, *Gill* was merely an exercise in evasion. G. Michael Parsons, "Dodge, Duck, Dip, Dive, and Dodge: The 5 D's of the *Gill v. Whitford* Decision," Modern Democracy Blog (June 19, 2018), https://moderndemocracyblog.com/2018/06/19/dodge-duck-dip-dive-and-dodge/.
[33] *Rucho v. Common Clause*, 139 S.Ct. 2484, 2507 (2019).
[34] Ibid., at 2524.

originalists, meanwhile, prefer a more cabined conception of what the constitutional structure, as opposed to immediate expressions of popular will (such as through legislation), can dictate regarding electoral structure. This debate should not obscure the reality that there is a consensus that there must be a plausible constitutional point of entry. One example of the limit is the ostensible futility of any claim that the Electoral College – which has endured extensive criticism from pundits on the left[35] – is unconstitutional. The Electoral College has explicit institutional potential (and lately, reality) to be countermajoritarian (though it can be defended as part of a broader federalist setup). But given that its role is explicitly articulated in the higher law of the Constitution, a purely judicial (as opposed to political) solution seems toothless.

3.4.2 Political Freedom and the Right to Equality

The most compelling alternative to contestation over freedom as the unifying axis of the law of elections is the right to equality. Both words in the phrase are important. The courts' institutional role can be best encapsulated as rights enforcement that defends against state action (rather than the more positive vision of engaging in debate over self-rule), and the principle of equality appears substantively pre-eminent. Equality and freedom are the two great substantive values of democracy. As John Rawls states, liberal democracy must "answer to the claims of both liberty and equality." Moreover, the equality of constituents is fundamental to legitimate democratic organization: "the basic institutions of a constitutional democracy" must "satisfy the fair terms of cooperation between citizens regarded as free and equal."[36] As Rawls, and the vast public reason scholarship he has engendered,[37] observe, the requirement that members of a democratic polity are free *and* equal poses a series of thorny dilemmas. When constituents freely choose policies and terms of state organization, it may result in the unequal distribution of resources and privilege as well as structures that perpetuate this inequality. However, mandating equality may deprive constituents of the full range of choices of governance.

Thus, why does the best account of election law invoke constituent autonomy, rather than constituent equality, or some synthetic concept that unifies them (as Rawls's own idea of public reason might be said to do)? There is no question that an account of election law would be woefully incomplete if it did not substantively and extensively engage with the norm of equality (as this project does, especially

---

[35] For a summary of one recent brickbat, see Josh Chafetz, "Why We Should Abolish the Electoral College," *The New York Times* (March 17, 2020), www.nytimes.com/2020/03/17/books/review/let-the-people-pick-the-president-jesse-wegman.html.
[36] Rawls, "Political Liberalism," 4.
[37] For a useful overview, see Samuel Freeman, "The Idea of Public Reason Revisited" (2003) 72 *Fordham Law Review* 2021.

in Chapter 4 on one person, one vote and Chapter 7 on race and elections). Yet the best unified account of the election law doctrine treats equality as an intermediary concept that informs the higher value of self-determination, rather than an alternative or equal partner. At the level of doctrine, each domain can be more readily understood to be concerned with self-determination at the individual and collective levels, rather than a personal right to equality (a point made by anti-entrenchment theorists as well as more general structuralists, such as Heather Gerken).[38] Furthermore, in asking why election law matters overall, the principle of self-determination offers a more compelling and meaningful answer: it matters because it allows constituents to express their capacity for self-rule. Equality may be necessary for this freedom, but it is a subsidiary feature that facilitates and serves the goal of autonomy.

This point can be adapted from Philip Pettit's discussion of non-domination (an analysis that can be generalized to most treatments of freedom). Pettit observes that "[f]reedom as nondomination does not call for [supplementation by other values] since…it already requires institutions that perform well in regard to values like equality and welfare; thus those values do not have to be introduced as distinct desiderata."[39] He elaborately conceptualizes why equality can be folded into a theory of freedom,[40] but in the electoral context the unity of the values is even easier. Since elections produce singular government action by aggregating the wills of individual constituents, any illegitimate excess power holding by a particular constituent will necessarily come at the cost of the self-determining capacity of another constituent. The unity of the good at issue – the capacity to contribute to self-rule – means that equality is an *aspect* of the liberty to engage in self-governance.

There are both purely doctrinal reasons and normative reasons to argue that equality is the best frame for election law. To address these, it is useful to consider a sophisticated and intelligent account of election case law, Richard Hasen's *The Supreme Court and Election Law*. Hasen maintains that equality is the unifying concept for the doctrine and offers a normative theory for when the Supreme Court should intervene. His account not only offers a compelling synthesis of the doctrine through equality, but it also argues that the law should be understood as a matter of individual right (rather than structuralism), offering a personal rights account as the basis for judicial review.[41] His guiding principles – distrust of the judiciary and a question of what the Constitution actually instructs judges to do – are reminiscent of the originalist interpretation, and echoes Scalia's belief that originalism is a

---

[38] Gerken, "Undiluted Vote."
[39] Philip Pettit, *Republicanism: A Theory of Freedom and Government* (Oxford: Oxford University Press, 1997), p. 81. Compare this to Tuck's defense of majoritarianism in Chapter 2.
[40] Ibid., p. 116.
[41] Richard Hasen, *The Supreme Court and Election Law: Judging Equality from Baker v. Carr to Bush v. Gore* (New York: New York University Press, 2003), pp. 153–5.

lesser evil than the broad judicial creativity that undergirds sophisticated structural intervention. The problem with this approach – in addition to the difficulty of deriving a "true" account of the constitutional instruction reviewed in Chapter 2 – is that at times the Court must assess the validity of political structures and terms of representation. Hasen's theory – that the Court should only robustly enforce election law rights when there is social consensus over their validity[42] – directly speaks to the counterpopular dilemma. He clearly speaks to one of its sides in arguing that the Court should be cautious in enforcing equal rights except where it has a clear mandate to do so.

I advocate an alternative to Hasen's prioritization of equality and analytic suggestion. His reliance on social consensus to ground Supreme Court intervention is not especially stable, and is particularly vulnerable in a highly polarized environment where there is fierce contestation over appropriate values of self-governance. Furthermore, an instance of social consensus runs into a definitional problem. Even if there is consensus over an ideal such as "rejecting unequal voting power" or "preventing disproportionate influence over campaigns by elites," the doctrinal application of a given ideal is itself likely to be contested. For example, as discussed previously, while both conservatives and progressives acknowledge the risk of elite domination in campaign finance, conservatives see it in the form of government regulation of speech, whereas progressives see it in the impact of disproportionate wealth. This disagreement means that even where there is consensus on a broad value, doctrinal resolution is likely to be far fiercer.[43] It is therefore preferable to identify ongoing contestation as a universal feature of election law, rather than merely an intermediary step (which Hasen calls an initial "murkiness")[44] that culminates in stable and decisive holdings. Achieving democracy – for reasons described in this chapter – is unlikely to ever reach the sort of settlement that he suggests.

Substantively, Hasen's emphasis on equality has a reasonable footing. The first and most immediate aspect of this is doctrinal. The constitutional basis for much judicial intervention in election law is grounded in rights that explicitly invoke equality, most centrally the Fourteenth Amendment's equal protection clause. This clause has been used to advance one person, one vote for state and local districting, and to challenge racial and partisan gerrymanders as well as practices such as poll taxes. Furthermore, scholars have reconceptualized domains of election law as oriented around equality even where it is not the most prominent principle in the doctrine. David Strauss and Cass Sunstein have offered influential arguments

---

[42] Ibid., p. 80.
[43] In fairness to Hasen, he wrote "Judging Equality" in 2003, before *Federal Election Commission v. Wisconsin Right to Life II*, 551 US 449 (2007), *Citizens United v. Federal Election Commission*, 558 US 310 (2010), and *McCutcheon* showed the fierceness of the partisan divide.
[44] Hasen, "Judging Equality," p. 49.

that campaign finance is about the equalization of spending power rather than the actual freedom to express ideas;[45] Daryl Levinson has argued that both voting and rights enforcement should be conceived of as protecting minorities from a tyranny of the majority.[46]

There is also a conceptual argument for preferring equality as the organizing axis of election law: the degree and nature of the right to political equality can be seen as the substance of what the Supreme Court actually contests. In one person, one vote, the Court had to determine whether (and on what terms) equality of voting power would be imposed; in racial and partisan districting, how equality is to be guaranteed to persons and groups based on certain protected criterion; and in campaign finance, the nature of the speech equality that persons are afforded in light of regulation of wealth disparities. According to this view, the dispute over the right to equality and the substance of such a right offers a more substantively meaningful description of judicial analysis. Liberty may be the ultimate goal, but the real playing field of judicial disputes is constituents' political equality in the process of self-rule.

Yet framing election law through equality is, in a complete assessment, less substantively accurate. Firstly, it lacks comprehensive doctrinal accuracy, at times openly deviating from the content of the doctrine. Equality is a central idea in much, but not all, election law litigation. For example, while Strauss's observation that campaign finance can be analytically cast as a matter of equality is an insightful abstract point, the justices have unequivocally rejected the idea that the equalization of speech is a legitimate goal of regulation. Even the progressive wing, as detailed above, has sought to justify regulation as a matter of freedom. Unless one identifies the Court as either blind to the real issue or engaged in a deceptive shadow debate, equality is not an accurate frame for the legal dispute. This challenge is even plainer in areas such as parties' ballot access (discussed in Chapter 6). While Hasen classifies minor party ballot access as an equality issue,[47] ballot access is only a matter of equality for parties in the most abstract and formalist sense. Even a topic that seems to more centrally address equality, partisan gerrymandering, benefits from being conceived *not* as a matter of equality, but of how constituents rule themselves in light of parties' influence. Equality under the equal protection clause may be one doctrinal means of analyzing partisan districting, but the issue quickly raises substantive questions of political arrangement. And in the context of race and elections, some areas cannot be accurately captured by the concept of equality. For instance, Section 5 of the Voting Rights Act contrasts the value of preventing the

---

[45] David A. Strauss, "Corruption, Equality, and Campaign Finance Reform" (1994) 94 *Columbia Law Review* 1370; Cass R. Sunstein, "Political Equality & Unintended Consequence" (1994) 94 *Columbia Law Review* 1390, 1397.
[46] Daryl J. Levinson, "Rights and Votes" (2012) 121 *Yale Law Journal* 1286.
[47] Hasen, "Judging Equality," p. 39.

retrogression (distinct from equality) of minority political power under the Fifteenth Amendment against the value of federalism, a debate that the concept of equality cannot fully capture.

This lack of doctrinal accuracy is linked to the deeper conceptual accuracy of equality as opposed to freedom. The ultimate question that courts face in resolving election law disputes is *what type of democratic arrangement would best allow constituents to rule themselves*. Equality is an intermediary concept in election law: it is equality *in the service* of constituent autonomy. This can be most vividly established where equality seems to be most central to the dispute. In racial gerrymandering, the key question is what minorities can demand in just voting arrangements through their constitutionally guaranteed right to equality. The Court has contested this question by asking *what terms of equality would best grant minorities a fair capacity in shaping political outcomes*.[48] The realities of self-rule are decisive. Likewise, the partisan gerrymandering debate has hinged not on equality, but on the role that parties play in affecting constituent self-determination. The most general expression of this ideal might be derived from Justice Breyer's concept of "active liberty." He argues that judges can resolve cases (including those related to equality)[49] by asking what types of outcomes would yield legitimate citizen control of politics. Breyer's view is unquestionably in the progressive/living constitutionalist mold – yet the conservative/originalist obverse would answer a query about equality by looking at what constituents freely agreed to in the text of the equal protection clause.[50] For both types of interpretations, the *method* of informing equality becomes an enquiry into what will best serve constituent self-determination.

However, the use of equality as a frame might in the final instance be defended as a universal feature of all judge-made law on elections: any successful claim ultimately depends on an assertion that, as a matter of law, the claimant should be treated equally by some relevant constitutional feature (e.g., a protected category, ability to engage in speech, right to association). This is unquestionably true, but the highly generalized, abstract nature of the claim paradoxically reveals the hollowness of the equality framing. In a rule of law regime, *every* right is a claim to equal treatment under the law. This neutrality distinguishes courts as the most appropriate institution to protect the rule of law. However, because of this level of generality, a framing concept that is more substantively specific and more tailored to elections offers a more meaningful analysis.

[48] Gerken, "Undiluted Vote"; cf. Richard H. Pildes and Richard G. Niemi, "Expressive Harms, Bizarre Districts, and Voting Rights: Evaluating Election-District Appearances after Shaw v. Reno" (1993) 92 *Michigan Law Review* 483. Gerken ultimately shows that expressive harm theory falls out of favor, and the fact that it does not point to freedom explains why.
[49] Stephen Breyer, *Active Liberty: Interpreting a Democratic Constitution* (Oxford: Oxford University Press, 2008), p. 49.
[50] For a magisterial example, one might consider Michael McConnell's originalist treatment of *Brown v. Board*. Michael W. McConnell, "Originalism and the Desegregation Decisions" (1995) 81 *Virginia Law Review* 947.

The suitability of freedom over equality as the framing concept for election law doctrine ultimately rests on two features: the superior ability of considering constituent self-determination to organize and illuminate the case law, and the fact that self-determination is the core of democratic process. Equality is an intermediary issue precisely because in democratic process, it is relevant for evaluating and debating the legitimacy of competing forms of democratic process. This is especially clear in Chapter 7, which considers the validity of two competing interpretations of equality as relevant *not* as a first-order good, but as determining what claim minorities can make to influence democratic outcomes. Yet the preferability of freedom in understanding election law is not necessarily applicable to other areas of law. For example, in areas such as access to types of final-order resources such as economic goods or access to education, equality *may* be a final order goal that need not serve some other value.[51] The universal utility of freedom is only claimed here with regard to election law.

---

[51] Such issues are debated on differing sides in, for example, *University of California v. Bakke*, 438 US 265 (1978) and *Richmond v. J.A. Croson*, 488 US 469 (1989).

4

One Person, One Vote

The Triumph of Minimal Procedural Equality

The right to vote freely for the candidate of one's choice is of the essence of a democratic society, and any restrictions on that right strike at the heart of representative government. And the right of suffrage can be denied by a debasement or dilution of the weight of a citizen's vote just as effectively as by wholly prohibiting the free exercise of the franchise.
–Earl Warren, Reynolds v. Sims

[W]hat the Court is doing reflects more an adventure in judicial experimentation than a solid piece of constitutional adjudication.
–John Marshall Harlan II, Baker v. Carr

The principle of one person, one vote catapulted the Supreme Court into the arena of electoral design. Introduced by a series of landmark cases in the 1960s, the one person, one vote rule is unique among election law doctrine in that its essential validity has been accepted on the bench for decades rather than the subject of contemporary dispute. While celebrated in popular opinion as a triumph for democratic fairness, scholars have criticized one person, one vote as irruptive, conceptually confused, and constitutionally unprincipled. This Chapter challenges this scholarly orthodoxy. The conventional view is that recognizing malapportionment as a constitutional wrong was a novel, sudden reversal. This Chapter demonstrates that the Supreme Court adopted this position only after decades of normative contestation over the importance of equality to democratic process. Similarly, the conventional scholarly view is that the equipopulousness rule that makes up the substance of one person, one vote is theoretically and practically deficient. This Chapter, however, shows that the adoption of a procedurally minimalist, mechanical principle reflected the Supreme Court's recognition that it was imposing a democratic norm upon the polity without a constitutional mandate. In light of this blatant imposition of a norm of self-rule upon the polity, the Court worked carefully to integrate and balance the one person, one vote jurisprudence with other constitutional values. The one person, one vote jurisprudence is ultimately characterized by an attempt to promulgate a bedrock precondition of democratic legitimacy while recognizing the importance of allocating the electorate authority over its own terms of self-rule. The law of one person, one vote thus epitomizes the Supreme Court's efforts to navigate the counterpopular dilemma.

4.1 ONE PERSON, ONE VOTE AND THE DECONTESTATION OF BARE EQUALITY

The one person, one vote rule remains an extraordinary and oft-celebrated entry into election law by the Supreme Court. Where representatives are allocated to subdivisions, district lines can be drawn that lead to disparities in how many voters select each representative. When a representative is selected by proportionally fewer voters, each of those voters has a proportionally stronger representative voice than the average voter. Likewise, where a representative is elected by an above-average number of voters, each of those voters has proportionally less representation in government. Such disparities (at least where they are not explicitly a function of constitutional design, as they are in the Senate) result in egregious democratic unfairness by violating the principle of equal citizen power.

Such malapportionment was endemic in America before the 1960s.[1] Legislatures had long been loath to redraw lines as voters moved between districts, in part because doing so might threaten the tenure of current representatives. Malapportionment can be a highly effective vehicle of entrenchment. It illustrates how legislatures can impede change by controlling the terms of their selection. With the dramatic consolidation of the US population into cities during the first half of the twentieth century, this became even more salient. Highly concentrated voters in cities were dramatically underrepresented in long-outdated districting plans.

In what Gordon Baker coined the "reapportionment revolution,"[2] the Supreme Court condemned such population-based malapportionment as illegal and declared that legislative districts must each contain an equivalent number of persons. As seminally stated in *Reynolds v. Sims*, "the fundamental principle of representative government in this country is one of equal representation for equal numbers of people."[3] This doctrine transformed the American electoral landscape, required

---

[1] For an accessible but detailed account of malapportionment, see J. Douglas Smith, *On Democracy's Doorstep: The Inside Story of How the Supreme Court Brought "One Person, One Vote" to the United States* (New York: Hill and Wang, 2014), Chapter 1.

[2] Gordon Baker, *The Reapportionment Revolution: Representation, Political Power, and the Supreme Court* (New York: Random House, 1966). For a description of the political effects of the wave of reapportionment, see Gary W. Cox and Jonathan N. Katz, *Elbridge Gerry's Salamander: The Electoral Consequences of the Reapportionment Revolution* (Cambridge: Cambridge University Press, 2002).

[3] *Reynolds v. Sims*, 377 US 533, 560–1 (1964). The opinion attributes this idea to *Wesberry v. Sanders*, 378 US 1, 15 (1964) which, while it observes the basic principle of "equal representation … for equal numbers of people," does not seem to provide quite the breadth or priority attributed to it by *Reynolds v. Sims*.

4.1 One Person, One Vote and the Decontestation of Bare Equality

many states to redraw long-standing districting plans, and eliminated gross superficial disparities in voter power. This bold step also marked the beginning of modern election law and set the stage for many of the subsequent battles over what terms courts should impose as necessary for fair democracy.

One person, one vote had a paradoxical legacy. Uniquely among domains of election law, its legal validity is a matter of near consensus on the bench and its policy benefits are widely celebrated.[4] Clarence Thomas is the only current justice who openly doubts the legitimacy of one person, one vote.[5] Former Chief Justice Earl Warren prized one person, one vote as his greatest legacy[6] and speculated that if it had been achieved earlier, it could have pre-empted many of the other civil rights challenges.[7] The tenuous foundations of one person, one vote make its veneration even more surprising. The one person, one vote rule lacks a clear prompt from constitutional text and arguably contradicts the Election Clause's clear allocation of authority over voting to the states; it also overturned prior Supreme Court precedent and long-established practice. These weaknesses have left it vulnerable to a variety of fierce scholarly criticisms. Some scholars have attacked the lack of constitutional foundations[8] and thereby challenged the norm's fundamental legal validity. Others have argued that the Court's enforcement of mechanical equipopulousness is deficient as a matter of political principle.[9]

However, I argue that the counterpopular dilemma is the real challenge to one person, one vote. If the judiciary imposes a norm based solely on moral authority, this suggests that the franchise cannot rule itself through accountable or autonomous processes. The one person, one vote norm has been "decontested," meaning that it has achieved a "stable meaning within a given framework."[10] In other words, it is the decisive and precedential resolution of an issue such that it is settled law. When an issue has been decontested, resolving core questions on the issue will not be a significant matter of legal or constitutional debate. In Hartian terms, it is the conclusion that a given rule is determinant.[11]

---

[4] Guy-Uriel E. Charles, "Constitutional Pluralism and Democratic Politics: Reflections on the Interpretive Approach of Baker v. Carr" (2003) 80 *North Carolina Law Review* 1104.
[5] *Evenwel v. Abbott*, 136 S.Ct. 1120, 1133 (2016).
[6] Pamela S. Karlan, "Democracy and Disdain" (2012) 126 *Harvard Law Review* 1, 4; Smith, "On Democracy's Doorstep," pp. 3–4.
[7] Guy-Uriel E. Charles and Luis Fuentes-Rohwer, "Reynolds Reconsidered" (2015) 67 *Alabama Law Review* 485.
[8] Derek T. Muller, "Perpetuating "One Person, One Vote" Errors" (2016) 39 *Harvard Journal of Law & Public Policy* 371.
[9] Heather K. Gerken, "Lost in the Political Thicket: The Court, Election Law, and the Doctrinal Interregnum" (2004) 153 *University of Pennsylvania Law Review* 503; Sanford Levinson, "One Person, One Vote: A Mantra in Need of Meaning" (2002) 80 *North Carolina Law Review* 1269; Grant M. Hayden, "The False Promise of One Person, One Vote" (2003) 102 *Michigan Law Review* 213.
[10] David Collier, Fernando Daniel Hidalgo, and Andra Olivia Maciuceanu, "Essentially Contested Concepts: Debates and Applications" (2006) 11 *Journal of Political Ideologies* 211, 218.
[11] H. L. A. Hart, *The Concept of Law* (Oxford: Oxford University Press, 2012), p. 135.

One person, one vote therefore lacks the typical quality that softens the counterpopular dilemma – the judiciary's continual debate of appropriate norms. The widespread and intractable presence of malapportionment prior to *Baker* shows why the judiciary felt compelled to act, yet it does not resolve the affront to popular self-determination raised by such judicial intervention.

The form and substance of one person, one vote reflects the Court's attempt to navigate through this difficulty. The norm inescapably imposes a procedural requirement for electoral process. However, given the judicial fabrication of the requirement, the Court advanced *the thinnest and least invasive possible requirement* for demanding citizen equality. The mechanical equipopulousness that one person, one vote demands looks *only* to persons' equality as bare members of a political community rather than any "thicker" attributes or aspects of justice. It also limits judicial enforcement to a readily and incontrovertibly falsifiable test rather than creating the opportunity for "thicker" normative reasoning. Furthermore, the Court framed its innovation in familiar modes of constitutional reasoning and substantively deferred to other constitutional principles where possible, while still advancing the equipopulousness requirement.

This chapter traces the history of one person, one vote as a constrained but unabashedly normative intervention into democratic process. *Baker v. Carr*, the watershed case that declared malapportionment illegal, is conventionally described as a sudden break with all previous doctrine. However, a review of past precedent through the lens of contestation shows that *Baker* was not a pitched battle over the justiciability of malapportionment, but rather its resolution. Prior research in this area has overlooked the real inflection point, *Colegrove v. Green*, in which a fiercely divided Court wrestled, through characteristically contestatory normative debate, with whether it should address malapportionment. Most justices were committed to reconciling one person, one vote with judicial review by the time of *Baker*; thus the majority opinion abstained from such open normative theorizing. *Baker*'s famous reformulation of the political question doctrine is best understood as framing the imposition of the democratic norm in recognizable constitutional terms. By doing so, the Court sought to deflect the critique that its entry into the political thicket was baldly anti-democratic.

The subsequent doctrinal development of one person, one vote ameliorated the counterpopular dilemma in two main ways: (1) using strict arithmetic equipopulousness to assess districts' legality and (2) gradually introducing a "safe harbor" for state and local deviations from this strictness. The mechanical equipopulousness test has been extensively criticized as undertheorized and failing to engage with the "thick" realities of democratic power. Yet the Court adopted the "thin" test precisely to avoid making highly tailored, normatively complex evaluations of the fairness of individual districting plans. The "thin" test cabined the Court's practical interference terms of self-governance. So long as equipopulousness was satisfied, districting plans satisfied one person, one vote. The "thin" test thereby granted the electorate broad authority to set its own terms of self-rule, so long as it conformed to a single clearly enunciated requirement. The safe harbor, meanwhile, showed respect for a competing constitutional principle – federalism.

However, the case law does not fully articulate the purely normative assertion underlying one person, one vote. If the Court was going to impose a single condition upon democratic organization, why select the minimalist equipopulousness requirement? This chapter answers this question by observing that, given the principle of democratic governance as self-rule, the equality of citizens is a precondition of freedom. Without such equality, claims that a polity realizes democratic freedom are hollow, for each member of the polity cannot be given the real power to shape the path of their own governance. Because such equality is a precondition for self-rule, it must be present in the political process prior to any more fully elaborated determination through subsequent lawmaking. But as such an externally imposed precondition of equality becomes richly substantive, it constrains the opportunity of the franchise to realize its autonomy by selecting its own democratic processes. Where an equality precondition is explicitly articulated in the Constitution (or through logical development of constitutional precedent), its validity can plausibly be attributed to the polity. However, where the judiciary advances a norm based wholly on a claim of intrinsic moral priority, it evokes the counterpopular dilemma. By adopting a thin and normatively minimal conception of equality, the Court minimized this dilemma. This conception requires no engagement with the outcomes of democratic process, but only the minimal starting condition for defining democracy – constituents' formal equality.

4.2 *BAKER V. CARR*: DECONTESTING ENTRY INTO THE POLITICAL THICKET THROUGH CONSTITUTIONAL INNOVATION

The foundation of the one person, one vote doctrine was forged across several opinions. *Baker v. Carr* established the justiciability of malapportionment, while *Gray v. Sanders*, *Wesberry v. Sanders*, and *Reynolds v. Sims* articulated the numerical equipopulousness rule. These two steps reflect different types of innovation. *Baker* required expanding the power of the judiciary against legislative discretion, which necessitated the normative proposition that self-determination by the polity must satisfy incontrovertible background conditions. In addition to lacking a clear constitutional grounding, this claim cut against pre-*Baker* precedent regarding how the legislature and judiciary should divide authority over electoral procedure. Perhaps sensitive to this background, the *Baker* majority opinion does not justify the decision by the superiority of the judiciary as a moral arbiter, but by a drily doctrinal approach – reworking the political question doctrine. In doing so, the Court couches and limits its two radical moral propositions, that electoral procedure must conform to judicial norms and that the Court has this type of moral insight, through typical constitutional reasoning.

4.2.1 Baker's About-face: From Legislative to Judicial Authority over Districting

Baker's practical impact – imposing a requirement of equality upon state districting – was a notorious legal fabrication by the Court, a "judicial sleight of hand."[12] Yet noting that *Baker* represents a fabrication ignores its relationship to prior doctrine. The Court did not invent a constitutional standard out of nothing; rather, it rejected (albeit through somewhat disingenuous phrasing) the previously accepted position that districting principles should be established by formally authoritative expressions of popular will. Scholarly accounts typically focus on how *Baker* challenges its immediate contradictory predecessor, *Colegrove v. Green*. Most such research identifies "overcoming the justiciability hurdle erected by *Colegrove*" as *Baker's* defining move.[13] Yet *Colegrove's* real relationship to *Baker* is best understood through the frame of contestation. Prior to *Colegrove*, the idea that malapportionment was an intrinsic wrong was not even present in the judicial imagination, as a careful review of the case law shows. *Colegrove's* fierce fracture in fact manifests contestation over this question, and *Baker* decontests this.

This doctrinal history is important for two reasons. First, it cogently demonstrates how a norm of popular self-rule can be contested and then decontested within election case law. Second, *Baker* and the *Colegrove* dissenters relied on distorted readings of pre-*Colegrove* precedent to make their case that the justiciability of malapportionment was a matter of precedent as well as a normative shift. Highlighting the inaccuracy of their readings confirms the purely normative character of one person, one vote and demonstrates how dedicated the *Baker* majority was to framing its normative intervention in the form of familiar common law reasoning.

4.2.1.1 The Pre-eminence of Popular Will under the Old Doctrine

Three early twentieth century cases exemplify the deference to popular determination of electoral procedure under the "old" regime, despite being cases that the *Baker* majority curiously asserts "sustain[] the federal courts' jurisdiction of the subject matter of federal constitutional claims of" malapportionment.[14] In *Davis v.*

---

[12] Richard L. Hasen, *The Supreme Court and Election Law: Judging Equality from Baker v. Carr to Bush v. Gore* (New York: New York University Press, 2003), p. 51. See also Michael W. McConnell, "The Redistricting Cases: Original Mistakes and Current Consequences" (2000) 24 *Harvard Journal of Law & Public Policy* 103, 106 (the Equal Protection Clause at the time of *Baker* "had never been applied to the districting question").

[13] Heather K. Gerken, "The Costs and Causes of Minimalism in Voting Cases: *Baker v. Carr* and Its Progeny" (2002) 80 *North Carolina Law Review* 1411, 1419. See also Charles and Fuentes-Rohwer, "Reynolds Reconsidered," 498; Samuel Issacharoff, "Political Judgments" (2001) 68 *University of Chicago Law Review* 637, 640. Both Charles and Fuentes-Rohwer, 494 and Issacharoff, 639 point to cases prior to *Colegrove v. Green*, 28 US 549 (1946) that establish the long legacy of judicial non-intervention in politics, *Giles v. Harris*, 89 US 475 (1903) and *Luther v. Borden*, 48 US 1 (1849), respectively.

[14] *Baker v. Carr*, 369 US 186, 201 (1962).

Hildebrant,[15] the Court evaluated whether a popular referendum could negate a districting plan adopted by representatives, in the context of federal legislation asserting that districting should be undertaken by state legislatures, but the state constitution incorporating the referendum as part of its legislative procedure. In concluding that the referendum could negate the legislature, the Court affirmed the referendum's authority over the districting process.[16] *Davis* thereby expresses the practical characteristic of deferring to popular determination of electoral procedure. The Court would not interfere with the state's internal determination of its democratic process as allocated to it by the Elections Clause.

Smiley v. Holm likewise affirmed the authority of state constitutions over electoral procedures on the basis of the Elections Clause.[17] The Court concluded that an attempt by Minnesota's state legislature to fast-track a districting bill despite the governor's veto had no legal force because it contravened the state constitution. *Smiley* confirmed elected governments' authority to structure elections (including districting), but concluded that within a state, the state constitution is the higher law to which any process of legislating must conform. This left Minnesota with no districting plan at the time it was expected to seat congressional representatives. The Court concluded that because the federal Constitution requires seating House representatives, they must be selected via an at-large election. *Smiley*'s legal foundation was that "because redistricting is lawmaking…the legislature must act through the normal legislative channels provided in its state constitution."[18] While the *Colegrove* dissenters[19] and the *Baker* majority[20] identified *Smiley* as a pivotal indicator of federal judicial authority over state elections, *Smiley* is uncontroversial as a matter of popular self-determination. It was not a "hard" case, as it required no normative interpretation of the relevant authoritative bases of state action. *Smiley* merely affirmed that lawmaking must be undertaken in accordance with appropriate formal procedures. Disregarding the executive veto of the districting plan contravened the state process for lawmaking, and nothing in the congressional legislation at issue suggested any attempt to challenge such state process.[21] *Smiley* affirms the authority

---

[15] *State of Ohio ex rel. Davis v. Hildebrant*, 241 US 565 (1916).
[16] The *Baker* majority invokes the case as support for federal oversight of districting on the grounds that the *Hildebrant* Court chose to affirm the state court decision rather than simply reject the appeal for want of jurisdiction. The *Hildebrant* Court, however, casually noted that which it relied upon was irrelevant to the result. The political question sting comes from *Hildebrant's* observation, 241 US at 569, that negating the referendum as an attack on the republican form of government under the Guaranty Clause lies outside the Court's jurisdiction as a political matter that can only be addressed by Congress.
[17] *Smiley v. Holm*, 285 US 355, 363 (1932).
[18] Benedict J. Schweigert, "'Now for a Clean Sweep!' Smiley v. Holm, Partisan Gerrymandering, and At-Large Congressional Elections" (2008) 107 *Michigan Law Review* 133, 152.
[19] *Colegrove*, 328 US at 564; *Baker*, 369 US at 573.
[20] *Baker*, 369 US at 232.
[21] *Smiley*, 285 US at 371.

of popular will over electoral procedures by observing that deviating from those formal procedures will lack legality.

The final and most decisive deference to political oversight of districting is *Wood v. Broom*. In the redistricting that followed the 1930 census, Mississippi created congressional districts that varied significantly in the number of constituents. Previous federal legislation requiring districts of equal population had not been renewed, and Mississippi citizens brought suits alleging various constitutional *and* legislative violations. The US Supreme Court unanimously found no violation and dismissed the suit. The opinion emphasized the absence of a congressional instruction to maintain equipopulous districts;[22] four of the justices would have dismissed the suit for general lack of equity. While later supporters of *Baker* sought to marginalize *Wood* on the grounds that it did no more than address the status of federal legislation,[23] this interpretation is implausible. While the Court in *Wood* did not specifically reject the assertion that the Constitution provides legal grounds for equipopulous districts,[24] the plaintiffs in *Wood* did advance a claim that malapportionment comprised a first-order constitutional wrong (using highly similar language to that later invoked in *Baker*).[25] The *Wood* opinion was silent on this point most plausibly because such a purely constitutional claim had so little basis it was not worth specifically rejecting. By failing to identify a freestanding constitutional wrong in the malapportionment at issue, the *Wood* case communicated that there was no legal right on that basis. If a right to equal representation had existed on the basis of judicially enforceable constitutional right, *Wood* would have been obligated to identify it.

Wood epitomizes the "traditional" Supreme Court attitude toward districting: it was wholly a matter of popular political determination, rather than an issue that must survive some deeper normative scrutiny. The Court demonstrated that while it would give legal force to explicit instruction (legislative or constitutional) that formally articulates such popular will, it would not interrogate the fairness or normative legitimacy of either the terms by which the popular will is expressed, or the content of formally correct popular will. As *Wood* demonstrates, in the most straightforward instance this will involve deferring to legislative instruction (and, in its absence, refusing to identify a legal wrong). *Hildebrant* and *Smiley* illustrate that parsing the popular will may require considering if a given districting obeyed explicit constitutional procedures for lawmaking, but in both cases the Court indicated that a districting plan is valid if legislation obeyed such formalities. The cases

---

[22] *Wood v. Broom*, 287 US 1 (1932).
[23] Charles L. Black, "Inequities in Districting for Congress: Baker v. Carr and Colegrove v. Green" (1962) 72 *Yale Law Journal* 13, 18.
[24] Jo Desha Lucas, "Legislative Apportionment and Representative Government: The Meaning of Baker v. Carr" (1962) 61 *Michigan Law Review* 711, 715, 717. This conclusion is buttressed by the Court's open rejection of this claim in *MacDougall v. Green*, 335 US 281, 284 (1948).
[25] Brief for Appellee, *Wood v. Broom*, 1932 WL 33449 (October 11, 1932) at 12–4.

lack any indication that the Court would make general evaluations of the fairness or legitimacy of electoral procedure, or enquire if the background conditions of lawmaking reflected the population's free will.

4.2.1.2 Colegrove and Contestation over Malapportionment

Colegrove v. Green represented a sudden and disruptive shift in the Supreme Court's approach to districting. While the law had previously been wholly concerned with the formal lawmaking authority of other institutions, the *Colegrove* dissenters showed novel interest in the substance of electoral procedure. The fractured 3-1-3 decision resolution of *Colegrove*, moreover, illustrates that the judicial imposition of electoral norms was controversial. The case considered a durable legislative malapportionment by the state of Illinois. The unequal districting had been perpetuated for four decades based on a 1901 Act, but did comply with formal requirements of the lawmaking. The Illinois Supreme Court had consistently asserted that districting was a matter of purely legislative authority and therefore not subject to judicial oversight,[26] and refused to identify a wrong under either the state or federal constitution.

Justice Frankfurter's plurality opinion unequivocally declared that solving malapportionment is "beyond [the Court's] competence."[27] He asserted that the dismissal could be handily affirmed by *Wood v. Broom* as directly controlling and on-point precedent. He also indicated that the case could be dismissed for want of equity (as some justices suggested in *Wood*). However, Frankfurter also clearly reacted to the novel arguments offered by the dissenters and theorized regarding oversight of political process. He asserted, "it is hostile to a democratic system to involve the judiciary in the politics of the people."[28] Underlying this was a theory of institutional allocation of democratic design; Frankfurter maintained that such judicial intervention "would cut very deep into the very being of Congress." This claim rests on an assertion that "the vigilance of the people" must be the champion of political rights.[29] This argument is based on the premise that addressing malapportionment lies on one side of the counterpopular dilemma. Given the constitutional role of the courts, legislative districting is a matter of political process; the judiciary has no part in evaluating its fairness. By raising this normative justification, Frankfurter's argument against the justiciability of malapportionment itself comprises a dramatic shift from the uncritical formalism of prior districting cases. Instead, Frankfurter argued that judicial oversight of malapportionment would upend the balance of power in the constitutional architecture and thereby interfere with political self-determination.

---

[26] *People ex rel. Woodyatt v. Thompson*, 155 Ill. 451, 474 (1895); *Daly v. Madison County*, 378 Ill. 357, 362 (1941).
[27] *Colegrove*, 328 US at 551.
[28] *Ibid.*, at 554.
[29] *Ibid.*, at 556.

Frankfurter was prompted to these normative arguments by the novelties of Justice Black's dissent. Black asserted that the malapportionment comprised both a violation of Fourteenth Amendment equal protection and Article I's guarantee that House representatives should be chosen by the people. He declared that individuals have a right to votes of "approximately equal weight,"[30] and perhaps most strikingly, that voters have the right to "cast an effective ballot."[31] To support this as a matter of precedent, Black cobbled together *Nixon v. Herndon* (which identified a violation of the equal protection clause in legislation that excluded Black voters from the franchise) to support the proposition that ballot access is a matter of judicial oversight and *Smiley*'s intervention into illegal districting. Yet both *Nixon* and *Smiley* can be understood as matters of formal enforcement. The legislation at issue in *Nixon* was a complete and unequivocal deprivation of explicitly protected, textually unambiguous legal right to racial non-discrimination,[32] and *Smiley*, as discussed above, enforced formalities of constitutional structure in the context of invalid legislation. Unlike the institutional background in *Smiley*, the various branches of the Illinois state government in *Colegrove*, including the courts, concurred that no justiciable wrong was present; thus, *Colegrove* cannot be interpreted as the judiciary arbitrating between competing democratic branches. Black's argument must rest on the principle that the judiciary should undertake principled evaluations of whether a districting scheme is fair. This shifts the nature of the legal reasoning from a formal assessment of complying with lawmaking requirements to evaluating whether a districting scheme allows voters to effectively rule themselves.

Justice Rutledge's solo but decisive concurrence subtly undertakes the same type of interpretive legerdemain as Black's. Rutledge does not identify general judicial authority to perform oversight for fairness in the constitutional text. He instead concludes that the text of the Election Clause demands deference to state and federal legislatures in House representative selection. However, he reads *Smiley* as a precedent that grants the federal judiciary broad oversight of districting.[33] *Smiley* is more accurately described as granting the Court the ability to enforce the terms of a constitution, rather than to enforce the terms of electoral fairness generally. However, despite this, Rutledge concurred with Frankfurter through a peculiar move. He observed that four justices in *Wood* would have refused to hear the case at all on the grounds of equity. His ultimate concurrence was based on the fact that intervening might be imprudent, a "cure… worse than the disease."[34] Nothing in *Wood* supports this application of the use of the principle of equity to grant judicial discretion; the decision was an addendum that four of the concurring justices in *Wood* would have refused to hear it *at all*.[35] Rutledge

[30] Ibid., at 570.
[31] Ibid., at 573.
[32] *Nixon v. Herndon*, 273 US 536, 541 (1927).
[33] *Colegrove*, 328 US at 564.
[34] Ibid., at 568.
[35] *Wood*, 287 US at 8–9.

flips this pre-substantive bar to afford the Court discretion to opine on the fairness of districting. Justice Rutledge's distorted readings of *Smiley* and *Wood* (parallel to Black's creative treatment of constitutional text) created the conceptual space for much greater judicial oversight of districting than any prior precedents. Rutledge's concurrence prefigured both (1) the broad expansion of judicial power to review districting and (2) the willingness to instrumentally and selectively read prior precedent that would be the mark of *Baker*.

Shortly after *Colegrove*, *MacDougall v. Green* revisited the issue of whether malapportionment is justiciable in the context of primary election ballot access. The *per curiam*[36] majority opinion reiterated Frankfurter's normative position in *Colegrove*:

> It would be strange indeed, and doctrinaire, for this Court, applying such broad constitutional concepts as due process and equal protection of the laws, to deny a State the power to assure a proper diffusion of political initiative as between its thinly populated counties and those having concentrated masses…The Constitution—a practical instrument of government—makes no such demands on the States.[37]

The split of *Colegrove* continued: Rutledge again invoked pragmatic concerns, formally couched in equity, to decline jurisdiction. And Justice Douglas, writing for the same three dissenters as in *Colegrove*, again offered a normative claim – "Free and honest elections are the very foundation of our republican form of government"[38] – based on tenuous readings of precedent that spoke to explicitly unconstitutional deprivation of legal right, rather than structural vote dilution.

Leading scholars of the political question doctrine treat *Colegrove* as a continuation of the status quo rather than a watershed case.[39] Yet Supreme Court cases that considered districting prior to *Colegrove*[40] only evaluated the unambiguous formal requirements of constitutional and legislative instruction; there was no suggestion that the Court might review the underlying political desirability of a districting. *Colegrove* shifted to the normative query of if malapportionment is so illegitimate that the judiciary must intervene to maintain democratic constitutionalism. Ironically, this switch to normative rather than legal–interpretive reasoning may be most apparent in Frankfurter's own reliance on democratic autonomy to vindicate abstaining from

---

[36] Despite being a *per curiam* opinion, *MacDougall*, 335 US 281 (1948) again had a concurrence by Rutledge and a dissent joined by Douglas, Black, and Murphy.
[37] *MacDougall*, 335 US at 284.
[38] *Ibid.*, at 288.
[39] Rachel E. Barkow, "More Supreme than Court? The Fall of the Political Question Doctrine and the Rise of Judicial Supremacy" (2002) 102 *Columbia Law Review* 237, 260. Tara Leigh Grove, "The Lost History of the Political Question Doctrine" (2015) 90 *New York University Law Review* 1908, 1946–7 observes that *Colegrove* follows in the wake of *Pacific States Telephone v. Oregon*, 223 US 118 (1912), which offered a general revision of the doctrine.
[40] The most influential parallel to such foundational reasoning may be in *Luther v. Borden*, 48 US 1, 36 (1849), which concludes that the Guaranty Clause is nonjusticiable.

matters of districting.[41] His fundamental argument is that accepting the justiciability of general malapportionment would paradoxically *impair* self-rule by displacing popular will. His argument, like that of the dissenters, addresses the prerequisites for popular autonomy. Furthermore, Frankfurter attempted to cabin the judicial remit in light of a previously unconsidered question of the normative status of districting generally. As Guy-Uriel Charles and Luis Fuentes-Rowher observe, Frankfurter's refusal to identify a legal wrong in districting only applied where general malapportionment was at issue. Where a districting reflected a violation of some other express constitutional right (i.e., non-discrimination), he would find it illegal – as manifest in his authorship of *Gomillion*.[42]

Under *Colegrove*, one person, one vote had all the hallmarks of contestation over electoral process. The justices were divided on what arrangements would best serve the ultimate principles of democracy. The plurality argued that judicial oversight beyond formalism would deprive the electorate of the opportunity to set its own terms of self-rule; the dissenters argued that democracy must conform to underlying terms of fairness before such self-determination is legitimate; and the decisive Rutledge, while sympathetic to claims of fairness, would limit intervention to circumstances of appropriate benefit given the costs of disruption. While the justices phrased such disputes in terms of constitutional instruction – e.g., what do Article I Sections 2 and 4 and the Equal Protection Clause entail? – the root of the divergence extends to norms of appropriate democratic arrangement. As Tara Leigh Grove has noted in her overview of the history of the political question doctrine, in the wake of *Colegrove* the Supreme Court typically declined to hear reapportionment cases.[43] Given that *Colegrove* was a sharply divided decision, this is a studied application of the passive virtues to avoid revisiting an unsettled question. *Baker* shows that the Court was ready to decisively resolve this unsettled question.

4.2.1.3 Decontestation under Baker

Baker famously concluded that population-based malapportionment comprised a constitutional wrong, and set the stage for the radical and enduring transformation of legislative districting. The opinion is an anomaly in at least three ways. First, while it rejects the holdings of prior cases, the factual scenarios are largely identical. Like *Colegrove*, the facts of *Baker* looked to a long-standing state legislative malapportionment that had stood since 1901 (this time in Tennessee).[44] As in *Colegrove*, the state Supreme Court had refused to find the districting unconstitutional.[45]

---

[41] *Wood*, *Smiley*, and the other family of districting cases did not consider such normative justifications; one must look back to *Luther* for such an argument.
[42] Charles and Fuentes-Rowher, "Reynolds Reconsidered," 496.
[43] Grove, "The Lost History," 1947 n. 201.
[44] *Baker*, 369 US at 187. For an extensive discussion of the context and history of *Baker*, see Muller, "Perpetuating," 375.
[45] *Baker*, 369 US at 325 (Frankfurter, dissenting) (collecting cases).

However, one critical feature had changed: The composition of the bench. Only three justices from the *Colegrove* Court remained – Black, Douglas, and the now-dissenting Frankfurter. Historically, the shift in *Baker* may be unsurprising as a more progressive and interventionist spirit emerged with the Warren Court. There are plenty of realist explanations for *Baker*, particularly as voting rights emerged during the Civil Rights era as a powerful tool to fight oppression.[46]

Second, despite its radical nature, the reasoning in the *Baker* opinion is formal and justifies its conclusion through technical doctrinal analysis. Justice Brennan's majority opinion carefully framed its reasoning as supported by doctrine. He declared that judicial authority over malapportionment is wholly derived from precedent and the plain meaning of the constitutional supremacy: the "question here is the consistency of state action with the Federal Constitution."[47] To support this proposition it deploys a number of precedents, most saliently *Gomillion*,[48] *Nixon v. Herndon*,[49] and *Smiley v. Holm* (and related cases).[50] Yet *Gomillion* and *Nixon* both involved blatant acts of racial discrimination and fell within the core of the equal protection clause, and *Smiley* involved judicial enforcement of an explicit constitutional command. *Baker* discussed *Wood* only to establish jurisdiction over matters related to elections (ignoring its precedential relevance), and wholly disregarded Frankfurter's conclusion in *Colegrove* that *Wood* was sufficient to reject the proposition that malapportionment comprises a constitutional harm. It further artificially recharacterized *Colegrove* addressing only the question of the Guarantee Clause,[51] which at the time was seen as presenting a non-justiciable political question.[52] By so pruning *Colegrove*'s significance, the *Baker* Court managed a problematic precedent by addressing a legal principle that would have been unhelpful for its desired holding. It managed *MacDougall* by constraining it to the barest of facts, suggesting that rather than speaking to a state's right to apportion as a whole, it addressed only the specific factual issue of nomination;[53] this yielded an analysis that was "clearly wrong."[54] Indeed, the *Baker* opinions include some statements that are factually false, such as Justice Clark's assertion that the plaintiffs in *Colegrove* had not asserted a Fourteenth Amendment argument and that *Colegrove* did nothing to foreclose it.[55]

---

[46] Smith, "On Democracy's Doorstep," 5; Muller, "Perpetuating," 375 n. 22. Cf. Samuel Issacharoff, "Judging Politics: The Elusive Quest for Judicial Review of Political Fairness" (1993) 71 *Texas Law Review* 1643, 1654 (describing the limits of prophylactic analysis).
[47] *Baker*, 369 US at 226.
[48] Ibid., at 229.
[49] Ibid., at 209.
[50] Ibid., at 232.
[51] US Constitution Article IV, Section 4 (guaranteeing every state a republican form of government).
[52] McConnell, "The Redistricting Cases," 106–7.
[53] *Baker*, 369 US at 234.
[54] Lucas, "Legislative Apportionment," 718.
[55] *Baker*, 369 US at 729; cf. *Colegrove*, 28 US at 569 (analyzing whether malapportionment impacts equal protection) (Black, dissenting). The majority in *Colegrove* apparently lumped the equal protection claim under the general head of "various provisions of the United States Constitution" upon which

This mixture of instrumental recharacterization and marginalization exemplifies *Baker*'s treatment of the law. To use the words of one scholarly commentator of the time, it "tortured the precedents beyond recognition."[56]

The absence of explicit normative reasoning in Brennan's opinion is especially remarkable in light of this untenable legal analysis. Brennan disposed of the justiciability of malapportionment on a purely technical level, without wrestling with the constitutional legitimacy of judicial intervention. He thus avoided addressing the legitimate source of electoral procedure – the very issue that *Colegrove* and *MacDougall* most hotly contested. Some of the concurring opinions offer such consideration of the realities of self-rule[57] or imply that morally laden interpretivism is the appropriate mode of constitutional understanding,[58] suggesting that some of the concurring justices reconciled themselves to the decision by considering appropriate terms of self-governance. Conversely, the Frankfurter and Harlan dissents ardently deploy normative principles (as well as more plausible doctrinal analysis) with explicit accounts of how popular freedom should be realized. Frankfurter bookends his legal analysis by arguing that relief from malapportionment must come from "an informed, civically militant electorate"[59] and warning of the dangers of excessive "judicial intervention into the very structure of government."[60] Harlan invoked the foundational structural norms of the "federal system" to argue that "those who have the responsibility for devising a system of representation may permissibly consider that factors other than bare numbers should be taken into account."[61] These are straightforward arguments that the counterpopular dilemma excludes the judiciary from intervention.

Why would Brennan's majority opinion so scrupulously avoid the dramatic, unabashedly normative nature of its reasoning, particularly given appeals to democratic structure by Frankfurter and Harlan? The answer is that *Baker* was the decontestation of a normative principle regarding electoral structure. As such, it can only be understood as a moment of disjunction or transformation. Such a transformational moment is deeply discomforting given the counterpopular dilemma. By advancing its holding as a result of familiar (if inaptly deployed) modes of legal reasoning, the opinion sought to mitigate the tension within this move. Ironically, the Court sought to frame the decision in the most traditional forms possible to avoid

---

the plaintiffs relied (and which was cited in the Plaintiff's appellate brief, *Colegrove v. Green*, Brief for Appellants, WL 50074 (1946) at 56; Justice Clark's assertion that it was not included in the appellate brief is an error), and which the *Colegrove* majority rejected en masse (*Colegrove*, 328 US at 550).

[56] Lucas, "Legislative Apportionment," 803.
[57] *Baker*, 369 US at 259 (Clark, concurring) (observing a lack of opportunity for the polity to exert its will through initiative and referendum).
[58] Ibid., at 245 (Douglas, concurring) (engaging in a parsing of the power of the judiciary to interpret clauses, thereby implicitly rejecting textualism in favor of a type of interpretivism).
[59] Ibid., at 270.
[60] Ibid., at 295.
[61] Ibid., at 332–3.

highlighting the institutional and constitutional tensions of *Baker*'s radical nature. As a corollary to this it avoided the very normative assertion of the Court's role that is *Baker*'s defining feature.

This points to the third remarkable aspect of *Baker*. Its normative nature makes it the first case characteristic of contemporary election law. The Supreme Court rejected its prior established role as a formalist arbiter of other institutions' authority and demonstrated that it could impose moral norms upon electoral procedure (though the full content of those norms would not be articulated until the successor cases). As such, *Baker* is the transformative moment that *defines* election law as a field, exemplifying the normative reasoning that has come to dominate it.

The one person, one vote rule initiated by *Baker* is unique within the field it has come to define, in that its normative conclusion is no longer a matter of contestation, and it was rapidly accepted on the bench as an authoritative statement of the Court's ability to impose a norm. This explains Brennan's reliance on narrow doctrinal reasoning, which disposes of the case (accurately or not as a matter of precedent) as settled descriptive truth, rather than contestable normative controversy. Relying on technical reasoning narrows the range of challenges within the bench by suggesting that the matter to be decontested is (ironically) not a matter of normative debate. A practical driving force in this quality of navigation may have been the need to make it palatable to the justices, as is apparent in the negotiation among justices in the *Baker* decision.[62] Brennan did not need, on the terms of his own doctrinal analysis, to address the dissenters' appeals to democratic principle. The opinion also signaled that despite its normative intervention, the Court remained cognizant of its institutional limits, rather than openly adopting the role of moral enforcer.

4.2.2 *Baker as an Exemplar of Decontestation*

This three-part narrative describes the path and substance of *Baker*, which elevated the judiciary's democratic values over aggregated precedent that prized the polity's authority to determine its own electoral procedure. This contrast is most apparent in the divergence between *Baker*, on one hand, and *Smiley* and *Wood* on the other. *Smiley* and *Wood* demonstrated that the Court would give force to the legal instructions derived from explicit and formally valid legislative and constitutional sources. As such, the Court indicated it would only act as a conduit for bestowing legality on procedures selected through the political process. While this raises issues of entrenchment and democracy's "drift" away from validity, as well as the problems of framing that generally face originalism, it addresses one aspect of counterpopulism: the Court only arbitrates among the rules the polity has decided for governing itself. This historical approach can rely on conventional rules for lawmaking to determine appropriate democratic procedure, trusting a "civically militant electorate" to effect

---

[62] Hasen, "The Supreme Court and Election Law," p. 52.

reforms and alter democratic process either through legislation or through constitutional amendment. Both stability (through the Court's enforcement of existing law) and changes in electoral procedure (from the electorate) come from the expression of popular will. *Baker* rejects this historical approach and redefines just electoral procedure as conforming to normative preconditions. More broadly, it suggests a reversal of the standard relationship between the judiciary and popular will. Prior to *Baker*, the Court perceived its treatment of electoral procedure as constrained by popular will. With *Baker*, it indicated that judicially identified fundamental norms may constrain any democratically accountable choices regarding electoral process.

Is this assertion that *Baker* cannot be considered typical constitutional interpretation excessive? Two of the constitutional theories discussed in Chapter 2, decisive living constitutionalism and representation reinforcement/anti-lockup theory, could plausibly be advanced to explain *Baker*'s radical shift. According to the former, the legitimacy of judicial intervention over malapportionment might have emerged from the country's changing socio-political fabric, with the Supreme Court acting as the conduit of this change. In this view, the new moral norms present in the broader social context would boost the significance of the equal protection clause. Representation reinforecement theory can make an even more straightforward case for justifying judicial oversight of malapportionment because it is precisely the type of legislative conduct at the core of the theory.[63] Those in power can draw district lines that overrepresent themselves on a per capita basis by placing their supporters in more sparsely populated districts (thereby diluting their opponents' votes). This explains why the underlying political concern in malapportionment was that it allowed rural interests to dominate politics.[64]

These arguments may be valid, even morally compelling. Judicial intervention when voting power is distributed unequally on a per capita basis may be justified as a matter of fundamental democratic norms (as in living constitutionalism) or as a matter of pragmatic power distribution (as in representation reinforcement). But it is difficult to accurately characterize such intervention as a type of truly *legal* constitutional lawmaking rather than pure norm imposition. As such, attempting to characterize *Baker* using either of these constitutional theories faces the basic problem described in Chapter 2. They create procedures that validate popular self-determination, while simultaneously imposing foundational terms for electoral processes from a non-accountable source, and thereby contradicting the very principle of popular autonomy the foundational terms are meant to serve.

It can be countered that equality as a constitutional requirement is no stranger to constitutional reasoning, especially in light of the equal protection clause. In this

---

[63] John Hart Ely, *Democracy and Distrust: A Theory of Judicial Review* (Cambridge: Harvard University Press, 1980), p. 120; Samuel Issacharoff and Richard H. Pildes, "Politics as Markets: Partisan Lockups of the Democratic Process" (1998) 50 *Stanford Law Review* 643, 716.
[64] Issacharoff, "Political Judgments," 655.

4.2 Baker v. Carr: Decontesting Constitutional Innovation

view, *Baker* and its progeny did no more than identify new implications of the text in the relevant provision of Article I and in the equal protection clause. This raises the problem of extracting novel meaning from settled text. Such a view requires, at a minimum, ready intelligibility in one domain: the linguistic commitments of the constitutional contract as expressed in the original document.[65] There is no such plain instruction that would justify *Baker*'s novelty (as might explain *Gomillion*'s as the Court finally having the temerity to appropriately enforce the equal protection clause). Nor is there sufficient ambiguity in the clauses that characterize identifying the constitutional illegality of malapportionment as a "hard case," at least given the Court's pre-*Colegrove* treatment of districting. *Baker* did not comprise a discretionary but "constrained normative choice"[66] in light of ambiguous textual provision. It was unvarnished innovation regarding the principles of democracy.

But if *Baker* comprised a bold principled stance on democratic organization, why did Brennan take such care to frame it as traditional precedential reasoning? The answer partly reflects universal institutional pressures on the optics of judicial decision-making. To establish that it is acting in line with rule-of-law neutrality, and even more generally that judging is a disinterested craft instead of mere value imposition, the Court couches its decisions in familiar judicial practices, such as interpretive consistency and respect for precedent. During decontestation of principles of democratic process, these pressures are particularly strong due to the ramifications of the decisions. A settled, judicially enforced conclusion regarding legitimate democratic process imposes future terms on self-determination by the polity, as discussed in Chapter 1 – and might encourage judges to be especially careful to couch decisions in technical legal reasoning.

The idea that judges use the optics of legal reasoning as a fig leaf for their policy preferences is prominent in legal realism. Yet judges have incentives to painstakingly couch their decisions in the formalities of technical judicial decision-making when decontesting norms. Moreover, their reasons for doing so do not need a foundational commitment to the skepticism of rule-of-law and judicial discipline that underlies legal realism. Judges might instead be typically committed to standard modalities of legal reasoning. When they decontest a judicially imposed norm because it is an anomalous type of analysis that contravenes the normal modes and properties of legal reasoning, they demonstrate a commitment to those standard modalities to establish that the norm is now internalized within, and as if achieved by conformity to, standard modalities.

Decontestation is the expression of a consensus regarding a norm that was previously disputed. When a court decontests a norm, it moves a principle that previously

---

[65] See the discussion of Michael J. Perry, *The Constitution in the Courts: Law or Politics?* (Oxford: Oxford University Press, 1994), p. 38 in the Introduction.
[66] Richard H. Fallon, "The Meaning of Legal 'Meaning' and its Implications for Theories of Legal Interpretation" (2015) 82 *The University of Chicago Law Review* 1235, 1307.

had a fundamentally – and reasonably – disputed meaning into the realm of settled consensus. The appropriate content of the norm may have been fiercely contested in the past (as is still the case in most areas of election law, as discussed in subsequent chapters). But once it has been decontested, such foundational disputes cease. The norm now has the same sort of power as a settled point of precedent or interpretation reached by normal modes of interpretation, which are not controversial. An illuminating parallel here may be drawn between Hart's conception of legal rulemaking – which maintains that close cases are resolved within the "open texture" of law, and reflect a reasoned but highly bounded process of judicial resolution[67] – and Dworkin's conception of hard cases that require a type of contextually rooted moral reasoning based on competing principles.[68] Standard modalities of legal interpretation can resolve differences within the open texture of settled law that is characteristic of Hart; norm contestation is more visibly akin to Dworkin's conception of moral reasoning.

The careful obedience to standard, conservative modes of legal reasoning in norm decontestation reflects the amount pressure to bring the norm "into the fold" of settled law. This is precisely the quality of the reasoning in *Baker*. *Baker* cites broad swathes of precedent (some of which it distorts) to argue that the justiciability of malapportionment is not controversial. Conspicuously, but unsurprisingly, this is also the quality of the reasoning in the pre-*Colegrove* cases, where the non-justiciability of malapportionment was non-controversial and settled. Of course, in the pre-*Colegrove* cases the reason was not because it was a point of decontestation, but because the basic principle of excluding districting from judicial oversight was a settled point of doctrine. As the narrative above shows, *Colegrove* differed markedly. Each understanding of the appropriate judicial posture toward malapportionment was justified on normative terms. This is precisely because *Colegrove* represents the period of contestation in which the justices adverted to competing incompatible understandings of a principle.

The closest parallel to *Baker* in recent jurisprudence may be partisan gerrymandering. The array of opinions in *Vieth* reflected the instability of the debate over whether federal courts might review the legality of partisan gerrymandering – much like the opinions of *Colegrove* comprised a battle over the legality of malapportionment. Similarly, the thin legal reasoning of *Rucho v. Common Cause* comprised an attempt to decontest the principle at issue. The parallels should not be drawn too strongly: *Rucho* seems like a much less convincing example of decontestation. On the surface, the 5–4 partisan split appears to indicate that a Court with a different composition could revisit the principle. However, the majority opinion in *Rucho* did not engage with the fundamental issue facing partisan gerrymandering

[67] Hart, "The Concept of Law," p. 129.
[68] Providing this account is arguably the goal of all of Ronald Dworkin, *Law's Empire* (Cambridge: Harvard University Press, 1986), but his pithiest expression is probably in the description of interpretative integrity on pp. 255–6.

(as *Baker* did for malapportionment, even if it did so by twisting precedent). Instead, it reflected an attempt to evade, rather than confront, the norm of party involvement at issue, and comprises a far less convincing instance of decontestation.

4.2.3 *The Political Question Doctrine as Mediation of Decontestation*

To cloak its sudden shift in direction, the *Baker* Court reworked the political question doctrine. As a general principle, this doctrine prevents federal courts from opining on matters that the Constitution allocates to the elected branches.[69] This doctrine advances the proposition that some matters are not only explicitly reserved for elected branches but there are some domains where the judiciary should not interfere for "prudential" reasons.[70] *Luther v. Borden* developed the doctrine as a "prudential bar on having courts adjudicate contested questions of electoral legitimacy."[71] By the early twentieth century, the Court interpreted the political question doctrine as eliminating first-order judicial review of the fairness of electoral procedure.[72] Scholars have long asserted that *Baker* was a dramatic inflection point regarding this doctrine – and perhaps even began to efface it. Recognizing that *Baker*'s treatment of the political question doctrine was a way to decontest a norm of self-rule changes the tenor of this perception. First, scholars have typically given *Colegrove* little attention; previous research has tended to classify it as in step with prior treatment of the doctrine. Considering the political question doctrine's shift as part of decontestation, however, requires re-evaluating the importance of the *Colegrove* opinions as well as contextualizing *Baker*'s own revision of the test. In *Colegrove* the justices disagreed whether an electorate has unlimited authority to set fair terms of electoral procedure, or if electoral procedure must first conform to certain standards of fairness (the very question at the root of the counterpopular dilemma). *Baker*'s revision of the political question doctrine softened the counterpopular imposition of a norm and demonstrated the Court's commitment to the constraints of the constitutional architecture.

4.2.3.1 The Scholarly Orthodoxy: Baker as the Inflection Point

Prior to *Baker*, the political question doctrine was a broad, even amorphous, instruction regarding when the Court could not opine on the merits of a particular dispute. While the "classical" version of the doctrine looked to explicit constitutional text

---

[69] Barkow, "More Supreme than Court?" 248 traces the political question doctrine back to *Marbury v. Madison* 5 US 137 (1803). As Grove, "The Lost History," 1918–25 notes, there was a transition from using the treatment of "political branches' determination as factual" to using them as non-justiciable, adapted from dicta in *Luther v. Borden*.
[70] Barkow, "More Supreme than Court?" 257.
[71] Issacharoff, "Political Judgements," 639.
[72] Frankfurter synthesizes this position in *Colegrove*, 328 US at 555, to argue against judicial "embroilment in politics".

to determine if a matter was allocated to a coordinate branch, the "prudential"[73] form inferred this information from the general constitutional architecture. The prudential form of the doctrine allowed the Court to avoid becoming engaged in politicized conflicts;[74] it resisted being "domesticated"[75] or delineated by a clear set of principles. The Court could therefore use it as a convenient escape hatch to avoid issues it found too politically volatile.

The *Baker* majority opinion described its treatment of the political question doctrine as categorizing and eliminating the "disorderliness" in existing jurisprudence.[76] But there is no question that it substantively altered the doctrine. It analytically formalized the doctrine, identifying it as a consequence of the separation of powers[77] and categorically delimiting it by reducing its scope to six delineated groups.

It is broadly held orthodoxy that *Baker*'s treatment of the political question doctrine represents a revolutionary disjunction. Mark Tushnet maintains that *Baker* brought about the "doctrinalization" of the political question doctrine,[78] transforming what had been a prudential doctrine by which the Court could decline legal engagement into a rigid test that identified narrower categories of non-judicial expertise. Rachel Barkow describes how it replaced a flexible approach to the political question doctrine that encouraged "judicial restraint and extreme deference"[79] with one that more narrowly stipulated when the Court could not intervene. Scholars have also described how *Baker* effected a higher-level transformation of the Court's role in shaping on the constitutional architecture. Grove asserts that this formalization advanced a type of procedural authority that increased the Court's power, as the Court would independently determine the extent of its ability to perform judicial review.[80] This expansion of the Court's procedural power coincided with a number of specific doctrinal conclusions that curtailed the extent of when a question was political.[81] The most significant of these was the political question doctrine's emphasis on the separation of powers[82] rather than federalism. After *Baker*, a state's assertion that under federalism the federal courts should not have authority would not

---

[73] Barkow, "More Supreme than Court?" 253; Mark V. Tushnet, "Law and Prudence in the Law of Justiciability: The Transformation and Disappearance of the Political Question Doctrine" (2002) 80 *North Carolina Law Review* 1203, 1212.

[74] This understanding is affiliated with political process theory, particularly as advanced by Alexander Bickel. See also Barkow, "More Supreme than Court?" 262.

[75] Ely, "Democracy and Distrust"; Tushnet, "Law and Prudence," 1204.

[76] *Baker*, 369 US at 210.

[77] Prior to *Baker* it had been identified as having a broader constitutional foundation. See Grove, "The Lost History," 202. See also Barkow, "More Supreme than Court?" 264 (identifying, prior to *Baker*, that the doctrine was also based on principles of federalism).

[78] Tushnet, "Law and Prudence," 1213.

[79] Barkow, "More Supreme than Court?" 263.

[80] Grove, "The Lost History," 335.

[81] Ibid., 1962–63; Barkow, "More Supreme than Court?" 264.

[82] *Baker*, 369 US at 210.

render a question political.⁸³ More generally, *Baker* required the assumption that the Court had the decisive authority to determine *when* a particular type of question was allocated to a coordinate branch, or not.⁸⁴ Grove also observes a more technical change in what she calls the "new political question" doctrine asserted by *Baker*. According to Grove, instead of dismissing political questions, under the pre-*Baker* political question doctrine the courts would enforce the political branch's decision. Post-*Baker*, such decisions were simply dismissed.⁸⁵ She notes that the technical underpinnings of this shift occurred prior to *Baker* in *Pacific States Telephone*, but that it was *Baker* that turned the political question doctrine from a tool of judicial restraint into a "source of judicial power."⁸⁶

4.2.3.2 Reintroducing *Colegrove* into the Narrative

Constitutional law scholars have generally not acknowledged a relationship between the transformation of the political question doctrine and the substantive equipopulousness rule advanced by the one person, one vote jurisprudence. Yet closer attention to the context of electoral procedure (and specifically *Baker* as a moment of decontestation) yields two significant insights about the relationship between the two dramatic changes.

The first relates to *Colegrove*. The magisterial analyses of the political question doctrine provided by Barkow⁸⁷ and Grove⁸⁸ treat *Colegrove* as a continuation of the "old" political question doctrine. With regard to Frankfurter's controlling plurality opinion this is a technically sensible move. Yet when seen as the site of the contestation over procedures of democratic self-determination, and with its remarkable 3-1-3 fracture, *Colegrove*'s treatment of the political question doctrine takes on a much weightier significance.

Frankfurter's invocation of the political question doctrine is, in one respect, completely in line with the precedent. He points to the core of the political question doctrine – allocating the issue at hand to a coordinate branch – to exclude districting from judicial review.⁸⁹ While this point had not been made as explicitly in prior districting cases, Frankfurter's technical analysis is reminiscent of *Luther v. Borden* through its reliance on explicit constitutional command.⁹⁰

Frankfurter's opinion makes one subtly pivotal contribution to the political question doctrine. His last sentence indicates that the doctrine ultimately relies upon "the

---

⁸³ Barkow, "More Supreme than Court?" 264.
⁸⁴ Grove, "The Lost History," 1964.
⁸⁵ Ibid., 1918, 1962.
⁸⁶ Ibid., 1960.
⁸⁷ Barkow, "More Supreme than Court?" 260.
⁸⁸ Grove, "The Lost History," 1946–47. Grove does note the splintered character of *Colegrove* and its shift from the traditional doctrine fact treating to the *Pacific States*' jurisdiction-declining version of the doctrine.
⁸⁹ *Colegrove*, 328 US at 554–5.
⁹⁰ *Luther*, 48 US at 35.

vigilance of the people in exercising their political rights."[91] Unlike *Luther*, which relied only on the basis for the political question doctrine that can be drawn from the constitutional structure, Frankfurter makes a principled argument: the political question doctrine should preserve popular autonomy (the same principle that underlies the counterpopular dilemma). Different facets of democratic organization are allocated to different institutional structures – some to that implement the will of the franchise, and others that protect the rule of law. Under the traditional understanding of the political question doctrine, the sources for this allocation are not first-order norms. Rather the traditional understanding basis the doctrine in constitutional text and in history and practice. However, the validity of this constitutional architecture itself must be attributed to some underlying normative root – in democracy, the autonomy of the constituency. By invoking the "vigilance of the people" to validate the muscular application of the political question doctrine, Frankfurter points to the ultimate moral foundation of democracy: the autonomy of self-rule.

The implication of Frankfurter's reasoning is that directly accountable representation should have primacy in setting terms of self-rule. Justice Black, conversely, asserts the judicial authority to supervise the terms of self-rule. While conceding that the subject matter is political, he declares the state law at issue "abridges the Constitutional rights of citizens to cast votes in such way as to obtain the kind of congressional representation the Constitution guarantees to them."[92] Yet Black's vague invocations of democratic constitutionalism – "the kind of Congressional representation" and "an effective ballot," – cannot get around the fact that his position would require the judiciary to impose first-order democratic norms. In this view, the very engines of democracy that have default legitimacy to shape governance – expressions of popular will, legislation, and constitutions – are only effective if they conform to normative preconditions that may not be fully articulated in the Constitution itself.

Black notes that on the surface, the dispute may appear semantic:[93] do the various constitutional provisions (Article 1 Section 2 and the equal protection clause) denote a legal requirement for equally sized districts? Yet attempting to parse the semantics alone is unfruitful.[94] More revealing to this question – and at the core of the political question doctrine – is the implication for the sweep of judicial authority based on the Constitution. The Constitution provides broad authority to address malapportionment despite the absence of any explicit instruction regarding whether the constitutional architecture works to expand the scope of judicial review, rather than bind it. Such a treatment of the political question doctrine

---

[91] *Colegrove*, 328 US at 556. This point of course anticipates Frankfurter's most plaintive claim in *Baker* (that districting must be solved by a "civically militant electorate").
[92] Ibid., at 572.
[93] Ibid. at 573, rejecting the possibility that it is a "play on words" to call it political.
[94] One could say it is precisely the type of constrained normative choice invoked by Fallon, "The Meaning of Legal Meaning," 1307.

would turn it from a source of "judicial restraint" into a source of "judicial power," to use Grove's terminology.[95]

Thus, in *Colegrove*, Frankfurter and Black were precisely debating the role of the political question doctrine that was later settled in *Baker*: should the political question doctrine constrain the sweep of judicial review? The urgency of this question obtains an additional layer of complexity due to the issue of electoral procedure. Frankfurter's invocation of the franchise self-determination suggests that authority over electoral procedure must as a starting principle reside with the electorate. Conversely, Black's willingness to give the judiciary the power to indicate normative requirements for fair elections suggests that it is conformity to such democratic preconditions that is the highest priority.

4.2.3.3 Political Question Doctrine Reformulation as Easing Decontestation

The second insight relates to *Baker*'s relationship to the dispute over the political question doctrine. As with the resolution of the justiciability of malapportionment, *Baker* was not the site of dispute over the political question doctrine, so much as the point of its decontestation. The fundamental dispute occurred in *Colegrove*. *Baker* obscured the radicalness of its change to the political question doctrine by adopting a technical, "doctrinalizing" approach. This evasiveness parallels the Court's treatment of the malapportionment, and is part of its use of a technical approach to mitigate its radical conclusion about democratic self-governance.

Yet the Court's reformulation of the political question doctrine in *Baker* did not change the explicit imposition of a normative requirement for electoral fairness (no more than the Court's strenuous attempts but distortive engagement with prior districting doctrine did). So why did the Court engage with the political question doctrine so extensively? If the goal of the *Baker* Court was to legitimate the judicial imposition of a norm of self-governance, the reformulation should be treated as instrumental to achieving this end. This understanding of *Baker* does much to explain why the Court chose this context to revise the political question doctrine.

Deploying the political question doctrine as the "shell" for the judicial imposition of electoral procedure operates at three distinct levels of abstraction. The first is optical. Had the Court explicitly stated in *Baker* that it deemed certain authoritative norms to be a precondition of legitimate democracy, it would have openly evoked the counterpopular dilemma. By framing the *Baker* decision as dictated by a clearer understanding of the political question doctrine, the Court blunted the suggestion that the judiciary has the moral insight to evaluate the terms of self-rule. This allowed the *Baker* Court to indicate that its decision was a function of a technical area of law, rather than a direct intervention into the terms of self-rule.

In a second level of abstraction, the basis of the political question doctrine – the constitutional architecture itself – indicates another, more directly substantive

---

[95] Grove, "The Lost History," 1960.

manner in which the doctrine blunts the counterpopular dilemma. Instead of asserting the judiciary's unique capacity, the Court's reliance on the political question doctrine frames battling malapportionment as the Court performing its designated role. This is apparent in at least two respects. First, *Baker*'s treatment of the doctrine is grounded in the principle of the separation of powers.[96] This allows the Court to assert that its subsequent conclusions are derived from constitutional instruction, rather than any freestanding view of democracy. Second, in *Baker* the Court affirms its "responsibility…as ultimate interpreter of the Constitution."[97] In this view, the Court's analysis of prior cases and constitutional architecture to determine how the political question doctrine would impact the justiciability of malapportionment was not merely a necessary justification (or pretext), but rather obligatory given the Court's assigned constitutional role. The elaborate attempts to ground its treatment in prior cases (which were arguably more obedient to constitutional constraint of the judiciary) reinforces this impression.

Fealty to the Constitution provides a final layer of significance to the political question doctrine's reformulation. The separation of powers is a bedrock structural commitment of the American polity and is made explicit in the Constitution. By identifying it as the basis for the political question doctrine, the Court can cast any subsequent identification of justiciability *not* as a discretionary choice by the Court, but as necessitated by the political architecture of the nation – a political architecture to which the polity must be fundamentally committed. Any findings under the enforcement of this architecture are therefore not counterpopular, but mandatory by the will of the constituency. On a basis of legitimacy akin to that claimed by originalist contractarianism, the Court can assert it is elevating a popularly acclaimed higher law, and giving force to the people's will. *Baker*'s questionable treatment of precedent and constitutional instruction undermines the convincingness of this claim. But as a matter of framing, it demonstrates the Court's formal subordination to democratic will.

None of these efforts to couch in the orthodoxy alter the radical character of *Baker*. It represents a dramatic break with prior precedent on both districting and the political question doctrine. *Baker* gave the Court the opportunity to reshape electoral procedure on normative terms. It also turned against the principle, seemingly uncontested prior to *Colegrove*, that the Elections Clause gives the federal and state legislatures the authority to structure elections. These efforts do signal that the Court sought to operate within the accepted bounds of the judicial role as much as possible. In particular, the *Baker* majority avoids the bedrock theorizing about the appropriate allocation of power that characterized the unsettled dispute in *Colegrove*.

Recognizing *Baker* as decontestatory highlights the Court's cautious posture when it dictates terms of self-rule to the polity. This caution has two high-level aspects.

---

[96] *Baker*, 369 US at 211.
[97] Ibid.

First, the Court seeks to avoid openly imposing normative judgments, because this would deviate from typical modalities of legal analysis. Second, to the extent that it does take on such a role and impose foundational terms of self-rule, the Court carefully couches this involvement in familiar constitutional analysis, whether as a cloak for its moralizing ambitions or out of genuine respect for the boundaries set by the Constitution.

4.3 DEVELOPING THE RULE: JUDICIAL RESTRAINT, THIN NORMATIVE REASONING, AND THE SHADOW OF THE COUNTERPOPULAR DILEMMA

Baker famously declined to articulate a standard for when malapportionment was illegal, leaving the question to later cases. The subsequent development of the one person, one vote rule has reflected two prevalent trends: (1) the establishment of the principle that an equal number of persons per district is required for legal districts and (2) the emergence of a margin of flexibility in the enforcement of this standard. Each of these features demonstrates the Court's struggle to balance popular authority over self-rule as expressed through legislation and the Constitution with the intrinsic demands of democratic fairness. The result is an unambiguous but substantively minimalist, mechanically applied rule that limits case by case judicial discretion and incorporates deference to federalism.

The one person, one vote doctrine advances equal self-rule without requiring the judiciary to generate a rich theory of democracy. This suggests that the minimalism of one person, one vote that has been so thoroughly criticized in the scholarship is an effort to minimize the counterpopularism that inevitably results from judicial imposition of norms of self-rule.

4.3.1 *The Cautious Doctrinal Construction of One Person, One Vote*

The core principle of equipopulousness was quickly and firmly established in the early 1960s. However, the Court's willingness to accommodate deviations from arithmetical precision in allocation of voters to districts – always greater in the state and local than the Congressional context – emerged more gradually.

4.3.1.1 The Development of the Rule

A trio of cases in 1963 and 1964 concluded that districts must be equipopulous. In *Gray v. Sanders*, the Court struck down a system that used unequally populated counties to select representatives for various political offices. *Gray* was the first case in which the Supreme Court indicated that the equal protection clause requires numerical per-person voter equality in districting.[98] *Wesberry v. Sanders* was the first

---

[98] *Gray v. Sanders*, 372 US 368, 379 (1963).

case to deem districts with gross disparities between numbers of voters per congressional district illegal. *Wesberry* interpreted Article I, Section 2 of the Constitution, with its indication that congressional representatives are to be chosen "by the People of the several States", to require that congressional districts must satisfy equipopulousness "as nearly as is practicable."[99] *Reynolds v. Sims* returned to the equal protection clause to conclude that one person, one vote applies to *all* state legislative districting. While *Reynolds* intimated that the one person, one vote rule might be less stringent in local and state contexts compared to congressional apportionment, the Court remained adamant that this did not dilute the applicability of the "equal-population principle."[100]

Together this troika (1) resolved the unanswered question of *Baker* (what, as a matter of law, correcting malapportionment requires) by affirming that equipopulousness is required and (2) asserted its breadth by applying the principle to legislative districting unless contraindicated by explicit federal constitutional demand (i.e., the Senate).[101] Furthermore, these cases established that one person, one vote apportionment was the *only* requirement that the Court would police as a matter of general political fairness.[102]

Despite the Court's commitment to one person, one vote, its reasoning is devoid of typical legal or constitutional reliance on prior precedent or textual analysis. Rather, it makes a pure normative assertion regarding the nature of equality in popular self-rule. *Gray* makes this normative assertion tersely in its rejection of the legitimacy of an established system that uses unequally populated counties to weight voting power. The closest it comes to invoking traditional precedent is citing a line of cases which establish that the right to vote may not be taken away illegally, and that the federal government has the authority to enforce such rights.[103] The cases the Court can cite only establish general federal jurisdiction over voting (the question in each case is if a federal statute had appropriate constitutional foundations).[104] None of the specific legal bases invoked by *Gray* – the Fourteenth Amendment or Seventeenth Amendment (with its requirement that senators are chosen "by the people") – provide any meaningful support for equipopulousness as a principle. The nearest *Gray* offers to an on-point legal foundation for one person, one vote is rhetoric: the Constitution invokes "we the people" and supports equality in voting.[105]

---

[99] *Wesberry v. Sanders*, 376 US 1, 8–9 (1964).
[100] *Reynolds*, 377 US at 578.
[101] Ibid., at 574.
[102] *Karcher v. Daggett*, 462 US 725, 730 (1983) (initial enquiry of one person, one vote violation is only activated if there has been a failure to draw districts in a manner that serves equality); *White v. Weiser*, 412 US 783, 796 (1973) (rejecting a Court's interest in considering other political features when assessing a districting plan).
[103] *Gray*, 372 US at 380.
[104] *U.S. v. Classic*, 313 US 299, 314 (1941); Ex parte Yarbrough, 110 US 651, 660 (1884); *U.S. v. Mosley*, 238 US 383, 386 (1915).
[105] *Gray*, 372 US at 380.

4.3 Developing the Rule

In *Wesberry v. Saunders*, the Court addressed how one person, one vote applies more generally to unequally populated congressional districts. Justice Black's majority opinion assayed to squeeze a legal justification from constitutional history and the Framers' debates. To do so, it made the peculiar strategic decision to locate the legal command for one person, one vote *not* in the equal protection clause (*Baker's* constitutional foundations), but rather in Article I, Section 2 of the Constitution (which commands that members of Congress shall by chosen "by the People of the several States…according to their respective Numbers").[106] The analysis, however, is characterized by rhetoric of equality rather than constitutionally grounding a legal right. Black cites historical statements from, for example, the Constitutional Convention and other debates surrounding the period of constitutional formation to support the observation that equality of per-person voting power was one value some Framers saw as important in fair representation.[107] Yet none of his statements establishes a link between the constitutional command and any specific form of representation. This "painful[ly]"[108] distortive analysis cannot support a principle as specific yet forceful as equipopulousness.[109] Even the concurring Justice Clark was unwilling to accord to Black's reasoning, instead identifying a freestanding normative principle through the equal protection clause.[110] Black's appeal to the "high standard of justice and common sense which the Founders set for us"[111] is, like *Gray's* invocation of constitutional rhetoric, no more than a cloak for a purely normative judgment.

The final foundational case of one person, one vote, *Reynolds v. Sims*, established that equipopulousness applies to state and local legislative districting.[112] The Court invoked the equal protection clause as the constitutional basis for the decision. However, Chief Justice Warren's opinion does little to extract a justification for equipopulousness from constitutional interpretation, constitutional history, or legal precedent. Subsequently *Reynolds* lays bare the nature of the one person, one vote rule: it is an independent normative conclusion regarding the nature of political organization, based on "democratic ideals of equality and majority rule" that are the "bedrock of the political system."[113] Contrary to Justice Holmes's famous

---

[106] *Ibid.*, at 17.
[107] *Wesberry*, 376 US at 10–18.
[108] Richard V. Carpenter, "Wesberry v. Sanders: A Case of Oversimplification" (1964) 9 *Villanova Law Review* 415 at 417.
[109] Justice Harlan makes this case compellingly enough in his dissent, *Wesberry*, 376 US at 30–42 to convince the concurring Justice Clark (who preferred the equal protection clause to enforce one person, one vote) that Article 1 Section 2 supports no such principle. *Wesberry*, 376 US at 18.
[110] *Wesberry*, 376 US at 18–19.
[111] *Ibid.*, at 19.
[112] In *Avery v. Midland County, Texas*, 390 US 474 (1968) the one person, one vote requirement was deemed to also apply to local government of "general governmental powers," 390 US 474, 485 (1968), though this requires a nuanced judgment of what comprises general powers. See Richard Briffault, "Who Rules at Home?: One Person/One Vote and Local Governments" (1993) 60 *University of Chicago Law Review* 339.
[113] *Reynolds*, 377 US at 562–6.

dictum,[114] it is the "logic[]"[115] of democratic organization, rather than precedential or constitutional instruction, that has guided the Court. The seminal reasoning – and most resonant rhetoric – of *Reynolds* appeals to the essence of political autonomy rather than legal reasoning:

> Legislators represent people, not trees or acres. Legislators are elected by voters, not farms or cities or economic interests. As long as ours is a representative form of government, and our legislatures are those instruments of government elected directly by and directly representative of the people, the right to elect legislators in a free and unimpaired fashion is a bedrock of our political system.[116]

Thus, across the foundational cases, one person, one vote is the pure expression of a norm of democratic governance.

4.3.1.2 Softening the Rule: Accommodation of a Margin of Deviation

The constitutional reasoning by which the Court developed one person, one vote has complicated the doctrine. *Wesberry* demanded that congressional districts must satisfy equal population "as nearly as practicable" under Article I Section 2. However, *Reynolds* indicated under the equal protection clause that state legislative districting must satisfy the lesser standard of being "substantially on a population basis and [with] the equal-population principle … not diluted in any significant way."[117] *Reynolds* indicated that if a deviation from perfect equality was in the service of "legitimate considerations incident to the effectuation of a rational state policy,"[118] the districting could survive judicial scrutiny. It further suggested the types of state policies that might be legitimate, particularly drawing state legislative boundaries to map on to political subdivisions. Yet *Reynolds* declined to articulate any specific test. It indicated that such evaluations may be highly particularized and delegated to the lower courts.

Subsequent doctrinal developments reveal the difficulty of balancing competing mandates. Initially, the Court treated equipopulousness as a sufficiently universal principle to cross-pollinate reasoning between contexts. Even as it recognized the different legal bases of Article I, Section 2 and the equal protection clause, *Reynolds* invoked *Wesberry* to support its normative thrust.[119] Likewise, the first case that elaborated the strict implications of the "as nearly as is practicable" equality rule in the congressional setting relied on the logic of *Reynolds* as much as that of *Wesberry*.[120] However, once the Court faced close cases, the jurisprudence of the

---

[114] Oliver Wendell Holmes Jr., *The Common Law* (1881), p. 1.
[115] *Reynolds*, 377 US at 565.
[116] Ibid., at 562.
[117] Ibid., at 578.
[118] Ibid., at 579.
[119] Ibid., at 563.
[120] *Kirkpatrick v. Preisler*, 394 US 526, 531, 533 (1969).

congressional and state contexts began to cleave apart. The Court must "as nearly as is practicable" require "absolute equality" in congressional districts.[121] A congressional districting *can* survive deviation from absolute equality, but only if it demonstrates (1) a good-faith effort to satisfy equality *and* (2) that any deviation is necessary to achieve a legitimate competing objective.[122] It was not until 2012 – half a century after *Reynolds* and 30 years after recognizing the possibility of an exception to absolute equality – that the Supreme Court tolerated a deviation (of less than 1 percent) as permissible.[123] The Court carefully scrutinized that deviation, the reasoning for it, and the viability of alternative districting plans. There appears to be a default presumption that only perfect equality is acceptable, and can only be overcome via a positive and compelling showing that the deviation, however slight, results from a scheme that is comprehensively preferable to any plan that better satisfies equipopulousness.

The Court has demonstrated a far greater tolerance for deviations from perfect equality in state and local districting. *Reynolds'* reasoning that such deviations were permissible if they effected a rational state policy is the root of this principle, but it was not until *Mahan v. Howell* that the divergence between the federal and state/local contexts in the implementation of one person, one vote was fully enumerated.[124] *Mahan* considered a state districting with a maximum deviation of 16.4 percent and found it constitutionally acceptable on the grounds that it was necessary to avoid fragmenting local government subdivisions.[125] *Mahan* illuminates the vast gulf between Article I *Wesberry* reasoning and equal protection *Reynolds* reasoning. In rejecting the *Mahan* district court's reliance on *Kirkpatrick* and other *Wesberry* progeny, the Supreme Court indicated that there is a "dichotomy"[126] between the two legal categories. A decade later, *Brown v. Thompson* elaborated the distinctive flexibility afforded state and local districting. If such plans had a maximum deviation below 10 percent, they would enjoy a safe harbor that made any such deviation *de minimis* and presumptively

---

[121] *Wesberry*, 376 US at 7.

[122] *Karcher v. Daggett*, 462 US at 731 (striking down a district with a deviation of less than 1 percent because the state had failed to justify its burden).

[123] *Tennant v. Jefferson County Commission*, 567 US 758 (2012) (permitting a 0.79 percent deviation due to minimal disruption to other *Karcher* factors). While *Tennant* "seemed to loosen[] the strict mathematical equality it had required states to use to draw congressional districts," dicta in *Evenwel v. Abbott*, 136 S. Ct. 1120, 1124 (2016) cited *Kirkpatrick* to reaffirm the principle that states must draw districts as close to perfect equality as possible. Richard L. Hasen, "Election Law's Path in the Roberts Court's First Decade: A Sharp Right Turn but with Speed Bumps and Surprising Twists" (2016) 68 *Stanford Law Review* 1597, 1613. For an account of the exactingness to which congressional districtings have traditionally been held, see Adam Raviv, "Unsafe Harbors: One Person, One Vote and Partisan Redistricting" (2005) 7 *University of Pennsylvania Journal of Constitutional Law* 1001, 1009 n. 33.

[124] *Abate v. Mundt*, 403 US 182 (1971) and *Sailors v. Board of Education of Kent County*, 387 US 105 (1967) anticipated this holding, but with narrower scope and in a manner that seemed particularized to the context.

[125] *Mahan v. Howell*, 410 US 315, 323 (1973). In doing so, *Mahan* seemed to vindicate, and extended the curt reasoning of, *Abate*, which involved similar justifications for deviations within a single county.

[126] *Mahan*, 410 US at 322.

constitutional.[127] *Brown* itself found a state plan with a maximum deviation of 89 percent legal, thanks to the sparsely populated Wyoming county districts.

The evolution of this jurisprudence conceals a deeper tension in the Court's reasoning. There is no intrinsic constitutional, let alone normative, reason why Article I, Section 2 and the equal protection clause should yield differing levels of stringency regarding one person, one vote.[128] Moreover, as the mingling of justifications in *Wesberry* and *Reynolds* (and the rejected district court reasoning in *Mahan*) suggested, the original normative logic of equipopulousness did not contain such a clear divergence. Rather, the Court fabricated it over time, relying on folk social science reasoning (the smaller per-person sizes and greater numbers of state and local districts, and the legitimacy of other interests, justifies tolerance of such deviations),[129] buttressed by the inevitable blurriness of census measuring.[130] Such logic conflicts with the origins of one person, one vote as well as the Court's own refusal to consider other interests when deciding if districting plans are fair.[131]

4.3.2 Accommodating the Counterpopular Dilemma

The development of the one person, one vote rule has yielded two high-order doctrinal puzzles. The first emerges from the evolution of the jurisprudence. Why has the one person, one vote rule forked in terms of its demandingness between the congressional and state/local contexts? The second puzzle is why, given the competing demands on fair voting arrangements, has as mechanical a principle as equipopulousness been adopted as the normative touchstone? Critics have observed that the primary virtue of one person, one vote rule is "manageability," yet given its conceptual inadequacy and its deviation from typical legal reasoning, this virtue seems insufficient.

Recognizing that the Court was engaged *not* in a typical act of constitutional interpretation but rather in advancing a normative precondition of electoral self-rule does much to clarify (though not resolve) these puzzles. This clarity comes from recognizing that judicial advancement of a freestanding normative commitment inevitably conflicts with the terms of self-rule that can be more readily understood as accountable (legislation, the Constitution, and, more rarely, referendum).[132]

---

[127] *Karcher*, 462 US at 842. For an authoritative account of the evolution of this 10 percent rule, see Raviv, "Unsafe Harbors,"1012–1014 (observing that *Brown*, perhaps inaccurately, formalized the Court's suggestion in *White v. Regester*, 412 US 755 (1973) that a prima facie case was not made by a 9.9 percent maximum deviation).

[128] Issacharoff, "Judging Politics," 1651 (characterizing the differing legal bases as "artificial").

[129] *Brown*, 462 US at 842.

[130] *Gaffney v. Cummings*, 412 US 735, 746 (1973).

[131] Weiser.

[132] *Lucas v. 44th General Assembly of the State of Colorado*, 377 US 713 (1964) shows that the Court held the norm of equality to dominate even direct expressions of terms of self-rule. I am thankful to Derek Muller to bringing this to my attention.

In short, the Court found it difficult to directly advance a norm of legitimate democracy in the face of the counterpopular dilemma. The result is that even when the Court firmly commits to a given norm of democracy (here, the wrongfulness of malapportionment), it still tries to balance other values (most centrally, popular authority over terms of self-rule). The tension from this balancing is apparent in both the conceptual thinness of the "manageability" justification (which reflects the judicial desire to avoid imposing a "thick" substantive conception of democracy) and the greater margin of deviation afforded to state and local districting (which reflects both the constitutional principle of federalism and the recognition of sub-national autonomy).

4.3.2.1 Redeeming the Thinness of One Person, One Vote

The sole content of one person, one vote is equipopulousness; the Court has declined to advance a concept of general fairness in voting that encompasses other features. At times, the Court has been explicit that its normative remit extends no further, as in *White v. Weiser* when it struck down a lower court that elected to advance its apportionment plan on the basis that it was fairer, even though it did not as precisely satisfy equal apportionment as the state's preferred alternative.[133]

The ostensible virtue of this minimalist conception is that there is little ambiguity regarding the rule. It is easy for a court to test (or for a legislature to know) whether a given districting plan satisfies the equipopulousness requirement. Scholars (and, early in its development, judges)[134] have frequently noted that "manageability"[135] or "administrability"[136] is insufficient to justify equipopulousness as the decisive norm. Sanford Levinson has offered the bluntest criticism. If there are moral demands of representation such that malapportionment is illegal, it is wholly unclear why equipopulousness is the best way to realize this morality.[137] Heather Gerken's critique offers an analytic parallel to Levinson's normative brickbat. She argues that because it lacks "an adequate mediating theory," the one person, one vote doctrine is "circular" and cannot be adapted to other political harms.[138] Likewise, Richard Hasen has emphasized the pragmatic limits of one person, one vote as a doctrinal solution, and argued for a standard that explicitly prefers a higher level of *unmanageability* because it would facilitate "experimentation" and trial-and-error assessments of the best policy.[139]

These critiques agree all exhort subtler, more nuanced more normative analysis on the bench. Yet they overlook the institutional pressure the Court faces from decontesting an electoral norm as it did following *Baker*. The Court instructed the

---

[133] *Weiser*, 412 US at 795–6.
[134] Justice Stewart dissenting in *Lucas*, 377 US at 750 (famously criticizing numerical equipopulousness as "sixth grade arithmetic").
[135] Hasen, "The Supreme Court and Election Law," p. 49.
[136] Levinson, "One Person, One Vote," 1270.
[137] *Ibid.*, 1273–7.
[138] Gerken, "The Costs and Causes of Minimalism in Voting Cases," 1430.
[139] Hasen, "The Supreme Court and Election Law," p. 58.

franchise *ex cathedra* on how it should arrange democracy without a clear source of constitutional authority. The blatantly counterpopular nature of such a claim incentivizes a minimalist approach. This feature has been noted by scholars who were writing near the time of the adoption of one person, one vote rule, including John Hart Ely and Jan Deutsch,[140] perhaps because they directly witnessed the drama of entering the political thicket.

The observations of Ely and Deutsch still have bite. Embracing a less settled standard would require the judiciary to expound a thicker vision of representative fairness and popular autonomy whenever it reviewed a districting plan. Each act of judicial review would elicit the counterpopular dilemma afresh, not merely as a matter of countervailing a legislative decision, but insofar as the judiciary's own democratic theorizing would become the dominant factor in resolution. The mechanical quality of one person, one vote allows the Court to make such a normative irruption only once. This demonstrates the cost of the wholly reasonable suggestion of Luis Fuentes-Rohwer[141] and Derek Muller[142] that a rational basis review of districting plans would be preferable to the rigid equipopulousness test. Such a test would risk recurring entanglements with democratic theory. Such entanglement poses a risk to the judiciary's legitimacy, as each normative assertion would elicit its claim to the normative priority of its own judgments over the electorate's setting its own terms of self-rule.

Critics will inevitably say the normative validity of one person, one vote's thinly justified arithmetic test nevertheless imposes a substantive democratic theory – just a poorly designed one. There is no question that a *complete* theory of democratic representation would suggest districting principles that go beyond mere equipopulousness. Yet the intrinsic tension of judicial review of election law demonstrates why the Court declines to advance such a theory: it would require (further) allocating power over procedures of self-rule to the courts, and away from voters, and even more problematically elicit the counterpopular dilemma. Conversely, the thin norm of equipopulousness comprises a less extensive intrusion, asserting only that sound democratic procedure entails minimal recognition of citizens as equal participants. This is a defensible imposition in a liberal democracy and a viable outcome of the bold decision to decontest a feature of democratic self-rule.

4.3.2.2 Conceding Federalist Flexibility to State and Local Districting

This argument for a rigidly arithmetic standard raises a question about the flexibility of state and local districting. If the very virtue of numerical equipopulousness is its fixedness, why introduce the uncertainty and discretion that the Court seemingly sought to avoid? The answer lies in the Court's recognition of the force of other principles – specifically those that have their own normative standing as expressive of self-rule, either

---

[140] Ely, "Democracy and Distrust," p. 124.
[141] Luis Fuentes-Rohwer, "Baker's Promise, Equal Protection, and the Modern Redistricting Revolution: A Plea for Rationality" (2002) 80 *North Carolina Law Review* 1353.
[142] Muller, "Perpetuating," 387.

as legislation or as a constitutional expression. These two concerns are synthesized by understanding the recognition of flexibility as a function of federalism.

This point is illustrated by the development of the "safe harbor" deviation from equipopulousness that the Supreme Court ultimately afforded states and localities. As Adam Raviv has observed, this margin is "not one that the Supreme Court declared definitely at any specific time, but rather one that it gradually backed into through a series of several opinions."[143] The origins of the principle can be traced to *Sailors v. Board of Education of Kent County*, in which the Court rejected a constitutional challenge to the selection of non-legislative government officials by appointment rather than by election. While the plaintiffs asserted a constitutional wrong on the basis of the one person, one vote principle, the Court determined that it did not apply, and that localities had significant discretion to determine their own political arrangements[144] as long as doing so does not constitute an attempt to circumvent what would otherwise be a political protected right.[145] Any possibility that *Sailors* stood for the proposition that one person, one vote did not apply to localities was brushed aside the following year by *Avery v. Midland County*, which confirmed that wherever there is voting to determine general government power, the districting arrangements must satisfy the one person, one vote requirement.[146] Rather, *Sailors* became the basis of the proposition that legislatures have a degree of autonomy in structuring their electoral districts.[147] They need not satisfy exacting equality under one person, one vote, so long as the basis for deviation effects some rational policy.[148]

While the Court has not justified the safe harbor in rigorous constitutional terms, its explanation – that universally applying the congressional districting standard may "impair the normal function of state and local governments"[149] – is best understood as a common-sense, practical instance of federalism, albeit with a unique institutional facet. Federalism is typically seen as setting the balance of power between the federal government and state governments, rather than between the federal courts and states (though it is the courts that strike such a balance).[150] The scholarship on

---

[143] Raviv, "Unsafe Habours," 1012.
[144] *Sailors*, 387 US at 109–11.
[145] Ibid., at 109.
[146] *Avery*, 390 US at 485. See Briffault, "Who Rules at Home?" 346. This point is made explicit in *Kramer v. Union Free School District*, 395 US 621, 628–9 (1969): "The need for exacting judicial scrutiny of statutes distributing the franchise is undiminished simply because, under a different statutory scheme, the offices subject to election might have been filled through appointment… 'once the franchise is granted to the electorate, lines may not be drawn which are inconsistent with the Equal Protection Clause of the Fourteenth Amendment.' Harper v. Virginia Bd. of Elections, supra, 383 US, at 665." See Briffault, "Who Rules at Home?" 354.
[147] *Abate*, 403 US at 185.
[148] *Mahan*, 410 US at 322.
[149] Ibid., at 323.
[150] See generally Heather K. Gerken, "Federalism 3.0" (2017) 105 *California Law Review* 1695. For a discussion of the contested degree of delegation of power over elections to Congress, see Franita Tolson,

election law and federalism has focused on the intersection between state autonomy and federal regulation.[151]

However, one person, one vote did not emerge from the political branches, but rather from the Court's own normative reasoning regarding the preconditions of democracy. Insofar as the safe harbor grants states more freedom as an aspect of federalism, it can be conceived in two ways. One is that the safe harbor recognizes a federalist balancing between state governments and the federal judiciary. The other is that the Court itself is balancing two competing constitutional principles – federalism and equal protection. The result is the same, but the Court's pragmatic approach to the safe harbor suggests the former. The Court recognizes it is imposing a normative standard for democracy on legislatures, yet will accommodate the force of other constitutional principles in the implementation of this norm.

The creation of the safe harbor thereby mitigates the counterpopular tension of the one person, one vote rule in the state and local context. In practice, it returns power to directly democratic modes of governance within the normative demand for equally populated districts. As a constitutional matter, it recognizes the need to give weight to the principle of federalism. Given that federalism facilitates self-rule, and is founded in the Constitution (and thus validated by the relevant principle that legitimates constitutionalism), the concession to federalism recognizes competing expressions of democratic autonomy.

4.3.2.3 The One Person, One Vote Rule as Minimizing Counterpopular Intrusion

Considered as standalone normative principles, the equipopulousness requirement and the safe harbor suffer from the same flaw: both appear arbitrary. Placing them in the context of the counterpopular dilemma explains why the judiciary adopted them.

By decontesting one person, one vote and imposing a specific norm of democratic organization, the Court took the remarkable step of determining that a value (pure procedural equality as a precondition of democratic freedom) is a necessary precondition if any popularly selected rules are to have validity. This is a moral proposition, asserting the character of freedom and representation as matters of objective truth, and thereby claiming epistemic authority regarding the nature of democracy.

The tensions that judicial imposition of a norm elicits for popular self-determination are obvious. The lack of contestation over one person, one vote on the bench exacerbates this tension by indicating the judiciary has no doubts regarding principle's normative authority. This chapter has, so far, established that the peculiar and oft-critiqued doctrinal features of one person, one vote reflect an attempt to manage this tension. Once *Baker* concluded that malapportionment comprised an unequivocal moral

---

"Reinventing Sovereignty?: Federalism as a Constraint on the Voting Rights Act" (2012) 65 *Vanderbilt Law Review* 1195.

[151] Justin Weinstein-Tull, "Election Law Federalism" (2016) 114 *Michigan Law Review* 747; Franita Tolson, "Election Law 'Federalism' and the Limits of the Antidiscrimination Framework" (2018) 59 *William and Mary Law Review* 2211.

wrong, the judiciary faced a dilemma. The Court was normatively obligated to strike down illicitly unequal districtings, yet the Constitution provides no guidance regarding what to do. This created a confrontation between the pure imposition of judicial norms that have no clear popular basis (even in the Constitution) and democratically accountable (if normatively unacceptable) state conduct. Advancing one person, one vote would be unabashedly counterpopular, even if normatively mandatory.

The thinness of the one person, one vote test and the state/local safe harbor represent different aspects of managing this dilemma. The thin equipopulousness test was not only manageable, it was theoretically minimalist – and eliminated the need for ongoing, multifaceted judicial evaluation of the legitimacy of non-equipopulous districting. The state/local safe harbor permitted another constitutional value space in the consideration of districting without requiring a formal retreat from theoretical minimalism. That the safe harbor has emerged gradually and without formally advancing a contrary principle of democracy is a virtue in light of the counterpopular dilemma. Instead of being required to rigorously and explicitly justify a competing democratic principle, the Supreme Court has been able to slowly introduce a value with little controversy. The alternative was to adopt a normatively "thicker" judicial test of whether a malapportionment is illegal. While many scholars have called for this approach, a thicker test would require the Court to develop a full theory of equality, and contextualize it within a full theory of democracy.

The Court has been willing to debate such topics – directly or indirectly – in other areas of election law. Remarkably, the post-*Baker* debate over one person, one vote has been largely absent and diminished over time. Having established a consensus that the Court has the power to shape democratic procedure based on its normative conclusions, an unstable test would constantly invoke the counterpopular dilemma. The Court would be placed in the situation of continuously evaluating democratic arrangements with no touchstone other than its own theorizing. This is discomforting in any judicial context, but particularly for election law. A judiciary that was required to continuously reflect upon a principle to determine the legitimacy of districting schemes, empowered by a principle the judiciary had itself invented, would indicate that the Court knows how the electorate ought to rule itself better than the electorate itself. A thick test, in short, would turn the illegality of malapportionment into a continual reminder of the Court's normative paternalism.

4.4 THE NORMATIVE CHARACTER OF ONE PERSON, ONE VOTE

This analysis has illustrated how the development of the one person, one vote doctrine has negotiated and softened the counterpopular dilemma. Given the Court's evasiveness in articulating its underlying normative principle, legal analysis does not capture the deeper substance of the one person, one vote rule, or whether it is valid. This section informs that philosophical endeavor. It first describes the "what" of one person, one vote – formal minimalist equality of persons as members of the polity.

It then turns to the "why" of one person, one vote – a form of pure procedural justice that advances such formal political equality with minimal determination of the outcomes of democratic process. This analysis demonstrates why one person, one vote may be uniquely decontested among areas of election law: the thin theory of democratic equality it advances is compatible with agnosticism toward liberal democracy.

4.4.1 The "What" of One Person, One Vote: Formal Respect for Equal Liberty

In this section I analyze the three cases that articulated the equipopulous standard in the one person, one vote doctrine – *Wesberry*, *Gray*, and *Reynolds*. *Baker* coyly suggests that the standards to tackle malapportionment were established in prior law ("well developed and familiar").[152] However, both the prior precedent[153] and the internal judicial politicking[154] surrounding one person, one vote indicate that this assertion simply deferred defining what standard districting must meet.

Tracing the development of the equipopulousness rule in these three cases mingles tangential legal and historical precedent,[155] feints at political theory,[156] and charged rhetoric. The opinions read as if the Court was bound to reach the rule that it did: "we see no constitutional way by which equality of voting power may be evaded" and thus "the conception of political equality ... can mean only one thing – one person, one vote."[157] Yet the requirement of equipopulousness the case law advances creates a condition necessary for democratic self-rule. The substance of the principle can be synthesized so:

i) democracy requires formal equality in representatives per person among members of the polity (the core idea of "one person, one vote")[158];

ii) this requirement of equality applies *only* to the bare status of membership,[159] and does not incorporate other circumstances or features of democratic membership or structure;[160]

iii) this minimal equality of voters is a necessary precondition for electoral freedom.[161]

---

[152] *Baker*, 369 US at 186.
[153] Ibid.; see also Muller, "Perpetuating," 387.
[154] Hasen, "The Supreme Court and Election Law," p. 52.
[155] *Gray*, 372 US at 381 clumps together the Declaration of Independence, the Gettysburg Address, and three constitutional amendments.
[156] *Wesberry*, 376 US at 8 (most saliently an invocation of "fundamental ideas of democratic government").
[157] *Gray*, 372 US at 381.
[158] Ibid.
[159] *Reynolds*, 377 US at 562 (persons, rather than any other features of the polity, are the only relevant feature); *Gray*, 372 US at 379 (rejecting the significance of other personal features for districting).
[160] *Lucas* (rejecting citizen affirmation of an alternative, not perfectly equipopulous plan); *Weiser* (rejecting a plan that satisfies equipopulousness less perfectly, but has other virtues as a system of representation).
[161] *Reynolds*, 377 US at 565 ("Since legislatures are responsible for enacting laws by which all citizens are to be governed, they should be bodies which are collectively responsive to the popular will.").

Members of a democracy are not free unless they enjoy equality vis-à-vis their status as *voters* with regard to each legislative election. Inequality of formal representation allows those with more proportional representation to dominate those with less voting power. The historical context that motivated the creation of the one person, one vote rule was the concern that sparsely populated rural areas were dominating urban areas.[162] Yet the Court does not articulate a *legal* requirement that districting must be equipopulous that is contingent upon pathological social circumstances (as, say, rational basis review might). Rather the Court asserts such equipopulousness as a *universal* requirement of legitimate districting.[163]

While the Court does not clearly articulate the philosophical foundations of why formal voting equality is a precondition of electoral freedom, this principle is central to liberal democratic thought. John Rawls classifies voting as one of the lexically prior equal basic liberties.[164] It is a first-order principle of a democratic regime of free and equal citizens. Such principles establish "just political procedures," and in Rawls's they view are subject to little legitimate variation in their implementation and typically little dispute regarding their importance.[165]

The lexically prior status of voting illuminates why the Supreme Court is comfortable imposing one person, one vote as a requirement against any contrary legislative or popular[166] decision. It also explains why one person, one vote could be so readily decontested as a principle of democracy. Equal voting power of citizens qua citizens is a precondition of democratic self-rule, rather than a valid subject of substantive dispute.

Philip Pettit's treatment of non-domination further[167] explains how malapportionment contravenes the liberty expressed by voting, and why strict equipopulousness is the appropriate solution. Malapportionment is problematic because voting power is hydraulic: "the intensity of freedom as non-domination which a person enjoys in a society is a function of other people's power as well as their own."[168] A political process that grants some persons in a polity disproportionately more formal access to political power (i.e., representation) on a per-population basis necessarily reduces the liberty of the persons who have disproportionately *less* power to undertake self-rule. Those with less proportional representation are less free to rule themselves.

---

[162] Smith, "On Democracy's Doorstep," Chapter 1.
[163] *Gray*, 372 US at 380 implies that this principle can only be dominated by explicit constitutional instruction with regard to the selection of senators and the president.
[164] John Rawls, *A Theory of Justice* (Cambridge: Harvard University Press, 1999), p. 53.
[165] John Rawls, *Political Liberalism* (New York: Columbia University Press, 1996), pp. 228–9.
[166] *Lucas*.
[167] Rawls's treatment of political liberties is notoriously terse. Harry Brighouse, "Political Equality in Justice as Fairness" (1997) 86 *Philosophical Studies: An International Journal for Philosophy in the Analytic Tradition* 155, 156.
[168] Philip Pettit, *Republicanism: A Theory of Freedom and Government* (Oxford: Oxford University Press, 1997), p. 113. Pettit's explanation looks to a "fuller" account of social factors than one person, one vote, however.

If democracy is defined as the collective self-rule of free and equal individuals, malapportionment is thereby illegitimate.

Rawls and Pettit wrote decades *after* the Warren Court articulated the core of one person, one vote. The close fit between the best account of one person, one vote and mainline liberal democratic accounts of the moral importance of voting demonstrates what the Court was doing: advancing a substantive political theory that is explicable within a well-established liberal democratic tradition. Rawls classifies republicanism, with which Pettit is mostly closely associated, as a type of liberal democracy.[169] Whether or not this is accurate, Pettit's account of the problem of inequality as touching freedom in the case of voting is readily compatible with Rawls. I do not assert here that one person, one vote necessarily advanced the *best* political theory. As Sanford Levinson (writing as a lawyer) and David Estlund (writing as a political theorist) argue,[170] a democratic theory that most highly prioritizes optimal policy outcomes may not support a strict understanding of the equality of voting power. But the very nature of such a critique affirms the nature of the Court's reasoning in the one person, one vote arena.

4.4.2 The "Why" of One Person, One Vote: Pure Procedural Justice, Formal Minimal Equality, and the Counterpopular Dilemma

The substantive critique of one person, one vote – that voting equality would be better protected by a less rigid and formalist principle – points to the next question: *why* has the Court advanced a political theory with the substance that it did? The answer, in short, is that the thinness of one person, one vote minimizes the degree to which it could dictate actual political outcomes. If the Court's normative impositions, it would evoke the core concern of the counterpopular dilemma. In calling for the Court to offer a "thicker" theory of democracy in advancing one person, one vote, this is precisely what the critiques of Gerken and Levinson might entail. The practical and institutional aspects of this argument are discussed above. However, to understand its theoretical aspect, it is helpful to return to political theory and characterize formal equipopulism as pure procedural justice. Understanding the norm in this way explains how it minimizes the degree to which it elicits the counterpopular dilemma. It thereby explains why the Court has been willing to impose one person, one vote as a requirement of self-rule: pure procedural justice does not speak to the *outcome* of procedures.

Pure procedural justice is attributed to the terms of the procedure rather than to subsequent outcomes.[171] It "obtains when there is no independent criterion for the right result: instead there is a correct or fair procedure such that the outcome is

---

[169] Rawls, "Political Liberalism," p. 204.
[170] David Estlund, "Political Quality" (2000) 17 *Social Philosophy and Policy* 127.
[171] The definitive account is in Rawls, "A Theory of Justice," pp. 74–5.

likewise correct or fair, whatever it is, provided that the procedure has been properly followed."[172] The fairness of pure procedural justice must derive from the "intrinsic features"[173] of the process itself, rather than from any output it yields. Rawls contrasts pure procedural justice with perfect and imperfect procedural justice, in which there is pre-existing knowledge of the fair outcome. As a matter of institutional design, perfect and imperfect procedures for justice are intrinsically self-justifying. Where there is a known just outcome and a procedure that is at least preferable to other procedures to generate it, that procedure needs no further validation. Rawls defines "perfect procedural justice" as "an independent and already given criterion of what is just (or fair)… the procedure can be designed to insure an outcome satisfying that criterion."[174] Since pure procedural justice has no such knowledge, "there are not criteria for the correct outcome, there is an ideal (or actual) set of procedures."[175]

By adopting a minimalist and mechanical rule, the Court's approach to one person, one vote conforms to pure procedural justice, rather than (im)perfect procedural justice. The Court only evaluates whether a given districting plan treats all persons as formally equal in their status qua citizens, and conforms to the criterion of constituent equality. The rule makes no "thicker" assessment regarding the wisdom of the plan, or how it will affect electoral results (including by considering what other features, such as race or party identity, a districting plan might use to allocate voters). The Court's commitment to this principle is particularly apparent in the cases in which it had the opportunity to advance more fulsome notions of democracy. This is most explicit in *Weiser*, where the Court struck down a lower court's attempt to prefer one districting design over another holistic approach. Similarly, in *Evenwel*, the Court left to the legislature's discretion a question regarding democratic membership and the construction of the electorate with direct bearing on application of the one person, one vote rule. The bench asks nothing of districting plans other than that they conform to a foundational starting commitment of liberal democracy: that all citizens are equal.

Given the vast injustices that can be perpetuated even if a districting plan obeys equipopulous one person, one vote, why would the Court hew to such a conception of pure procedural justice? The answer lies in the intersection of three factors: (1) one person, one vote has no apparent basis in legal–constitutional analysis (unlike, say, *Gomillion*'s prohibition on clear racial malapportionment); (2) one person, one vote was decontested and made an entrenched prerequisite of democratic procedure; and (3) the counterpopular dilemma as grounded in the electorate's capacity to self-determine (including by setting its own districting plans). If the Court was going to impose a pure norm on the polity with no typical basis of legal authority,

---

[172] *Ibid.*, p. 75.
[173] *Ibid.*, 260.
[174] Rawls, "Political Liberalism," p. 72.
[175] See Lawrence B. Solum, "Procedural Justice" (2004) 78 *Southern California Law Review* 181, 240.

it needed to advance a norm that was incontrovertibly essential to democracy. Because democracy is fundamentally a mechanism by which the electorate selects its own path of governance, any such norm would have to be part of pure proceduralism, rather than speak to the validity of any outcome. Outcomes of democratic process are the domain of a free electorate. If the Court decisively advanced a notion of one person, one vote that went beyond the minimum of equality as required for democratic legitimacy, it would suggest the Court had some special moral knowledge of just outcomes, such that it could deny a range of outcomes *without* a constitutional basis. The Court could only speak with certitude to the justice of what norm is necessary for starting conditions, regardless of the outcome. This norm is basic constituent equality.

A purely procedural approach to one person, one vote has a justification very similar to certain familiar arguments regarding the limits on the nature of judicial review generally: a purely procedural norm is less likely to result in the judiciary making decisions that appear to emulate (and displace) political decision-making. In practical terms, advancing a purely procedural norm shields the Court from concerns that it is seeking to achieve certain types of political outcomes with any level of particularity.

The judges who crafted one person, one vote were certainly not aiming, in any conscious way, to achieve pure proceduralist justice (to use Gerken's phrasing, typical analysis of cases does not aspire to a "psychoanalytic account of judicial decisionmaking").[176] However, understanding one person, one vote as pure procedural justice so as to minimize counterpopular tension explains why one person, one vote reflects such a seemingly "atheoretical" approach to representation.[177] The Court could commit to this approach to democratic equality without making any commitment regarding the desirable *outcome* of democratic process, only its necessary fair starting conditions.

4.5 REAPPRAISING ONE PERSON, ONE VOTE

None of this analysis argues that mechanical equipopulousness is the ideal starting point for representative democracy. This is hardly a novel claim. From one direction, one person, one vote is assailed for having shoddy constitutional foundations;[178] from another, it is attacked for advancing a theory of democracy that is theoretically lacking and insufficiently ambitious.[179]

Yet this chapter has shown these critiques miss the context of institutionalized democratic autonomy that framed the development of one person, one vote. The counterpopular dilemma indicates that direct judicial imposition of electoral norms

---

[176] Heather K. Gerken, "The Costs and Causes of Minimalism in Voting Cases: Baker v. Carr and Its Progeny." (2002) 80 *North Carolina Law Review* 1411, 1420.
[177] Gerken, "The Costs and Causes of Minimalism in Voting Cases," 1427.
[178] McConnell, "The Redistricting Cases"; Muller, "Perpetuating."
[179] Levinson, "One Person, One Vote"; Gerken, "The Costs and Causes of Minimalism in Voting Cases."

comes with great institutional onus. The nature of one person, one vote – which the Court intimated, rather than articulated, as formal and minimalist procedural egalitarianism – reflects this onus. Such a minimalist norm is the incontrovertible baseline of liberal democratic fairness, and can be advanced with little controversy. The constitutional framing that contextualizes this normative imposition – the careful entry into malapportionment through the reconstruction of the political question doctrine and the deference to federalism – further demonstrates that the Supreme Court has threaded a needle, asserting a foundational norm of democratic legitimacy while accommodating other constitutional commands. While the substance of one person, one vote may be a rigid and mechanical, this substance minimizes constitutional and moral objections based on the judiciary's institutional role. Alternative principles might be substantively sounder, but would, if imposed by an unelected entity such as the Court, more directly infringe upon popular self-determination.

This account of one person, one vote operates within the narrative that election law is characterized by contestation. The decontested nature of one person, one vote is its distinguishing feature compared to other jurisprudence on election law. In other areas, judges have advanced much richer and more robust theories of democracy and its practice. These theories have generated fierce contestation, as the understandings of democracy they rely on are far from incontrovertible as a matter of democratic theory and electoral practice.

The oft-critiqued aspects of one person, one vote therefore reflect various types of institutional constraints on the judiciary. By advancing a principle that only has legitimacy because of its normative force rather than as a constitutional command, the Court was pressured to adopt the thin form of a principle – the formal equality of citizens – the substance of which could not be disputed (at least in a polity that resembles a liberal constitutional democracy). By advancing such a "thin" principle, the Court not only ameliorated the counterpopular dilemma, but it also adopted a principle that minimized dissent on the Court. It is not accidental that one person, one vote is both theoretically minimalist and, uniquely, a point of consensus on the bench.

5

Campaign Finance

Contesting Voters' Cognitive Capacities

[T]he American people... have recognized a need to prevent corporations from undermining self-government since the founding, and who have fought against the distinctive corrupting potential of corporate electioneering since the days of Theodore Roosevelt.
  –John Paul Stevens, Citizens United v. Federal Election Commission

The first instinct of power is the retention of power, and, under a Constitution that requires periodic elections, that is best achieved by the suppression of election-time speech.
  –Antonin Scalia, McConnell v. Federal Election Commission

Campaign finance and its regulation speak to the transformation, and perhaps the distortion, of the political views and preferences of constituents and representatives. While typically (and unhelpfully) framed as a balance between free speech rights and preventing corruption, the real question more closely relates to human freedom: what influences distort cognition such that political actors are unfree? In *Buckley v. Valeo*, the Court sought to cleave to a middle ground, concluding that campaign finance contributions can be distortive, but that expenditures are not. This middle ground has become a no-man's-land of contestation. Progressives have sought to establish a broader conception of how private wealth in politics distorts free will, while conservatives have argued that the state's looming power to restrict speech represents a far greater threat to constituent decision-making. In the context of individual constituents' personal will, the campaign finance debate epitomizes the battle between egalitarian-public and libertarian-private conceptions of popular self-rule.

5.1 THE UNIQUE CORE OF CAMPAIGN FINANCE: THE MORAL AUTONOMY OF PREFERENCE FORMATION

Most voting jurisprudence seeks to indirectly ensure that voter preferences (the engine of the people's will) are accurately translated into governance, for example by limiting voter *suppression* (e.g. via literacy tests, poll taxes, and racialized districting in the pre-Civil Rights South). The case law seldom addresses voter preferences directly.¹ Conversely, campaign financing and its regulation do not directly change voters' selection of representatives. Campaigns instead shape how voters *form* their political beliefs, influencing voters as reasoning agents. At its core, the campaign finance jurisprudence wrestles with what it means for a person to be autonomous as a morally reasoning individual.

The Supreme Court has not directly confronted this deontological core of campaign finance. Instead, it has asked a subsidiary question: what is the greater threat to free preference formation? The now-ascendant conservative position is that state regulation of speech threatens tyranny, and therefore the judiciary should invoke the First Amendment to tightly constrain regulation. The progressive position is that economic inequality represents a grave threat to politics, so the government should be given significant leeway to curb the influence of money on elections. However, both positions depend upon accounts of how the application of reason yields personal self-determination, and what circumstances facilitate or obstruct that process of reasoning.

Constitutional reasoning typically focuses on rights and institutions rather than the mysteries of free will, so it is unsurprising that the judiciary has not directly addressed the philosophical root of autonomous preference formation. However, the result has been obfuscation and imprecision in the legal treatment of campaign finance. The initial formulation of *Buckley v. Valeo* framed the threat of wealth as influence over officials via corruption. This framing has elaborately shaped campaign finance lawmaking, as the Court weighs the benefits of anti-corruption legislation against the chilling of speech. Samuel Issacharoff describes the result as "a regulatory structure created by the Court."² Although widely condemned,³ the anti-corruption rationale remains the dominant justification for regulating campaign finance. However, campaign finance and its regulation directly impact voters' decision-making, rather than shifting the underlying terms by which they select representatives. Any pathology of campaign finance itself – whether in the use of wealth or its regulation – must be directly linked to *voter reasoning*. Identifying the appropriate campaign finance regime thus requires a robust theory of personal autonomy, which judges (perhaps unsurprisingly) and scholars (more surprisingly) have been loath to articulate.⁴

---

[1] As discussed in Chapter 7, one of the exceptional features of *Shaw v. Reno*, 509 US 630, 657 (1993) in its discussion of how the Court hopes voter preferences themselves will change to become less racially polarized. It is an exception that proves the rule.
[2] Samuel Issacharoff, "On Political Corruption" (2010) 124 *Harvard Law Review* 118, 119.
[3] At the time of *Colorado Republican v. Federal Election Commission* (*Colorado Republican I*), 518 US 604 (1996), it seemed a majority of justices wished to overrule the *Buckley* compromise, but could not agree on which side to fall. For a more extensive description of this deadlock, *see generally* Pamela Karlan "New Beginnings and Dead Ends in the Law of Democracy" (2007) 68 *Ohio State Law Journal* 743.
[4] Samuel Issacharoff and Pamela S Karlan, "The Hydraulics of Campaign Finance Reform" (1999) 77 *Texas Law Review* 1705, 1723–4 (preference formation vs. preference expression). Elizabeth Reese, "The Inexplicable Absence of the Voters in the Campaign Finance Debate" (2018) 56 *Houston Law*

Immanuel Kant's conception of autonomy as independence from illegitimate external circumstance captures the philosophical question at the heart of campaign finance: what conditions in campaign finance and its regulation threaten to yield governance that does not depend upon the genuine will of voters? Conservatives assert that it is the risk of state tyranny that could make constituents heteronomous; progressives argue that some form of overdetermination from wealth in politics could yield such heteronomy.

Critically, both perspectives hang on a subtle premise of campaign finance that has been oddly underexplored: any pathology in campaign finance (whether inequality or regulation) must be traceable to a fundamental weakness in the expression of *political* self-determination as a matter of moral autonomy. If inequality can impair popular self-rule, this means that leaders and constituents are already tractable to plutocratic influence and that the body politic is no longer self-guiding – in other words, that that political actors are heteronomous. Yet if regulation can have this effect, it suggests that voters have already lost control of their representatives (or that representatives have turned against the voters). In both cases, the loss of freedom generated by campaign finance indicates a deeper political pathology. The ills of campaign finance are thus both subsidiary (in that they cannot be the first-order problem in political self-determination through electoral self-governance) and revelatory (in that they indicate what those first-order problems must be).

The correct judicial posture toward these problems must further be situated within the role of the courts in the constitutional order. This facet of the debate has also been surprisingly neglected. Reasoning on campaign finance has instead taken on the tone of a policy debate, with conservatives arguing that the state is the threat and progressives countering that plutocratic inequality is the threat. The progressives seem to have the upper hand. Martin Gilens, Christopher Achen, and Lawrence Bartels have detailed how wealthy persons have vastly disproportionate power in politics.[5] Furthermore, the electorate overwhelmingly desires campaign finance reform.[6] Strangely, the conservatives have chosen to reply *not* by adverting to the unique role of the judiciary, but by responding in kind with policy arguments and denying that economic inequality is a problem in politics. Yet the stronger conservative reply would identify the appropriate limits of the judiciary to solve social problems (similar to the conservative tack regarding partisan gerrymandering). Even

---

Review 123 reiterates the point that campaign finance law has failed to take into account actual voter behavior, but likewise does not explore the philosophical root.

[5] For a synthesis of this scholarship, see Nicholas O. Stephanopoulos, "Aligning Campaign Finance Law" (2015) 101 *Virginia Law Review* 1425, 1468.

[6] See Nathaniel Persily and Kelli Lammi, "Perceptions of Corruption and Campaign Finance: When Public Opinion Determines Constitutional Law" (2004) 153 *University of Pennsylvania Law Review* 119; Bradley Jones, "Most Americans want to limit campaign spending, say big donors have greater political influence," Pew Research Center (May 8, 2018), www.pewresearch.org/fact-tank/2018/05/08/most-americans-want-to-limit-campaign-spending-say-big-donors-have-greater-political-influence/.

if economic inequality disrupts politics, it is contestable that the judiciary should modulate the First Amendment's constraint on state power. Even if more robustly egalitarian campaign finance arrangements might be socially optimal, it is not obvious that the judiciary is the institution best suited to identify them.

As this chapter shows, constituent autonomy must thus be advanced by ensuring the Court has the appropriate institutional role within the freedom-serving democratic infrastructure. This is a doctrinally specified version of the counterpopular dilemma. The final interpretive problem of campaign finance is minimizing counterpopularism. Should the judiciary enforce the First Amendment with the rigid formality demanded of an initial commitment, even if this enforcement (beyond being counterpopular) harms the polity's political capacities? Or should the judiciary reinterpret its remit in response to social circumstances[7] and drift away from classical guardianship of constitutional rights meant to be durable against majority opinion and the vagaries of circumstance?

This chapter explores these nested problems. Section 5.2 describes how the doctrinal development has concealed as much as clarified the stakes of campaign finance regulation. The framing of the law through corruption tilted the debate away from the necessary impact of campaign finance on voter preference formation and instead created a one-sided consideration of representative integrity. While the debate has become increasingly fierce, the dominance of corruption as the analytic lens has resulted in a debate about whether unequal wealth can corrupt governance and society more broadly. Section 5.3 demonstrates the real question at issue in campaign finance: whether the more imminent threat to voter autonomy is the state action or the inequality of wealth in politics. Section 5.4 observes how this debate over the appropriate legal posture toward the regulation of campaign finance is based on how the courts impact freedom. Section 5.5 considers the types of rigorous philosophical and constitutional analyses to which campaign finance law must be subject to further progress and observes how this question organizes and exposes the limits of dominant scholarly debates.

5.2 THE DEVELOPMENT OF THE CAMPAIGN FINANCE REGIME: A CRITICAL RECAP

The law of campaign finance regulation has had a twisting path. The foundational case in the doctrine, *Buckley v. Valeo*, frames constitutional analysis as balancing the First Amendment against preventing corruption. Yet in the past two decades, the contours of corruption have become the battleground. If campaign finance spending can only corrupt through directly bribing representatives, then regulations that do not target such explicit transactions illegitimately constrain

---

[7] Sunstein highlights the risk that campaign finance becomes a type of regulatory equality-enforcing "Lochnerism." Cass R. Sunstein, "Lochner's Legacy" (1987) 87 *Columbia Law Review* 873.

free speech (the conservative view). But if massively unequal infusions of wealth into campaigns corrupt politics (and perhaps even constituents) more pervasively, then more expansive regulation is justified (the progressive view). Each of these positions elicits puzzles as to precisely how each of the threats at issue (state over-regulation and the corrosive effects of wealth) can have such effects on democratic self-governance.

5.2.1 Buckley's Doomed Architecture

The contemporary campaign finance regime was born out of a collision between a corruption scandal and constitutional rights. Investigations of the Nixon administration's burglary of the Democratic Party National Committee headquarters (the Watergate scandal) revealed that Richard Nixon's campaign had received significant illegal campaign contributions.[8] This led Congress to conclude that the disclosure-based campaign finance regime of the time (based on the assumption that voter awareness of contributions ensures political integrity) was inadequate[9] and to pass the Federal Election Campaign Finance Act (FECA).[10] The 1974 FECA established a far more robust framework for campaign financing. It imposed strict limits on (1) contributions to candidates and parties and (2) campaign expenditures by candidates and independent supporters.[11] This limitation of private media expenditure was paired with expanded government subsidizes for campaigns. The intention and result of the reforms were to ensure campaigns occur largely through governmental rather than private channels.[12]

Buckley v. Valeo fractured this elaborately designed system. The decision struck down expenditure restrictions but upheld contribution restrictions.[13] This split was driven by two propositions. First, the Court reasoned that since contributions were more likely to be used as bribes in a *quid pro quo* exchange, their strict regulation had

---

[8] For a detailed account, see John Samples, *The Fallacy of Campaign Finance Reform* (Chicago: University of Chicago Press, 2006), pp. 213–5.

[9] See S. Rep. No. 93–689, at 2 (1974), as reprinted in 1974 U.S.C.C.A.N. 5587, 5588. See generally J. Skelly Wright, "Politics and the Constitution: Is Money Speech?" (1976) 85 *Yale Law Journal* 1001, 1002 (origins of current campaign finance regime in reaction to Watergate); George D. Brown, "Putting Watergate Behind Us – Salinas, Sun-Diamond, and Two Views of the Anticorruption Model" (2000) 74 *Tulane Law Review* 747 (describing Watergate as an anticorruption threshold).

[10] See Jacob Eisler, "The Unspoken Institutional Battle over Anti-Corruption: Citizens United, Honest Services, and the Legislative-Judicial Divide" (2010) 9 *First Amendment Law Review* 363, 388–93.

[11] Federal Election Campaign Act of 1974, Pub. L. No. 93–443, § 101(b), 88 Stat. 1263, 1263–4 (1974) (codified as amended at 2 U.S.C. §§ 431–55 (Supp. 2004)), describes contribution limits; § 101(c) describes expenditure limits; and key terminology for contribution and expenditure limits are articulated by §§ 201, 204–309.

[12] S. Rep. No. 93–689, at 5 (the "election of federal officials is not a private affair.").

[13] *Buckley v. Valeo*, 424 US 1, 25–59 (1976) (describes the logical apparatus behind the expenditure–contribution divide). See also Issacharoff and Karlan, "The Hydraulics of Campaign Finance Reform" (providing one of the most influential analyses of the structural logic of the contribution–expenditure divide, particularly that it simply induces candidates to dedicate too much time to fundraising).

a stronger anti-corruption justification. Second, expenditures would only provide information to voters. In this role, expenditures could not serve as bribes, and had a weaker anti-corruption rationale. This Court's evaluation of each measure's constitutionality tracked this assessment of their political impact. By preventing only the interpersonal transfer of money, contribution expenditures did little to restrict speech; expenditure restrictions, however, could inhibit speakers' ability to propagate their messages and limit the exchange of information by voters, thereby constraining free speech.

The *Buckley* compromise seeks to protect the central aspects of constituent self-governance. In a representative democracy, elected agents of the people hold effective (though not final) power. If the electorate ceases to have final authority over these representative agents, constituents no longer self-govern. Such accountability comprises a central relationship of democratic self-governance. As the Court recognized in *Buckley*, the essence of corruption is the assumption of control over representatives by competing non-democratic principals (i.e. the bribe payers).

The other hinge of democratic self-governance is the electorate's capacity to make political choices freely and independently. Central to this freedom is the opportunity to engage in discourse and debate. *Buckley*'s decision to strike down expenditure limits was designed to protect this aspect of self-governance by refusing to allow direct state curation of discourse and debate.

Thus, the spirit of *Buckley* is that the state may police the conduct of representatives but not voters' preference formation. As an abstract principle, this is reasonable enough and accords with the concerns of the counterpopular dilemma. This quality may explain the durability of the *Buckley* formula, despite its unpopularity. It also coordinates the character of campaign finance jurisprudence with other areas of election law. Under *Buckley*, the Court will ensure that the state is guided by the will of the electorate, and strike down lawmaking that cleaves apart popular will and legitimate representative governance. But it will not inquire into the substance or generation of that popular will.

History has proven the *Buckley* compromise woefully naïve.[14] The *Buckley* precedent failed to recognize the subtle interplay between political and economic influence in campaigns, as the need for the Bipartisan Campaign Reform Act (BCRA) almost 30 years later demonstrated. The contribution–expenditure divide presumed

---

[14] *Buckley v. Valeo*, 424 US at 235. The inadequacy of the framing would not be a surprising outcome even to many justices on the bench when *Buckley* was decided, as the minority *Buckley* opinions acknowledged this over-simplification and anticipated the current conservative–progressive divide. Rejecting the constitutionality of contribution limits, small donor disclosure, and the public financing regime, Justice Burger anticipated the conservative distrust of the state and saw these efforts as "an impermissible intrusion by the Government into the traditionally private political process." Remarkably, Burger's *Buckley* opinion also anticipated the later scholarly innovation that campaign finance corruption cannot be about bribe-like corruption as representatives: "The Court's attempt to distinguish the communication inherent in political contributions from the speech aspects of political expenditures simply 'will not wash.' We do little but engage in word games unless we recognize that people candidates and contributors spend money on political activity because they wish to

that the impact of campaign funding could be neatly separated into corrupting effects on representatives and edifying effects on voters. Scholars have observed that categorizing the impact of campaign funding as either affecting representatives or voters is flawed because *campaign* contributions cannot directly enrich representatives in the same way as typical bribes, but are part of the complex ecosystem of voter preference formation. David Strauss notes that since the only target of such regulation is *campaign* money, its real concern cannot be representative corruption. Unlike in typical cases of corruption (where an official converts public wealth into private gain), campaign finance wealth can only be converted into the good of voter approval. The only benefit from a campaign finance payoff is improved chances of re-election.[15]

Thus, obtaining campaign contributions can only be understood as part of a broader narrative that is directed at shifting the preferences of the electorate. Daniel Ortiz elaborates on this difficulty with the *Buckley* divide. Given this limitation, campaign financing is a political pathology in which the funds obtained through "corrupt" contributions only sway voters. Ortiz has argued that voters who are so easily swayed must be "slackers," who are presumably too civically disengaged to enquire into candidates' real allegiances and commitments.[16] In short, *all* campaign finance resources are used to try to sway voters and win elections. If campaign money corrupts politics, it must do so much more systematically – and progressive scholars have offered many accounts of how it might do so. Yet the contribution–expenditure divide remains good law, despite being long viewed as "a rotten tree just waiting to be pushed over."[17]

5.2.2 *From Bellotti to BCRA: Struggles over the Campaign– Expenditure Boundary and the Progressive Trust of the State*

After *Buckley*, the Court sought to refine and buttress the contribution–expenditure divide. This involved technical questions such as how to differentiate issue advertisements from express advocacy that acts as a contribution[18] and the legal

---

communicate ideas, and their constitutional interest in doing so is precisely the same whether they or someone else utters the words." *Ibid.*, at 244. Justice White, prefiguring *Austin* and the progressive view, rejected the Court's ruling that expenditure divides are unconstitutional, observing that Congress has reasonably concluded that "other steps must be taken to counter the corrosive effects of money in federal election campaigns," *ibid.*, at 260, and presciently observing how politics would become dominated by fundraising, *ibid.*, at 265.

[15] David A. Strauss, "Corruption, Equality, and Campaign Finance Reform" (1994) 94 *Columbia Law Review* 1369, 1372.

[16] Daniel R. Ortiz, "The Democratic Paradox of Campaign Finance Reform" (1998) 50 *Stanford Law Review* 893, 903.

[17] Burt Neuborne, "Money and American Democracy," in Paul D. Carrington and Trina Jones (eds.), *Law and Class in America* (New York: New York University Press, 2006), pp. 37–59.

[18] *Federal Election Commission v. Massachusetts Citizens for Life*, 479 US 238 (1986) (concluding that a corporation that circulated a document advocating against a candidate based on an issue violated a FECA provision against express advertising, but as applied the FECA was itself unconstitutional).

status of campaign money passed through the conduit of political parties.[19] While a full review of the divide is beyond the scope of this chapter, one early post-*Buckley* decision emphasized that the Court was committed to the core principle of voter autonomy. In *First National Bank v. Bellotti,* the Court struck down an expenditure restriction that limited corporate expenditures during a popular referendum directly relevant to that corporation's interests. The Court's reasoning was consistent with the *Buckley* structure. With no candidate to corrupt, the anti-corruption rationale vanished. The point of the restriction at issue was to prevent the corporation's advertisements from influencing the election results, but this is just a euphemism for the anti-liberal assumption that voters could be tainted by speech. As the *Bellotti* Court states, "the fact that advocacy may persuade the electorate is hardly a reason to suppress it."[20]

However, the Court softened this position in *Austin v. Michigan,* which considered the constitutionality of a statute that prohibited the use of corporations' general treasury funds to finance independent campaign advocacy. Allowing the statute to stand even though it restricted campaigning that appealed directly to voters, the *Austin* Court infamously introduced the (now overruled) "distortion" rationale, suggesting that expenditures that "have little or no correlation to the public's support"[21] can harm governance. By suggesting voter susceptibility to campaign speech, *Austin* dramatically deviated from the faith in voter capacity that comprises half of the *Buckley* divide. Competent voters could presumably incorporate knowledge of such spending into their electoral choices, thereby correcting for any distortive effect.

However, the *Buckley* approach faced its most tangible challenges from attempts by donors and candidates to circumvent the divide and the subsequent legislative response. In 2002, Congress passed the BCRA,[22] which sought to "plug"[23] holes in the regime to combat the use of campaign money that could comprise "indirect" corruption. The BCRA tightened regulations of two categories of spending to prevent more diffuse forms of influence over representatives. The first was "soft

---

[19] *Colorado Republican Federal Campaign Committee v. Federal Election Commission,* 518 US 604 (1996) (concluding that money spent by a political party to attack an opposing candidate but not aid a particular candidate is protected by the First Amendment). For a more extensive discussion, see Jacob Eisler, "The Deep Patterns of Campaign Finance Law" (2016) 49 *Connecticut Law Review* 57 and Jacob Eisler, "The Unspoken Institutional Battle over Anticorruption: Citizens United, Honest Services, and the Legislative-Judicial Divide" (2011) 9 *First Amendment Law Review* 363.

[20] *First National Bank of Boston v. Bellotti,* 435 US 765, 790 (1978).

[21] *Austin v. Michigan Chamber of Commerce,* 494 US 652, 660 (1990). Attempts to resuscitate, justify, or preserve the distortion rationale have become an academic cause célèbre. See, e.g., Stephanopoulos, "Aligning Campaign Finance" (advancing an "alignment" rationale).

[22] Pub. L. No. 107–155, 116 Stat. 81 (codified in scattered sections of 2 U.S.C., 18 U.S.C., 28 U.S.C., 36 U.S.C., and 47 U.S.C. (2002). See generally Richard Briffault, "McConnell v. FEC and the Transformation of Campaign Finance Law" (2004) 3 *Election Law Journal* 147 (offering a comprehensive measure-by-measure description of BCRA).

[23] *McConnell v. Federal Election Commission,* 540 US 93, 133 (2003).

money" – funding donated to parties without an instruction to promote a specific candidate. This type of spending does not readily contribute to *quid pro quo* corruption. The presumptive bribe-like benefit to the donor is a general sense of gratitude from members of, and a stronger relationship with, the recipient political party. The second spending category was electioneering spending, which refers to ads that support a candidate but are not coordinated with them. While such electioneering advertisements are clearly "intended to influence the election,"[24] such expenditures cannot operate directly as bribes. Electioneering has a weaker "pro" component than classical transactional bribery, as the *quids* and *quos* are correspondingly less explicit. Determining when a given advertisement is electioneering also requires differentiating between "advocacy" speech (which directly promotes a candidate) and "issue" speech (which speaks to an issue more generally). In a sop to candidates, the BCRA also raised "hard money" contribution limits (i.e. allowed candidates to raise more money from individuals directly).

BCRA recognized the complexity of the campaign finance regime and concluded that wealth could have an influence beyond the bribe-like control of representatives that is *Buckley*'s sole concern. It demonstrated Congressional skepticism of the (naïve) liberalism of the *Buckley* détente, which, for example, maintains that electioneering by independent groups cannot have the "typical" corrupting effect on leaders. According to *Buckley*'s reasoning, electioneering can only impact the electorate, and thus there is no way it can aggrandize representatives other than by helping them get re-elected. If electioneering has a corrupting effect, either the electorate cannot exert effective control over leaders (even when they know exactly which plutocratic influences are trying to pander to them, as this influence is targeted at the electorate) or the electorate can be corrupted by media bombardment (or both).

McConnell v. FEC was the Court's initial and most comprehensive assessment of BCRA. It left most of the regulatory structure intact and largely accepted the animating logic of the reforms. The complex opinion is the progressive high-water mark, with a broadened conception of corruption that vindicates more extensive regulation of campaigns. This is exemplified in the majority opinion's approval of expanded regulation of soft money and electioneering expenditures.[25] Because of the attenuation of the connection between a donor and a candidate, it is difficult to see how soft money can corrupt representatives with *quid pro quo* granularity. Likewise, the Court upheld more extensive regulation of expenditures directly by donors, whether they were coordinated with a candidate or directly targeted against a candidate.

Both BCRA and *McConnell* were, as contributions to the campaign finance debate, subjected to substantial criticism. Some argued that BCRA did not do

---

[24] Ibid., at 193.
[25] Ibid., at 138.

enough to truly fix the campaign finance system,[26] while others attacked *McConnell* for failing to take the First Amendment protection of free speech seriously enough and for capitulating to the legislation's self-serving political motivations.[27]

Regardless, it is indisputable that *McConnell* demonstrated the progressive justices' willingness to identify the toxic effects of wealth on democratic representation. Obtaining wealth or gratifying donors for the purpose of campaigns can jeopardize the commitment of party leaders and officials to civic welfare and their constituents. Yet such impairment operates through generally transforming political leaders' ideological and moral commitments to civic interests. In accepting this as a legitimate basis for regulation, *McConnell* internalizes *Austin*'s distortion rationale. This occurs despite *McConnell*'s ostensible commitment to *Buckley*'s original reasoning, with the risk of private wealth identified as erosion of leaders' commitments rather than any direct harm to voter preference formation.

If campaign wealth can make leaders less responsive to the public interest in a non-bribe-like way, then the causal mechanism of such impairment must pass through voters' vulnerability to such funded appeals, or at least their incapacity to hold representatives accountable for generalized plutocratic influence. Elite domination may be how plutocratic corruption operates *in practice* (as discussed below, this is precisely what Lessig, Teachout, and Kuhner warn), but this requires a deeper structural failure in democracy. This structural failure could be traced to voters' ultimate susceptibility to campaign spending; it could also be because campaign financing is an aspect of Schumpeterian elite coordination that facilitates the non-democratic domination of politics.[28] But *McConnell* does not specify which of these alternatives explains its expanded vision of corruption.

When the conservatives began to deconstruct the campaign finance regime, the progressive dissents intimated such a theory of the impact of unequal wealth and a corresponding solution through novel constitutional interpretation. Justice Breyer's *McCutcheon* dissent summarizes this position:

> Corruption breaks the constitutionally necessary chain of communication between the people and their representatives. It derails the essential speech-to-government-action tie. Where enough money calls the tune, the general public will not be heard. Insofar as corruption cuts the link between political thought and political

---

[26] See, e.g., Richard Briffault, "Reforming Campaign Finance Reform: A Review of Voting with Dollars" (2003) 91 *California Law Review* 643, 645 (arguing that even after the BCRA was passed, candidates still needed large donors to be competitive).

[27] See, e.g., Richard L. Hasen, "Buckley is Dead, Long Live Buckley: The New Campaign Finance Incoherence of McConnell v. Federal Election Commission" (2004) 153 *University of Pennsylvania Law Review* 31, 60–3 (criticizing the Court's "blanket calls for deference" toward the legislature in the *McConnell* majority opinion); Bruce Cain, "Reasoning to Desired Outcomes: Making Sense of McConnell v. FEC" (2004) 3 *Election Law Journal* 217 (describing the Court's analysis and backwards reasoning in *McConnell* as political, making the Court susceptible to political control).

[28] Joseph Schumpeter, *Capitalism and Democracy* [1976] (Oxford: Routledge, 2010); Sabeel Rahman, *Democracy against Domination* (Oxford: Oxford University Press, 2017).

action, a free marketplace of political ideas loses its point. That is one reason why the Court has stressed the constitutional importance of Congress' concern that a few large donations not drown out the voices of the many.[29]

The progressives support this theory of diffusive corruption with legal and theoretical commitments that facilitate robust and expansive regulation. The progressives trust Congress to confront the ills of campaign spending, and adjust their level of constitutional scrutiny accordingly.[30] As a normative matter, this goes far beyond technically expanding what a "contribution" means under the *Buckley* formula. When the progressives shifted from addressing the corruption of representatives' motives to the corruption of the system as a whole, this forced them to take a position on the social preconditions of autonomous self-rule in a capitalist democracy. The bedrock theory necessary to sustain this is elaborated in Section 5.3.2.2 below.

5.2.3 *The Conservative Triumph: Libertarian Ideals and Regulatory Anxieties*

Conservatives reacted to the progressives' broad approval of regulation in *McConnell* with a mix of derision and alarm. Justice Thomas went so far as to see *McConnell* as anticipating a totalitarian regime marked by "outright regulation of the press."[31] Justice Kennedy located this concern within constitutional commitments. For example, he maintained that the First Amendment establishes "that the Government cannot be trusted to moderate its own rules for suppression of speech."[32] This suspicion of the state was twinned with the assertion that since additional campaign expenditures can only "convince voters of the correctness of [the spenders'] ideas,"[33] they cannot harm voters. Indeed, where speech is persuasive – whether or not it is funded by wealthy corporate entities or takes the form of vicious attacks on politicians[34] – it is achieving the end intended by the First Amendment. Thus infusions of wealth suit, rather than challenge, a classically liberal understanding of electoral self-determination.

The *McConnell* dissents exemplify the conservative position. Since the electorate (who are "neither sheep nor fools" according to Justice Scalia)[35] cannot be harmed by speech, the only legitimate purpose of campaign finance regulation is to prevent the bribery of representatives. Yet even this legitimate goal must be counterbalanced against what the conservatives perceive to be the greater threat: self-aggrandizing

---

[29] *McCutcheon*, 572 US 185, 237 (2014).
[30] *McConnell*, 540 US at 137.
[31] Ibid., at 283 (Thomas, dissenting), 355 (Rehnquist, dissenting, doubted that the Court would permit regulation of the press even though it is the logical consequence of *McConnell's* reasoning).
[32] Ibid., at 288 (Kennedy, dissenting).
[33] Ibid., at 274 (Thomas, dissenting).
[34] Ibid., at 261 (Scalia, dissenting).
[35] Ibid., at 258 (Scalia, dissenting).

state censorship. When incumbent representatives pass legislation that regulates the very speech that could threaten their own positions, that threat is strongest, as the representatives have both the opportunity and the incentive to curate speech to their own advantage.[36] Given this concern, while the conservatives (aside from Thomas) accept the *Buckley* anti-corruption rationale, they are skeptical of any expansive conception of corruption.

When Justice Alito replaced O'Connor in 2006, this gave the conservatives a majority that has since aggressively pruned the campaign finance regime. The first shot across the bow was *FEC v. Wisconsin Right to Life (WRTL II)*. This case considered an as-applied challenge to a limitation of corporate electioneering under Section 203 of BCRA. The ads, funded by a non-profit corporation, mentioned candidates by name but did not explicitly advocate voting for or against them. The conservatives concluded this was "not the 'functional equivalent' of express campaign speech,"[37] could not act as a *quid* in a bribe transaction,[38] and thus could not be legitimately regulated. Underlying Justice Roberts' majority opinion was suspicion of speech regulation that attenuates the possibility of directly hijacking representatives through bribery, and of any anti-bribery rationale that can only be explained by stringing together an elaborate daisy chain of corrupting influence.[39] As the progressive view makes clear, this concern of chained corruption justifies regulation to address the distortion of politics through unequal use of wealth, but such regulation cannot be integrated into the classical *Buckley* anticorruption framework. Justice Scalia was blunter in accusing representatives of self-serving legislation. He maintains that the electioneering restriction allowed representatives to "muzzle…a small, grassroots organization" to prevent criticism of politicians.[40]

Three years later in *Citizens United v. FEC*, the regulation of corporate electioneering met its predictable fate. Considering a challenge to the same provision at issue in *Wisconsin Right to Life*, a five-justice conservative majority declared it an unconstitutional restriction of speech and overturned the anti-distortion rationale of *Austin*. *Citizens United* reiterated the familiar conservative logic. Limitations on electioneering speech represent a direct and extensive constraint on speech and lack a material connection to the anti-bribery rationale that has justified such campaign finance measures. Kennedy classified Section 203 as "an outright ban, backed by criminal sanctions…[a] classic example[] of censorship."[41] He invoked

---

[36] See Samuel Issacharoff, "Throwing in the Towel: The Constitutional Morass of Campaign Finance," in Keith Ewing and Samuel Issacharoff (eds.), *Party Funding and Campaign Finance in International Perspective* (London: Bloomsbury Publishing, 2006) at 190 (identifying Scalia's challenge to *McConnell* as incumbent protection, discussed above, as "basically unanswered").
[37] *Federal Election Commission v. Wisconsin Right to Life, Inc.*, 551 US 449 (2007) at 457.
[38] *Ibid.*, at 478.
[39] *Ibid.*, at 479 (expressing suspicion of a "prophylaxis-upon-prophylaxis approach to regulating expression").
[40] *Ibid.*, at 503–4.
[41] *Citizens United*, 558 US at 337.

"mistrust of governmental power"[42] as the touchstone of the First Amendment, and condemned the discretion of the Federal Election Commission to evaluate "what political speech is safe for public consumption."[43] He declared that BCRA gives the state so much power to curate the speech environment that it comprises "censorship to control thought."[44] Scalia likewise rejected the legitimacy of broad state discretion to shape campaigns. His attack on Zephyr Teachout's influential suggestion that the idea of corruption should be expanded beyond narrowly defined bribery to justify campaign finance regulation is particularly revealing. Scalia retorted that "if speech can be prohibited because, in the view of the Government, it leads to 'moral decay' or does not serve 'public ends', then there is no limit to the Government's censorship power."[45]

The conservative majority could have based *Citizens United* exclusively on this distrust of the state. Such a solution would have recognized the Court's specific remit to advance certain constitutional principles while avoiding a broader assertion regarding the appropriate arrangements to address unequal wealth. Neutrality on the broader issue – the uncomfortable dual identities of citizens who are politically equal yet economically stratified – would have shown sensitivity to the judicial role. Yet Kennedy notoriously differentiated non-coordinated expenditures from bribes on the grounds that "influence or access [by donors]…will not cause the electorate to lose faith in our democracy" so long as the mode of influence is not *quid pro quo*.[46] Furthermore, the conservatives embraced the idea that spending on speech (even when the source is a corporate entity) is a social good. Kennedy speculated that corporations may play a unique role in the rapidly evolving communication landscape;[47] Scalia, emphasizing a theme from his *McConnell* dissent, declared "to exclude or impede corporate speech is to muzzle the principal agents of the modern free economy. We should celebrate rather than condemn the addition of this speech to the public debate."[48]

These themes were reiterated in *McCutcheon v. FEC*, in which the five-justice conservative majority struck down a campaign finance limit for lacking a sufficiently close connection to the core *Buckley* rationale. At issue in *McCutcheon* were aggregate limits on contributions. Mirroring *Citizens United*'s doctrinal logic, Justice Roberts concluded that vast sums of money distributed among many different officials and entities do not pose a material threat of *quid pro quo* corruption.[49] He extended *Citizens United*'s logic to observe that the purpose of the First

---

[42] Ibid., at 340.
[43] Ibid., at 336.
[44] Ibid., at 356.
[45] Ibid., at 391.
[46] Ibid., at 360.
[47] Ibid., at 364.
[48] Ibid., at 393.
[49] *McCutcheon*, 572 US at 208, 225.

5.2 The Development of the Campaign Finance Regime

Amendment is to protect individuals against the state – including when the state reflects the will of the majority – rather than to advance any "generalized conception of the public good."⁵⁰

The conservative view goes beyond a vigorous interpretation of the First Amendment to assert a highly competent electorate threatened only by an overbearing state. According to this perspective, any influence that operates through campaigns, including unequal wealth, affects the electorate. And since any such influence is processed by voter decision-making rationality, it is by definition noncoercive. The only way campaign finance money can disrupt politics is by directly hijacking state accountability – *bribery*. If voters are presumed to have complete autonomy in the formation and expression of their preferences, regardless of the informational ecosystem, then it is true that wealth cannot corrupt them. Conversely, when the state intervenes to regulate speech, it directly impinges on voters' ability to gain information and form political views – *censorship*. The only threat to such voters is actual coercion, and the source of such coercion is the state, with its monopoly on violence.

Yet the conservative view poses a paradox. If voters are as capable as the conservatives posit, why are they incapable of using the ballot box to punish the representatives who pass oppressive legislation? Either voters can sort through a complex campaign environment or they are vulnerable to the manipulation of campaigns (which might occur through wealth or through state oppression). If voters are capable, the best shield against dangerous, self-serving legislation is the will of the electorate itself. Being neither "sheep nor fools," voters will be able to identify when legislation is undesirable state oppression, and electorally punish the representatives who passed such noxious legislation. If voters are not wise and capable enough to identify when campaign legislation is noxious, then judicial rights intervention may be necessary – but if voters are not wise and capable, then the influence of unequal wealth on campaigns is likewise a prospective danger, justifying more extensive regulation.

Conservatives might try to escape this dilemma by invoking the Court's constitutional remit. First Amendment rights protection is valuable precisely because it is not subject to the vagaries of typical political process, thereby protecting the ability of minority groups and fringe speakers to advance unpopular views.⁵¹ Yet the practical enforcement of such rights protection must be balanced against its constraint of popularly responsive and accountable policymaking. The dilemma is at its sharpest in the campaign context, as the Court is denying the electorate the "power of self-protection"⁵² against what it has identified as a threat: "corporate domination

---

⁵⁰ Ibid., at 205.
⁵¹ Ibid., at 191 ("Money in politics may at times seem repugnant to some, but so too does much of what the First Amendment vigorously protects. If the First Amendment protects flag burning, funeral protests, and Nazi parades – despite the profound offense such spectacles cause – it surely protects political campaign speech despite popular opposition.").
⁵² *McConnell*, 540 US at 224 (citation omitted).

of the electoral process."[53] This suggests that the electorate may not select its own rules regarding the informational environment of campaigns. Yet the polity has chosen these rules precisely because of the conclusion that corruption or inequality are greater problems than the marginal loss of funded campaign information. Furthermore, in the first instance at least, the polity makes these decisions before any such campaign-modulating legislation is put into force. The result is paradoxical: *the electorate must be prevented, by the counterpopular judiciary, from enjoying the full range of possible political arrangements in order to be free.*

This internal paradox is in effect the obverse of the paradox facing the progressive position. The progressives struggle to explain how campaign expenditures that are not bribe-like can distort politics. They can of course indict the entire campaign infrastructure of democratic self-rule to suggest that voters have lost control over their representatives, and that accountability has broken down. But in this case the flows of campaign funding are only a small intermediate part of this breakdown, which indicts American governance through and through. The conservatives face a parallel problem: how can marginal restrictions on wealth be such a vast threat to democracy if voters are as competent and capable as the conservatives assert?

Conservatives can reply that regardless of these social realities, the Constitution delineates the role of the Court and the norms it must enforce. This position narrows the normative basis of the conservative claim and undermines its gratuitous assertions regarding the beneficial impact of wealth and corporations. But it also allows the conservatives to draw a line in the sand.

However, this justification faces further difficulties. Nothing in campaign finance regulation targets unpopular viewpoints or marginalizes a specific group (other than, arguably, the wealthy, who enjoy disproportionate social power).[54] If the campaign regulations at issue, for example, substantively favored the views of the sitting government or silenced a specific and identifiable class or the capacity of a class of actors, the conservative alarmism of censorship might be more justified. Yet these regulations only modulate the resources those with an economic advantage in a deeply unequal society may deploy. The conservatives assert that the substantive neutrality of campaign finance regulation does not matter. They maintain that since restrictions constrain political speech, the First Amendment's limitation of state power and the logic of politics unequivocally prohibit this type of threat to personal freedom. This proposition only has real force if two conditions are met: (1) such regulation is a toehold for substantive censorship and (2) the Court (or some other institution, such as the electorate) would be unable to intervene to prevent further expansion. In short, the conservative view is only plausible if it is the beginning of a slippery slope that will in fact lead to "outright regulation of the press" (and which cannot be stopped at any point along the way).

---

[53] *Citizens United*, 558 US at 475 (Stevens, J., dissenting).
[54] Aaron Tang, "Reverse Political Process Theory" (2017) 70 *Vanderbilt Law Review* 1427.

If the conservatives cannot demonstrate a genuine threat of creeping censorship, their policy view and constitutional method are one-sided and myopic. Constitutional self-rule is situated in a broader economic and social context. The threat of the state to free speech cannot be considered wholly in isolation from the impact of wealth – which is created and protected by the state's protections of property, and, as an aspect of this, of the corporate form. Scholars fiercely contest whether the state, as expressive of the popular will, should be imagined as the bedrock of this social organization, or whether individual rights to property and wealth can be imagined in isolation (as a Nozickian might). The Court's function within this framework, and its role in protecting rights, is likewise a matter of the chosen analytic frame (as I discuss extensively in Chapters 1–3). The Court can be imagined as either an originalist guardian of individual liberties or an adaptive participant in the process of self-governance. The former view risks rigidity, while the latter risks transforming the Court into a quasi-regulatory body that lacks political oversight. Both elicit the counterpopular dilemma, and choosing between them requires a foundational justification, rather than the mere presumption that one view is correct. The distortion of self-governance by unequal wealth and plutocratic influence is the type of factor that might influence which frame is selected.

5.3 PRECONDITIONS OF FREEDOM: THE JUDICIAL STRUGGLE OVER AUTONOMOUS SOCIAL ORGANIZATION

The conservative and progressive approaches to campaign finance reflect irreconcilable starting presumptions and divergent core anxieties. This section seeks to identify the point of consensus in the campaign finance debate – facilitating voter self-rule. Contestation over freedom thereby provides the lens for understanding the campaign finance debate.

5.3.1 *Points of Divergence*

The claim that autonomy best frames campaign finance may seem to marginalize the conventional analysis of the hard-fought doctrine. This is most apparent in the fever pitch of *Citizens United*. While Kennedy recognized in his majority opinion that he had to overrule *Austin*, he justified this by characterizing *Austin* (and anything from *McConnell* that rests upon it) as an anomalous outlier. The conservatives sought to establish their conclusion as the only appropriate heir to the jurisprudence, systemically undermining even marginal comments in any prior opinions that might be used to vindicate restrictions on corporate speech.[55] Yet Justice Steven's *Citizens United* dissent defends *Austin*'s with the same fervor, characterizing the conservative

---

[55] *Citizens United*, 558 US at 358.

view as "a dramatic break from our past"[56] and at odds with a long legacy of permitting congressional legislation that limited "undue influence"[57] from corporate speech. The same dissonance can be identified in the different treatments of modes of legal analysis. While this divergence reflects the long-running conservative–progressive dispute over methodology exemplified by the originalism versus living constitutionalism divide, the two factions disagree even over what these approaches mean on their own terms (particularly the Framers' intent with regard to corruption).[58]

The mid-level concepts at issue manifest similar dissonance. Corruption has become the fulcrum of campaign finance law, but the two factions assign it different meanings. The conservatives define corruption narrowly as illicit *quid pro quo* transactions – trades of public power for private gain. This view accords with the traditional social science meaning of corruption.[59] Progressive scholars have championed their view by conceiving of corruption as diffuse undue influence or distortion. Lawrence Lessig and Zephyr Teachout, building on work by Dennis Thompson, have defined corruption as non-specific interruption of the relationship between the franchise and the representative.[60] Insofar as the campaign finance jurisprudence reflects a meaningful debate, it cannot be about corruption, because the two sides use the word to describe different phenomena. Other concepts in the debate likewise reveal vast substantive divergence. Conservatives posit that corporations are legitimate participants in political discourse, and progressives respond by arguing that corporations in fact pose a greater threat as conduits of inequality, and as such deserve less vigorous rights protection.[61] This type of descriptive divergence is repeated, for example, in the way the contribution–expenditure divide should be conceived.[62] What progressives treat as contribution-like corporate funding the conservatives define as mere speech-advancing expenditures.

---

[56] Ibid., at 394.
[57] Ibid., at 449 (Stevens, dissenting).
[58] Ibid., at 432 (Stevens, dissenting) (suggesting the majority opinion disregards the Framers' substantive commitments); cf. 353, 387 (Scalia, concurring) (suggesting the progressive view engages in a "bait and switch" between the content of the First Amendment and the Framers' view of the corporations).
[59] The most influential definition of corruption as *quid pro quo* is J. S. Nye, "Corruption and Political Development: A Cost-Benefit Analysis" (1967) 61 *American Political Science Review* 417, which has been broadly adopted in the social science scholarship. Nye's definition of exchanging public benefit for private gain may be somewhat broader than the "narrow, crabbed view" in *Citizens United*, but it is certainly closer to the conservative view than the progressive view. Richard L. Hasen, "Citizens United and the Illusion of Coherence" (2011) 109 *Michigan Law Review* 581, 583.
[60] Lawrence Lessig, *Republic, Lost: How Money Corrupts Congress – And a Plan to Stop it* (New York: Twelve, 2012); Zephyr Teachout, *Corruption in America: From Benjamin Franklin's Snuff Box to Citizens United* (Cambridge: Harvard University Press, 2015). But see Seth Barrett Tillman, "Citizens United and the Scope of Professor Teachout's Anti-Corruption Principle" (2015) 107 *Northwestern University Law Review* 399 (querying the extent of the principle).
[61] *Citizens United*, 558 US at 466.
[62] Ibid., at 436 (progressive view that a ban on corporate contributions is well established); cf. 558 US at 379 (relying on the contribution–expenditure divide as the first principle that justifies rejecting *Austin*).

5.3 The Judicial Struggle over Social Organization

Scholars have framed the broader struggle as a confrontation between egalitarian and libertarian worldviews. The progressive (egalitarian) position argues that democracy is fundamentally a project between equals who should aspire to richly engaged, mutually regarding self-rule; thus campaigns should be regulated to reflect this ideal.[63] This mutualist, civically substantive vision, which resonates with civic republicanism, validates limiting the impact of wealth and advancing an ethos of self-rule that prizes cooperation among equals. The libertarian (conservative) position asserts that politics is competitive and zero-sum and thus campaigns can do no more than provide information to voters who make rational but typically self-interested or faction-serving decisions.[64] The libertarian position is compatible with a conception of democracy as interest group pluralism. Libertarians are skeptical of campaign finance regulations that aggrandize a particular ideological agenda (even one as laudable as egalitarianism). They perceive such regulations as just another lever in cutthroat power politics. Scholars have offered many related conceptions that track or contextualize this distinction. For example, Dworkin differentiates between a competitive theory of "majoritarian" democracy and a richly civic "partnership" conception.[65] Jim Gardner differentiates between a "tabulative" understanding of electoral process that simply aggregates citizen's self-interested preferences and a "deliberative" conception that seeks to use campaigns to reach consensus through reason.[66] There are analogues to these conceptions of campaigns in democratic theory more generally. For example, Richard Posner and Jürgen Habermas offer ideologically opposed schemas of democracy that correspond to egalitarian and libertarian positions.[67]

When campaign finance jurisprudence is located within systematizing, ideologically expansive theories of democracy, it becomes a useful lens on general theory. But it does little to identify the unique nature of campaign finance law on its own

---

[63] Salient examples include J. Skelly Wright, "Money and the Pollution of Politics: Is the First Amendment an Obstacle to Political Equality" (1982) 82 *Columbia Law Review* 609; Frank Pasquale, "Reclaiming Egalitarianism in the Political Theory of Campaign Finance Reform" (2008) *University of Illinois Law Review* 599; Edward B. Foley, "Philosophy, the Constitution, and Campaign Finance" (1999) 10 *Stanford Law & Policy Review* 23. This view is more broadly associated with civic republicanism as a democratic ideal. See Frank I. Michelman, "Law's Republic" (1988) 97 *Yale Law Journal* 1493, 1495; Cass R. Sunstein, "Beyond the Republican Revival" (1988) 97 *Yale Law Journal* 1539, 1576–89.

[64] Kathleen M. Sullivan provides a relatively sympathetic account of this constitutional legacy in "Two Concepts of Freedom of Speech" (2010) 124 *Harvard Law Review* 143, 158. Bruce Cain demonstrates that this contrast has been long established. Bruce E. Cain, *Moralism and Realism in Campaign Finance Reform*, (1995) 1995 *University of Chicago Legal Forum* 111, 122.

[65] Ronald Dworkin, *Sovereign Virtue: The Theory and Practice of Equality* (Cambridge, MA: Harvard University Press, 2002), pp. 357–8.

[66] Jim Gardner, *What Are Campaigns For? The Role of Persuasion in Electoral Law and Politics* (Oxford: Oxford University Press, 2009), p. 3.

[67] Richard A. Posner, *Law, Pragmatism and Democracy* (Cambridge: Harvard University Press, 2003), pp. 130–212; cf. Jürgen Habermas, "Three Normative Models of Democracy" (1994) 1 *Constellations* 1 (describing "republican" and "liberal" models that correspond to Posner's "Concept 1" and "Concept 2," respectively).

terms. Moreover, concluding that campaign finance can only reflect competition between contrasting ideologies suggests a dire future for the law.

5.3.2 *The Aspiration of Campaign Finance Law: An Autonomous (not Heteronomous) Electorate*

Given that the factions within the Court are at substantive loggerheads, identifying the point of convergence in campaign finance law, and thus the true core of the doctrine, requires examining the basic purpose of campaigns in elections. Campaigns are meant to help voters engage in free self-rule. Thus, the mutual aspiration of both the progressives and conservatives is to protect voters' political autonomy from the most dangerous threat; they merely disagree over what this threat is.

5.3.2.1 Autonomy and Heteronomy

Autonomy is the linchpin of this book. It is the core of individual morality,[68] a central value that political regimes must reflect and advance in their relationship with the members of the polity,[69] and the seminal quality of moral standing considering the polity as a self-defined entity.[70] Autonomy is lost when outside circumstances or influences dominate or dictate a path or outcome. This state of being determined by outside forces is heteronomy. The point of transition from autonomous to heteronomous is itself highly contested, and perhaps mysterious.[71]

Under liberal democracy, meaningful personal discretion is necessary for freedom – at a minimum, the absence of threats of physical violence or extreme material privation.[72] Responses to such coercive external conditions render a person heteronomous. Likewise, for a polity to be autonomous, it must choose its own course of affairs through an internal political process. As in the individual context,

---

[68] Immanuel Kant, *Groundwork for the Metaphysics of Morals*, Mary Gregor (trans.), 4th ed. (Cambridge: Cambridge University Press, 1998).
[69] John Rawls, *A Theory of Justice* (Cambridge, MA: Harvard University Press, 1999); John Rawls, *Political Liberalism* (New York: Columbia University Press, 1996).
[70] Philip Pettit, *Republicanism: A Theory of Freedom and Government* (Oxford: Oxford University Press, 1997).
[71] Even a materialist determinist such as Hobbes recognizes blunt physical restraint as a condition of unfreedom. Thomas Hobbes, *Leviathan: Or the Matter, Forme and Power of a Commonwealth, Ecclesiasticall and Civil* (1650), ed. Michael Oakeshott (New York: Simon and Schuster, 1997). Some philosophical traditions, such as Stoicism, would argue that the only form of freedom is correct alignment of the mind or soul in a fundamentally coercive phenomenal world. See Peter Garnsey, *Ideas of Slavery from Aristotle to Augustine* (Cambridge: Cambridge University Press, 1996). This has relatively little bite in the practice of contemporary democratic politics.
[72] Hobbes, "Leviathan," p. 103. is committed to a wholly negative theory of freedom, and famously argues that even an agreement in response to immediate physical violence is in fact freely given. For a more extensive account of Hobbes's treatment of freedom as internally coherent, if fundamentally deterministic, see David van Mill, *Liberty, Rationality, and Agency in Hobbes's Leviathan* (Albany: State University of New York Press, 2001).

the line between a state that autonomously self-rules as sovereign and one that is heteronomously ruled as a subject is contestable. A polity whose policies are formally set by a superior and unaccountable entity is not sovereign, but an unequivocally heteronomous subject or colony. A polity whose foremost goal is appeasing an economically or militarily imposing neighboring state may be formally autonomous but is practically heteronomous.

This puzzle is the subject of the most compelling account of freedom in modern Western philosophy.[73] Immanuel Kant declares "autonomy of the will is the property of the will by which it is a law to itself (independently of any property of the objects of volition)."[74] Or as Steven Darwall synthesizes, "there is a distinctive moral goodness that can be achieved only by a morally autonomous agent, one who self-reflectively governs herself as a moral agent by her own moral convictions."[75] A person is free (and acts morally) when the sole basis of their conduct is the cognitively reflective conformity of will to self-made law. When a person acts – or, perhaps more instructively, *reacts* – to an outside influence or consideration other than reasoned contemplation of morality, "heteronomy always results."[76] When conduct is reactive to such external conditions, it is by definition unfree.

Kant's account exposes the problem of heteronomy. What does it mean for a person to act only according to self-made law? A realistic account of human motivation primarily explains decisions as reactive to the outside world. Individuals' political decisions are influenced by their personal values, social identity, and self-interested incentives. They vote based on what they believe, what groups they ally themselves with, and what they think will be most personally beneficial.[77] Yet according to Kant, such political decisions are unfree. When persons act in response to such motivations, they are not internally guided by reason (the sole basis of morality) but rather subordinate to (morally arbitrary) circumstance. Because they are responding to the outside world, their conduct is as heteronomous as a person who responds to an immediate physical threat or is physically restrained.

---

[73] Kant has an ancient parallel in Plato, who indicates that freedom (and justice) consist of the conformity of human thought and action to reason. *Republic*, Paul Shorey (trans.), 441e in Edith Hamilton and Huntington Cairns (eds.), *The Collected Dialogues of Plato* (New York: Pantheon Books, 1961). In justifying why conformity to reason (as opposed to another impulse, particularly appetite) yields freedom, Plato faces the same basic problem as Kant: why is conformity to whatever informs reason itself not a type of heteronomy? His answer, articulated in the last books of the *Republic*, while less intricate than Kant's, may have the same metaphysical foundations: reason has a type of spiritual (or noumenal) origin. See R. F. Stalley, "Plato's Doctrine of Freedom" (1998) 98 *Proceedings of the Aristotelian Society* 145.

[74] Kant, "Groundwork," p. 47, 4:440.

[75] Stephen Darwall, "The Value of Autonomy and Autonomy of the Will" (2006) 116 *Ethics* 263, 272.

[76] Kant, "Groundwork," p. 48; 4:441.

[77] Darwall, "The Value of Autonomy," 272 explains, some theorists such as Hume are contrasted with Kant by identifying morality by the quality of motivations rather than conformity to an abstract moral rule.

The challenge posed by the Kantian understanding of heteronomy is that it constrains the range of action that is morally free to an infinitesimally narrow range. Almost every reason that motivates individuals to act is externally determined by the stringent Kantian test and is thus heteronomous – and morally arbitrary. As Thomas Nagel summarizes, "The area of genuine agency, and therefore of legitimate moral judgment, seems to shrink under this scrutiny to an extensionless point. Everything seems to result from the combined influence of factors, antecedent and posterior to action, that are not within the agent's control."[78] Kant himself has a sophisticated but onerously demanding and philosophically intricate solution: the will is free when it acts in accordance with universal law that abstracts from particular circumstances and only considers what would be moral *regardless* of particular contingent circumstances. This solution – which echoes the Rawlsian veil of ignorance as a tool for the design of just societies – demands that persons completely abjure incorporating personal features (let alone self-interest) into decision-making.

This brief survey of one of the most studied problems in philosophy sets the stage for a reconsideration of the campaign finance debate. No realistic lawyer, legal scholar, or judge deploys the stringency of the Kantian test of autonomy to assign moral weight to political freedom. Yet a softened version of the autonomy–heteronomy distinction is useful because legal thinkers are typically interested in identifying the *realistic* point at which it is appropriate to determine when a person acts freely as opposed to when they act in a manner that is heteronomously determined by external circumstances. Both personal moral significance and legal responsibility are assigned where a person is deemed to act freely.

How unequal wealth in campaigns, or its regulation by the state, threatens political autonomy is the heart of the law. Progressives are concerned that the decisions of a monied elite, rather than the properly reasoned choices of the electorate, will overdetermine political outcomes – precisely the type of domination that characterizes heteronomy in a polity that adheres to democratic norms. Conservatives worry that state censorship may prevent citizens from freely forming views about candidates' political views. Both are concerned about some power (wealthy elites, or the state) outside of self-determining popular will hijacking the course of politics. Both of these outcomes involve the domination of political choice by an illegitimate, binding outside influence: heteronomy.

5.3.2.2 The Progressive Position: Political Heteronomy from the Influence of Wealth

Progressives argue that unequal campaign money somehow degrades popular control of representation. Yet campaign spending does not *coercively* interrupt this relationship in the way that voter suppression does, for instance. Regardless of how

---

[78] Thomas Nagel, *Mortal Questions* (New York: Cambridge University Press, 1979), p. 35.

much campaign speech there is funded by those with disproportionate wealth, voters can still select their preferred representatives; and if they suspect their representatives of being corrupt or in the pocket of wealthy interests, they can eject them. The progressive opinions do not clearly articulate how wealth could nonetheless deprive constituents of their autonomy. Progressive assertions of "undue influence" and the "corrosive effects of wealth" imply, but do not specify, how this deprivation occurs. *Austin* suggests it occurs through the operation of wealth upon the electorate; *McConnell* hews more closely to the *Buckley* rationale by suggesting that representatives are influenced by money even when they are not directly bribed.[79] Progressive dissents are more plaintive, but still do not address the mechanics of autonomy deprivation. The presence of excessive wealth in campaigns destroys the "'chain of communication' between the people and their representatives" and ruptures "the link between [public opinion] and [governmental] action."[80] These indicate a symptom of unequal wealth: The loss of popular control over politics. But beyond vague assertions of popular "cynicism"[81] and diffused corruption of leaders' motives, progressives fail to provide a particularized causal account of how wealth dominates governance.

A claim of heteronomy must point to an external force that determines an otherwise free agent. This explains the appeal of *Buckley*'s concern with corruption, because one clearly illegitimate way in which wealth could render a democratic polity heteronomous is through the bribery of representatives. The causal account is unequivocal: those who bribe the representatives rule the people, rather than the people ruling themselves. For all its analytic deficiencies, this explanatory clarity is the virtue of *Buckley*. Yet the progressive position is that wealth can dictate governance through some other means.

Progressive scholars have pursued three approaches to address this lacuna. The first group has worked within the *Buckley* tradition to advocate a more expansive conception of corruption. Sympathetic to *McConnell*'s "undue influence" concept, these "institutional corruption" scholars argue that wealth can hijack governance through a mechanism other than direct bribery. Lessig describes a type of corruption in which the power of money in politics makes representatives dependent on some influence other than the will of the people.[82] Lessig concedes that such corruption (what he calls "dependence corruption") is less causally granular than *quid pro quo*. It can take entrenched structural forms such as "preliminary primaries" that vet candidate viability according to how much money they have raised instead of their popularity with the franchise. Dependence corruption can also take more subtle forms, such as pervasive anxiety that wealthy donors may intercede to

---

[79] *McConnell*, 540 US at 143, 185, 205.
[80] *McCutcheon*, 134 US at 1467 (Breyer, dissenting).
[81] Ibid., at 1468 (Breyer, dissenting).
[82] Lessig, "Republic Lost," p. 231.

influence campaigns if candidates do not do enough to appease them.[83] Teachout vividly describes how such influence can operate. As the prospect of private self-enrichment infiltrates representatives' minds, "Congress is now dominated by people who are casting a longing eye on highly paid lobbying jobs."[84] The result of such prospective "gifts" looming in the future is that representatives will cease to serve their constituents, and instead aggrandize prospective benefactors[85] – including by participating in a money-dominated campaign finance regime. The Court's narrow definition of corruption in *Citizens United* has insulated the diffuse influence of wealth from constitutionally permissible regulation.

According to the second group of progressive scholars, "anti-plutocrats," socio-economic inequality may generally disrupt accountable politics. Ganesh Sitaraman has argued that "economic inequality" inevitably translates into "political inequality" and rigs the political system. One aspect of a rigged system is inculcated allegiance (rather than outright bribery) of representatives to wealthy donors rather than the franchise.[86] Sitaraman further argues that the Constitution includes economic equality as a substantive value; deviation from this equality is intrinsically pathological (and unfree).[87] Courts could address inequality in campaign finance spending by querying how a given regime contributes to inequality with knock-on political effects. In a vein evocative of civic republicanism, Sabeel Rahman has argued that unequal economic power yields domination, "concentrati[ng] arbitrary power [to] undermine[] economic freedom and opportunity for individuals and communities."[88] Rahman elaborates that this domination can occur through either direct oppression (dyadic domination) or systemic conditions that prevent individuals from realizing their true liberty (structural domination).[89] Likewise, Joseph Fishkin and William Forbath argue that excessive inequality generates oligarchic political as well as economic relationships, and that oligarchic wealth has long posed a tangible threat to democratic self-rule. They further argue that there is a long tradition in America of addressing such threats through constitutionally legitimate regulation.[90] These anti-plutocrat accounts characterize inequality in

---

[83] *Ibid.*, pp. 232–4; Lawrence Lessig, "What an Originalist Would Understand 'Corruption' to Mean" (2014) 102 *California Law Review* 1.
[84] Teachout, "Corruption in American" p. 247.
[85] *Ibid.*, p. 253.
[86] Ganesh Sitaraman, *The Crisis of the Middle-Class Constitution: Why Economic Inequality Threatens Our Republic* (New York: Alfred A. Knopf, 2017), p. 247.
[87] *Ibid.*, pp. 5, 224.
[88] Sabeel Rahman, *Democracy against Domination* (Oxford: Oxford University Press, 2017), p. 80.
[89] Rahman, "Democracy against Domination," pp. 82–6. It could be argued that Rahman's analysis could be parsed along the negative/positive liberty divide advanced by Isaiah Berlin, *Two Concepts of Liberty* (Oxford: Oxford University Press, 2002) in that preventing dyadic domination simply requires the lack of obstruction whereas preventing structural domination requires actively facultative conditions.
[90] Joseph Fishkin and William E. Forbath, "The Anti-Oligarchy Constitution" (2014) 94 *Boston University Law Review* 671.

campaign funding as reflecting a deeper problem. Economic elites convert their privileged financial status into political power. Campaign financing is among the blunter instruments that economic elites use to achieve this conversion. It gives elites a means of exerting control over politicians and signaling which ones they favor. It may also allow elites to collectively signal their priorities to leaders. Antiplutocrats share much ground with those who offer a broader definition of corruption but are distinguished by their suggestion that the pathology of unequal wealth is pervasively systemic, rather than an interruption of specific relationships of political accountability.

The third group of scholars maintains that campaign spending might corrupt voters themselves. This perspective challenges the presumption of voter capacity that underlies liberal democracy, and scholars as well as the judiciary have been reluctant to advance it. The exception is Timothy Kuhner, who argues that "the judgment that corporate advertising campaigns are good for democracy rests on the assumption that citizens are sophisticated political consumers who are not easily manipulated or misled by big spenders."[91] Because individuals are malleable and responsive to conditions, they are the real locus of plutocratic manipulation of democracy. This occurs not only when voters are bombarded with media that disproportionately advocates certain viewpoints, but also when voters acclimate to a political environment dominated by market-style relationships. In Kuhner's view, *Citizens United* blessed this type of market logic, most explicitly by recognizing that influence via wealth is a legitimate aspect of democratic governance. In a diverse society beset by vast gulfs in economic power, market logic deviates from the democratic ideal of autonomous equals ruling one another. At the extreme, individuals who are "socialized under neoliberal conditions" undergo a moral transformation into civically and morally vacant "*homo economicus*."[92] Such persons are not only more vulnerable to the appeals of plutocratically funded campaigns; they are committed to a view of social organization that prizes rapacious capitalism over civic virtue.

A deeper explanatory link is missing in each of these narratives: *how* campaign money obstructs constituent self-rule. If money can somehow infiltrate and disrupt democratic self-rule, the story cannot be as simple as "those with unequal wealth were able to exert illegitimate political control." There must be a prior, purely political feature that explains *how* wealth was able to intrude into the sphere of political autonomy. From an abstract perspective, political autonomy indicates that a state's governance is directed by and accountable to the legitimate source of instruction. In a liberal democracy, where the people rule themselves as free equals, this means the state is guided by (and responsive to) the voters. If some other influence is capable of

---

[91] Timothy K. Kuhner, *Capitalism v. Democracy: Money in Politics and the Free Market Constitution* (Palo Alto: Stanford University Press, 2014), p. 173.
[92] Timothy K. Kuhner, *Tyranny of Greed: Trump, Corruption, and the Revolution to Come* (Palo Alto: Stanford University Press, 2020), p. 111.

directing politics, there is a prior, distinctly political flaw that allows non-legitimate influences (i.e. an entity other than popular will) to guide politics.

Thus, the assertion that "wealth (or unequal wealth) hijacks democratic politics" must be the compression of two steps. The first is that democratic politics must have some general vulnerability or susceptibility to non-legitimate influence (i.e. influence other than the sole legitimate influence in democracy, popular self-determination). This initial vulnerability or susceptibility of some aspect of governance to non-legitimate influence is a prerequisite for the second step. This second step is identifying the specific pathological effects of wealth – and explaining how it is *internal* to governance. In other words, it is a flaw within the condition of a democracy as politically autonomous. This internal susceptibility is what permits an external intruding force, like wealth, to disrupt politics.

A return to the Kantian understanding of morality clarifies the problematic nature of this progressive causal story. According to Kant, personal moral autonomy requires an individual's conduct to be guided by conformity to self-willed, moral law that is independent of circumstance. He would argue that a person is rendered heteronomous *not* because they are susceptible to a particular influence, but because they react to a contingent external influence at all. For a person to be heteronomous, the first characteristic is not susceptibility to a particular contingent influence, but the person's preconditional failure to adhere to self-willed morality. This general loss of autonomy (i.e. failure to adhere to moral law as the determinant of conduct) creates an opportunity for a *particular* circumstance to hold sway over the individual. This circumstance need not be visibly morally "bad" to render a person heteronomous. A person is obviously rendered heteronomous when they give into a vicious appetite such as sadism and follow that instead of moral instruction. Yet, they are also heteronomous if they perform an action that may seem outwardly "good," such as donating to charity, because of an emotional pull. In both cases, the person is subordinate to an outside circumstance instead of a servant to moral law. This general susceptibility to outside circumstances is a critical failing in individual moral decision-making. This failing is internal to the person's moral adherence to self-willed law and distinct from the impact of the outside influence (whether a vicious appetite or a noble sentiment) that later manifests that failing.

Translating this analogy into politics, a democratic system is expected to retain its moral legitimacy when it is guided by appropriate influence – the will of the franchise. This is the democratic equivalent of personal adherence to self-willed law. Much as a person is morally autonomous only when they adhere to self-made law, a democratic polity is politically autonomous only when popular will is the sole source of governance (which explains the applicability of the counterpopular dilemma). When a democratic polity is governed by a non-popular source of power, this is the condition of heteronomy – even if this non-popular source seems to yield beneficial policy (say, a benevolent bureaucrat who intervenes to override a less expert or prudent democratic will). The initial precondition in this heteronomy, however, is not the intervention of the outside source, but rather the breakdown in democratic accountability. This occurs *internal* to democratic politics. If money dominates democratic governance, it must "take advantage" of some internal political breakdown in democracy that has already made it heteronomous, in the same way, a contingent influence exerts heteronomizing power on a person due to their prior failure to adhere to moral law.

Synthesizing the scholarly progressive explanations clarifies the practical implications of this observation. According to progressive accounts, there are two ways that money makes democratic politics heteronomous: hijacking of leadership and influencing voters. Yet for money to have these effects, there must be an initial characteristic, internal to the values of democracy, that deviates from political autonomy for any actor. For leaders, that feature is straightforward. They must already have abandoned a commitment to accountability and service to the electorate as their polestar. The initial failing of the intrusion of wealth through hijacking leadership is not the impact of money, but a deviation from good service that makes leaders susceptible to *any* non-accountable influence. This explanation broadly parallels Lessig's idea of dependence corruption, which posits that leaders' susceptibility to such influence has already made democratic politics heteronomous. The essence of this moral-political heteronomy is that leaders' delegated use of state power is no longer directed toward the correct source, the will of the constituency. The intrusion of wealth is the second step in this process. Given the interdependent relationship between economic and political power in a liberal capitalist democracy, it is unsurprisingly a prominent influence. But it can only act by exploiting a preliminary deviation of leaders from a commitment to accountable governance that is necessary for democratic autonomy.

For voters, the initial step of heteronomy is more mysterious. Realistically, voters must be assumed to have a reasonable level of cognitive competence and personal autonomy for democracy to work. For voters to be undermined by the influence of money indicates the limit of this cognitively based personal autonomy. For the influence of campaign spending *specifically* to undermine voter autonomy, there must be some *general* conditions that can render voters *personally* heteronomous; campaign spending is simply one example. In Kantian terms, there must be an initial capacity for the loss of rational political decision-making that campaign finance somehow activates. Some conditions that would strip away this rationality (i.e. direct threats of violence at polling stations) are non-controversial. Yet recognizing a limit to free conduct based on simply exposure to disproportionate media or a diffusely capitalist ecosystem is in tension with liberal understandings of self-rule (though some scholars would assert that the preconditions for mutualist, egalitarian self-rule were never truly present).[93]

---

[93] See, e.g., Martin Gilens, *Economic Inequality and Politics Power in America* (Princeton: Princeton University Press, 2012); Bertrall L. Ross II and Douglas M. Spencer, "Passive Voter Suppression: Campaign Mobilization and the Effective Disfranchisement of the Poor" (2019) 114 *Northwestern University Law Review* 633; Burt Neuborne, "Money and American Democracy," in Paul D.

This theoretical analysis does nothing to challenge the prospective accuracy of the progressive accounts. Much descriptive social science has shown that democratic governance is to some degree heteronomously overdetermined by wealthy elites, rather than autonomously determined by popular will. Yet progressives still must offer a more explicit account of the initial step by which politics becomes susceptible to such outside influence. Lessig's account of wealth-driven shadow primaries provides a compelling explanation of how wealthy donors can influence policy by pre-vetting candidates, largely through indirect cooperation with the party system. His narrative explains how the polity is heteronomous insofar as any candidates presented to voters have already been approved by a wealthy elite, and thus the franchise does not in fact choose freely. Yet his account does not adequately explain what political factors make candidates susceptible to non-democratic forces in the first place. Lessig uses an analogy of funder vetting via racist "White" primaries to establish that deviation from democratic values has long been an unfortunate feature of American politics.[94] Yet for this to be true, there must be some failing or defect in the accountability of the democratic selection process that illegitimate factors exploit to render the franchise heteronomous. The representatives must in the first instance fail to obey democratic accountability. Lessig does not specify what this failing is; he only indicates that it occurs, and that money is the particular non-democratic influence to which leaders are beholden. Leaders, and a system of representative selection committed to democratic autonomy, would ignore such illegitimate outside influences in the same way that a person of moral integrity only obeys self-made moral law. While wealth may be the temptation that has captured political elites, there must be an initial democratic failure that makes the state prospectively responsive to factors other than a popular will. This is the great unanswered challenge facing both progressive jurists and scholars. It must be answered in a manner that continues to sustain the basic premises and plausibility of democratic autonomy.

The great project for the progressive account is to explain what type of political arrangements would satisfy democratic autonomy, and then show what internal political failure makes the polity vulnerable to heteronomy in general. This would explain how money can become the particularly dangerous heteronomous influence. To date, progressive scholars have offered superficial descriptions of the effects of money, elaborating on the symptoms without identifying the underlying disease. Furthermore, as discussed in Section 5.4 below, this account would then need to be integrated into a specific account of why the nature of the heteronomy at issue is of *constitutional* importance and why it should be addressed through judicial interpretation. Reformers could fairly argue that the loss of autonomy by the

---

Carrington and Trina Jones (eds.), *Law and Class in America* (New York: New York University Press, 2006), p. 37 (observing that the campaign finance system perpetuates a historically elitist and discriminatory American power structure).

[94] Lessig, "What an Originalist Would Understand 'Corruption' to Mean," 16.

electorate occurs in a context of blurred distinctions between economic and political power, populated by elites who rotate between the private and public spheres. Yet an explanation of how money can deprive the electorate's political autonomy must differentiate between legitimate political and illegitimate economic influences; simply asserting that the two are impossibly tangled makes effective regulation and constitutionally bounded judicial intervention impossible.

Two final contextualizing features reinforce the idea that the source of the problem cannot be unequal wealth, but instead some failure internal to political self-governance. First, wealth is channeled through (and organized by) the state. Corporations are a creation of the state that are granted special legal rights; modifying their legal standing would be just as effective as implementing campaign finance regulation. Second, fiat currency and the presence of wealth are not (unless one is a committed Nozickian property rights libertarian) a freestanding social phenomenon, but structured by politics. If the electorate is politically autonomous, it has ample tools with which to control the presence of wealth. If the electorate is not capable of doing so, this represents a far more damning structural failure of politics.

5.3.2.3 The State and Heteronomy

The conservative anxiety is more direct: tyranny. Thomas's concern is that the "chilling endpoint" of a permissive attitude toward campaign finance regulation is "outright regulation of the press;"[95] Kennedy's is that the electioneering ban "silence[s] entities whose voices the Government deems to be suspect;"[96] and Scalia's is that a broadened understanding of corruption would produce "no limit to the Government's censorship power."[97] The conservative opinions in *Citizens United* and *McCutcheon* assert that the First Amendment provides a critical bulwark against such tyrannical state power by creating a constitutional barrier, "[p]remised on mistrust of governmental power,"[98] that "afford individuals protections against such infringements."[99] Conservative fears of an oppressive state evoke a foundational concern in American constitutional design. How can democratic representatives be prevented from using their delegated, conditionally held power to dominate the polity they are meant to serve? Vast swaths of the Constitution are understood to serve this purpose – the protection of individual rights, the separation of powers (which makes the representatives compete, rather than cooperate), and federalism.[100]

---

[95] *McConnell*, 540 US at 284.
[96] *Citizens United*, 558 US at 339.
[97] Ibid., at 391.
[98] Ibid., at 340.
[99] *McCutcheon*, 572 US at 206.
[100] For a high-level account of these features, see Tom Ginsberg and Aziz Z. Huq, *How to Save a Constitutional Democracy* (Chicago: University of Chicago Press, 2019), pp. 8–14.

If the state abuses its power to dominate the electorate, it inverts the relationship by which an autonomous franchise controls the state. State control of the people is unequivocal heteronomy. According to conservatives, campaign finance threatens this ill. If the state uses its power to regulate the speech that determines which future leaders the electorate selects, current leaders control the terms of their own selection. This in turn violates the fundamental purpose of elections, which is to allow voters to freely select leaders, not to give leaders a pretext to retain power. This possibility underlies the concern that campaign finance regulation will be used to "lock up" elections.[101] Bradley Smith raises a more direct concern that campaign finance regulation reform "favor[s] certain political elites, support[s] the status quo, and discourage[s] grassroots political activity."[102] Compared to the amount of scholarship dedicated to explaining why the progressive position is the legitimate one, the conservative position has received remarkably little scholarly support, perhaps due to the wide alarm in the academy with the effects of economic inequality, or because the conservative position is, in some respects, fairly straightforward. While the descriptive accuracy of the conservative stance can be challenged, this has primarily taken the form of pointing out the toxic effects of wealth, a critique which dovetails with the progressive position. Yet the directness of this progressive critique shows how the conservative understanding of campaign finance regulation avoids one of the complexities of the progressive account. Unlike the need of the progressive account to locate itself in a society-wide account, the conservative account identifies the abuse of power to regulate campaign finance as internal to politics.

If the conservative case is that campaign finance threatens autonomy more directly, the critique of the conservative position is correspondingly straightforward. The conservative account treats the marginal case of the state addressing a particular facet of campaigns as the one-sided domination of the electorate's autonomy. If campaign regulation at the margins (as opposed to pervasively Orwellian propaganda) can deprive the polity of autonomy, this suggests the electorate's capacity to rule itself is profoundly limited to begin with. The campaign regulations at issue do not achieve a complete (or even especially dramatic) deprivation of political freedom. Voters still have the autonomy to eject representatives through the ballot box; indeed, they would be expected to do so if they conclude representatives have made moves toward tyranny in campaign finance legislation. None of the legislation at issue squelches dissent in a manner typically associated with tyranny; it merely gives incumbents a marginal advantage.[103] Such marginal advantages would not

---

[101] Issacharoff and Karlan, "The Hydraulics of Campaign Finance Reform."

[102] Bradley A. Smith, "Faulty Assumptions and Undemocratic Consequences of Campaign Finance Reform" (1996) 105 *Yale Law Journal* 1049, 1051.

[103] Issacharoff, "Throwing in the Towel: The Constitutional Morass of Campaign Finance," p. 190 (identifying Scalia's challenge to *McConnell* as incumbent protection, discussed above, as "basically unanswered").

jeopardize the decision-making capacities of a competent, autonomous electorate of the type conservatives posit is capable of processing large amounts of information. Furthermore, most Western democracies *do* regulate campaign speech and have not devolved into tyranny. Conservatives might argue that American democracy is uniquely free and that these other polities are not truly self-determining, but this would challenge common sense.[104]

An electorate that can so easily be rendered heteronomous by campaign circumstances would be far from independently autonomous. Rather, its capacity to rule would itself be contingent on circumstances that, according to the conservatives, are readily disrupted. This suggests either that the political structure is far from intrinsically robust (and is heteronomous on the outside factors necessary to sustain it) or that voters are fragile and require highly curated circumstances to make decisions (and are heteronomous on being provided with these circumstances). Both suggest that the electorate's capacity to rule depends on highly specified conditions beyond the electorate's control. Such a fragile franchise would already be deeply heteronomous.

Further, comparing this fearful conservative vision of state domination with the alternative of the extraordinary influence of private media reveals an internally contradictory view of democracy. If conservatives truly believe that marginally limiting vast expenditures on campaigns represents a threat to democracy, they must believe the franchise's autonomy is extremely fragile. Yet according to the conservative account, this same fragile electorate is capable of processing vast amounts of media and parsing the motive of representatives under the sway of donors. A more sensible and coherent view would be that the electorate either (1) *cannot* be dominated by marginal regulation or (2) *can* be dominated by vastly unequal media.

The strongest conservative argument is that the issue is not the political impact of campaign financing, but rather the appropriate conception of the First Amendment. If, as the progressives argue, the First Amendment were reconceived to include the state's theory of good governance, it would presumably weaken its role in defending constituent against confrontations with the state. This faces the same obstacle of treating the marginal case as the final case. But the presumption that this understanding of speech does the most to enhance constituent autonomy requires deep priors about the nature of the social organization that is caricatured and unrealistic, based on an idealized portrait of the individual.

Furthermore, the conservatives ignore a political reality – that campaign finance regulation is (at least until it is blatantly tyrannical) an attempt *by an initially self-determining electorate* (or so it must be presumed, if the conservatives wish to protect a status quo ante regulation of an autonomous polity through rights protection) to

---

[104] See Stephen Ansolabehere, "Arizona Free Enterprise v. Bennett and the Problem of Campaign Speech" (2011) 39 *The Supreme Court Review* 39; C. Edwin Baker, "Campaign Expenditures and Free Speech" (1998) 33 *Harvard Civil Rights-Civil Liberties Law Review* 1, 53.

set the terms of its own self-rule. The conservatives already make the most straightforward argument against this: such legislation is (presumably) supported by a majority of voters, and that allowing a majority to potentially constrain dissenting minorities is extraordinarily dangerous.[105] Constitutional rights of course create bulwarks against such majoritarian oppression. But the constitutional right cannot be interpreted to hobble the electorate's capacity to set the terms of its own future processes of governance, particularly when a weaker majority (the poor) hopes to defend itself from a stronger minority (the rich). To do so misconceives (or degrades through mistrust), the relationship between the state and constituents. The democratic state must ultimately be considered an agent of the people, and to deny this in any meaningful manner is to deny the people the capacity for self-rule – and thus to make them heteronomous on such a principle. When courts act to deny the people the power to set the terms of their own future elections through self-governance, they evoke the counterpopular dilemma.

5.4 THE JUDICIARY AS AN INSTITUTIONAL INTERCESSOR IN POLITICAL AUTONOMY

Contemporary campaign finance law has a strikingly non-jurisprudential character. Progressives and conservatives dispute whether unequal wealth or censorship poses the greater threat to voter autonomy. This battle over optimal policy is often described as outside the judicial remit. At first glance, the conservative–progressive contestation over campaign finance fits with their debate over constitutional interpretation described in Chapter 2. The standard originalist[106] understanding of the Constitution supports a classically liberal, state-limiting understanding of First Amendment rights; it accords (at least in a post-*Buckley* world)[107] with constraining the state from restricting campaign speech. Conversely, a living constitutionalist understanding could, as Breyer suggests, adapt the meaning of the First Amendment to consider contemporary concerns of plutocratic influence and economic inequality, enabling rights interpretation that is more permissive of regulation.[108]

---

[105] *McCutcheon*, 572 US at 205 (laws, including campaign finance laws, reflect "the will of the majority").
[106] Teachout's argument in "Corruption in America" that the Founders were deeply concerned with corruption, while compelling, does not directly bear on a tightly constrained constitutional reading favored by the conservative originalist-textualist approach. The Founders may have been worried about corruption and woven this throughout the Constitution, but the First Amendment comprises a far blunter and more explicit articulation that the Court should be suspicious of the state. See Seth Barrett Tillman, "Why Professor Lessig's 'Dependence Corruption' Is Not a Founding-Era Concept" (2014) 13 *Election Law Journal* 336.
[107] The Court could have used its interpretive tools at the time of *Buckley* to completely reframe the debate. For example, it could have simply concluded (as Justice White did at the time) that money is not speech, and upheld all of FECA 1974. But the conclusion that campaign finance regulation activates the First Amendment is now precedentially entrenched.
[108] *McCutcheon*, 572 US at 239.

Considering the campaign finance debate as contestation over popular autonomy enriches this narrative. Both conservatives and progressives wish to maximize voter autonomy in the arrangement of campaign finance regimes. The unique institutional role of the judiciary should, however, inflect how the Supreme Court engages in this process. Given that judicial intervention in campaign finance strikes down legislation, it raises the question of how a counterpopular act can contribute to popular self-rule. The more cautious explanation is that such intervention is sustained by the higher-priority commitment to constitutional rights (essentially an originalist justification). A more ambitious explanation is that the Court should intervene in the campaign finance realm as appropriate to ensure that the electorate retains autonomy.

5.4.1 *The Progressive Case: Letting Voters Freely Police Contemporary Neoliberalism*

Progressives have two compelling real-world arguments at their disposal. They can convincingly argue that wealth inequality is a serious threat to fair representation. They can also argue that democratic representation, not the judiciary, has greater institutional competence to address the impact of economic inequality on politics.

The first point has been extensively covered by social scientists and more recently adopted by legal scholars. As Larry Bartels summarizes, "elected officials and public policy are largely unresponsive to the policy preferences of millions of low-income citizens, leaving their political interests to be served or ignored as the ideological whims of incumbent elites may dictate."[109] Marty Gilens examines evidence across different types of political party holders and declares that American governance resembles a plutocracy more than a democracy.[110] Further work by Bartels and Christopher Achen has demonstrated that the problem is not merely present through the capture of representatives and elite structures; economic elites can use their resources to exploit direct democratic mechanisms such as initiatives and referendums to make "selective appeals" on issues and then exploit "agenda-setting and framing" to obtain desired outcomes.[111] The result, as Nicholas Stephanopoulos describes in a useful summary of the scholarship, is that the influence of wealth generates a misalignment between the rank-and-file electorate and political outcomes.[112] Campaign finance is a central mechanism by which money enters the political system and allows the wealthy to exert this influence.[113]

---

[109] Larry M. Bartels, *Unequal Democracy: The Political Economy of the New Gilded Age*, 2nd ed. (Princeton: Princeton University Press, 2018), p. 3.
[110] Martin Gilens, *Affluence and Influence: Economic Inequality and Political Power in America* (Princeton: Princeton University Press, 2012), p. 235.
[111] Achen and Bartels, "Democracy for Realists," p. 75.
[112] Stephanopoulos, "Aligning Campaign Finance," 1468–74.
[113] Gilens, "Affluence and Influence," pp. 243–50; Bartels, "Unequal Democracy," p. 245.

The disproportionate power of the wealthy is an affront to equality. Those with money are senior partners in a political project that is meant to be self-rule by political equals. This inequality is an affront to autonomy, for the reasons provided by Philip Pettit and detailed in Chapter 3. Since the wealthy exert more control over policy, they effectively "rule" more than the poor(er). The rich do not merely engage in self-rule but rule over others thanks to a feature (wealth) that has no legitimate democratic weight. The result is that a (morally and politically) arbitrary few rules over the many.

The question for jurists is, what should courts do about this problem? The progressive answer is simple and passive: avoid getting in the way. As the progressive justices stated in *Citizens United* and *McCutcheon*, the Supreme Court should respect "the common sense of the American people"[114] and avoid "substitut[ing] judges' understandings of how the political process works for the understandings of Congress."[115] The Court need only recognize that it should not meddle in popular efforts to handle the problem of unequal wealth in politics.

Moreover, as Sunstein observes, judicial nullification of campaign finance regulation is a type of Lochnerism.[116] It enforces "a constitutional requirement of neutrality that commands preservation of the status quo as reflected in market outcomes,"[117] in this case the distribution of economic power that can be converted into political speech. Thus, judicial intervention in campaign finance is fundamentally an attack on redistributive efforts. To avoid such Lochnerism, the Court need merely avoid restricting Congress's efforts.

Conceived as a matter of autonomy, this argument applies even more broadly. Campaign finance regulation can be fairly described as the franchise's attempt to uphold democratic autonomy against economic inequality. When the Court strikes down efforts to maintain democratic autonomy that have been undertaken through the democratic process, it prevents the electorate from preserving its own freedom against inimical social forces. In such circumstances, judicial counterpopularism becomes part of the very pathology by which autonomy-undermining social forces intrude upon democratic self-determination. The judiciary could use this argument to explain how wealth intrudes upon politics. But the Court need not advance it with authoritative decisiveness. The Court could simply observe that such a pathology is plausible and concede the greater legitimacy of the people to address it.

To avoid sabotaging efforts by the people to maintain their own freedom, the Court should have allowed reasonable campaign finance legislation to stand – and respected the people's autonomy to police their own terms of self-rule. The Court had many ways of doing so prior to *Buckley*. For example, it could have exerted the passive virtues in some form or concluded that as long as regulations do not target

---

[114] *Citizens United*, 558 US at 479.
[115] *McCutcheon*, 572 US at 260.
[116] Sunstein, "Lochner's Legacy," 914; Cass R. Sunstein, *Democracy and the Problem of Free Speech* (New York: The Free Press, 1995), p. 98.
[117] Sunstein, "Lochner's Legacy," 918–9.

particular viewpoints they do not elicit First Amendment concerns. Alternatively, it could have adopted Justice White's conclusion that the entire regulatory apparatus must stand together, and is on the whole constitutional. Instead, the *Buckley* compromise elevated the concept of corruption and peculiarly marginalized the concept of inequality. The result has been enormous interest, from progressive scholars, in justifying the anti-corruption (Teachout, Lessig, and Kuhner) and pro-equality (Sitaraman, Rahman, and Fishkin and Forbath) interests.

Identifying the true heart of the campaign finance debate – the autonomy of the electorate – points to a less elaborate, more foundational justification for judicial acceptance of reasonable campaign finance regulation. Campaign finance regulation is a mechanism by which the electorate, acting through its representatives, acts freely to preserve its own freedom. Judicial oversight that meddles with such efforts by a polity to exercise its own autonomy risks rendering the polity subject not only to the outside influence at issue (here, wealth) but also subject to the will of the Court. Such oversight doubly threatens to make the polity heteronomous and contravenes the central value of democracy.

5.4.2 *The Conservative Argument: Foundational Commitments as a Bulwark against Tyranny*

The essence of the conservative response is a unitary – and arguably inflexible – understanding of the judiciary's institutional role. Conservatives' social science counterargument to the claim that the great threat is unequal wealth is that incumbents enjoy a significant, and growing, advantage over challengers in elections.[118] This advantage interacts with wealth in complex ways. For instance, incumbents may have an easier time fundraising due to their broader political access. The empirical evidence on[119] and theoretical analysis[120] of this conjecture are mixed, and certainly less robustly established than the disproportionate effect that wealth has on politics. Yet the fear that incumbents will exploit their power over the state to entrench themselves features in both the conservative argument[121] about anxieties

---

[118] For a magisterial account, see Stephen Ansolabehere and James M. Snyder Jr., "The Incumbency Advantage in U.S. Elections: An Analysis of State and Federal Offices, 1942–2000" (2004) 1 *Election Law Journal* 315.

[119] Cf. Thomas Stratmann, "Do Low Contribution Limits Insulate Incumbents from Competition?" (2010) 9 *Election Law Journal* 125 (finding that more stringent campaign finance regulation enhances competitiveness); Jordan Butcher and Jeffrey Milyo, "Do Campaign Finance Reforms Insulate Incumbents from Competition? New Evidence from State Legislative Elections" (2020) 53 *PS: Political Science & Politics* 460 (finding that extensive regulations, including prohibitions on corporate spending, benefit incumbents and reduce competitiveness).

[120] Adam Meirowitz, "Electoral Contests, Incumbency Advantages, and Campaign Finance" (2008) 70 *Journal of Politics* 681, 693 (modelling to find an enhanced incumbent advantage under some circumstances from campaign finance regulation).

[121] See *McConnell*, 540 US at 248 (Scalia, dissenting); Issacharoff, "Throwing in the Towel."

over censorship as well as prominent scholarly arguments that identify campaign finance as a key mechanism for achieving lockup that the judiciary is well positioned to combat.[122]

The incumbent protection concern, however, faces two challenges. The first is that if incumbent advantage *is* the core practical result of campaign finance, the issue is not, in fact, campaign financing, but representatives who are fundamentally disloyal and unaccountable to their constituents. Much like the progressive case faces the difficulty of identifying the internal point of political failure to justify money as the problem, if the real problem surrounding *regulation* is incumbency protection, then campaign finance regulation is a secondary issue. There is a more fundamental breakdown in the machinery of democratic accountability and electorate–representative relations if incumbency advantage itself impairs autonomy. Moreover, as discussed in Chapter 6, there are vivid examples of incumbent-protecting practices (such as partisan gerrymandering) that conservatives have been unwilling to identify as constitutional wrongs.

The second challenge is that adverting to the realities of politics does not fit well with the typical methods of conservative reasoning. Modulating constitutional interpretation to address a given political practice resonates more with living constitutionalism than with the conservative approach and its fixed understanding of the judicial role.

The conservatives' most compelling argument comes from constitutional principle. Regardless of the consequential policy concerns surrounding regulation, if the steadfast application of First Amendment rights would limit regulation, campaign regulation should be limited. Rights are meant to be consistently enforced against state action regardless of the compelling character of policy arguments (which Ronald Dworkin calls "trumps").[123] As such, as Chief Justice Roberts reasonably notes in *McCutcheon*, the possibility that a consistent and even unpopular application of a right may cut against the collective perception of the good suggests the right is performing its proper state-and-majority limiting function.[124] Moreover, if the Court more expansively considered the wisdom of applying a right to a particular policy, it would deviate from its distinct role as the interpreter of the Constitution.

This entire argument is premised on the Court's ability to justify a fixed meaning of a right. Conservatives are, in principle, well-positioned to do so. Originalism legitimizes rights by asserting that the Constitution expresses the most authoritative and, in its foundational character, autonomous expression of popular preferences. While this justification faces the general objections to the legitimacy of originalist understandings, it grants a potential internal consistency to the conservative position.

---

[122] Issacharoff and Pildes, "Politics as Markets," 688; Issacharoff and Karlan, "The Hydraulics of Campaign Finance Reform," 1735.

[123] Ronald Dworkin, "Rights as Trumps," in Jeremy Waldron (ed.), *Theories of Rights* (Oxford: Oxford University Press, 1984), pp. 154–9.

[124] *McCutcheon*, 572 US at 205. This argument is a calmer relative of Scalia's vociferous rejection of Teachout's view of corruption, *Citizens United*, 558 US at 391.

An anti-tyranny, state-constraining understanding of the First Amendment is not just a prudent approach, but a foundational value of American constitutionalism that must stand up to less morally authoritative legislative affronts. This protection of higher-order foundational values is the obligate remit of the Court; if the Court fails to protect these values (as the conservatives would accuse the progressives of doing), this represents a dire failure of institutional responsibility.

The practical effect of the conservative position is to disrupt immediate popular efforts to address democratic crisis. It is legitimate so long as the right is sustained by a higher-order normative commitment that can vindicate legislative counterpopularism. Thus, the conservative position is under enormous normative pressure to explain why the electorate freely commits to a fixed vision of the Constitution.

5.4.3 Autonomy as Aligning the Positions

Discussions of which campaign finance policy best maximizes autonomy as a practical matter correspond to the respective progressive and conservative positions on judicial review of campaign finance. The progressive position conceives of a constitutional and political structure menaced by economic inequality. According to this view, the influence of unequal wealth is extra-constitutional both in the broad sense that it undermines a just constitutional order and in the narrow sense that deployment of plutocratic wealth does not fall within the judicial remit of rights protection. The appropriate posture of the Court is to permit the people, operating through the elected branches, to address this alien threat to democratic autonomy. By bringing certain facets of politicized wealth (campaign expenditures) into the constitutional remit, the *Buckley* formula has complicated the progressive position. Both justices and scholars have felt obligated to frame their analysis in terms *internal* to the Constitution, either by expanding the concept of corruption or by arguing that the Constitution includes, as a legal matter, some concept of substantive equality.

Maneuvering around *Buckley* has obscured the true nature of the progressive position – that the electorate has the power to autonomously protect its democratic norms, and the Court lacks the authority to intervene. If such interventions took a form that contravened viewpoint neutrality, progressive justices would likely take a different tack, but the legislation advanced by Congress has not raised this concern.

The conservative position characterizes popular autonomy as fundamentally distinct from the state, and conceives of the judiciary's role as maintaining a balance between them. The underlying difference from the progressive viewpoint is that, rather than conceiving of popular autonomy as being *within* the political structure, the conservatives regard electoral self-rule as a "natural" event that must be *protected from* the political structure. The conservatives view the Court as an entity entrusted by the people (conceived separately from the state, or at least the state as operating through the typical representative political structure) to monitor and enforce this relationship to preserve popular autonomy. The threat conceived by progressives – unequal wealth – is simply not of interest to the judiciary in the conservative view (and when the conservatives seek to make social science arguments regarding the benefits of wealth in politics, their arguments become materially less compelling). While the state may address the problem of unequal wealth, the conservative Court grants it no exceptional terms to do so; any such efforts still face an insurmountable constitutional obstacle if they tread on rights.

Conservatives perceive any attempt by the state (or progressives) to advocate such exceptional terms as a dangerous attack on the balance between the state and the people that the Court must maintain. The Court's view of its institutional role, and the state's prospective threat to the electorate, are aspects of the appropriate protection of popular autonomy *within* the constitutional dynamic. Outside threats do not affect the Court's scrutiny of the state.

5.5 THE MYSTERIOUS FRONTIER OF CAMPAIGN FINANCE: PERSONAL AUTONOMY IN POLITICS AND THE LIKELIHOOD OF CONTINUED CONTESTATION

Recognizing that campaign finance law has been primarily concerned with evaluating threats to free self-governance poses a challenge. A complete resolution of the campaign finance dilemma would require not merely sensible policy, but rather an exhaustive understanding of how individuals contribute to political decision-making in complex social environments. While this challenge is daunting, it must be faced for the law to move forward. Yet recognizing that the contestation over human autonomy is the core of the law also provides an organizational framework for the current policy and critical struggles over campaign finance. Campaign finance lawmaking has been beset from its inception by competing worldviews. Recognizing the shared value is human freedom does not resolve these differences, but at least identifies the shared terrain. The view of this project, applied to campaign finance, points the way forward both in principle and in the context of existing battles.

5.5.1 *Personal Freedom as the Crux of Campaign Finance Law*

This chapter has established the following propositions:

i) Campaign finance or its regulation, considered as an independent pathology that impairs franchise self-rule, operates through influencing individual voters' decision-making processes;

ii) any damaging effect of campaign finance or its regulation has at its root a failure wholly internal to politics that impairs free self-rule by voters (a failure of either leaders' legitimate political accountability or of voters' decision-making capacity);

iii) the impact of unequal or constrained campaigning merely exploits this internal-to-politics weakness; and
iv) the judicial posture toward campaign finance regulation depends on how rights enforcement should facilitate self-rule.

Together, these propositions demonstrate that achieving a comprehensively just approach to campaign finance regulation is a ferociously complex undertaking. The choke point is that campaign finance (and its regulation) inevitably affects *voters*. A decisive account requires an authoritative understanding of how voters process information to make political decisions and the circumstances that make those decisions (sufficiently) free.

Determining how judges should address campaign finance regulation requires a satisfactory theory of voter cognition in the context of representative constitutional democracy. This involves addressing a number of issues, including how voters react to unequal or regulated campaign discourse; how this impacts representative accountability, and the degree to which other aspects of campaign finance (i.e. its direct corruption of representatives) impair voters' ability to control representatives; and how the intervention of courts changes the extent to which campaign finance regulation affects voters' ability to rule themselves. Each of these dizzyingly complex factors impacts voter autonomy in preference formation.

The inevitable starting point is adequately free preference formation by voters, and how economic inequality versus state intervention affects it in the campaign context. This must be satisfactorily (if not authoritatively) addressed. Otherwise, the debate remains stuck on the character of voters, and which type of influence (inequality or censorship) is more likely to yield political outcomes that are shaped by outside forces rather than free choice.

However, even a remotely definitive account of personal cognition seems to remain far beyond current understandings. A survey of the scholarship is beyond the scope of this chapter, but it is illuminating to consider the depth of some of the challenges. One particularly serious challenge is the inadequate scientific understanding of how humans make decisions. Yet a decisive account – which *might* entail materialist determinism – may simply be an inaccurate way of conceiving of how people think at all. Indeed, whether such a computationalist account is valid is itself fiercely debated.[125] Whether such a decisive account would leave space for moral free will is also contestable. As Nagel suggests, as an account of autonomy becomes more robustly causal and explanatorily exhaustive, the more the account actually erodes the breadth and significance of autonomy through its determinism. Such determinism diminishes autonomy's moral importance. From a Kantian perspective, this is demonstrated by the fact that an individual who imagines themselves as a moral actor necessarily imagines themselves *not* as part

---

[125] See, e.g., Jerry Fodor, *The Mind Doesn't Work That Way: The Scope and Limits of Computational Psychology* (Cambridge: The MIT Press, 2001).

of the causally driven material world, but as possessing a noumenal self-generated capacity for free action.[126] An *externally* decisive account of human preference formation might be intrinsically incompatible with treating persons as morally free, self-motivating beings.

Even if it was possible to inform the morality of human cognition and preference formation, an account would then have to be made of collective preference expression in the context of a constitutional democracy operating in capitalist neoliberal social settings. There are few such accounts; they are inevitably based on propositions that can themselves be disputed. Classical analogues include Plato's *Republic* (which weaves together a theory of a human virtue and a full concept of the state) and Thomas Hobbes's *Leviathan* (which builds up from a materialist account of the individual to a theory of sovereignty). Contemporary examples include Rawls's description of a just liberal democracy hypothetically joined by the agreement of rational citizens[127] and Philip Pettit's theory of republicanism that works up from a foundational theory of individuals as intentional actors in a social setting.[128] These theories are distinguished by integrating a defensible philosophical theory of humans as free moral agents with an account of social organization that builds up from that theory of freedom. Yet they all include fiercely contested propositions, both as foundational starting assumptions and in the analytic moves they use to elevate their theories of freedom to the level of social theory.

Furthermore, these accounts are not specific enough to resolve the granular campaign finance questions. Nor do they delineate a jurisprudential theory that can do so. Rawls may come closest in his discussion of courts as exemplars of public reason.[129] But his observation that they should "prevent [constitutional] law from being eroded by the legislation of transient majorities" while offering "in their reasoned opinions the best interpretation of the constitution they can"[130] is still not specific enough to resolve the campaign finance debate. Conservatives see themselves as defending the Constitution from the transient wishes of a majority (that is perhaps in the thrall of self-interested legislators), while progressives view their modulation of the First Amendment as necessary to best interpret the Constitution and protect public reason during a crisis of economic inequality. That Rawls – a redistributionist liberal who would certainly wish to limit the effects of unequal wealth – could be plausibly employed to support either side's argument illustrates the limits of trying to use a foundational theory.

Beyond these difficulties of parsing individual freedom and seeking to integrate it into a full theory of constitutional self-rule, there are two further difficulties of

---

[126] Christine Korsgaard, Introduction to Kant, "Groundwork," p. xxviii.
[127] Rawls, "Political Liberalism" and, even more so, "A Theory of Justice."
[128] Philip Pettit, *The Common Mind: An Essay on Psychology, Society, and Politics* (Oxford: Oxford University Press, 1996).
[129] Rawls, "Political Liberalism," 233.
[130] Ibid., 236.

institutional operation. The first is institutional competency. Courts are not the type of institutions that undertake this type of philosophical analysis; nor are judges necessarily trained in the relevant social science disciplines. If judges were to seek positions on these types of matters, they would risk acting as a type of broadly legislative body. This is a perpetual bugbear of the judiciary that is closely linked to the counterpopular dilemma. Yet it is difficult to crack the nut of the campaign finance debate without it. The second difficulty is that it is unrealistic to expect judges with diverse moral and philosophical outlooks to meaningfully debate – let alone come to a consensus on – foundational matters of social organization and the nature of moral autonomy. Moving the terrain of the campaign finance debate toward its true foundations – moral autonomy in the context of democratic self-rule – and away from mid-level, oblique questions of constitutional interpretation seems unlikely to yield calm resolution.

5.5.2 Framing the Debates through Contestation over Autonomy

If conceiving campaign finance as a dispute over freedom elicits this cascade of challenges, why do so? The answer is that, beyond offering an organizing axis regarding the case law, such a perspective unifies the broader debate. The cleavage between libertarian and egalitarian approaches to democracy broadly, and campaign finance specifically, aims to protect the franchise's political autonomy. Advocates of the two approaches disagree over what preconditions are necessary to achieve this autonomy,[131] and what pathology represents the greater threat – an overbearing state, or the influence of unequal wealth. But underlying this disagreement is a fundamental debate over how persons actualize this freedom by forming and expressing political views. Likewise, the corruption debate is a parallel concern of how a loss of accountability by agents of the franchise undermines this freedom. There is no question that corruption makes constituents less free. The question is whether such unfreedom only occurs when an agent is directly hijacked, or if more pervasive (or even constituent-focused) economic influence can bring it about.

At the granular policy level, each of these debates involves social realities of mass democratic governance in the context of economic stratification as well as the status of humans as moral agents. These disagreements often appear to be intractable because they involve questions of descriptive social fact. Either voters are problematically susceptible to campaign spending, or they are not. Either leaders are led astray from democratic accountability in the practice of governance, or they are not.

Yet these questions of social fact are not conclusive for the relevant questions. Rather, they are wholly encapsulated by the autonomy of individuals as moral

---

[131] Cf., e.g., Wright, "Money and the Pollution of Politics," 626 ("political equality and self-government stand or fall together"); Sullivan, "Two Concepts," 176 ("The libertarian strand…emphasizes that freedom of speech is a negative command that protects a system of speech").

agents, and this question of autonomy is ultimately exhaustive of the granular policy issues. The libertarian–egalitarian debate centers on the question of whether the absence of constraint or equality of power is more essential for persons to be politically free. The corruption debate queries when autonomy-facilitating anti-corruption regulation begins to impair autonomy by limiting constituent engagement. Furthermore, the relevance of the social facts is exhaustively contextualized and wholly determined by the moral character of the persons they act upon. The effects of state constraint of speech, unequal spending, corrupt representative behavior, and anti-corruption regulation only have meaning insofar as they impact persons as free moral agents. The character of human freedom is not only an initial question about which postulations must be made; it is exhaustive of the ultimate relevance of these social facts.

The substantive claim that freedom is a fundamentally contested concept allows this approach to encompass opposing viewpoints. Such contestation is likely to remain a property of the law; whether unequal wealth or censorship represents the greater threat to democracy seems resistant to philosophical resolution. If the debate is ever resolved, it will come about not from any breakthrough regarding noumenal truth that resolves the nature of freedom, but through development of a more rigorously developed conception of democracy that casts campaigns, corruption, and inequality in a new light.

The centrality of such a foundational philosophical question to judging indicates the limits of using freedom to interrogate the campaign finance jurisprudence. Unlike more partisan and policy-oriented treatments of the topic, when freedom is used as the lens, it does not indicate which policy direction (deregulation or more aggressive regulation) is preferable. But this approach also offers an important advantage. Orienting campaign finance law around human freedom illuminates the real political significance of topics such as the influence of plutocratic wealth – which occur not only through campaign finance but through far less readily visible intrusions of wealth into politics. It is only through their impact on autonomy that the specific consequences that are celebrated or (more often) mourned are politically relevant. Recognizing that the Supreme Court doctrine draws out broader social challenges that bear upon freedom further confirms the legitimacy of the philosophical gloss. It specifically shows that that the campaign finance jurisprudence satisfies one of Rawls's desiderata for constitutional courts. By highlighting pressing issues of how constituents as political beings can best achieve self-rule in an economically stratified mass democracy, the Court reveals and contests various aspects of contemporary social crises. It acts as a less idealized version of an "exemplar of public reason,"[132] debating contrasting approaches to social crises rather than seeking their synthetic resolution.

The clarity brought by the philosophical perspective exemplifies the virtue of freedom as a broader approach to election law. Because freedom itself is a contestable

---

[132] Rawls, "Political Liberalism," 235.

concept, it is unlikely to indicate the direction of unsettled law (except where it is uncontestably determined by settled norms). By focusing on individual autonomy, this chapter makes clear that this is because the nature of freedom is noumenal. Rather than being a falsifiable aspect of the descriptive social world, freedom is a moral concept. Its social manifestation has multiple, radically different interpretations and aspects. Interrogating the case law through freedom offers a virtue that is different from settling how questions should be resolved. Rather, it clarifies the true stakes of legal disputes and indicates the most important issues underlying mid-level questions of doctrine and policy. It shows how the law can reveal the dominant social questions in a democracy undergoing significant social stresses and clarifies how the law can act as a locus of social change.

6

Parties in Democracy

Facilitators or Usurpers of Popular Self-Rule?

[Partisan] gerrymanders enabled politicians to entrench themselves in office as against voters' preferences. They promoted partisanship above respect for the popular will. They encouraged a politics of polarization and dysfunction. If left unchecked, gerrymanders like the ones here may irreparably damage our system of government.
–Elena Kagan, Rucho v. Common Cause

[W]hen States regulate parties' internal processes they must act within limits imposed by the Constitution.
–Antonin Scalia, California v. Jones

Parties perform a dual role in constitutional self-governance. They are private intermediaries by which rank-and-file constituents organize themselves to control the state. They are also a means by which elite government actors coordinate to enhance their public power. Given their lack of formal accommodation in the Constitution, this duality has forced the Court to duel over their nature. Should parties be protected as private organizations that serve constituent interests, or should they be treated as privileged state-like powerholders and held to constitutional scrutiny? While this question has been analyzed through a number of constitutional frames – including associational rights and the question of justiciability – the underlying dispute is singular: does party organization facilitate or hinder constituent rule of the state? The diversity of contexts in which parties operate, and of the effects they have, has yielded a complex and unruly jurisprudence, ranging from the White Primary cases to the struggle over partisan gerrymandering, that can obscure the unity of this issue.

6.1 EXTRA-CONSTITUTIONAL PARTY GOVERNANCE AND THE PUZZLE OF JUDICIAL OVERSIGHT

American democratic process is inextricable from party governance. Representatives are elected and make political choices as members of major political parties. Voters overwhelmingly support candidates from the party with which they identify. Party organization presents many different faces. Parties are alliances of private constituents bound together by personal loyalty; elite-led organizations with formal structure and standing, but which lie outside the government structure; and cliques of representatives that coordinate formal governance.

The ubiquity of party governance highlights a puzzle for judicial oversight of election law: the Constitution does not formally accommodate parties. One explanation is historical. The Framers condemned parties. Another explanation may be intrinsic to parties' role in politics. They provide a mechanism for the expression of both mass and individual impulses (such as group loyalty and personal ambition) that cannot be fully articulated within formal structures. Parties' development without constitutionalized interference is thereby arguably a critical expression of free self-rule.

Because parties are extra-constitutional and emergent rather than informed by constitutional mandate, the federal judiciary lacks clear guidance regarding (or an explicit remit to supervise) their role in electoral process. Yet parties exert enormous power over political outcomes, and can be manipulated, suppressed, or weaponized by those in power, including those who control the state. The Court has therefore struggled with two competing pressures (both of which reflect the primacy of popular self-determination): (1) the benefits of judicial curation to promote party governance that serves popular autonomy; and (2) the tenuous constitutional and normative foundations for judicial review, because parties are an extra-constitutional expression of political will.

This tension has driven the case law. Three distinct doctrinal arcs are apparent, and together they illustrate the Courts' normative priorities, some of which are settled, and some that remain contested. The White Primaries cases established that use of party governance to achieve a morally repugnant aim distinct from party governance – the exclusion of minority voters from the political process – is illicit. These cases make explicit that certain democratic norms have absolute priority over parties' status as extra-constitutional. However, when the Court has considered legislation that only speaks to the nature of party governance, it demonstrates a far more prudential approach. Regulations stand or fall based on the Courts' intuitions regarding the desirable features of party organization – competition, party cohesion and integrity (i.e., anti-splintering and anti-raiding), and party autonomy. This prudential character reflects a paradox facing judicial oversight of state regulation of parties. Parties are an extra-constitutional venue for political expression and struggle, which justifies their protection from state interference, but judicial review itself is one such form of state interference (a tension complicated by the fact that parties operate within as well as outside of the state apparatus). In the most fiercely contested domain of party practice, partisan gerrymandering, the Court has faced a subtly different problem. When the state exploits partisan affiliation in electoral design but does not specifically dictate the terms of party practice, should the judiciary intervene? This calls into question whether the judiciary should impose certain conditions regarding parties' "natural" development, despite their extra-constitutional and self-structuring nature. Partisan gerrymandering, in short, queries if free self-rule requires that party governance adhere to certain internal norms to contribute to free self-rule.

Together, these three topics show that in the realm of party governance, the Supreme Court remains focused on advancing popular autonomy. However, compared to other domains of election law, the contestation over parties has expressed two values that point in opposite directions: (1) ensuring that parties, given that they can be hierarchical and elite driven, do not dominate the franchise's self-governance while simultaneously (2) respecting parties' as extra-constitutional expressions of popular political negotiation and conflict.

6.2 THE EVALUATION OF PARTIES IN AMERICAN DEMOCRACY

Scholarly perception of parties provides useful context regarding their constitutional status. The Framers condemned parties as factions and sought to exclude them from American governance. When parties first emerged early in American history they were largely neglected by scholars;[1] the prevalent response was to dismiss them as implements of patronage.[2] Intensive and often approbative study of parties, and recognition that they are central to popular self-rule, began in the mid-twentieth century. Parties have retained their champions even as new anxieties regarding hyperpolarization and elite domination evoke traditional concerns about faction.

6.2.1 *Madisonian Anti-factionalism*

The long history of distaste for parties in the US expresses the concern that advocacy for factional interests deviates from the unitary common good.[3] As Jim Gardner has shown, the Framers embraced the (at the time conventional) "idea of an objective, and objectively knowable, common good,"[4] and arranged electoral institutions accordingly. James Madison most famously articulated the subsequent "traditional teaching – that parties are evil"[5] in *Federalist* 10.[6] He argued that parties are

---

[1] E.E. Schattschneider, *American Government in Action Party Government* (1942) (London: Routledge, 2004), pp. 3–8.
[2] Leon Epstein, *Political Parties in the American Mold* (Madison: University of Wisconsin Press, 1986), pp. 10–18.
[3] Russell Muirhead, *The Promise of Party in a Polarized Age* (Cambridge, MA: Harvard University Press, 2014), p. x; James A. Gardner, "Madison's Hope: Virtue, Self-Interest, and the Design of Electoral Systems" (2000) 86 *Iowa Law Review* 87 at 116, 120.
[4] Gardner, "Madison's Hope," 116.
[5] Muirhead, "The Promise of Party," p. 5.
[6] S. C. Stokes, "Political Parties and Democracy" (1999) 2 *Annual Review of Political Science* 243–67 at 245; Muirhead, "The Promise of Party," pp. 32–3.

undesirable as part of governance because they uphold the wrong fundamental value – particularized self-interest instead of universal virtue. This critique resonates with a Kantian-deontological vindication of democracy, which defines freedom as the pursuit of objective and detached moral goodness rather than aggrandizing self-interest (a contingent aim that relinquishes true autonomy).[7]

6.2.2 Mid-Twentieth-Century Redemption

The benefits of party governance were not widely recognized until E.E. Schattschneider's seminal *Party Government*, which began with the now-canonical observation that "modern democracy is unthinkable save in terms of the parties."[8] Since its publication in 1942, American political science has delved deeply into how parties shape the American political process. This trend has been approbative of parties as coordinating intermediaries. In this view, parties are invaluable because they create stable coalitions that allow political actors to convert preferences (voters' policy preferences and candidates' desire to win) into government action.[9]

As a descriptive matter, political scientists have identified parties as necessary to aggregate the diverse, often conflicting, preferences of representatives and their constituents. Taking action where power is distributed among multiple actors with conflicting preferences poses a nigh-insurmountable coordination problem (most familiarly articulated by Arrow's impossibility theorem). The organizational framework provided by parties ameliorates this collective action problem. Gary Cox and Matthew McCubbins specify two broad sets of benefits. The first is internal legislative organization, as parties provide "durable coalitions" to manage an otherwise "chaotic and unpredictable agenda" that lacks longitudinal stability. The second set of benefits is party affiliation, which provides a signaling mechanism to the franchise.[10] Voters rely on party affiliation as a heuristic shortcut to understand the values and commitments of representatives in complicated policy environments,[11] and as a signal that they are supporting representatives who might be part of a

---

[7] For contemporary correlates, see Rosenblum, "On the Side of the Angels," pp. 2–3.
[8] Schattschneider, "Party Government," p. 1. This passage is quoted by Muirhead, "The Promise of Party," p. 8; John H. Aldrich, *Why Parties? A Second Look* (Chicago: University of Chicago Press, 2011), p. 3; Marty Cohen, David Karol, Hans Noel, and John Zaller, *The Party Decides: Presidential Nominations Before and After Reform* (Chicago: University of Chicago Press, 2008), p. 19; and the epigraph to Stokes, "Political Parties."
[9] V.O. Key, *Politics, Parties, and Pressure Groups* (New York: Crowell, 1958), p. 12.
[10] Gary W. Cox and Mathew D. McCubbins, *Setting the Agenda: Responsible Party Government in the U.S. House of Representatives* (Cambridge: Cambridge University Press, 2005), pp. 17–18. Aldrich, "Why Parties" offers a parallel specification of the social choice problems as manifesting "within government," p. 35, and with regard to "electoral mobilization," p. 43.
[11] Michael Kang, "Democratizing Direct Democracy: Restoring Voter Competence Through Heuristic Cues and "Disclosure Plus"" (2003) 50 *UCLA Law Review* 1141; Aldrich, "Why Parties," p. 45.

successful majority coalition. Party leaders value this signaling benefit because it helps rally voter support.[12]

Paralleling this descriptive account, scholars have recognized that functional and responsive parties are normatively desirable because they express "people's interests and solidarities."[13] John H. Aldrich has been among the most prominent successors to Schattschneider's view, arguing that a "necessary condition for effective democracy…is that there must be a *party system*, an ongoing set of parties in sustained competition."[14] Without such a structure, democracy faces problems of the "ambition, collective action, and social choice theory sorts."[15] Durable, persistent, and longitudinally recognizable parties (in contrast to coalitions of factions) structure, discipline, and counterbalance the competing and diverse interests in a democratic polity (both substantively and in terms of differing types of political agendas held by candidates, activists, and rank-and-file voters). In particular, they allow ordinary voters to discipline interest groups and elites. Indeed, the lack of such affiliation can impair democratic representation. In the 1980s, Leon Epstein articulated widely held fears that voters' affiliations were too weak, and that representatives were focused on their own brands rather than party loyalty.[16] He was motivated by concerns about maintaining effective party competition; ironically his anxieties were the obverse of contemporary concerns of hyperpolarization and domination by party rule.

Parties also provide a mechanism to facilitate and modulate sustainable and mutually respectful conflict. Contrary to Madison's condemnation of partisan interference with the pursuit of unitary virtue, parties provide constituents with flexibly structured affiliations with likeminded individuals. Those affiliations coordinate healthy disagreement and conflictual discourse, as well as effective coalitions. Schattschneider was writing in the 1940s when democracy was being challenged by systems (communism and fascism) that claimed to be founded in objective, unequivocal truth and rejected the pluralist diversity of political positions supported by party competition; democracy's ability to handle pluralist conflict through party governance is a comparative and unique virtue. Russ Muirhead has argued that healthy (or what he calls "high") partisanship is critical to allow "[s]erious disagreements about the common good."[17] Nancy Rosenblum offers a similar perspective. To facilitate "deliberation, partisanship is desirable as well as unavoidable…the framework for political deliberation requires the rough process of a struggle among combatants fighting under

---

[12] Joseph Schlesinger, *Political Parties and the Winning of Office* (Ann Arbor: University of Michigan Press, 1994), p. 33, is the most prominent advocate of the view that desire for victory drives party affiliation.
[13] Stokes, "Political Parties," 246.
[14] Aldrich, "Why Parties," p. 4.
[15] *Ibid.*, p. 310.
[16] *Ibid.*, pp. 4, 37, 262.
[17] Muirhead, "The Promise of Party," p. 256.

hostile banners."[18] Muirhead and Rosenblum thereby clarify how parties facilitate reasoning in a complex, large-scale democracy. Organized and coherent ideological disagreement and reconciliation could not occur without them.

There is a deeper parallel between the structural (a party system makes democratic competition stable) and discourse-based (partisanship provides a framework for discursive reasoning) justifications for parties, in that both at root identify party governance as benefiting popular self-rule. At the mass scale, democracy is characterized by competition for power among elites. By acting as intermediaries between ordinary constituents (whose ultimate political authority gives democracy validity) and elites, parties make this fierce competition accessible and responsive to rank-and-file voters. Collectively, parties give the franchise a mechanism for controlling elites, and thereby sustain democracy's foundations in popular autonomy. This is paralleled by parties' impact on personal political participation. They make the terms of collective competition transparent, predictable, and consistent, such that individuals can reason about policy effectively.

6.2.3 Contemporary Anxieties: Elite Capture and Hyperpolarization

Recent scholarship has emphasized parties' excesses and pathologies. There have been concerns that partisan polarization has fragmented civic identity, and that corrupt elites have exploited the party system. These concerns harken back to Madison's objection to factions as deviating from the public good, but identify specific failings of parties rather than condemn their existence generally. These pathologies are excesses of what are, in a healthy party system, virtues. *Hyperpolarization* occurs when party identity dominates, rather than facilitates the expression of, substantive political interests. *Elite domination* occurs when the party structure lets leaders impose their will on the people, rather than facilitate the rank-and-file oversight of representatives.

6.2.3.1 Hyperpolarization

The past decade has exhibited a rising interest in hyperpolarization, in which party affiliation dominates political behavior. "[T]he major parties have transformed from heterogeneous coalitions into internally unified teams."[19] The phenomenon affects both elites and rank-and-file voters, though there is debate if the rank-and-file experience polarization to the same degree.[20] Polarization among elites reduces

---

[18] Nancy L. Rosenblum, *On the Side of the Angels: An Appreciation of Parties and Partisanship* (Princeton: Princeton University Press, 2010), p. 307.
[19] Michael S. Kang, "Hyperpartisan Gerrymandering" (2020) 61 *Boston College Law Review* 1379, 1381.
[20] Cf. Cynthia R. Farina, "Congressional Polarization: Terminal Constitutional Dysfunction?" (2015) 115 *Columbia Law Review* 1689, 1692, 1711 (describing hyperpolarization as primarily affecting Congress); Richard H. Pildes, "Why the Center Does Not Hold: The Causes of Hyperpolarized Democracy in

governance to conflict between opposing camps; representatives become unwilling to cooperate with the other party and engage in governance resembling "tribal warfare."[21] Hyperpolarization causes partisan identity to dominate voters' substantive policy and value commitments.[22] Such "affective polarization" makes opposing party identity an intractable basis of negative sentiment.[23] This inverts the desirable effect of partisanship. Instead of providing a nexus by which individuals can form beneficial coalitions, it fragments the electorate. Some evidence suggests that such hyperpolarization has leaked into personal identity more generally.[24] Furthermore, rank-and-file affective polarization exacerbates representative polarization, as representatives face a significant backlash if they are perceived to betray their partisan team.[25] This has been particularly salient following the 2020 presidential election, as constituents have punished Republicans who criticized Donald Trump after Trump failed to accord with norms of succession and sought to discredit Joe Biden's victory by declaring it to be the result of fraud.[26]

6.2.3.2 Elite Misappropriation of Party Power

An additional concern is that parties can help elites dominate politics. The coordination of leadership into coherent groups also makes the abuse of delegated power easier, because it provides a further venue for centralization. The most brazenly undemocratic type of practice involves the infiltration of plutocratic wealth into representation through donations to parties (mostly notoriously through soft money).[27] More normatively ambiguous is that special interest groups may use affiliation with (or special access to) parties to give their interests disproportionate weight in

---

America" (2011) 99 *California Law Review* 273, 279 (summarizing the debate over if polarization is an elite or rank-and-file phenomenon); Shanto Iyengar and Sean J. Westwood, "Fear and Loathing across Party Lines: New Evidence on Group Polarization" (2015) 59 *American Journal of Political Science* 690 (observing a broad presence of affective polarization in the population).

[21] Farina, "Congressional Polarization," 1701.
[22] Iyengar and Westwood, "Fear and Loathing," 704 (partisanship becomes an intrinsic basis for identification, rather than being driven by instrumental or ideological ends); Pildes, "Hyperpolarized Democracy," 277–8; Howard G. Lavine, Christopher D. Johnston, and Marco R. Steenbergen, *The Ambivalent Partisan: How Critical Loyalty Promotes Democracy* (New York: Oxford University Press USA, 2012), p. 84 (collecting sources).
[23] Kang, "Hyperpartisan Gerrymandering," 1381.
[24] Shanto Iyengar, Yphtach Lelkes, Matthew Levendusky, Neil Malhotra, and Sean J. Westwood, "The Origins and Consequences of Affective Polarization in the United States" (2019) 22 *Annual Review of Political Science* 129, 136.
[25] Iyengar and Westwood, "Fear and Loathing across Party Lines," 705.
[26] Reid J. Epstein and Katie Glueck, "10 Republicans Voted to Impeach Trump. The Backlash Has Been Swift," *The New York Times* (January 21, 2021), www.nytimes.com/2021/01/23/us/politics/republican-who-wont-vote-to-impeach-trump.html.
[27] Lawrence Lessig, *Republic, Lost: How Money Corrupts Congress – and a Plan to Stop It* (New York: Twelve, 2015), pp. 94–5.

governance.²⁸ Some ways that special interest groups exert power over parties (such as using cash to support campaigns) are clearly anti-democratic. Other means of special interest group access, such as interest groups ensuring higher turnout or consistent support from their constituent members from the affiliated party, may be considered parties performing their valid coordinating role, particularly if interest group pluralism is considered the most accurate account of democratic politics.

Whether such influence comprises undesirable elite access ultimately depends on whether the practice facilitates the power of rank-and-file voters (by organizing them into coherent blocks), or gives a select group of insiders disproportionate access. The role of parties in government leadership selection makes electoral process particularly vulnerable to elite influence and is a major concern of the anti-lockup approach.²⁹ The available evidence suggests that elites often dominate leadership selection processes that operate through parties. One group of scholars has offered extensive evidence that despite the popularization of the nomination process in the 1970s and the ostensible switch to candidate-centered campaigns, the ultimate choice of a party's presidential candidate is typically under the sway of a small group of party elites through "invisible primaries."³⁰

6.2.4 Parties as Facilitating Self-determination

Given these competing assessments, how should parties' role be conceived? Social scientists' structural descriptions of parties are redemptive because they show that without parties, modern mass representative democracy could not express the popular will. Underlying this function is parties' capacity to facilitate sound political reasoning, both in the power context of enabling constituent evaluation and control of representatives, and at the substantive personal level of voters reflecting on their own preferences and values. Partisan apologists show how the absence of the structured conflict facilitated by meaningful partisanship can indicate a lack of freedom. Muirhead observes that "bipartisan accommodation [was] possible" in the pre-Civil Rights era because racial minorities suffered the outright deprivation of political power,³¹ a claim strongly supported by evidence that during this period the South in particular lacked functional democratic choice.³² Silencing the political voice of a large chunk of the population allowed otherwise substantively opposed northern Republicans and southern Democrats to form an alliance of convenience.

---

²⁸ For a magisterial account of this process, see Gene Grossman and Elhanan Helpman, *Special Interest Politics* (Cambridge: MIT Press, 2002).
²⁹ Samuel Issacharoff and Richard H. Pildes, "Politics as Markets: Partisan Lockups of the Democratic Process" (1998) 50 *Stanford Law Review* 643; Samuel Issacharoff, "Gerrymandering and Political Cartels" (2002) 116 *Harvard Law Review* 593.
³⁰ Cohen et. al., "The Party Decides," pp. 1, 232.
³¹ Muirhead, "The Promise of Party," p. 245.
³² Aldrich, "Why Parties," p. 311.

Rosenblum observes that the absence of partisanship removes a critical fulcrum for the sustained and robust development of political positions among citizens. Political engagement without partisanship leaves citizens with only "amorphous and episodic"[33] opportunities for political engagement. Perpetual, preoccupying engagement with the political good and policymaking may be a real possibility for professional philosophers and the political elite. But it is unrealistic for most citizens.[34] Partisanship thus provides the fertile context for practical political freedom by affording accessible and meaningful opportunity to debate and organize to realize substantive political choices. There is empirical support for this claim, which suggests that "strongly attached citizens" – i.e., those with the strongest partisan affiliations – are the most likely to critically reflect on issues.[35]

When parties perform their appropriate role, they facilitate constituents' autonomous governance – particularly in a democracy that would otherwise alienate the electorate based on its sheer scale. Each pathology (hyperpolarization and elite domination) manifest a different manner in which party organization can undermine, rather than facilitate, popular autonomy as free self-determination. Affective polarization runs the risk of undermining political reasoning as reflective deontological engagement. Where citizens act as reactive, identity-driven partisans, they no longer engage in the free exercise of reason. They are instead heteronomously overdetermined by a feature that should coordinate politics rather than serve as a substantive moral commitment. Likewise, where leaders exploit the centralization of power granted by party organization, this impairs rather than facilitates popular self-rule. In each case the failure is one of excess, such that both reason as self-determination and practical popular control of politics are diminished due to structuring of democracy through parties. Parties are meant to be a subordinate, facultative institution, not a dominant commitment that crowds out the moral rationality that undergirds self-determination.

6.3 TOWARD PRINCIPLED JUDICIAL OVERSIGHT OF PARTY POLITICS

Judicial oversight faces a dilemma summarized by Epstein: While parties can be defined as "private political associations," their centrality to public governance, particularly in organizing direct primaries,[36] justifies their treatment as "state agencies."[37] The constitutional significance of this tension has been oddly neglected in the scholarship.

---

[33] Rosenblum, "On the Side of Angels," p. 308.
[34] Kang, "Heuristic Cues."
[35] Lavine et al., "The Ambivalent Partisan," pp. 209–11.
[36] Epstein, "Political Parties," p. 167.
[37] Ibid., p. 155.

6.3.1 Threshold and Framing Challenges

Parties' "extralegal character" outside the constitutional framework creates an initial analytic hurdle, though experience has shown that Schattschneider's claim that "parties and the law are nonassimilable" may be an exaggeration.[38] The legitimacy of subjecting parties to constitutional oversight depends on a substantive assessment of their character and role. If parties are organizations of private constituents that counterbalance and discipline the state, they should receive First Amendment associational and expressive protections and activate individual rights (as they sometimes do),[39] but if parties are instrumentalities of state actors, their conduct should be subject to the standard gauntlet of constitutional scrutiny (as it sometimes is).[40]

This difficulty occurs at two levels. The first level is the intrinsically multifaceted nature of parties. The second is the unique challenge of courts taking action to regulate or protect parties in light of this nature. As Issacharoff describes, a party is "an unstable amalgam of voter preferences, an internal apparatus driven by activists, and a structure through which party affiliates participate in government."[41] Each of these components of a party is necessary but not sufficient to define it, particularly in the American context. Regarding voter preference, compared to members of other democracies, Americans traditionally have relatively weak or malleable party affiliations.[42] American voters do not pay dues to join a party; compared to wedge bloc-aligned parliamentary systems, voters may find that different parties cater to various aspects of their identity;[43] and their willingness to switch parties is, as exemplified by Duverger's law, a major driver of party responsiveness to voter preference.[44] Yet voter loyalty remains the essential prerequisite for party success. Given the relative ease and reasonableness of switching allegiances in the US (compared to, for

---

[38] Schattschneider, "Party Government," p. 11. See also Stokes, "Political Parties," 245.
[39] *Cousins v. Wigoda*, 419 US 477 (1975); *California Democratic Party v. Jones*, 530 US 567 (2000); *Kusper v. Pontikes*, 414 US 51, 94 (1973).
[40] The most striking example in the doctrine is in the White Primary cases. *Smith v. Allwright*, 321 US 649 (1944); *Terry v. Adams*, 345 US 461 (1953). See also *Williams v. Rhodes*, 393 US 23 (1968); cf. *Nixon v. Herndon*, 237 US 536 (1927) (striking down legislation with such discriminatory effect) and *New York State Board of Elections v. Lopez-Torres*, 552 US 196 (2008) (refusing to police purely internal party selection procedures). As Nathaniel Persily, "Toward A Functional Defense of Political Autonomy" (2001) 76 *New York University Law Review* 750, 758–9 observes, the principle of the White Primary cases has not entered the wider doctrine.
[41] Samuel Issacharoff, "Private Parties with Public Purposes: Political Parties, Associational Freedoms, and Partisan Competition" (2001) 101 *Columbia Law Review* 274, 279. The authoritative source for this point is Key, "Politics, Parties, and Pressure Groups," pp. 163–5; Nathaniel Persily and Bruce E. Cain, "The Legal Status of Political Parties: A Reassessment of Competing Paradigms" (2000) 100 *Columbia Law Review* 775, 778.
[42] Epstein, "Political Parties," p. 4; Stokes, "Political Parties," 247.
[43] Jacob Eisler, "Constitutional Formalities, Power Realities, and Comparative Anglophone Responses to Foreign Campaign Meddling" (2021) 20 *Election Law Journal* 32.
[44] Stokes, "Political Parties," 248.

example, parliamentary wedge bloc parties that give clearly defined groups, such as union workers, only one viable option), the durability of some parties suggests that American voters are uniquely committed to their parties on their own terms – what Frank Sorauf evocatively calls "the party *within* the elector."[45] Elites in the party engage voters in a complicated dance, seeking to advance their own agendas – policy outcomes for activists, re-election for representatives – while maintaining popular support. Activists help develop a party's policy positions and facilitate party coherence and continuity, but they are neither the bedrock of the franchise nor hold formal power in governance. Representatives provide power in governance, and the rise of hostile polarization in Congress shows the influence of party allegiance. Yet America has long been characterized by personal rather than party candidacies, and since candidates are typically described as ultimately election (rather than party) oriented, the commitment to parties seems instrumental. It is thus difficult to see representatives as granting parties the resilient coherence they have exhibited in American politics.

This complexity has ramifications for judicial review of action by parties or that affects parties. Which aspect of party identity is dominant for a given issue will determine if the "state actor toggle" is flipped,[46] and subsequently whether parties should be subject to constitutional scrutiny or enjoy constitutional protection as civic associations. The answer to this question is inevitably contextual. When parties serve as private venues for constituent organization, they help hold the state accountable to popular will. In this role party governance can oppose the state, for example when rank-and-file constituents switch party affiliation, put forward new primary challengers, or form new coalitions to challenge existing political dynamics. Given that representatives can entrench themselves by obtaining control over parties and interrupting these dynamics, parties must be protected from state domination. Yet parties' externality from and antagonism toward the state is leavened by their extensive, mutually beneficial collaboration. Deeming them "quasi-governmental agencies," Leon Epstein has influentially classified parties as "public utilities."[47] This manifests most plainly in the fact that representatives are both party leaders and state servants. Through their party affiliation, representatives both obtain power (via party support in elections) and coordinate state action within government. Their continued appeal to both their party and voters depends on their successful cooperation with other party members and the realization of the party's goals. Furthermore, state action facilitates party power. The state administers the elections that bring parties to power, and parties' ongoing influence as a coordinating mechanism for representatives is ultimately realized through formal mechanisms, such as legislation.

---

[45] Frank Sourauf, *Party Politics in America* (Boston: Little Brown, 1933), p. 133.
[46] Cain and Persily, "The Legal Status of Political Parties," 777.
[47] Epstein, "Political Parties," p. 155.

6.3.2 Contemporary Constitutional Scholarship: The Ascendence of Instrumentalism

Despite periodic calls to identify deeper constitutional principles in considering parties,[48] the scholarship has tended to gloss over these complexities. The trend has been to describe desirable modes of party governance and reverse engineer constitutional reasoning to match. This approach encourages judicial review of parties that emulates direct policymaking.[49] The prevalent view is that parties possess so much institutional power that they should be treated as state organs. The main concern is that parties can use their representatives in government to introduce electoral procedures to help the party stay in power and reduce political competition – a core anxiety of anti-lockup theory.[50] Samuel Issacharoff, one of the staunchest advocates of this view, has argued that party "insiders [may act] to lessen competitive pressures."[51] This echoes the concern of elite domination and leads Issacharoff to call for judicial review guided by "contextual and institutional"[52] prudence rather than constitutional logic. This instrumentalizes judicial review.[53] The validity of the instrumentalizing approach is often simply presumed, with the dominant focus on measuring the asserted signs of pathologies.[54] The most influential example is Nicholas Stephanopoulos's argument that the efficiency gap can identify unconstitutional gerrymanders without any principled explanation of the constitutional

---

[48] Heather K. Gerken, "Lost in the Political Thicket: The Court, Election Law, and the Doctrinal Interregnum" (2004) 153 *University of Pennsylvania Law Review* 503, 530 (asserting the need for "structural analysis" that goes beyond an individual rights framework, maintaining a certain instrumentalist tendency); Persily and Cain, "The Legal Status of Political Parties," 799 (identifying "decision rules" based on existing paradigms that are not decisive or foundational).

[49] The exception is Michael S. Kang, "Gerrymandering and the Constitutional Norm Against Government Partisanship" (2018) 116 *Michigan Law Review* 351, argues for the illegality of partisan animus through a careful reconstruction of the doctrine. But Kang's doctrinal-focused approach is the exception, rather than the rule.

[50] Issacharoff and Pildes, "Politics as Markets," 646, 651.

[51] Issacharoff, "Gerrymandering and Political Cartels," 600. Other scholars have echoed or adapted Issacharoff's position. See, e.g., Richard L. Hasen, "Do the Parties or the People Own the Electoral Process Point/Counterpoint" (2001) 149 *University of Pennsylvania Law Review* 815; Michael S. Kang, "Sore Loser Laws and Democratic Contestation" (2010) 99 *Georgetown Law Journal* 1013, 1075.

[52] Samuel Issacharoff, "Private Parties with Public Purposes: Political Parties, Associational Freedoms, and Partisan Competition" (2001) 101 *Columbia Law Review* 274, 313.

[53] Some have noted these difficulties. See Daniel Lowenstein, "Vieth's Gap: Has the Supreme Court Gone from Bad to Worse on Partisan Gerrymandering?" (2005) 14 *Cornell Journal of Law & Public Policy* 367; Richard Briffault, "Defining the Constitutional Question in Partisan Gerrymandering" (2005) 14 *Cornell Journal of Law and Public Policy* 397; Yunsieg Kim and Jowei Chen, "Gerrymandered by Definition: The Distortion of 'Traditional' Districting Criteria and a Proposal for Their Empirical Redefinition." (2021) 2021 *Wisconsin Law Review* 101.

[54] For an extended summary of this trend, see Jacob Eisler, "Partisan Gerrymandering and the Constitutionalization of Statistics" (2019) 68 *Emory Law Journal* 979.

character of partisan affiliation.⁵⁵ Other scholars have similarly made effects-based arguments regarding hyperpolarization.⁵⁶

Scholars have likewise relied on institutional arguments to uphold the contrary position – that parties should benefit from, rather than be policed by, constitutional review. For example, Nathaniel Persily challenges both Issacharoff's condemnation of partisan gerrymandering⁵⁷ and his defense of party autonomy in primary design.⁵⁸ Yet Persily's arguments relate almost entirely to the *consequences* of protecting parties. Because partisan influence over electoral procedure can be reconciled with efficacious representation, he argues against restricting party influence and advocates protecting parties when the state seeks to curb their sway. This speaks to the Schattschneiderean political justification that parties facilitate and organize the expression of popular autonomy. But it does not address the puzzle of the judiciary, as an institution, having a coherent posture towards parties.

By neglecting the uniquely constitutional dimension that must discipline judicial review of party practice, past studies in this area have failed to address the Court's unique institutional posture and normative mandate.⁵⁹ Such an instrumentalized approach also destabilizes any analysis, because it makes appropriate constitutional treatment of parties contingent upon political circumstances. Fifteen years after his initial concerns that parties could dominate the electorate process (and following Donald Trump's ascent to the presidency through the Republican Party), Issacharoff mourned that "[w]eakened political parties do not have the institutional fortitude to withstand hostile challenges from outsiders" and indicted a lack of "institutional support."⁶⁰ Issacharoff's analysis points to particular weak junctures in the electoral ecosystem that has dethroned parties as central coordinators of governance.⁶¹ Yet according to Persily, partisan gerrymandering and control over primaries are the sorts of practices that could return some power to such parties. The fact that Issacharoff's position on the desirability of party power has shifted with political

---

⁵⁵ Nicholas Stephanopoulos and Eric McGhee, "Partisan Gerrymandering and the Efficiency Gap" (2015) 82 *University of Chicago Law Review* 1, 41.
⁵⁶ Kang, "Hyperpartisan Gerrymandering."
⁵⁷ Nathaniel Persily, "In Defense of Foxes Guarding Henhouses: The Case for Judicial Acquiescence to Incumbent-Protecting Gerrymanders" (2002) 116 *Harvard Law Review* 649. See also Peter H. Schuck, "The Thickest Thicket: Partisan Gerrymandering and Judicial Regulation of Politics" (1987) 87 *Columbia Law Review* 1325; Michael S. Kang, "The Bright Side of Partisan Gerrymandering" (2005) 14 *Cornell Journal of Law and Public Policy* 443 (2005); Jacob Eisler, "Partisan Gerrymandering and the Illusion of Unfairness" (2018) 67 *Catholic University Law Review* 229.
⁵⁸ Persily, "Toward A Functional Defense of Political Autonomy."
⁵⁹ Ironically this point may have received more attention earlier in the novel Court's intervention into party practice. See Schuck, "The Thickest Thicket," 1378 (observing the Court is now a political combatant).
⁶⁰ Samuel Issacharoff, "Democracy's Deficits" (2018) 85 *The University of Chicago Law Review* 485, 492, 495.
⁶¹ Samuel Issacharoff, "Outsourcing Politics: The Hostile Takeover of Our Hollowed-Out Political Parties" (2017) 54 *Houston Law Review* 845, 862–79.

fortunes suggests that an instrumental analysis of party impact on elections does not provide a stable basis for constitutional review.

6.3.3 Counterpopularity and Self-determination through Party Politics

Focusing on political consequences obscures the real challenge for judicial review. Since party governance has emerged organically despite having no formal constitutional status, judicial review has no obvious basis for evaluating it. Where the judiciary opines on such an "emergent" practice, it imposes a counterpopular view of how the electorate should govern itself, with no apparent legitimation of such review by the franchise. As Peter Schuck quips (alluding to Justice Frankfurter's opposition to the one person, one vote rule), this makes judicial review of party practice the "thickest thicket."

The counterpopular tension is particularly great because of parties' unique contribution to self-rule. They are an extra-constitutional response to the structural challenges and exigencies of mass democratic rule, accommodating a need not explicitly addressed, and perhaps not even capable of being addressed, in the formalized legal structure. The lack of formal constitutionalization means that, absent some specific feature that means the state conduct of action violates some *other* independently protected right, judicial review of parties and partisanship is a judicial declaration of how a franchise should rule itself as a prudential or normative matter.

This puzzle is complicated by parties' multi-faceted nature, as described above. Should parties be identified with rank-and-file members, the private but elite party apparatus,[62] or the party in government? Making such a threshold constitutional determination only shifts the onus on judicial review, because it is a prospective imposition of values regarding parties' appropriate role in governance.

The contrast between the one person, one vote jurisprudence and the judicial oversight of parties illuminates this problem and how the scholarship has neglected it. Scholars have historically treated judicial oversight of party practice as a logical extension of *Baker v. Carr*.[63] Yet the state action at issue in *Baker* – malapportionment of voters by legislators acting in their state capacity, subsequently unequal distribution of political power, and contravention of a basic liberal democratic norm of equal self-determination, as described in Chapter 4 – was an unequivocal use of government power by representatives to control constituents' relationship to the state. The power effects of malapportionment run in one direction, enabling state domination of constituents. The Court's tangled, messy efforts to enforce fairness in the partisan arena (most clearly exemplified by the ignominious fate of the foray

---

[62] Issacharoff, "Private Parties"; Richard L. Hasen, "Do the Parties or the People Own the Electoral Process Point/Counterpoint" (2001) 149 *University of Pennsylvania Law Review* 815.

[63] Luis Fuentes-Rohwer, "Doing Our Politics in Court: Gerrymandering, Fair Representation and an Exegesis into the Judicial Role" (2003) 78 *Notre Dame Law Review* 527; Schuck, "The Thickest Thicket," 1325.

into partisan gerrymandering) demonstrate that reviewing the electoral procedures according to party affiliation is less straightforward due to the ambiguous or multi-faceted character of parties themselves. Parties act both outside and against (but also within and in concert with) the state, and party action inevitably reflects meaningful popular sentiment, even when the party acts through the state. As Schuck has argued, these choices may include adopting procedures that change how a victorious party – a group that has achieved dominance over the state, but corresponds to a set of constituents – rules itself.[64] Deciding when party action moderated through the state crosses the line of being state conduct that violates rights will necessarily involve interrogating the underlying terms of legitimate self-rule.

This is not to suggest that the judiciary cannot review electoral procedure that discriminates on party grounds. For instance, the state clearly uses partisanship or party identification (even if it reflects partisan impulses) against individuals in their private capacity. Michael Kang has provided egregious examples of partisan and partisan-like discrimination that would fail to pass constitutional muster.[65] However, the ambiguous status of parties and persons as party members as acting to facilitate or collaborate with the state in some contexts, and in opposition to or outside the state in others, means that judicial review of law that is based on partisan affiliation must take into account this multi-faceted, category-crossing character. Some uses of partisanship – for example, abusive treatment of individuals for being from a "losing" party such as denying them jobs (i.e., patronage punishment) – clearly entail the deployment of state power against an individual. But the struggle among parties to set terms of electoral process cannot be so readily condemned as state oppression of private persons, because the coordinating intermediaries (including constituents as members of such intermediaries) are the actual participants in the struggle. Were the judiciary to simply instruct parties as to the appropriate terms of their contestation, it would be unequivocally counterpopular. If the judiciary intervened to protect a party or party members whenever they suffered a political defeat or were disadvantaged in some way, the emergent value of parties as mediating democratic conflict would be lost.

The difficulty of extending *Baker*'s structural logic to parties indicates the need for a distinct, party-specific approach. The core of such a principle must cut beyond the political effects of party self-rule (i.e., whether parties act as facilitators or dominators; whether they are of the people or of the state) because these questions themselves require substantive political judgments, with no clear "right" answer (including from constitutional instruction). A satisfactory approach engages with

---

[64] Schuck, "The Thickest Thicket," 1350.
[65] Kang, "Gerrymandering and the Constitutional Norm," 351, 379 (discussing official government endorsement of candidates and parties); Kang, "Gerrymandering and the Constitutional Norm," 391 (discussing the application of the Elections Clause to limit substantive state interference in particular issues).

the thorny cross-over quality of parties as mediating between the state and private constituents, and will revert to the fact that all democratic state action is accountable to (and empowered by) popular will. As discussed in Chapters 1 and 2, some popular decisions are higher-order constitutional commitments that constrain typical lawmaking, which is reinforced by judicial scrutiny. Because parties cannot be neatly classified as either of the state or private, this complicates the account that describes courts as simply protecting constituents' higher-order commitments to the organization of the state. Thus, in addition to making a prudential decision about how parties should contribute to party governance, there is a question of whether they are a subject of constitutional interest at all. Any judicial oversight of party electoral practice must evaluate (1) the desirability of the practice for constitutional democracy (which will resemble standard rights enforcement, and has been the dominant lens via which most have understood the judicial oversight of parties) and (2) whether the category of practice is a matter of constitutional–judicial interest at all (which recognizes the unique counterpopular onus borne by judicial review of party practice).

6.4 PARTIES BEFORE THE COURTS

The case law on parties reflects the judiciary's struggle with advancing free self-rule in party governance while also recognizing the extra-constitutional and multifaceted nature of parties. This presents as contestation on the bench over how party governance can best contribute to free self-rule, but also involves even fiercer contestation over how the judiciary can legitimately opine on an extra-constitutional aspect of governance in light of the counterpopular dilemma. The result is a jurisprudence that operates at two levels: (1) a query regarding if a particular practice of party governance can be reconciled with popular autonomy and (2) an even more foundational query regarding whether the judiciary is authorized to address any ills that emerge from party governance while still respecting the primacy of democratic self-governance.

The doctrine illustrates the struggle to answer these queries through three groups of cases. In concluding that the primary process could not be exploited to exclude racial minorities from the franchise – albeit only after fierce contestation over the problem of extra-constitutionality – the Court demonstrated that some democratic norms have absolute priority over autonomy of party governance. In addressing direct state regulation of party electoral process, the Court sought to balance a variety of prudential values. Since this requires disentangling parties-in-the-state from parties as private organizations, it epitomizes the difficulty of specifying the norms by which political intermediaries should operate. Most recently, in the fierce battle over partisan gerrymandering, the justices grappled with the question of whether political conflict that *exploited* the centrality of parties to American democracy, but did not explicitly aim to regulate parties, should be subject to judicial review. Since the effect of such districtings does nothing to prevent parties from adapting to new circumstances (as does direct party regulation), the debate highlights the fact that the emergent nature of parties makes the counterpopular dilemma especially sharp. The pivotal question – frustratingly dodged by the Court – is whether the Court is morally bound to enforce any norms internal to party governance.

6.4.1 The Decontested Beachhead of Party Regulation: The White Primaries Cases

One doctrinal domain of party governance is fully settled. Between 1927 and 1953, a series of Supreme Court rulings (the White Primary cases) unequivocally concluded that the explicit racist exclusion of voters from participation in major party primaries is unconstitutional, even where the exclusion was effected through private organization. At one level, the opinions address if parties should be treated as public utilities or private entities. Yet if this were the decisive issue, the Court would be expected to more clearly articulate the conditions under which private organizations qualify as state actors. The real struggle was over which norm is valued more highly in democratic process: the autonomy of party governance or ensuring non-discriminatory access to electoral process. The White Primaries cases demonstrate normative analysis similar to that of one person, one vote jurisprudence. The Court was willing to impose a liberal democratic norm, even if the constitutional remit for doing so (and the authority derived from the electorate) is thin.

The White Primary cases addressed the dispiritingly persistent efforts of the Democratic Party of Texas (which at the time was functionally a one-party state) to exclude African American voters from effective political participation. The first case, *Nixon v. Herndon*, ruled that a legislative act which excluded African American voters from the Democratic primary was unconstitutional. Michael Klarman describes the unanimous *Herndon* opinion as "by far the easiest of the three pre-*Smith* cases for the Court because state action was unquestionably present."[66] In response to *Herndon*, the Texas legislature promptly passed a statute that gave parties the explicit right to set their own constituencies. Although it appeared to be neutral, the provision was unabashedly designed to give Democratic Party leaders the power to exclude voters on the basis of race and achieve the same illicit aim as the initial statute. In the much more fiercely contested *Nixon v. Condon*, a bare five-justice majority found that this statute was also unconstitutional, because "Whatever power of exclusion has been exercised by members of the committee has come to them…not as the delegates of the party, but as the delegates of the state."[67] In the next case, *Grovey v. Townsend*, a unanimous bench refused to find

---

[66] Michael J. Klarman, "The White Primary Rulings: A Case Study in the Consequences of Supreme Court Decisionmaking" (2001) 29 *Florida State University Law Review* 55, 57.
[67] *Nixon v. Condon*, 286 US 73, 85 (1932).

unconstitutionality where a party excluded voters without state involvement in the exclusion (though this ruling has been criticized for failing to recognize the general role of the state in enabling primaries).[68] However, *Grovey* was not a durable opinion: Six years later, *U.S. v. Classic* established that the right to participate in primary congressional elections is "secured by the Constitution," even where the potentially oppressive actor is a party rather than a state agent.[69] *Classic* cleared the path for *Smith v. Allwright*, which returned to the question of if the Democratic Party of Texas could exclude non-White voters from primary participation, and functionally overturned *Grovey*. Though recognizing that parties are private organizations, the Court concluded when "that privilege [of party membership] is also the essential qualification for voting in a primary to select nominees for a general election, the state makes the action of the party the action of the state."[70] The Court therefore concluded that the conduct violated the Equal Protection Clause. A final attempt by the Texas Democratic Party to exclude African American voters was to conduct pre-emptive quasi-primaries through a civic organization called the Jaybirds, which would hold a "shadow primary" that was functionally decisive for the Democratic primary victor. The Jaybirds adopted the exclusionary policy that *Smith* had held to be illicit when effected by a party. In *Terry v. Adams*, the Court brushed aside this formalist attempt at circumvention in an 8–1 ruling, and held the conduct to be a violation of the Fifteenth Amendment.

In 25 years, the Court went from the initial step of prohibiting unequivocally racist voter exclusion by legislation to prohibiting it when non-party private organizations engaged in the practice. Various contextual factors explain this arc. For example, Darlene Clark Hine has emphasized the dedicated efforts of African American activists.[71] Klarman has highlighted the role of historical events and associated cultural changes, particularly the drive for greater racial equity following World War II.[72] Issacharoff and Pildes argue the later cases reflect a shift from legal formalism to political functionalism.[73] Echoing Muirhead's condemnation of the lack of partisan competition in the pre-Civil Rights era, they suggest that the White

---

[68] Klarman, "The White Primary Rulings,"59 calls *Grovey* "confused and confusing." Most strangely, it articulates the ways in which (per Epstein, "Political Parties," p. 175) party primaries are state functions, before declaring a lack of a state nexus. *Grovey v. Townsend*, 295 US 45, 50 (1935).

[69] *U.S. v. Classic*, 313 U.S. 299, 314 (1941). *Classic* addresses arcane facts regarding fraudulent action by party agents that deprived a voter of electoral participation; as such its relevance is establishing general judicial oversight of primaries. Klarman, "The White Primary Rulings," 61 suggests that *Classic* is distinguishable from *Grovey* on technical grounds, a distinguishing that the Court in *Smith v. Allwright* confirms as a technical matter, 341 US 649, 660 (1944). However the path of the law shows that *Classic* provided a point of entry for expanding substantive party regulation.

[70] *Smith*, 321 US at 664–5.

[71] Darlene Clark Hine, *Black Victory: The Rise and Fall of the White Primary in Texas* (Milwood, New York: KTO Press, 1979).

[72] Klarman, "The White Primary Rulings," 64.

[73] Issacharoff and Pildes, "Politics as Markets," 660.

Primary cases were driven by the realization that party elites orchestrated the suppression of African American voters to prevent shifting wedge bloc allegiances that could challenge the entrenched leadership – a classic political lockup.[74]

These compelling explanations contribute to the causal story. Yet none speaks to the tenuous constitutional justification for judicial oversight of party action. Scholars have recognized this tenuousness, largely conceding that there is no constitutionally adequate account. Issacharoff and Pildes assert that "the Court's legal analysis breaks down completely" in *Terry*; this motivated the authors to adopt a functionalist anti-lockup approach to election law.[75] Likewise, Klarman observes "None of the rationales articulated by the three separate opinions in support of the conclusion that the Jaybirds' scheme involved the requisite state action for a constitutional violation was terribly persuasive,"[76] leading him to accept a sociohistorical account.

However, these moves gloss over the Court's internal struggle over dictating the terms of democratic self-rule without a clear constitutional mandate. The judiciary's legitimate authority to dictate the terms of democratic procedure requires voters to bind themselves to higher law. Because parties lie outside the constitutional structure, they seem to fall outside such higher law unless they clearly act through the state. To make objectionability of a party practice the sole basis for legal oversight would suggest that the judiciary is not disciplined by any articulated constitutional remit and has a general authority to dictate the terms of legitimate self-rule.

Issacharoff and Pildes as well as Klarman provide explanations that ameliorate these qualities by showing how the Court's decisions align with popular will. Klarman describes the Court as a direct agent of the franchise and maintains that by the time of *Smith*, "ordinary white citizens, lacking in any particular political incentive, tolerated or even supported black suffrage because they could not see how to justify continued disfranchisement in a democratic age."[77] For Issacharoff and Pildes, racial disenfranchisement allowed political elites to maintain an anticompetitive stranglehold on power, effectively depriving even White voters of meaningful political autonomy. Yet relying on these explanations to support *judicial* intervention disregards the defining and vindicating features of parties as responsive to popular will (most classically manifested in Duverger's law). If the electorate had objected to minority disenfranchisement, it could have prevented such discrimination it through direct politics, demanding that party leadership support their efforts. As Klarman notes, there is no reason to believe the judiciary is likely to be better than the legislature at identifying consensus.[78] As a matter of party dynamics,

---

[74] Ibid., 662–6.
[75] Ibid., 658.
[76] Klarman, "The White Primary Rulings," 68.
[77] Ibid., 73.
[78] Michael J. Klarman, "The Puzzling Resistance to Political Process Theory" (1991) 77 *Virginia Law Review* 747, 771.

nothing prevents an allegiance of voters (drawing from across races) from creating a new party that could undertake the necessary primary procedures (gathering signatures, holding their own primary, and so forth). The demand this would make on the party-in-the-electorate is the necessary tradeoff of an extra-constitutional party system, and a feature of the governmental–constitutional order. An alternative would be to use a constitutional amendment to declare parties a formal part of the governmental structure, subjecting them to the relevant discrimination-prohibiting requirements. But attributing constitutional weight on the basis of popular approbation or the normative status of a given political practice without the relevant constitutional "hook" (which is itself traceable back to some form of popular delegation to the judiciary) challenges the judiciary's broader institutional position and destabilizes the primacy of popular self-rule.

The competing concerns of the normative objectionability of such discrimination and the thin constitutional nexus for the oversight of parties drove the doctrinal evolution of the White Primary cases.[79] The exclusion of minority voters from the political process was without doubt normatively wrongful, whether it was undertaken by the state or the party as a private organization. Even Justice Minton, the sole dissenter in *Terry v. Adams*, derided the continuation of the practice by the Jaybirds as an "unworthy scheme."[80]

Herndon, in which identifying a state nexus was trivial, was a terse and unanimous decision. Conversely, *Condon*, where the legislature sought to conceal its discriminatory end through superficially neutral legislation, was fiercely contested. The political context left no doubt that the statutory transfer of power to the party executive committees was meant to perpetuate the blatantly racist dynamic, but Justice McReynolds's dissent noted that this objectionable end was accomplished through "voluntary action" by a political party. By arguing such extra-state party organization is "essential to free government,"[81] McReynolds classified the parties as emergent intermediaries of citizen will, arguing that where the fulcrum of an objectionable electoral dynamic is private rather than state action, the appropriate solution is corresponding private citizen organization, into new parties or new allegiances as politics dictates. The suggestion that the free organization of private citizens is the solution to bad party conduct anticipates Frankfurter's assertion that political questions should be answered by a civically militant electorate. The *Condon* majority, however, argued that the legislature's enablement of the party

---

[79] The Court disregarded one particularly decisive and coherent solution. It could have asserted the general rule that parties (or at least major parties that regularly qualify for access to the general ballot as a result of primary participation) are government actors and generally subject to constitutional scrutiny. Epstein, "Political Parties," p. 175. This conclusion would be transparent and coherent, though it would come at the cost of diminishing or complicating the status of parties as private associations.

[80] *Terry*, 345 US at 484.

[81] *Nixon v. Condon*, 286 US at 104.

made the party's executive committee members "delegates of the state."[82] This disagreement over the status of parties in *Condon* tracks the divergent understanding of parties as either in government or private actors (whether elites or rank-and-file voters). According to the *Condon* majority, statutory authorization gave the relevant party action enough of a quality of being in government to justify constitutional scrutiny. The anomalous holding in *Grovey* continues to parse partisanship on its own terms. Where the party action denied access to the party as an organization, but did not, in itself, deny formal access to the ballot (circumventing the claim that the state's instrumentalities were activated), the Court refused to define the party as a "mere instrumentality or agency for expressing the voice or will of the state."[83] *Herndon*, *Condon*, and *Grovey* are functionally a prolonged debate about how to balance judicial prohibition of normatively condemnable racial exclusion with formal constitutional logic that places party action outside the judicial ken.

Smith and *Terry* decontested this question[84] by unequivocally declaring that non-discrimination in electoral access is a greater normative priority than unconstrained party organization, and that regardless of the formal allocation of institutional authority, the Court will advance this norm. The formal basis is that since the state organizes party primaries, parties in this context can be held to constitutional scrutiny.[85] Such a conclusion would presumably advert to a rule about when parties should be classified as public or private when they collaborate with the state. However, instead of such a doctrinal solution, the *Smith* majority opinion offers a richly substantive conception of American democracy: "organic law grants to all citizens a right to participate in the choice of elected officials without restriction by any state because of race. This grant to the people of the opportunity for choice is not to be nullified by a state through casting its electoral process in a form which permits a private organization to practice racial discrimination in the election."[86] This is a normative commitment to both a first-order democratic principle and the Court's authority to enforce such principles. The broader integrity of democratic process drives the Court, rather than the formal question of if the state is the entity that effects such functional political deprivation (the distinction invoked in *Grovey*), or if the particular aspect of democratic integrity at issue had been allocated to the judiciary to champion. Once *Smith* had made this commitment clear, *Terry* is a logical extension. Justice Black's leading opinion precisely advances this norm. The Jaybird's racist exclusion was condemned on the basis that it denied minorities

---

[82] Ibid., at 85.
[83] *Grovey*, 295 US at 54.
[84] Doctrinally, the Court was willing to simply contradict *Grovey*. *Smith*, 321 US at 670 (Roberts, dissenting).
[85] *Smith*, 321 US at 661–2.
[86] Ibid., at 664.

the vote as a practical matter, "equivalent," because "the damage has been done," to state action.[87] Yet as the dissents of Roberts in *Smith* and Minton in *Terry* observe, the entities effecting the discrimination were private associations, and any attribution to the state is, from a formal perspective, artificial.

The lesson of the White Primary opinions is that the Court will advance terms of legitimate popular autonomy even if this subordinates consistent constitutional analysis (of both first-order substance and the Court's remit). The closest analogue to the White Primary cases is one person, one vote doctrine. In both sets of cases, following fierce contestation over whether the lack of a clear formal constitutional hook prevents judicial prohibition of a normatively undesirable practice, the Court concluded that democratic legitimacy requires conforming to bedrock democratic norms. In the one person, one vote doctrine, the norm was a minimum of political equality; in the White Primary cases, it was a norm prohibiting blatant racial exclusion. By resolving the question through the synthesis of desirable democratic arrangements and the party's role in the practice, the Court declined to adopt a consistent framework for classifying parties and party action. The White Primary cases therefore demonstrate that the Court's treatment of party practice is driven by normative reflection on popular self-rule rather than technical constitutional analysis.

6.4.2 *Party Regulation in Contemporary Election Law*

In the decades following the White Primary cases, the Court opined on a variety of state legislative efforts to dictate or constrain party conduct. It is challenging to identify a consistent practical goal in the Court's reasoning, since the opinions are guided by political intuition and folk assessment of good democratic practice. Underlying this is a lack of consistency of constitutional principle, which can largely be attributed to parties' operating both within the state (and thus being subject to scrutiny) and outside it (and thus deserving associational rights protection). The difficulty of a consistent rights-protecting approach is that the relationships at issue cannot be characterized as simply oppositional, with private organizations struggling to express constituent will against an oppressive state apparatus. The state and the parties typically collaborate, including to run elections. The subsequent legal conflicts link the relevant actors – the state, parties, and the individual constituents who have relationships with both – in shifting constellations of power relationships. Parties often act as quasi-regulatory bodies as much as private organizations, particularly in primaries. As in the White Primary cases, the Court has avoided adopted a strong or coherent perspective on the nature of parties. It has instead advanced a scattered collection of principles of good party governance.

---

[87] *Terry*, 345 US at 469. See also Clark's concurrence, *Terry*, 345 US at 482 (describing the Jaybirds as operating as "part and parcel of the Democratic party," and thus having state standing).

The dominant scholarly response to the regulation of political parties has addressed this lack of consistency by critiquing the rights-based frame as an awkward fit and advancing a structuralist–institutionalist approach directed toward increasing competitiveness.[88] The irony is that the Supreme Court doctrine reflects precisely such instrumentalism. However, the Court, rather than advancing a single specific electoral virtue (such as competitiveness), has sought to balance multiple competing goals. The Court has justified its decisions with party cohesion, minor party competitiveness, and voters' right to switch parties, each of which points in a different direction. A sufficiently broad perspective shows the Court has engaged with these principles with the aim of ensuring free self-rule through party governance, but this is apparent only from a synthesis of the doctrine.

6.4.2.1 Doctrine on Party Regulation

The Court has assayed multiple contexts when statutes that dictate party process could cause constitutional harms. While associational rights provide the primary point of entry, the jurisprudence functionally contests intuitions regarding what regulatory approach to party governance best allows the electorate to use parties as intermediaries to rule themselves (rather than be ruled by parties).

BALLOT ACCESS FOR PARTIES AND CANDIDATES The first question to receive extensive attention was the legality of regulations that limit access to the general ballot. State law typically gives major parties (those that receive a high enough percentage of a vote in the previous election) access to the ballot. If other parties wish to have their candidate on the general election ballot, they must satisfy more procedurally onerous requirements. In evaluating whether such requirements are legal, the Supreme Court has taken a middle course. In *Williams v. Rhodes* it ruled that legislation that makes it extremely difficult even for a party with significant support and resources to gain access violates associational rights[89] because it gives established parties a "complete monopoly" and thereby undermines the "[c]ompetition in ideas and governmental [that] is at the core of our electoral process."[90] This is a classic anti-lockup decision that seeks to advance certain practical qualities in the electoral process. Likewise, excessively onerous rules that condition ballot access on some feature that is not directly correlated with political validity – such as excessively high filing fees – will not pass constitutional muster.[91] Yet as

---

[88] Daniel R. Ortiz, "Duopoly versus Autonomy: How the Two-Party System Harms the Major Parties" (2000) 1000 *Columbia Law Review* 753; Issacharoff, "Private Parties"; Persily, "Political Autonomy"; Michael S. Kang, "Sore Loser Laws and Democratic Contestation" (2011) 99 *Georgetown Law Journal* 1013.
[89] *Williams v. Rhodes*, 393 US 23, 32 (1968).
[90] Ibid., at 32.
[91] *Bullock v. Carter*, 405 US 134 (1972).

long as such statutes are not "excessive or impractical" in conditioning ballot access on a show of popular political support, they will survive.[92] The Court's driving logic is a prudential balancing of competing interests in the electoral process. A ballot access regime must accommodate the "potential fluidity of American political life"[93] by giving organizations with sufficient support viable access to the ballot. But at the same time, governments must have the capacity to "preserv[e] the integrity of the electoral process and regulat[e] the number of candidates on the ballot to avoid undue voter confusion."[94] The Court characterized two schemes with broadly similar structures but different numerical thresholds for petition-based ballot access and different write-in rules as "vastly different"[95] because of how the different features are assessed in this balancing process. Instrumental effects rather than a perceptible principle determine when a statutory ballot access regime serves the facultative, organizational purpose of parties, and when it obstructs it. The Court evaluates when a given legislative rule of party governance aids popular self-rule, and when such a rule shades into exclusionary and anti-competitive domination.

PARTY AFFILIATION BY VOTERS AND CANDIDATES States have also sought to regulate how individuals can affiliate themselves in the electoral process as both voters and candidates. These areas have likewise been dominated by instrumental folk political theorizing. One question has been how long the state may require voters to be registered with a party before participating in its primary election. The Court ruled that a functional lockout of 11 months is acceptable,[96] but that 23 months is not.[97] For candidates, a one-year lockout was deemed constitutional,[98] as was an anti-fusion law that prohibited candidates from being listed as candidates for multiple parties.[99] The Court's reasoning, while framed through associational rights, is driven by a practical assessment of voter access to primaries. Lockouts of a limited duration and scope prevent "raiding" (disruption of party selection processes by hostile voters) and "splintering" (fragmentation of party cohesion due to a lack of stable affiliation). Preventing these phenomena aids useful party cohesion. But excessive restrictions interrupt the fluidity of voter affiliation that makes parties responsive. The dissents in the party affiliation cases are primarily driven by concerns that these practical considerations are not sufficiently well proven to justify the impact of the regulation,

---

[92] *American Party of Texas v. White*, 415 US 767, 783 (1974); see also *Munro v. Socialist Workers Party*, 479 US 189 (1986) (1 percent voter support threshold in blanket primary as limitation for general ballot listing not unconstitutional).
[93] *Jenness v. Fortson*, 403 US 431, 439 (1971).
[94] *American Party of Texas v. White*, 415 US at 782 n. 14 (settled points accepted by all parties and established by case law).
[95] *Jenness*, 403 US at 438.
[96] *Rosario v. Rockefeller*, 410 US 752 (1973).
[97] *Kusper*.
[98] *Storer v. Brown*, 415 US 724 (1974).
[99] *Timmons v. Twin Cities Area New Party*, 520 US 351 (1997).

or are different than the majority opinions anticipate.[100] Yet there is a fundamental peculiarity in the Court becoming intimately involved in assessing how a given practice will affect the granular operation of party politics, given that parties have no formal status in the constitutional structure, and in practice simultaneously act upon the state, within it, and in opposition to it. The result is that these judicial conclusions are based on claims regarding how party politics should operate in the service of popular autonomy.

PARTY SELF-GOVERNANCE State law can also bear more directly on internal party organization where the Court has been more unequivocally protective of party autonomy. The Court has deemed that a party's choice of which delegates to seat at a party convention will trump those dictated by state electoral rules. Yet while framed as a topic of associational rights, the underlying justification is one of political structure. Independent parties are essential facilitators of democratic self-rule: "The Convention services the pervasive national interest in the selection of candidates for national office, and this national interest is greater than any interest of an individual State."[101] In short, the Court's constitutional protection of party autonomy is informed by the need to protect their "essential functions" of "collective decision"-making.[102] The Court has also asserted that associational rights protect parties, but do not impose obligations upon them.[103] As discussed below, this may overlook the blended private–public nature of parties, including their action as state agents. The major point of contestation among the justices is over how to ensure that parties are effective intermediaries for the will of rank-and-file voters. For example, Powell's dissent in *La Follette* is forged in the substantive assessment that the major parties do not have "monolithic ideological identity" but are instead coalitions, such that if the state mandates more inclusive primaries, there is no material threat to parties' intrinsically adaptable associational purpose.[104] Likewise, Rehnquist's concurrence in *Cousins* expresses concerns that the Court is basing its decisions on an intrusively expansive conception of parties that may undercut their practical independence.

PRIMARY DESIGN The question of what institution has the authority to design primaries – the state or parties – has received the most attention from the bench and from scholars. Primaries exemplify state–party collaboration in running elections. The state often recognizes and allocates formal power and resources to parties, but parties retain the ultimate authority and responsibility to select candidates.

---

[100] *Kusper*, 414 US 69 (Rehnquist, dissenting). *Storer*, 415 US at 761; *Timmons*, 520 US at 374–5.
[101] *Cousins*, 419 US at 490.
[102] *Democratic Party v. Wisconsin ex rel. La Follette*, 450 US 107, 123 (1981); see also *Eu v. San Francisco County Democratic Central Committee*, 489 US 214, 232 (1989) (prohibiting statutory "regulation of internal party governance").
[103] *New York State Board of Elections v. Lopez Torres*, 552 US 196, 203 (2008).
[104] *Wisconsin ex rel. Law Follette*, 450 US at 132.

The Supreme Court has sought a prudentially moderated middle ground regarding this collaboration. The Court ruled in *Tashjian* that statutorily mandated primary regimes that deprive parties of the power to select their own constituencies – such as closed primaries that prohibit parties from inviting independent voters or blanket primaries that allow voters from any party to help choose nominees for other parties – are unconstitutional.[105] It also stated in *Tashjian* that party members should "determine for themselves with whom they will associate, and whose support they will seek."[106] Yet the state retains some power to impose primary designs on parties. A statutory semi-closed regime (which allowed parties to adopt closed primaries or invite independents, but prevented voters from crossing party lines to vote in primaries) survived constitutional scrutiny in *Clingman v. Beaver*,[107] as did a modified blanket primary in *Washington State Grange* that allowed any voter to vote for any candidate in a primary (with candidate self-designated party affiliations) and then advanced the top two vote getters to a general election on the basis that the statutorily constructed primary system "does not, by its terms, choose parties' nominees."[108] The Court assesses primary regulation according to its impact on parties' facilitation of voter preference into political action.

6.4.2.2 Evaluating Judicial Oversight of Party Regulation

The politically pragmatic, structural character of the doctrine on the regulation of parties is not incidental. Statutes that dictate the terms of party involvement in elections are an awkward fit for constitutional oversight, and not merely because, as the scholarship has emphasized, rights do not clearly indicate the desirable structures of election law. Rather, the Court's approach is muddled by the intrinsically ambiguous status of parties as both private organizations *and* the entities that coordinate action within the state. Representatives and candidates are simultaneously *members of parties* as private organizations that provide them with partisan support to enter politics and *public servants* (current or prospective) who rely on parties in government to coordinate political decisions. All voters share an identity through the state (mostly as citizens); most also advance a partisan agenda and identity through affiliation with a party and helping to select party nominees.

Because parties stand on both sides of the public–private divide, the standard rights dynamic of protecting private entities from state domination breaks down. For example, when a statute imposes barriers on a minor party's ballot access, the immediate actor is of course the state; but as the Court emphasizes, the underlying concern is that dominant parties exploit the states to enhance their own advantage.

---

[105] *Tashjian v. Republican Party of Connecticut*, 479 US 208 (1986).
[106] Ibid., at 214.
[107] *Clingman v. Beaver*, 544 US 581, 588 (2005).
[108] *Washington State Grange v. Washington State Republican Party*, 552 US 442, 453 (2008).

When a legislature passes such statutes, it acts as an agent of parties (while legislators formally wear their "representative" hats when passing the statute, their "party member" hats provide the underlying motivation), so the conflict could more accurately be characterized as powerful private organizations using their positional advantage to limit the power of weaker organizations. Furthermore, since parties also have a necessary concurrent existence as informed by voters, if voters disliked such statutes, they could communicate this to the major parties either by clamoring for reform through the party or by seeking alternate venues for reform (e.g., party switching or referendums and initiatives). This raises an underlying issue. Where party action changes the terms of representative struggle but does not actually deprive voters of ultimate authority, popular will may seem to offer sufficient recourse. This forms the core of Justice Stevens' dissent in *California Democratic Party v. Jones*, where he defends the constitutionality of the initiative-adopted blanket primary for being chosen directly by the people. Stevens asserts that such a popular decision regarding electoral structure articulates the bedrock of democratic autonomy, which he calls "a quintessential attribute of sovereignty."[109]

Stevens' dissent in *California v. Jones* hints at the broader circularity of judicial oversight of party regulation. Parties' political value is as coordinating intermediaries for the people; parties' power within the state should facilitate popular authority over state action. If this dynamic is operating as it should, when the state enforces terms regarding party conduct, it is merely the people selecting the conditions of their own mediated self-rule. For parties, there is no unambiguous point of transition from public to private, because their purpose (on behalf of the people) is to effect and act through the state (again on behalf of the people). This ambiguity upsets the doctrine of party regulation because it raises the question of whether party action (at least where a party has any real power) could plausibly *always* be identified with the party-in-government and thereby the state, and make parties subject to constitutional scrutiny rather than protection. Such analysis could undermine, for example, *New York State Board of Elections v. Lopez Torres*, according to which individual party members have no constitutional rights against the apparatus of a major party.[110]

Parties' extra-constitutional status further complicates coherent judicial identification of party regulation. If certain aspects, obligations, or capacities of parties were constitutionally delineated, the Court would have some guidance regarding when to treat them as public actors subject to scrutiny and when to treat them as private organizations deserving of rights protection. With no specific substantive guidance from the Constitution, the judiciary has had to adapt associational rights to make sense of parties' multidimensional and cross-cutting ontology. This contributes to the Court's prudential, politically instrumental reasoning. As discussed above, the

---

[109] *California Democratic Party*, 530 US at 590.
[110] *Lopez Torres*, 552 US at 209 (emphasizing "the distinction between constitutionality and wise policy" where a law enables a party to undertake internally questionable practices) (Stevens, concurring).

crux of the party regulation jurisprudence consists of, for example, weighing the anti-splintering interest against the value of voter flexibility, and interrogating granular policy concerns, such as the presence of write-in options,[111] the question of who funds a nominee selection process,[112] and if voters would be confused by a given nominee selection scheme.[113] Such analysis is characteristic of discretionary technocratic regulation, not principled constitutional review. As such, it runs a high risk of lacking clear constitutional imprimatur, and thus being counterpopular.

Two features soften this critique of judicial policymaking. First, such oversight is necessary for the Court to perform its institutional role as a check on state action and the self-interested use of power. The fact that parties are both public and private cuts in both directions and can be used to justify rather than marginalize judicial intervention in party governance. When state–party collaboration serves to diminish opportunities for outsiders, the technical distinction between public and private becomes less relevant than the reality of political exclusion that diminishes the electorate's real political access.

This points to the second quality that reduces the normative onus on the Court: Its lawmaking has sought to advance the redeeming foundation of parties. While the Court's involvement in party regulation may reflect judgments of political prudence rather than constitutional principle, the Court has nonetheless sought to treat parties as facilitators and police them when they act through the state to dominate the expression of popular will. The interests that have been taken to justify state regulation – preventing parties from breaking up and facilitating their coherence and intelligibility to voters in general elections – are precisely those that allow parties to coordinate popular democratic will. Conversely, judges challenge the legality of regulations precisely because they perceive them as impairing parties' capacity to serve such facilitating ends (typically by obstructing them from acting as genuine mechanisms for aggregating genuine coalitions)[114] or exploiting the role of parties to dominate, rather than facilitate, the genuine expression of popular political will.[115] Where judges disagree, it is generally over differing assessments of how a

---

[111] Cf. *Williams v. Rhodes* with *Jenness v. Fortson*.
[112] *Tashjian*, 479 US at 236 (Scalia, dissenting); cf. at 212 (observing that since primaries are publicly funded, the state should have statutory authority over their design).
[113] *Washington State Grange*.
[114] *Eu*; *California Democratic Party*, 530 US at 574; *Wisconsin ex rel. La Follette*, 450 US at 122; *Cousins*, 419 US at 490 (party authority over conventions critical to broader process of self-rule); *Kusper*, 414 US at 56; *Rosario*, 410 US at 769 (lockout period prevents citizens from exploiting fluidity of party affiliation to express political affiliation) (Powell, dissenting).
[115] *Williams v. Rhodes*; *Timmons*, 520 US at 379 (Stevens, dissenting, identifying excessive protectiveness of the two-party system at the cost of political freedom); *Clingman v. Beaver*, 544 US at 619 ("the interests asserted by the State are...protectionist measures that benefit the parties in power") (Stevens, dissenting); *Washington State Grange*, 552 US at 470 (legislation motivated by legislative desire "to blunt the ability of political parties with noncentrist views to endorse and advocate their own candidates") (Scalia, dissenting).

given regulation will influence the facilitating effect of parties. The dissenters in *Storer* and *Timmons*, for example, found insufficient evidence to support an antisplintering rationale; Scalia's dissent in *Washington State Grange* was based on the concern that the statute sought to act as a mechanism for advancing a particular view of partisan competition.[116] With no principled way to parse associational rights, such debates over how parties best advance freedom become the core basis for judicial analysis.

6.4.2.3 The Peculiarity of the Judicial Constitutionalization of Parties

The unique challenge of the Court's oversight of party regulation can be attributed to a distinct quality of parties – their emergent, self-organizing character. While the origin of this quality may be the Constitution's lack of formal accommodation of parties, its greater practical significance is that parties provide a mechanism for political dialogue and conflict that occurs outside formal legal mechanisms. Schattschneider's observation that "parties are able to compel public officers to behave in ways that the law does not contemplate, by methods of which the law is ignorant, without in any way affecting the validity of their official acts"[117] has been updated with the observation that parties accommodate leaders' personal ambitions[118] and mobilize constituents[119] in ways that stand, and ought to stand, beyond formal structure. It would be difficult to conceive of how regulation could (or should) coherently direct the nuanced blend of self-interest and loyalty that inspires leaders, dedicated activists, and constituents to rely on parties to coordinate democratic governance.

Because parties to some extent exist within and through the state, some of this self-organization occurs by law, contrary to Schattschneider's claim that parties operate beyond the law. The thorny question is when regulation of party governance should face judicial constitutional scrutiny. Where such legislation violates some other basis of right (as was unequivocally so in the White Primaries cases), the centrality of party organization poses no difficulty. The other right must simply be protected, and party organization (which has no particular privileged status in the Constitution) has no particular weight. Yet where the state action can only be described as acting on party rule, judicial review is only a commentary on the appropriate conditions of emergent party self-organization. The pragmatic character of judicial oversight of party regulation is not only distinctly political. It also addresses direct, pre-legal political organization that would seem to fall precisely *outside* the constitutionalized, judicially curated domain.

---

[116] *Washington State Grange*, 552 US at 470.
[117] Schattschneider, "Party Government," p. 12.
[118] Schlesinger, "Political Parties," p. 33
[119] Aldrich, "Why Parties," p. 310.

When courts substantively opine on statutes that set the terms of party politics, they formalize the conditions of political self-organization. This is most evident when the judges assert a statute should be struck down, for this defines the minimum conditions for party organization. *Jones* and *Eu*, for example, declare that certain party decisions must occur through constituent organization, rather than through public governance. The *Williams* decision and Stevens's dissent in *Clingman*[120] are explicit declarations that party governance should not excessively benefit major parties. Conversely, when a statute survives, it is often because the Court identifies desirable conditions for party governance.

Because the Court's pronouncements are eminently legal, and thus eminently of the state, judicial oversight of party practices comprises a uniquely assertive constitutionalization of politics. By undertaking judicial review of party regulation, the Court not only imposes, as Richard Pildes accurately notes, "implicit visions of democracy with which all judges must necessarily work,"[121] but it also imposes such substance upon entities that reside outside formal constitutionalism in the state structure of which the judiciary is a part. There is an intrinsic alienness to the Court asserting as a matter of law that an aspect of democracy that is outside the constitutional structure should be evaluated by the standards of that structure, and by an institution (the judiciary) squarely situated within it. If a polity asserts through partisan struggle that a two-party system is preferable, or that certain procedures for selecting partisan nominees are preferable, the legitimacy of the judicial review, limited by the Court's constitutional remit, is tenuous. Even the substantive judicial focus on making parties a locus of freedom cannot resolve the peculiarity of imposing constitutional expectations upon a constituent part of governance located outside of formal constitutional governance.

6.4.3 The Shadow Battle over Emergent Politics: Partisan Gerrymandering and the Ambiguity of Affiliation

The difficulties posed by judicial oversight of the relationship between parties and the state is heightened the fierce, recent struggle over partisan gerrymandering.[122] Partisan gerrymandering allocates voters to electoral districts by party identity, typically to the advantage of the party in power. While it may seem to be another variety of party regulation, at least two differences complicate treating it as such, particularly for the purposes of judicial review. First, districting is wholly under the authority of the state, even though such decisions may impact parties. Second, and relatedly, it

---

[120] *Clingman*, 544 US at 620.
[121] Richard H. Pildes, "The Constitutionalization of Democratic Politics" (2004) 118 *Harvard Law Review* 29, 126.
[122] This section adapts and updates material from two previous articles, Eisler, "Constitutionalization of Statistics" and Eisler, "Partisan Gerrymandering and the Illusion of Unfairness."

is distinguished by not directly bearing on party practice or access to the political process. Unlike a ballot access or voter registration rule, partisan districting does nothing to directly obstruct parties (including the ordinary voters who comprise the party) from performing their coordinating intermediary function; an effective party (and responsive, savvy voters) will adapt in response to a partisan gerrymander.[123] Unlike in the context of racial gerrymandering, there is no unequivocal constitutional or explicit federal legislative mandate that addresses the impact of districting on party identity.

Determining the legitimacy of judicial review of partisan gerrymanders is far murkier than for direct party regulation. The state legitimately deploys the power at issue; the political institution affected by the practice lies outside typical constitutional supervision. Judicial intervention can only be justified as the innovative and self-motivated (rather than constitutionally grounded) assertion of a norm regarding how democratic autonomy dictates the terms of party governance. By imposing such a substantive and independently generated condition of popular autonomy, striking down districtings for their partisan implications would risk an egregious type of counterpopularism. Countervailing this risk is broad acceptance that partisan gerrymanders are *normatively* objectionable.[124] Even the majority in *Rucho* that denied judicial oversight of partisan gerrymanders declared the practice was "incompatible with democratic principles."[125] Such districtings are an abuse of power undertaken by the dominant actor to consolidate their control.

The judicial review of partisan gerrymandering thus comprises one of the trickiest instantiations of counterpopularism. The Court must balance the limits of its own institutional participation against the normative undesirability of a practice. While the jurisprudence reflects this foundational struggle, the evolution of both the law and the scholarship has tended to obscure it. The past two decades of partisan gerrymandering litigation have predominantly focused on the unhelpful question of standards of review, rather than the fundamental question of the appropriate locus of power for setting electoral process to ensure sound popular self-rule.

6.4.3.1 The Substance and Puzzle of Partisan Gerrymandering

Partisan gerrymandering consists of drawing political districts to enhance or diminish voters' power by political affiliation. It exploits the fact that most representatives must win within a given geographic subdivision (such as a congressional district). It is possible to exploit knowledge of where voters with particular party loyalties reside

---

[123] For a full theoretical account, see Eisler, "Partisan Gerrymandering and the Illusion of Unfairness."
[124] See, e.g., Michael J. Klarman, "Majoritarian Judicial Review: The Entrenchment Problem" (1997) 85 *Georgetown Law Journal* 491, 516 ("indefensibly anti-majoritarian").
[125] *Rucho v. Common Cause* 139 S. Ct. 2484, 2506 (2019), citing *Arizona State Legislature v. Arizona Independent Redistricting Comm'n*, 135 S.Ct. 2652, 2586 (2015).

to manipulate the constituency boundaries to impact election outcomes. The artificially drawn districts will not reflect the actual levels of support for parties across an entire polity. Its equivalent for race is racial vote dilution, which is unequivocally illicit (see Chapter 7).

Technically, partisan gerrymandering is accomplished by "cracking" districts where disfavored voters have a narrow majority apart, and "packing" these voters into districts where the disfavored party has disproportionate supermajorities.[126] As Nicholas Stephanopoulos and Eric McGhee explain,[127] this "wastes" votes from the disfavored party. A simple example illustrates the force of partisan gerrymandering.[128] Imagine a polity with five representative districts split 52–48 percent between two parties, "R" and "D." While a completely homogeneous distribution of voters would lead to five R seats (each district would be 52–48 percent R, and thus, the R candidate would narrowly win in each), as is typical in real polities there is some "clustering" to the distributions. For example, if D voters are concentrated in a small number of cities (two for the sake of simplicity), a neutral, "natural" districting plan would likely lead to R candidates winning three seats and D candidates winning two.

If, however, following the election the 3–2 R majority engages in sufficiently aggressive partisan gerrymandering, it could create oddly shaped districts that "lumped" as many D voters into one district as possible. A "barbell"–shaped district linking the two cities, for example, could lump most of the D voters into one district (packing this district) and distribute the remaining D voters equally among other districts ("cracking" a district that previously had a majority of these D voters). If the R map makers could create a district that was almost wholly D (say entirely D for simplicity's sake, so 20 percent of the total voters in the state), and remaining D voters were equally distributed among other districts, this would leave four districts that were 65 percent R and 35 percent D. The new, aggressively gerrymandered plan would yield four R seats and one D seat. Thus, the gerrymander gives R members disproportionately greater power, impairs the D voters' power, and jeopardizes the efficacy and meaning of their political association. In addition to distorting the allocation of seats, the new districts tend to be uncompetitive; four of them are comfortable majority R and one is overwhelmingly D. This is an example of how partisan gerrymandering is not only an affront to fair partisan conflict, but also facilitates

---

[126] See Samuel Issacharoff, and Pamela S. Karlan, "Where to Draw the Line: Judicial Review of Political Gerrymanders" (2004) 153 *University of Pennsylvania Law Review* 541, 551; Bruce E. Cain, *The Reapportionment Puzzle* (California: University of California Press, 1984), pp. 148–50.

[127] Stephanopoulos and McGhee. "Efficiency Gap."

[128] Cain," The Reapportionment Puzzle," pp. 148–60 offers some other readily accessible examples and illustrations of this process. For a more technical statistical analysis that identifies partisan gerrymanders by their artificiality, see Jowei Chen and Jonathan Rodden, "Cutting Through the Thicket: Redistricting Simulations and the Detection of Partisan Gerrymanders" (2015) 14 *Election Law Journal: Rules, Politics, and Policy* 331.

anti-competitive entrenchment.[129] Finally, obtaining such power gives the R leadership the potential to eventually thwart majority will. It can draw and redraw districts as new demographic and census data arrives, potentially maintaining an R representative majority even if the slight edge in voter approval is lost. A 3–2 R advantage in representatives could be maintained so long as R voters comprise more than 30 percent of the electorate (two districts of 100 percent D voters, plus three districts that are very marginally R, though the R hold over such districts would be extremely vulnerable, and a savvy D party strategy could flip at least one).

Other scholars and activists have developed a dizzying array of methods for generating, identifying, and evaluating districting plans as partisan gerrymanders.[130] From a technical perspective, it is particularly relevant to note that more accurate and extensive data on the character and intensity of voter affiliation and increasingly subtle computer programs for effecting gerrymanders have made such districtings more aggressive and more durable.

6.4.3.2 The Tangled History of Partisan Gerrymandering Before the Court

In one of the anomalies of the case law, the impact of partisan gerrymandering on popular self-rule has become increasingly distant from the face of the doctrine (and the scholarship) over time, even as it has remained the unresolved stumbling block. A critical analysis of the cases shows it remains at the core, but with increasing layers of obfuscation.

THE STUMBLING EMERGENCE OF THE PARTISAN GERRYMANDERING DOCTRINE
The first case to address partisanship in districting, *Gaffney v. Cummings*, did so briefly and in passing, but indicated the challenges to come. The districting plan at issue, generated by a bipartisan districting board,[131] used information on voters' political preferences to create "a rough scheme of proportional representation of the two major political parties."[132] The decision established that districting that incorporates voters' political identity is, in the absence of some other wrong, constitutionally acceptable. The Court's reasoning in *Gaffney* is quite circumspect; it

---

[129] *League of United Latin American Citizens v. Perry*, 548 US 399 (2006) provides one of the most vivid illustrations of how parties use gerrymandering to attempt to hold on to political power even after popular opinion has changed. See also Daryl Levinson and Benjamin I. Sachs, "Political Entrenchment and Public Law" (2015) 125 *Yale Law Journal* 400, 416–8.

[130] Stephanopoulos and McGhee, "Efficiency Gap" (using "wasted votes" as the basis for assessing partisan gerrymandering); Chen and Rodden, "Cutting Through the Thicket" (using simulations to assess partisan gerrymandering); Bernard Grofman and Gary King, "The Future of Partisan Symmetry as a Judicial Test for Partisan Gerrymandering after *LULAC v. Perry*" (2007) 6 *Election Law Journal: Rules, Politics, and Policy* 2 (using partisan symmetry, which compares the vote–seat ratio, to assess partisan gerrymandering).

[131] *Gaffney*, 412 US at 736.

[132] Ibid., at 738.

reserves judgment regarding the conditions under which disempowering voters on the grounds of political identity might be a constitutional wrong. It only observes that the judiciary should not pursue "the impossible task of extirpating politics from what are the essentially political processes of the sovereign States," and suggests that "judicial interest should be at the lowest ebb" when a state seeks proportional allocation of voter power by party.[133]

Scholars have expressed increasing skepticism of *Gaffney*, particularly as polarization has increased and partisan gerrymandering has been deployed with greater aggression. For example, Issacharoff and Karlan have condemned *Gaffney*-style bipartisan gerrymanders as "shacking," (use of gerrymanders to achieve entrenchment of sitting representatives regardless of party), a practice which "renders elections... immune to voter preferences."[134] This critique has bite, but only if certain pessimistic assumptions are met regarding party politics. It presumes the defining pathologies of contemporary partisanship: that voters are polarized and committed to their parties, and that party elites exploit party structures to illicitly dominate politics. If these assumptions are incorrect, and if parties are instead under the sway of voters as much as elites, and voters are willing to switch parties to express their political will and hold representatives accountable,[135] such bipartisan gerrymanders may be less effective (or may produce an alternate mode of accountability if representatives maintain power simply by adapting to their constituents wishes). Indeed, without a baseline theory of democracy, it is difficult to condemn such a districting as pathological at all; it might be a hypothetically valid alternative form of democratic structure.[136] In safe districts, the struggle for power and expression of popular will may move into new venues, particularly within parties. Voters might express their preferences and contest current policy by selecting leaders and platforms from the dominant party, rather than switching to competing parties. If such alternative modes of democratic self-rule are not available, this suggests the presence of the pathologies of parties. If the presence of these pathologies is a precondition for bipartisan gerrymanders to be an ill, such districtings are only conditionally problematic.

A decade later, *Davis v. Bandemer* queried the legality of partisan gerrymanders that, instead of reflecting a bipartisan consensus, sought to aggrandize the party in power and disadvantage its competitors. A plurality of the Supreme Court concluded that partisan gerrymandering *could* violate the EPC, but that the districting in question (in Indiana) did not constitute such a violation.[137] The test

---

[133] Ibid., at 754.
[134] Issacharoff and Karlan, "Judicial Review of Political Gerrymanders," 571.
[135] See *Vieth v. Jubelirer* 541 US 267, 289 (2004) (non-determinativeness of party identity). For the argument that it is a function of political contestation, see Daniel Lowenstein and Jonathan Steinberg, "The Quest for Legislative Districting in the Public Interest: Elusive or Illusory" (1985) 33 *UCLA Law Review* 1, 74–6.
[136] Persily, "Foxes Guarding Henhouses."
[137] *Bandemer*, 478 US at 129.

for identifying illegal gerrymanders articulated in *Bandemer* is vague and difficult to satisfy:

> [A]n equal protection violation may be found only where the electoral system substantially disadvantages certain voters in their opportunity to influence the political process effectively...such a finding of unconstitutionality must be supported by evidence of continued frustration of the will of a majority of the voters or effective denial to a minority of voters of a fair chance to influence the political process.[138]

The *Bandemer* test exemplifies the challenge facing judicial oversight of politicized districting, and of partisan struggle in general. The plurality articulates democratic ideals – majority rule, "fair" influence for all voters – but without further specification, they offer little useful guidance because they will be clearly contravened only in the most egregious electoral arrangements. Recognizing that parties can be an internal venue of contestation highlights this lack of clarity regarding what makes a gerrymander illicitly egregious. Since the popular will can be expressed through either internal party selection mechanisms or voters' partisan affiliation,[139] it is extraordinarily difficult to determine whether partisan districting has deprived voters of political access unless some voters are excluded from a major party (as in the White Primaries cases). Where the party system is open to all voters, partisan gerrymandering can only be condemned through a more elaborately specified delineation of the norms of party governance. This in turn requires a vision of how party governance should contribute to democratic self-rule.

The *Bandemer* plurality fails to provide such a vision. Both O'Connor's concurrence (which rejects judicial oversight of partisan gerrymandering) and Powell's dissent (which asserted the partisan gerrymandering at issue should have been held unconstitutional) advance clearer visions of party governance. O'Connor argues that parties, "the dominant groups" in the political process, can "fend[] for themselves," and that judicially imposed terms of partisan struggle will, if coherent, "evolve towards some loose form of proportionality," a principle beyond the judicial remit.[140] In effect, she argues that emergent political struggle (including through partisan gerrymandering) is self-regulating, and that the judiciary has no basis for imposing its own conception of appropriate partisan contestation. Conversely, Powell asserts that "the State should treat its voters as standing in the same position, regardless of their political beliefs or party affiliation."[141] This declares that the norm of inter-group equality dominates group affiliation. O'Connor and Powell present two opposing views of the appropriate treatment of partisan struggle and if the judiciary ought to demand it conform to higher-priority norms.

---

[138] *Ibid.*, at 128, 133.
[139] Eisler, "Illusion of Unfairness."
[140] *Bandemer*, 478 US at 152–6. O'Connor's former point is elaborated in the argument that gerrymandering might be part of a legitimate political struggle. Schuck, "The Thickest Thicket," 1350.
[141] *Bandemer*, 478 US at 166.

The *Bandemer* test is so vague in articulation and demanding in character that lower courts largely allowed partisan gerrymanders to stand. As legislatures became increasingly bold and sophisticated in crafting partisan districting plans, the Supreme Court came under increasing pressure to offer guidance. However, the Court's first attempt to do so in *Vieth v. Jubelirer*, addressing an aggressive Republican gerrymander of Pennsylvania following the 2000 census, yielded a fiercely contested 4-1-4 split on the bench. This fractured decision left the law in an even more confused condition. The *Vieth* plurality decision, penned by Scalia on behalf of the four conservative justices, not only denied a constitutional wrong in the districting at issue, but also sought to overturn *Bandemer* and reject judicial oversight of partisan gerrymandering. Scalia asserted a "lack of judicially discoverable and manageable standards."[142] Two core assertions underpin his argument: (1) that nothing in the Constitution identifies politicized districting as wrongful and (2) that judicial attempts to craft one lack institutional legitimacy. In his concurrence, Kennedy agreed the gerrymander at issue was not unconstitutional, but was unwilling to reject the *possibility* that partisan gerrymanders might be found to be illicit in the future. He speculated it might be possible to prove a gerrymander was illicit under either the EPC or by associational rights.[143] The progressive dissenters offered an array of tests. Stevens argued that gerrymanders should be illegal when a districting seeks to effect a partisan gerrymander; Souter advocated adopting a burden-shifting test similar to that used in employment discrimination cases, which require plaintiffs to make an initial prima facie case that satisfies five technical criterion; and Breyer stated that such districtings violate the EPC if they effect "unjustified entrenchment."[144]

The great irony of *Vieth* is that the justices wrestle over the same questions at issue in *Bandemer*, but with even less analytic commonality. As this chapter has established, the decisive issue in deciding if courts should prohibit partisan gerrymandering is the normative priority of emergent party organization compared to other norms of popular autonomy, and the legitimacy of the judiciary enforcing this priority. The rejection of manageable standards is a refusal to articulate a theory of democracy that delineates the appropriate role of parties, at least from the Court's institutional position. The foundational argument for this refusal is the fluid and emergent nature of party composition (a point O'Connor made more straightforwardly in *Bandemer*),[145] which Scalia evoked with unhelpful obliqueness by maintaining that it is impossible to *measure* appropriate terms of partisanship.[146] Conversely, each of the progressive dissents is willing to advance some norm – of

---

[142] *Vieth*, 541 US at 277, quoting *Baker*, 369 US 186, 217 (1962).
[143] *Vieth*, 541 US at 314.
[144] *Ibid.*, at 361.
[145] *Bandemer*, 478 US at 156.
[146] *Vieth*, 541 US at 296.

representative integrity and disinterest (Stevens), political practice (Souter), or competitive majority rule (Breyer) – that should be prioritized over emergent party organization. Each of these progressive proposals is a more elaborate version of Powell's more direct declaration that equality should be prioritized over party governance.

SCHOLARLY INNOVATION AND CONSERVATIVE REJECTION According to Michael Kang, *Vieth's* 4-1-4 split "[left] it bizarrely unclear where the law of partisan gerrymandering st[ood]."[147] The result was an effusion of activist and scholarly innovation. Shortly after *Vieth*, a messy race-and-party conflict over Texas districting in *League of United Latin American Citizens v. Perry* (*LULAC*)[148] created a first opportunity to revisit the question. Liberal justices suggested a "bloodfeud" gerrymander was grounds for legal intervention[149] and proposed adoption of new tests.[150] Kennedy, remaining a swing justice, indicated he still saw no workable standard, and the conservative justices ignored the topic altogether. Justice Kennedy rejected the partisan symmetry standard proposed by Gary King for lacking "a reliable measure of fairness," not accommodating possible vote switching, and suggesting that the Court invalidate plans based on "a hypothetical state of affairs."[151] Yet Kennedy's engagement tantalized scholars by suggesting that an adequate technical standard could convince him.

In the interim, the Court addressed a case tangential to the legality of partisan gerrymanders that further illuminated the analytic battle lines in the justices' own approach to the problem. Given the judiciary's unwillingness to prevent partisan gerrymanders, one solution would be to address the issue through alternate non-judicial mechanisms such as independent redistricting commissions.[152] Exploiting the capacity for popular initiative-based lawmaking under the state constitution, voters in Arizona transferred power over districting to a neutral commission. In *Arizona State Legislature v. Arizona Independent Redistricting Commission*, the Arizona legislature protested, arguing that the Elections Clause of the federal Constitution gives state legislatures, rather than the electorate, power over districting. A bare majority of justices (progressives plus Kennedy) interpreted the word "legislature" in the Elections Clause to plausibly incorporate the electorate, when vested with lawmaking power. This point is buttressed by their invocation of the "importance of direct democracy as a means to control election regulations."[153] Thus, popular state

---

[147] Michael S. Kang, "When Courts Won't Make Law: Partisan Gerrymandering and a Structural Approach to the Law of Democracy" (2007) 68 *Ohio State Law Journal* 1097, 1111 (2007).
[148] *LULAC*, 548 US 399.
[149] *Ibid.*, at 456 (Stevens, dissenting).
[150] *Ibid.*, at 456 (Stevens, dissenting); at 483 (Souter, dissenting).
[151] *Ibid.*, at 419–20 (Kennedy, concurring).
[152] See Issacharoff, "Gerrymandering and Political Cartels," 644; cf. Persily, "Foxes Guarding Henhouses," 667.
[153] *Arizona State Legislature*, 135 S.Ct. at 2677.

referendums provide a possible way for the electorate to set its own terms of self-rule. The four conservatives dissented on the grounds that this reading was textually untenable (though two would have rejected the Arizona legislature's standing as a threshold matter, leaving the law in place). The substantive dissent, while based on a close technical reading of the word "legislature,"[154] would have deprived the polity of a practical means to fight partisan gerrymandering. Advanced by the same justices who deny that the federal Constitution provides grounds for addressing partisan gerrymandering, this position would further narrow the array of options available to the electorate to limit self-serving districting by legislators – and do so from both sides, refusing a constitutional solution but interpreting the Constitution to preclude solutions advanced through other political mechanisms. While it might be possible to argue that this suggests party rule must occur through particular modalities of conflict permitted by the Constitution, in practice, the conservative view shows little appreciation for the popular desire to prevent gerrymandering. While not directly bearing on the illegality of partisan gerrymanders, *Arizona State Legislature* emphasized a number of strategic points from *Vieth*. It showed the level of divergence between the progressives and conservatives in their perception of the danger of partisan gerrymanders and in their willingness to tolerate the weaponization of party organization. It further emphasized the degree to which Kennedy's vote was, at the time, decisive of the state of the law.

Inspired by Kennedy's concession in *Vieth* that he *might*, with a sufficiently convincing measure, identify an illegal partisan gerrymander, scholars redoubled their efforts, focusing on new, more analytically compelling metrics. The method that received the most attention, the efficiency gap metric championed by Nicholas Stephanopoulos and Eric McGhee and advanced by plaintiffs in post-*Vieth* litigation,[155] prefers simplicity to complexity, and does not require consideration of a hypothetical state of affairs.[156] The formula compares the number of votes cast for a party with the number of seats obtained,[157] thereby calculating "wasted" votes. Jowei Chen and Jonathan Rodden used traditional redistricting criteria to create multiple simulations of "neutral" maps[158] and compared them to real districtings to determine the likelihood of a partisan gerrymander.[159] Gary King continued to refine partisan symmetry as a metric.[160] While these methods offer sophisticated means of

---

[154] Ibid., at 2680.
[155] Simon Jackman, *Assessing the Current Wisconsin State Legislative Districting Plan*, exhibit for appellees, 3:15-cv-0:421 (July 7, 2015).
[156] Jackman, "Assessing," at 845.
[157] The formula is detailed in Stephanopoulos and McGhee, "Efficiency Gap," 851 (The efficiency gap is "the difference between the parties' respective wasted votes, divided by the total number of votes cast in the election. Wasted votes include both "lost" votes (those cast for a losing candidate) and "surplus" votes (those cast for a winning candidate but in excess of what she needed to prevail)") (emphasis omitted).
[158] Chen and Rodden, "Cutting Through the Thicket," 332.
[159] Ibid., 338–9.
[160] Grofman and King, "The Future of Partisan Symmetry."

identifying gerrymanders, they do little to justify their constitutional status. Other scholars have offered principled arguments against the legality of the practice based on the due process clause,[161] associational rights,[162] and partisan neutrality embedded in constitutional doctrine.[163]

Yet when the Court decisively opined on partisan gerrymandering in *Rucho v. Common Cause*, these nuanced analyses were brushed aside. Kennedy had been replaced by Justice Kavanaugh, giving the conservatives a five-justice majority. The Roberts-penned opinion condemned partisan gerrymandering as a moral matter,[164] but denied the judiciary should intervene:

> partisan gerrymandering claims present political questions beyond the reach of the federal courts. Federal judges have no license to reallocate political power between the two major political parties, with no plausible grant of authority in the Constitution, and no legal standards to limit and direct their decisions. Judicial action must be governed by standard, by rule, and must be principled, rational, and based upon reasoned distinctions found in the Constitution or laws.[165]

This statement blends two ideas: (1) it is institutionally inappropriate for the judiciary to meddle in partisan struggle and the contours of party identity (a normative claim about the position of party governance, in democratic self-rule, and the Court's power to police it) and (2) the federal judiciary cannot consistently identify partisan gerrymandering (a descriptive claim regarding technical limitations). In doing so, the majority combines a defensible (if contestable) assertion regarding the norms of democratic self-rule with a conceptually deficient descriptive assertion. The idea that parties ought to develop their political identity free from constitutional interference advances a principled understanding of parties as extra-constitutional and popularly emergent. However, the claim that no consistent test is available is false. Given that the Court developed holistic and context-sensitive tests for malapportionment and racial gerrymandering that include discretion or holistic evaluation, it could do the same for partisan gerrymanders. Whether any such test would involve an inappropriate deployment of judicial institutional authority or expertise, or would indefensibly complicate legislative districting, is a normative question of democratic self-rule rather than technical limitations. The relatively recent focus on the manageability of standards and the purported impossibility of a consistent test, as opposed to this bedrock normative question, has become a pretext or distraction in the case law. Had the third political question prong from *Baker v. Carr*, that a

---

[161] Edward B. Foley, "Due Process, Fair Play, and Excessive Partisanship: A New Principle for Judicial Review of Election Laws" (2017) 84 *University of Chicago Law Review* 655.
[162] Daniel P. Tokaji, "Voting Is Association" (2017) 43 *Florida State University Law Review* 763, 790.
[163] Kang, "Gerrymandering and the Constitutional Norm against Government Partisanship."
[164] *Rucho*, 139 S.Ct. at 2506.
[165] *Rucho*, 139 S. Ct. at 2506–7 (quoting *Vieth*, 541 US at 278–9, quotation marks and emendations omitted).

question is an initial policy determination better left to non-judicial discretion, been used to guide judicial analysis, the law might have developed far more clearly.[166] *Bandemer* gave roughly equal attention to the initial policy determination question and the manageability question;[167] the second *Baker* prong and manageability did not become the dominant focus of the jurisprudence until *Vieth*.

Framed by the second political question prong from *Baker* that identifies manageable standards as a basis for justiciability, the *Rucho* dissent passionately advanced two points: (1) partisan gerrymandering is an inexcusable affront to democracy (a point of consensus with the majority) and (2) several tests are available to identify partisan gerrymanders. This latter point is accurate, but the dissent goes too far in suggesting that such a test can be normatively neutral. The dissent argues that standards are already available that "do[] not use any judge made conception of electoral fairness" and thus "[do] not have to … choose among competing visions of electoral fairness."[168] This is obviously untrue, for in doing so the Court would be required to choose between "contested notions" and "competing visions of electoral fairness."[169] Such a test (including to check for a familiar legal threshold such as whether partisan self-interest was the "predominant purpose") would necessarily advance a contestable norm of how partisanship makes demands of electoral arrangements. At a minimum, any declaration that "excessive" partisan gerrymanders are illegal commits to the principle that partisan neutrality is a norm that should have constitutional weight enforced by the courts, as opposed to (as the majority suggests) a pathology with only non-judicial remedies.

6.4.3.3 Partisan Gerrymandering and the Insoluble Complexities of Party Character

The partisan gerrymandering jurisprudence exemplifies a general feature of the law on party governance. Faced with a multi-layered and complex social phenomenon of ambiguous constitutional status, the justices seek to reduce the problem to one of familiar legal tests. In the context of party regulation, this took the form of associational rights, which, if it cannot inform the complexity of the issues at stake, at least does not point in the wrong direction. In the partisan gerrymandering space, however, by transmuting the issue into the judiciary's ability to identify appropriate standards, the Court has obscured the topics at hand: (1) what is the relevant nature of parties in the districting context; and (2) does the judiciary have an institutional mandate to intervene? If these questions are answered in the affirmative, developing an appropriate test would become a relatively trivial exercise of technical discretion

---

[166] *Baker*, 369 US at 217.
[167] *Bandemer*, 478 US at 125.
[168] *Rucho*, 139 S. Ct. at 2516.
[169] Ibid., at 2519; cf. Pildes, "Constitutionalization," 126.

(as the plethora of sophisticated tests indicates); and if the Court is not deemed to have the authority to intervene, or the character of parties in the districting context is deemed beyond the judicial ken, the question is moot.

Answering these two questions requires engaging with some of the thorniest questions of the operation of party governance within democratic self-rule. Whether partisan gerrymandering causes sufficient harm to democratic freedom to justify the judiciary policing electoral process depends on assertions regarding the basic composition of parties. Unlike malapportionment, the vote dilution inherent in partisan gerrymandering does not deprive voters of basic access to political process. Unlike racial gerrymandering, it does not act upon an immutable characteristic that oppresses a minority group. Rather, parties are malleable, fluid intermediaries (at least under healthy conditions of party governance). Their identities should adapt to various conditions to best translate voter preferences into political action. Voters who believe a party affiliation no longer serves their interest may switch parties, or seek to form new coalitions with other voters (including those on the margins of the dominant party who may be tempted away). Conversely, party leaders might realize that a party becoming competitive might require luring voters away from a dominant party in "cracked" districts by changing policies to appease them. While these party platform changes might alienate some members of the gerrymandered party, the margin in "packed" districts give it the buffer to do so.[170]

Where such adaptation is possible, partisan gerrymanders might induce a party to adapt to ensure it represents the popular will. An effective partisan gerrymander must leave some districts controlled by the dominant party vulnerable to effective adaptation by the gerrymandered party.[171] However, certain political conditions could stymie such adaptation. For example, where party identity is strongly associated with some other feature, voters might be loath to abandon their affiliation with a party. The partisan gerrymander, and partisan affiliation itself, may simply be an intermediary to diluting the vote of some other group. This could also assume more subtle forms. If gerrymandered districts lump together voters with many disparate interests (what Nicholas Stephanopoulos calls "spatial diversity"),[172] it may be harder for them to respond by forming new allegiances due to the breadth of interests representatives would need to address.

Whether such conditions apply, however, speaks to far more than the mere presence of a partisan districting. Where parties are performing their effective role as adaptive intermediaries, partisan districtings could create new opportunities for adaptation.[173] Moreover, voter-led initiatives have shown that the electorate can

---

[170] Eisler, "Partisan Gerrymandering and the Illusion of Unfairness."
[171] Cain, "The Reapportionment Puzzle."
[172] Nicholas O. Stephanopoulos, "Spatial Diversity" (2012) 125 *Harvard Law Review* 1903.
[173] Kang, "Bright Side of Partisan Gerrymandering"; Jacob Eisler, "Partisan Gerrymandering and the Illusion of Unfairness."

effectively address partisan districting on its own terms. Yet where voters and leaders are hyperpolarized and unlikely to adapt (either by switching parties or changing the party platform or composition) to district borders that disadvantage them, a partisan gerrymander can deprive some constituents of equal political voice. Thus, evaluating the harm that partisan gerrymander causes to free self-rule cannot be assessed based on the districting's immediate partisan effects, but instead on how parties can respond in their vindicating role as facultative intermediaries of political will. The Court has already demonstrated some sensitivity to these questions in the party regulation domain by incorporating the contrasting values of fluidity of access and party cohesion, but determining the impact of partisan gerrymandering requires a far more comprehensive assessment of the operation of parties and when their conduct is harmful to constituent self-rule. Moreover, since partisan gerrymandering, unlike party regulation, does not *directly* affect individuals' capacity to affiliate and pursue representation, without a position regarding these contextual factors it is impossible to opine on its normative wrongfulness.

These factors are influenced by social realities. This highlights the multi-layered challenge facing judicial review of partisan gerrymandering. To legitimately strike down legislative districtings as partisan gerrymanders, the judiciary must assert positions on how parties *should* operate, how they *do* operate, and how partisan gerrymandering affects their desirable and actual functioning. Each of these questions is deeply and independently contestable, and the answer to whether and when the Court should strike down partisan districtings depends on their *intersection*. For example, it could be argued that parties only perform their proper roles as intermediaries when the process of affiliation and organization occurs with no external interference, in which case any disruptive adaptation caused by gerrymanders might be perceived as an infringement on voter freedom. If, however, party governance is seen as legitimately comprising a robust struggle between partisans, including "bloodfeud" gerrymanders, disruptive gerrymanders might be a legitimate – or even desirable – aspect of party governance.[174] The conditions considered necessary for parties to perform their roles will interact with the descriptive conditions of politics to determine whether partisan gerrymanders inhibit effective representation.

An appropriate legal approach to partisan gerrymandering would need to address the second-order question of legitimate judicial intervention, which itself is a multi-layered enquiry. The first question is the Court's legitimacy to assess the two ingredients that permit the identification of problematic gerrymanders: (1) the appropriate functioning of parties (particularly given their extra-constitutional origins); and (2) the descriptive conditions of politics. But underneath this lies the question of whether the judiciary has the authority to make assertions regarding these matters, and at this level of comprehensiveness. In short, the Court must establish not only the correct answers to these first-order questions, but do so while vindicating its

---

[174] See, e.g., Persily, "Foxes Guarding Henhouses"; Schuck, "The Thickest Thicket."

authority over this particular domain of democratic process. The question that has dominated the jurisprudence – that of judge-made standards – unhelpfully conflates these two questions.

Popular autonomy frames this enquiry and provides a polestar for the bench. The question of whether parties traditionally fall under constitutional supervision is contestable; yet it is uncontestable that their legitimate role is facilitating free self-rule by the electorate. The entire domain of election law is characterized by the judiciary's willingness to fiercely contest which norms would do the most to advance free self-rule. This also applies to the muddled partisan gerrymandering debate. Recognizing the centrality of popular autonomy clarifies the terms of this debate, particularly the most pressing layered questions facing the judiciary in its oversight of parties. Party governance, like judicial intervention in election law, is redeemed by parties' contribution to popular self-rule. This places the judiciary in the particularly delicate situation of balancing its own benefit to the electorate's free self-rule against the constraint of an institution whose own contribution to popular autonomy is defined by its emergent quality.

6.5 COUNTERPOPULAR OVERSIGHT OF PARTIES AND TERMS OF POPULAR SELF-RULE

The complexity of evaluating partisan gerrymandering, and the analytically jumbled debate about it on the bench, epitomizes the judicial response to party governance more broadly. The justices advance their pragmatic intuitions about what approach to party governance yields an electoral system that best advances popular autonomy. Yet because the Court has failed to parse the character of party governance (and its various possible relationships to constitutional oversight), the facial contestation has not reflected the norms at issue. The sole exception is the arc of the White Primaries cases, in which an external value was strictly prioritized over party governance. But where the Court has contested the nature of parties as an internal matter, it has been hesitant to directly address the critical norms of party governance. The decisive norms of the contestable nature of parties, and the parallel contestable propriety of judicial intervention, can be discerned underneath the opaque debates, as discussed above, but they are not at the forefront of contestation.

This may reflect the Court's tendency, understandable under the common law tradition, to use familiar constitutional categories. Association has dominated the party regulatory space, and the political question doctrine has come to dominate partisan gerrymandering. Yet while association may provide a point of entry, it offers nowhere near the structural complexity necessary to make sense of party governance, and the political question doctrine is an excessively narrow lens for understanding its complexities. In sum, the Court's doctrinal tendency has led to gross simplification when considering party as an internal matter.

However, simply suggesting the Court should embrace complexity poses its own challenges. The multiplicity of issues necessary to even make contestation over party governance coherent distinguishes it from the other domains of judicial election law. For instance, the one person, one vote doctrine was a debate over the primacy of minimal procedural equality; campaign finance has reflected a long-running struggle over free preference formation; and race in election law has reflected a fierce debate over substantive equality. It is far harder to pose a unitary question of whether judicially enforced norms would ensure party governance successfully facilitates free self-rule. There are too many shifting (and reasonably contestable) variables, such as how best to conceive of parties (e.g., made of voters, of elites, of representatives in government); to what degree should parties' extra-constitutional aspects be weighed, linked to their status as both within and outside the state; to what degree should parties be treated as organically emergent and organically popular, rather than elite-led; and the descriptive question of the degree to which they are tainted by hyperpolarization and elite domination. The answers to these contestable questions further inform the legitimacy of judicial review, comprising a conceptually separate layer of analysis. Each emerges at certain points in the relevant debate, but none is consistently or explicitly developed by the doctrine.

Decisive answers to this set of questions might be conclusive, but unrealistic. If (major) parties are deemed elite-fabricated state entities primarily exploited for representative entrenchment and elite aggrandizement, this would vindicate, both normatively and from a constitutional perspective, robust judicial oversight. However, if parties are deemed to be rank-and-file guided bands of voters, organized to exert control over representatives, this would suggest judicial review should be minimal, invoked only when some other clear constitutional priority is contravened (as in the White Primary cases). Yet if the Court offered such decisive answers, this would pose two problems: (1) the Court would contravene the reality that parties are multifaceted and fluid, defying decisive or unitary categorization; and (2) such a conclusion would comprise an extraordinary level of judicial imposition on democratic governance, just to establish a basis for consistent judicial review. The result is that contestation is the appropriate posture – but with an additional layer of complexity in every judicial enquiry into party governance. The Court might contest the relevant party characteristics with regard to a specific legal question, but this would not necessarily answer the question. It would merely establish the terms by which the legal question at issue could itself be contested.

The Court's contestation over party governance therefore poses unique challenges that are best met head on, even if the result is greater complexity in analysis and perhaps discomforting social science foundations to legal reasoning. By recognizing the issues at the root of party governance, the Court could begin to construct resilient and flexible doctrinal foundations that permit analysis of the issues that determine whether parties help the electorate rule itself.

7

Race and Elections

Equity of Access or Equity of Power?

[L]itigation in this Court demonstrates the variety and persistence of these and similar institutions designed to deprive [Black constituents] of the right to vote.
  –Earl Warren, South Carolina v. Katzenbach

The preclearance requirement [of the Voting Rights Act] abridges the voting rights of *all* citizens.
  –Lewis F. Powell, City of Rome

The ugly history of racial oppression in America has made racial justice the most transformative domain of election law. It should seemingly be the subject of the easiest constitutional analysis. The Fourteenth Amendment guarantees "equal protection of the laws," a provision that is unequivocally directed toward racial discrimination,[1] and the Fifteenth Amendment prohibits abridging the right to vote on the grounds of race.

Yet the guarantees of equality and nondiscrimination have generated a dispute of ferocious complexity. Does "equality" in the electoral context mean formal race blindness and thus prohibit attempts by legislatures (including Congress) and courts to advance the substantive power of oppressed minorities? Or does equality mean substantive political equality, and thus tolerate – or even demand – that minorities have access to electoral procedures that substantively benefit their role in governance?

This chapter examines this conflict in each of the major doctrinal arenas in which racial discrimination has been disputed – the equal protection clause (EPC), Section 2 of the Voting Rights Act (VRA), and the VRA preclearance requirement. It shows that, as in other areas of contested law, the conflict on the bench between

---

[1] A unanimous bench in *Shelley v. Kraemer*, 334 US 1, 23 (1948) held that it is "clear that the matter of primary concern [of the Fourteenth Amendment] was the establishment of equality in the enjoyment of basic civil and political rights and the preservation of those rights from discriminatory action on the part of the States based on considerations of race or color."

progressives and conservatives reflects a dispute between a collective, other-regarding conception of democracy and a private, endowment-protecting view.

7.1 THE NORMATIVE CORE OF JUDICIAL REVIEW OF RACE IN ELECTION LAW

Racial equity[2] is the most influential domain of election law for two reasons: (1) the tectonic impact of race on American law and politics generally and (2) clear constitutional commands that prohibit racial discrimination. The law of race and elections has been processed through three significant doctrinal lineages: (1) applying the EPC to state voting law; (2) judicial interpretation of Section 2 of the VRA; and (3) judicial interpretation of the preclearance requirement under VRA Sections 4 and 5.

Social science scholarship has thoroughly examined racially equitable representation. The fulcrum of this debate has been the legitimacy and scope of descriptive representation – the notion that groups should be represented by those who share their characteristics. Jane Mansbridge summarizes this as "women represent women or Blacks represent Blacks."[3] The legitimacy of the principle of descriptive representation has been fiercely debated as a matter of pure democratic design.[4] The doctrinal analogue to the theoretical debate over descriptive representation is when can minorities assert a right to decisively select a candidate (most familiarly with regard to the question of majority–minority districts).

However, the Supreme Court does not debate this as a question of pure theory (despite Justice Thomas's protestations to the contrary in, for example, *Holder v. Hall*), but within the context of constitutional adjudication. Subsequently, democratic design alone cannot inform legal reasoning. Judges must take the broader judicial remit into account, including competing constitutional obligations and the limits of constitutional right. Judicial interventions have long been justified as advancing racial equity, most seminally in John Hart Ely's conception of protecting

---

[2] I use the term "equity" to characterize the nature of the desirable but contested aim of the law with regard to race and elections. More specific terms, such as equality and anti-discrimination, are too narrow to capture the wide range of implications of the EPC and Fifteenth Amendment. The anti-retrogression standard that governs Section 5, for example, is not one of equality, and it can be disputed whether the current application of the EPC is dedicated to anti-discrimination or merely pure race neutrality. Nor do I use a more general term, such as justice or fairness, which would encompass aspects of social organization and policy that reach beyond election law.

[3] Jane Mansbridge, "Should Blacks Represent Blacks and Women Represent Women? A Contingent 'Yes'" (1999) 61 *The Journal of Politics* 628.

[4] For a summary, see Michael Rabinder James, "The Priority of Racial Constituency over Descriptive Representation" (2011) 73 *Journal of Politics* 899. James observes that the desirability of descriptive constituencies has received much less attention (though this question lies at the heart of the law). For an account of how descriptive representation seemed poised to take a leading role in legal analysis (but ultimately was not adopted), see Su Li and Bertrall Ross, "Measuring Political Power: Suspect Class Determinations and the Poor" (2016) 104 *California Law Review* 323.

insular and discrete minorities to justify representation reinforcement.[5] However, the intersection of (1) legitimate minority claims to representation and (2) the nature of judicial–constitutional interpretation to dictate the terms of legitimate electoral procedure has been neglected.

This intersection frames the hard question. In a polity committed to majoritarian self-rule but with a legacy of oppressing racial minorities, how should the judiciary advance the position of minorities? The failure to meaningfully advance the political position of minority groups will result in their continued subordination (including through majoritarian manipulation of electoral procedure), delegitimizing the democratic character of the entire polity. But, "given the zero-sum quality of representation," advancing minorities' position beyond guaranteeing minimal procedural equality (i.e., prohibiting first-order ballot access discrimination) must constrain the representation of other groups of voters.[6] The question that confronts the Court is thus what makes the polity *as a collective* free, given the competing mandates of majority rule[7] and minority protection.

The case law reveals two competing constitutional understandings of racial equity.[8] The conservative justices have advanced a minimalist–formalist interpretation of racial equity as equal access to the process of voting. This view conceives of equity as requiring only equal opportunity to *input* into the electoral process; it does not command (or permit) that law be deployed to ensure that minorities have guaranteed outputs from electoral process in terms of representation or policymaking power. Indeed, conservatives have become increasingly muscular in identifying intrusion upon the polity's free self-rule where government actors seek to protect minority representation if it displaces the default means of setting electoral procedure. Conversely, progressives have advanced a thicker substantive conception of constitutional racial equity that affords minorities meaningful protections of their actual power in governance (a view resonant with Ely's conception of representation reinforcement of insular and discrete minorities). In addition to advancing this understanding through constitutional interpretation of the meaning of equality, the progressive view is more permissive of congressional efforts to ensure that minorities are guaranteed some level of practical power.

---

[5] See Chapter 2 for Ely's account and critiques leveled against it.
[6] T. Alexander Aleinikoff and Samuel Issacharoff, "Race and Redistricting: Drawing Constitutional Lines after *Shaw v. Reno*" (1993) 92 *Michigan Law Review* 588, 601.
[7] For an analysis of this point, see the discussion of Richard Tuck, *The Sleeping Sovereign: The Invention of Modern Democracy* (Cambridge: Cambridge University Press, 2016) in Chapter 2.
[8] These competing visions echo the contrast between the formalist and anti-subordination views of antidiscrimination summarized in Michael C. Dorf, "Same-Sex Marriage, Second-Class Citizenship, and Law's Social Meanings" (2011) 97 *Virginia Law Review* 1267, 1293 and, in a more doctrinal frame, the distinction between effect-based minority-harming legislation and minority-protecting explicit legislation identified by Reva Siegel, "Equality Divided" (2013) 127 *Harvard Law Review* 1 (discussed more extensively in this chapter's conclusion).

Reflecting the judiciary's nuanced position in advancing racial equity, doctrinal contestation over this question operates at two levels. The first is purely substantive: what conception of racial equity is preferable, one that merely ensures minorities can access the political process on equal terms, or one that protects power in governance? This query manifests in the case law as judicial speculation over questions such as racial essentialization, the circumstances necessary for a desirably race-blind polity, and so forth. Yet this can be debated as purely a question of democratic design. The second level reflects the judiciary's institutional remit, which is informed (and limited) by constitutional enforcement as well as its counterpopular character. These two elements speak to different questions – substantive racial equity and the complexities of the judicial role – but they do not present as cleanly distinct issues. Rather, they are interwoven throughout the case law.

The remainder of this chapter explores the increasingly fierce doctrinal struggle between the formal-input and substantive–output conceptions of the constitutional requirements for racial equity. This necessitates a careful review of each of the extensively contested case law lineages in race in elections: applying the EPC as a debate over the pure parsing of the constitutional command for equality; VRA Section 2 as a battle over the nature of vote dilution as regulating ballot access or regulating the actual allocation of representatives through districting; and VRA Section 5 as balancing the constitutional commitment to federalism with a more robust remit of racial equity. This doctrinal analysis interrogates diverse legal questions (e.g., the legal status of coalition districts, or whether the Fifteenth Amendment gives Congress the power to prohibit second-order discrimination through districting) as well as a set of shared themes that cut across them. Does advancing minority power exacerbate racial essentialism (an evergreen conservative concern)? Should race be an organizing axis for representation? Most fundamentally, should racial inequality in democracy be resolved through political struggle (the conservative view) or constitutional structure (the progressive view)? A review of the scholarship shows that despite the cogent, often policy-focused insights, a unified perspective of race and election law is lacking. The chapter ends with an analogy from political theory. The contrasting conservative and progressive treatments of race can be analogized to the differing treatments of unequal property distribution advanced by Robert Nozick and John Rawls. The driving question is whether racial equity should be handled by accepting the existing distribution of political power as a baseline and only protecting the fairness of further struggle, or if the Constitution demands meaningful redistribution of power to protect less well-off minority groups.[9]

Finally, this chapter must be contextualized by the shameful legacy of racial oppression in America. It resonated (and arguably contaminated) the framing of the Constitution; it was the central causal factor in the Civil War; it currently shapes all

---

[9] One synthetic view of this is offered by Michael S. Kang, "Race and Democratic Contestation" (2008) 117 *Yale Law Journal* 734, who argues that the Court should in fact a richer conception of contestation. However, this has not infiltrated the case law.

aspects of American society. A recent trend in scholarship, critical race theory, has synthesized the overarching influence of race on American society as bedrock and ontological, shaping both institutions and persons.[10] Other scholars have focused on more specific social science manifestations of race, such as electoral participation[11] and outcomes.[12] The impact of race on the development of American legal doctrine in general and constitutional law in particular has been widely studied,[13] including the evolution of democratic procedure. As Samuel Issacharoff notes, "the prospect for goal-oriented abuse of election processes has been directed largely – though never exclusively – at black Americans...voters' vulnerability to disenfranchisement played out largely along race lines. Because of this, the defining law of democracy in America is heavily the law of black enfranchisement, either directly or even indirectly as in *Baker v. Carr*."[14] Chief Justice Warren's praise of one person, one vote as part of a broader program of advancing civil rights reinforces this point,[15] and Derek Muller has identified a specific strand in the scholarship that identifies *Baker* as a pre-VRA effort to limit racialized gerrymandering.[16]

Another perspective on the centrality of race to election law is the importance of race-focused election law legislation as the tip of the spear in civil rights legislation. The VRA has been described as "iconic," "a superstatute amid a world of ordinary legislation," "the crown jewel of the civil rights era,"[17] and the "most successful civil rights statute ever enacted."[18] Furthermore scholars have often shown how race shapes other areas of election law – particularly partisan affiliation,[19] but also campaign finance[20] – even if they are nominally informed by distinct legal questions. The centrality of race to American law and American democracy raises

---

[10] Charles W. Mills, *The Racial Contract* (Ithaca: Cornell University Press, 1997); Kimberlé W. Crenshaw, "Race, Reform, and Retrenchment: Transformation and Legitimation in Antidiscrimination Law" (1988) 101 *Harvard Law Review* 1331.

[11] Bernard L. Fraga, *The Turnout Gap* (Cambridge: Cambridge University Press, 2018).

[12] Zoltan L. Hajnal, *Dangerously Divided: How Race and Class Shape Winning and Losing in American Politics* (Cambridge: Cambridge University Press, 2020).

[13] Michael J. Klarman, *From Jim Crow to Civil Rights: The Supreme Court and the Struggle for Racial Equality* (Oxford: Oxford University Press, 2004); Reva Siegal, "Why Equal Protection No Longer Protects: The Evolving Forms of Status-Enforcing State Action" (1997) 49 *Stanford Law Review* 1111.

[14] Samuel Issacharoff, "Beyond the Discrimination Model on Voting" (2013) 127 *Harvard Law Review* 95, 97.

[15] See Pamela S. Karlan, "Democracy and Disdain" (2012) 126 *Harvard Law Review* 1, 4–5.

[16] Derek T. Muller, "Perpetuating 'One Person, One Vote' Errors" (2016) 39 *Harvard Journal of Law and Public Policy* 371, 375 n. 22.

[17] Issacharoff, "Discrimination Model on Voting," 95.

[18] Guy-Uriel E. Charles and Luis E. Fuentes-Rohwer, "The Voting Rights Act in Winter: The Death of a Superstatute" (2015) 100 *Iowa Law Review* 1389.

[19] Richard L. Hasen, "Race or Party, Race as Party, or Party All the Time: Three Uneasy Approaches to Conjoined Polarization in Redistricting and Voting Cases" (2018) 59 *William and Mary Law Review* 1837; Nicholas O. Stephanopoulos, "Spatial Diversity" (2012) 125 *Harvard Law Review* 1903.

[20] Jacob M. Grumbach and Alexander Sahn, "Race and Representation in Campaign Finance" (2020) 114 *American Political Science Review* 206; Spencer Overton, "The Donor Class: Campaign Finance, Democracy, and Participation" (2004) 153 *University of Pennsylvania Law Review* 73, 102.

the challenge of trying to analyze election law doctrine internally. It is beyond the scope of the book to present a comprehensive social account of the influence of race in American democracy. This chapter instead treats the case law as a self-contained expression of normative struggle over what makes a polity free.

7.2 STANDALONE CONSTITUTIONAL INTERVENTION TO PROTECT RACIAL MINORITIES: THE SETTLED TERRAIN AND THE UNSETTLED QUESTION OF DISTRICTING UNDER THE EPC

This section examines two lineages of the case law. The first includes explicit constitutional commands in the Fourteenth (prohibiting racial classifications) and Fifteenth (prohibiting racialized abridgment of voting) Amendments, with a corresponding lineage of direct judicial oversight. Prior to and during the early days of the Civil Rights movement, the Court (with a few shameful moral and analytical failures) directly applied the Reconstruction Amendments to prohibit blatant racial disenfranchisement. While the Fifteenth Amendment is now primarily advanced through Section 2 of the VRA, the purely constitutional question remains contested in the second lineage via applying the EPC to districting. The bench is riven by the question of whether the constitutional prohibition of racial classification advances formal race blindness in the drawing of districts or accommodates the recognition of race to protect minority representation.

7.2.1 *The Settled Terrain: The Constitutional Prohibition of Blatant Racial Oppression*

With *Nixon v. Herndon* (the first of the White Primaries cases, discussed in Chapter 6), the Court established in 1927 that denying ballot access on the grounds of race is a "direct and obvious infringement of the Fourteenth Amendment."[21] The pre-Civil Rights era Court also struck down unequivocally (if not textually explicit) racialized denial of Black citizens' access to the ballot. In *Guinn v. US* and *Lane v. Wilson*, the Court found that grandfather clauses – which applied voting prerequisites such as literacy tests to voters, but exempted those who could have voted prior to emancipation – were bald attempts to prohibit voting based on race, and therefore illicit. Other cases from the early Civil Rights era established that other efforts to impair or distort the voting process through explicit use of race would be deemed illegal.[22]

As *Katzenbach* describes, such formalist enforcement of racial neutrality was insufficient to even create a plausible minimum of racial equity in electoral process,

---

[21] *Nixon v. Herndon*, 273 US 536, 541 (1927).
[22] See, e.g., *Anderson v. Martin*, 375 US 399 (1964) (holding unconstitutional a state law requiring that required the race of candidates be printed on the ballot).

as states found less overt mechanisms for depriving minorities of their voting rights[23] Rather than effect social change, these "easy" cases[24] established that the Court would demand an uncontestable minimum of formal equality in voting procedure. The Court's recognition of this baseline, while insufficient to create the racial equity needed for free self-rule, contributed to ensuring, along with robust congressional action during the Civil Rights era, that "first order impediments simply to getting registered to vote" were eliminated.[25]

While there have been a few anomalous deviations from this settled core, their constitutional legacy (or lack thereof) is the exception that proves the rule. The most shameful and inexplicable example is *Giles v. Harris*, in which the Court refused to rule that a bill that excluded Blacks but enfranchised Whites in Alabama was unconstitutional. While conceding it was a "great political wrong,"[26] Holmes's opinion concluded it was a political question that the Court could not cure without negating the Alabama's entire voter registration plan, which is beyond the Court's jurisdiction (a pointed rightly challenged by the dissents). As Richard Pildes has aptly noted, this is "the most legally disingenuous analysis in the pages of the U.S. Reports."[27] Yet Pildes begins his analysis with perhaps the more striking point for contextualizing *Giles* within the current law: it has been "airbrushed out of the constitutional canon."[28] It was never decisively challenged, overruled, or contested. It was simply ignored.[29]

Similarly, in *Lassiter v. Northampton County*, just prior to the efflorescence of great civil rights cases, the Court concluded that literacy tests (historically used as a pretext for racial discrimination) could be constitutional since they have a rational relationship to voting.[30] *Lassiter* has never been directly challenged or

---

[23] *South Carolina v. Katzenbach*, 383 US 301, 313–5 (1966).
[24] Michael Selmi, "Proving Intentional Discrimination: The Reality of Supreme Court Rhetoric" (1997) 86 *Georgetown Law Journal* 279, 298. While adopting his language, this analysis deviates from Selmi's classification. Selmi refers specifically to the cases of the 1960s, but the description also applies to *Guinn v. U.S.*, 238 US 347 (1915), *Nixon v. Herndon*, and *Lane v. Wilson*, 307 US 268 (1939). Furthermore, Selmi characterizes *Gomillion* as the first of the "hard" cases rather than the last of the "easy" ones.
[25] Issacharoff, "Discrimination Model on Voting," 97. See also Samuel Issacharoff, "Polarized Voting and the Political Process: The Transformation of Voting Rights Jurisprudence" (1992) 90 *Michigan Law Review* 1833, 1838–9 (describing the "first generation" of voting rights cases that removed "barriers to black registration and the casting of ballots.").
[26] *Giles v. Harris*, 189 US 475, 488 (1903).
[27] Richard H. Pildes, "Democracy, Anti-Democracy, and the Canon" (2000) 17 *Constitutional Commentary* 295, 306.
[28] Ibid., 297. One of the only notable invocations of *Giles* was by Justice Frankfurter in *Colegrove* for the principle of the nonjusticiability of political questions, *Colegrove v. Green*, 328 US 549, 552 (1946). However, *Baker v. Carr* challenged *Colegrove*, whereas *Guinn* did not discuss *Giles* at all, and *Lane v. Wilson* sidelined it in a technicality by observing that unlike *Giles*, *Lane* adverted to congressional legislation that enforced the Fifteenth Amendment.
[29] Strangely, Pildes reduces this observation to a footnote, "Democracy, Anti-Democracy, and the Canon," 298–9 n. 15.
[30] *Lassiter v. Northampton*, 360 US 45, 51 (1959).

contested by the courts. It has simply been papered over. Scholars attribute this smothering of *Lassiter* to different cases. Richard Hasen points to the Court's generally more expansive application of equal protection exemplified by *Kramer v. Union Free School District*,[31] and Michael Selmi to the Court's conclusion that literacy tests violated Section 4 of the VRA in *Gaston County v. United States*.[32] In any case, the Court had already begun to narrow the breadth of *Lassiter*'s application in *Harper v. Virginia Board of Elections*, which found a poll tax (a similar mechanism of pretextual racist discrimination) to be unconstitutional because it lacked any relation to voting competency.[33] That *Giles* and *Lassiter* have been largely bypassed and papered over, rather than meaningfully contested, indicates their marginal status as what Pildes calls "anti-canon." Their largely silent marginalization confirms the bedrock status of some minimum of racial equality in election law. As I discuss in the book's Conclusion, they are analogs to *Bush v. Gore* because they are driven explicitly by politics and fail to contest the meaning of freedom.

7.2.2 *Contesting Second-Generation Barriers to Minority Representation: Dilution and Districting*

With the "first generation" of racial discrimination deemed illegal, the law has become dominated by "second-generation" questions regarding *vote dilution*. Vote dilution does not directly deny access to the ballot box, but unjustly limits actual political power. It typically uses the same mechanism of operation as partisan gerrymandering. By allocating voters in ways that artificially pack them together or thin them out, it is possible to reduce the number of representatives that minorities can elect, or to distort their ability to influence electoral choices. Minority groups are, however, far more vulnerable to such dilution than party members. While parties are adaptive entities from both the institution side and the voter side and the nature of such "dilution" is itself contestable (as Chapter 6 explains), minority groups have no such recourse to adapt their identities in response to discrimination.

Despite the clear threat and moral illegitimacy of racial vote dilution, it poses a far thornier normative problem than denial of ballot access because it speaks to the appropriate allocation of representation. It raises at least two contestable normative questions of democratic design. First, given that American electoral process does not guarantee proportional representation (and it would be a gross intrusion into electoral design if the Court were to mandate this), what can any vulnerable racial group assert as a right of minimum representation (or protection

---

[31] Richard Hasen, *The Supreme Court and Election Law: Judging Equality from Baker v. Carr to Bush v. Gore* (New York: NYU Press, 2003), p. 26.
[32] Selmi, "Proving Intentional Discrimination," 298.
[33] *Katzenbach*, 383 US 663, 666 (1966), though it might be noted this limitation of *Lassiter* was contested in *Harper* 383 U.S. 663 (1966) at 673 (Black, dissenting); 685 (Stewart, dissenting).

of process that determines representation)? The minimalist possibility is that racial equity requires formalist neutrality, and that districting that takes race into account (including to correct past injustices) is an illicit racial classification. Yet this view of racial equity disregards the historical and ongoing disadvantages suffered by minorities in seeking to elect their preferred representatives. The second normative question is to what degree should representation be presumed to be determined by racial affiliation (a presumption that some conservatives criticize as racial essentialism)? These issues speak to institutional design (particularly of a two-party system in which voters switching parties serves as the lubricant) and to deeper questions of social organization (particularly racial polarization). The answers to these questions do not merely involve descriptive social science, but what principles of representation best advance self-rule for a racially heterogeneous franchise.

7.2.2.1 Advancing Racial Equity in Districting: From Preventing Exclusion to Contesting the Meaning of Racial Neutrality

The Court's first engagement with districting confronted blatant racial discrimination. *Gomillion* set an uncontestable floor for when districting comprises unconstitutional vote dilution: when "districting legislation is solely concerned with segregating… voters [by race]…so as to deprive [minority voters] of their pre-existing…vote."[34] There are multiple ways of identifying the districting as illicit, confirming its status as egregious violation. Justice Frankfurter's majority opinion in *Gomillion* refers to violations of both the Fourteenth and Fifteenth Amendments from the districting, but leans more heavily on the Fifteenth to establish constitutional authority over the state. Justice Whittaker's concurrence, which relies more heavily on the Fourteenth Amendment, has become more emblematic of *Gomillion*'s meaning in the jurisprudence.[35] Furthermore, the conduct was facially indefensible. As the *Gomillion* opinion notes, the defendants "never suggested…any countervailing municipal function" of the districting, but only principled arguments based on total legislative discretion in districting so as to preclude judicial-constitutional oversight.[36] Pildes and Richard Niemi maintain that *Gomillion* is "exceptional" because "this particular pattern of line drawing had such a racially differential effect that it could only be a blatant example of a racist design to exclude black residents."[37] Where a districting otherwise inexplicably deprives minorities of their voting power, the Court will declare it

---

[34] *Gomillion v. Lightfoot*, 364 US 339, 342 (1960).
[35] Pamela Karlan and Richard H. Pildes, *The Law of Democracy: Legal Structure of the Political Process*, 4th ed. (New York: Foundation Press, 2012), p. 575.
[36] *Gomillion*, 364 US at 342.
[37] Richard H. Pildes and Richard G. Niemi, "Expressive Harms, Bizarre Districts, and Voting Rights: Evaluating Election-District Appearances after Shaw v. Reno" (1993) 92 *Michigan Law Review* 483, 552.

unconstitutional. *Gomillion* shows that some instances of vote dilution are so egregious that they are as easy to resolve as first-generation deprivations of access to the franchise. The denial of collective right in *Gomillion* was an open perpetuation of egregious mistreatment of individuals, even if the mechanism by which the legislation perpetuated this wrong was collective.

The Court subsequently struggled with districting plans that lessened the power of minority voters but without clear discriminatory intent. The contestation over the issue was exemplified by the Court's wrestling over the legality of multimember (also known as at-large) districts, which may in some circumstances result in the underrepresentation of minority voters.[38] In *Whitcomb v. Chavis*, the Court concluded that multimember districts that result in disproportionate power for a (White) majority bloc do not comprise discriminatory electoral practice in the absence of an *intent* to dilute minority votes or effects that impaired participation in the political process.[39]

Whitcomb indicates that the Court will only deem electoral procedures unconstitutional if they reflect racially discriminatory purpose. As Issacharoff notes, *Whitcomb* "wavered uneasily" between individual-focused (i.e., ballot access) concerns and group effects of electoral procedure that could achieve vote dilution.[40] Two years later, *White v. Regester* asserted that even where a particular practice was not ostensibly attributable to racial animus, it could be illegal if it threatened minority political power. Where there is a "history of official racial discrimination" and evidence that the members of the minority group had "less opportunity than did other residents in the district to participate in the political processes and to elect legislators of their choice," multimember districts could be unconstitutional if "used invidiously to cancel out or minimize the voting strength of racial groups."[41] *White* recognized vote dilution as violating a "group-based right" to *collective* minority ability to participate in the political process.[42]

White was the Court's most ambitious declaration of the constitutional demands of racial equity. It could have been a first step in a firm constitutional demand that electoral procedure advance minority voting power, as opposed to merely serve as

---

[38] Social science studies have not concluded that this is generally the case. See Richard G. Niemi, Jeffrey S. Hill, and Bernard Grofman, "The Impact of Multimember Districts on Party Representation in U.S. State Legislatures" (1985) 10 *Legislative Studies Quarterly* 441, 454 (evaluating electoral results to conclude "Multimember districts do not invariably, or even generally, underrepresent the statewide minority party in state legislative elections."); Elisabeth R. Gerber, Rebecca B. Morton, and Thomas A. Rietz, "Minority Representation in Multimember Districts" (1998) 92 *American Political Science Review* 127, 141 (observing that the impact of multimember districts on minority representation will vary based on the distribution of voter preferences among candidates, including minority voter preferences).

[39] *Whitcomb v. Chavis*, 403 US 124, 149 (1971).

[40] Samuel Issacharoff, "Polarized Voting and the Political Process: The Transformation of Voting Rights Jurisprudence" (1992) 90 *Michigan Law Review* 1833, 1840.

[41] *White v. Regester*, 412 US 755, 766 (1973).

[42] Issacharoff, "Polarized Voting and the Political Process," 1842.

a check on intentional legislative racial animus. It was a unanimous decision,[43] and maintained the Court's trajectory of expanding what (in terms of both legal technicalities and sensitivity to social context) equal protection required for electoral design. It continued the trend of *Gomillion* and, generalizing beyond the context of race, the one person, one vote jurisprudence. Yet its vague "totality of the circumstances"[44] test identified neither the precise character of illegal effects-based vote dilution that would make it illegal – it stated it was *not* proportional results, but some unspecified measure of minority power – nor the marker of unconstitutional legislative reasoning.[45] It required further elaboration.

Yet rather than serving as a beachhead, *White* became a doctrinal anomaly. This was most apparent in *City of Mobile v. Bolden*, in which a fragmented Court concluded that an at-large districting scheme was legal because minorities could "register and vote without hindrance."[46] By stating that "In only one case has the Court sustained a claim that multimember legislative districts unconstitutionally diluted the voting strength of a discrete group," *Mobile* implied that *White* was an outlier.[47] More directly damning to the possibility that the Court might find in the EPC a purely constitutional command to police discriminatory effect, *Mobile* interpreted *White*'s concept of "invidious use" of districting to refer only to "purposeful dilution."[48]

Mobile spelled the end of the promise, apparent in *White*, that the bench might interpret the Constitution as demanding that electoral process directly ensure minority political power. It harmonized the EPC elections jurisprudence with the requirement of discriminatory intent established by *Washington v. Davis*.[49] This synchronized the districting jurisprudence with the broader treatment of equal protection, but disregarded the unique characteristic of elections as the gateway to groups' access to power in governance. This point offers a normative justification for the Court advancing racial equity in electoral procedure in a more substantive way than the technical requirement of racial animus advanced in *Washington*.

As such, *Mobile* marks the beginning of the contemporary battle over what constitutional racial equity demands of electoral procedure – formal race blindness in legislation, guaranteeing only equal access, or substantive protection of minority power? Justice Marshall's full-throated *Mobile* dissent that *White* made "a showing of discriminatory intent...unnecessary"[50] captures the progressive doctrinal position.

---

[43] Justice Brennan's dissent in *White v. Regester*, 412 US at 773 was in "full agreement" with the finding of unconstitutional racial discrimination, disagreeing only with a related decision regarding partisan gerrymandering.
[44] *White v. Regester*, 412 US at 769.
[45] Issacharoff, "Polarized Voting and the Political Process," 1844–45.
[46] *City of Mobile v. Bolden*, 446 US 55, 65 (1980).
[47] *Mobile*, 446 US at 68 (citing *White*).
[48] Ibid., at 69.
[49] See Richard A. Primus, "Equal Protection and Disparate Impact: Round Three" (2003) 117 *Harvard Law Review* 494.
[50] *Mobile*, 446 US at 112.

The meaning of *White*'s own test for holistic "invidiousness" has itself been a battleground. This test has survived as precedent by being interpreted as requiring the same "standard of proof generally applicable to Equal Protection Clause cases,"[51] but its potential to offer a more expansive basis for identifying illegal intent beyond that which is purposefully discriminatory has been challenged as inconsistent with *Mobile*.[52]

Following this apparent return to an intent requirement, the next point of contention was how the requirement of racial neutrality would intersect with the demands of the VRA.[53] As described in more detail below, the VRA requires states to avoid electoral procedures that impair minority voting power. As states redistrict after each new census, they must comply with various constitutional and practical demands: one person, one vote; maintaining boundaries of existing communities; protecting incumbents; and the VRA. While a plurality of the Court initially suggested it might tolerate race-conscious districting motivated by VRA compliance as long as it did not leave any racial group "underrepresented relative to their share of the population,"[54] in *Shaw v. Reno* the Court indicated its lack of tolerance for (predominantly) race-conscious districting on *any* terms. The bench has therefore not only declined to advance the power-protecting promise of *White*, but it has turned against it by adopting a formalist understanding of what qualifies as illicit racial categorization.[55]

Shaw v. Reno addressed a North Carolina districting that, instigated by VRA preclearance requirements, created an additional majority–minority district (in which minorities comprise a majority of voters). The district connected two geographically disparate clusters of Black voters. The Court found an EPC violation, asserting "a plaintiff challenging a reapportionment statute under the Equal Protection Clause may state a claim by alleging that the legislation, though race-neutral on its face, rationally cannot be understood as anything other than an effort to separate voters into different districts on the basis of race, and that the separation lacks sufficient justification."[56]

The basis of the decision is the established illegality of "statutes that, although race neutral, are, on their face, unexplainable on grounds other than race."[57] Yet underlying the decision is discomfort with constitutional approbation of electoral

---

[51] *Rogers v. Lodge*, 458 US 613, 617 (1982).
[52] *Rogers*, 458 US at 629 (Powell, dissenting); 632 (Stevens, dissenting).
[53] Richard H. Pildes, "Is Voting-Rights Law Now at War with Itself – Social Science and Voting Rights in the 2000s" (2002) 80 *North Carolina Law Review* 1517.
[54] *United Jewish Organizations v. Carey*, 430 US 144, 166 (1977).
[55] Subsequent cases have confirmed that *Shaw v. Reno*, 509 US 630 (1993) is leading precedent: *Miller v. Johnson*, 515 US 900 (1995) and *Shaw v. Hunt*, 517 US 899 (1996). Further cases have struggled with the application of this test, particularly regarding evidentiary standards and standards of review, *Hunt v. Cromartie*, 526 US 541 (1999), *Easley v. Cromartie*, 532 US 234 (2001), and *Bethune-Hill v. Virginia State Board of Elections*, 137 S.Ct. 788, 802 (2017) (affirming the precedential status of *Miller* and *Shaw v. Hunt*).
[56] *Shaw*, 509 US at 649.
[57] Ibid., at 643 (quoting *Arlington Heights v. Metropolitan Housing Development Corp*, 429 US 252, 266 (1977)).

design for pursuing substantive racial equity (rather than merely guaranteeing formal neutrality). Digging a bit further reveals a collision between representation based on "physical territory" and the "organiz[ation of] political representation around the concept of [racial] interest."[58] The Court asserted that where districts reflect a racialized purpose of *any* sort, the district boundaries suggest to representatives "that their primary obligation is to represent only the members of that group, rather than their constituency as a whole. This is altogether antithetical to our system of representative democracy...the individual is important, not his race, his creed, or his color."[59]

Underlying *Shaw* is a theory of representative duty and citizen identity.[60] The opinion finds racially motivated design of electoral process to be suspect, even where the categorization protects, rather than oppresses, vulnerable minorities. The Court has in effect come full circle from *Gomillion* to the current state of the law, but asking the obverse question – is a racial classification that is meant to correct rather than perpetuate injustice wrongful? This suggests the core point of dispute is the nature of equality itself. The immediate concern is racial essentialism. If electoral process advances minority power, rather than merely guarantees formally equivalent access, it will ossify racial divides and undermine the spirit of racial egalitarianism that should flow upwards from citizens to representatives.

7.2.2.2 Judicial Delineation of Democratic Outcomes in a Racialized Polity

Scholars have reacted to the *Shaw* framework with dubiousness. Heather Gerken summarizes the practical difficulty: "a remedy for an aggregate harm like dilution simply cannot be squeezed into a conventional individual rights framework."[61]

---

[58] Pildes and Niemi, "Expressive Harms, Bizarre Districts, and Voting Rights," 483.

[59] Shaw v. Reno, 509 US at 648. The post-ellipses phrase quotes the dissent of Justice Douglas in *Wright v. Rockefeller*, 376 US 52, 66 (1964).

[60] The focus on the appearance of the district led Pildes and Niemi, "Expressive Harms, Bizarre Districts, and Voting Rights" to coin the concept of "expressive harms," that is constitutional harms whose sole characteristic is that they optically reflect an awareness of race even if they do not apparently cause practical disadvantage to persons based on racial classifications. As Heather K. Gerken, "Understanding the Right to an Undiluted Vote" (2001) 114 *Harvard Law Review* 1663, 1693 noted, the idea of expressive harms did not remain the core of the doctrine, as the Court has moved back to a more traditional focus on racialized intent as the touchstone of illegality. Pildes himself has conceded, at "Social Science and Voting Rights", 1544, "Since *Shaw*, the Court has also shifted the discourse of the constitutional violation at issue toward a more formulaic, purpose-based mode of equal protection inquiry." Moreover, as T. Alexander Aleinikoff and Samuel Issacharoff, "Race and Redistricting: Drawing Constitutional Lines after *Shaw v. Reno*" (1993) 92 *Michigan Law Review* 588, 606, observe, the harm in *Gomillion* was, likewise, an expressive harm – but one so unequivocally wrongful and oppressive that assessing its constitutionality raised few difficulties. The expressive harms concept, whether in *Shaw* or *Gomillion*, is only a vehicle for the Court to enquire into what equality demands of electoral procedure.

[61] Gerken, "Understanding the Right to an Undiluted Vote,"1998. See also Richard H. Pildes, "Principled Limitations on Racial and Partisan Redistricting" (1997) 106 *Yale Law Journal* 2505, 2544 (same point). This difficulty was predicted by Issacharoff, "Polarized Voting and the Political Process," 1858.

Vote dilution, unlike first-generation ballot denial, does not deprive an individual of a right (as no individual voter can assert a right to be in a district where their preferred candidate is elected). Rather, vote dilution requires querying what *groups* can demand as fair representation when they participate in the democratic process.

The root of the problem is intrinsic to democracy: the state can legitimately impose its will upon persons and groups who disagree with a particular policy, unless the process by which the collective decision was reached was illegitimate. For the purposes of judicial analysis, the Constitution describes the requirements of such process legitimacy. The challenge of electoral procedure is that a victorious majority can use its power to deny or diminish an opponent's access to the franchise; this is a central anxiety of the anti-lockup account. Ballot access denial on the grounds of race is an openly illegal form of such franchise denial. Vote dilution, however, cannot be so neatly resolved, because determining the appropriate power allocation among groups requires a full theory of legitimate democratic representation. Without explicit constitutional guidance, if the judiciary were to advance such a full theory of representation, it would risk usurping the electorate's power to set its own terms of self-rule, and would artificially overdetermine the terms of democratic self-realization. This underlies the conservative advancement of a formalist reading of racial equity, as manifest in Kennedy's concern regarding racial essentialism articulated in *Shaw*.

Yet such a drily acontextual reading of racial equity ignores the history and present reality. The Reconstruction Amendments, recognizing that the White majority in Southern states would seek to maintain *post bellum* racial dynamics by permanently depriving minority voters of access to democratic process, were an attempt to embed racial equity into the constitutional order. The necessity of the VRA showed that the Court alone was unwilling (or institutionally unable) to take robust, creative, and proactive steps to realize this constitutional instruction. *White* was a watershed missed opportunity precisely because it was a tentative first step toward such substantive delineation of the terms of baseline democratic legitimacy, with the Court evaluating procedure by referencing socio-historical racial inequality rather than abstract and normatively denatured formal categories. However, the Court could only do so by advancing a vision of substantive racial equity in the design of democratic process. Such a substantive declaration would dramatically expand the role of the Court – a classical counterpopular concern. *Mobile* and *Shaw* each accelerated the retreat from this possibility.

Post-*Shaw*, the EPC jurisprudence is a formalist query of the use of racial categories, distilling the conservative view of the judicial role in protecting racial equity. The progressive dissents in these cases have largely reiterated the point that such formalism will result in the continued subordination of minorities and articulate the need for the judiciary to take a meaningful role in advancing substantive racial equity in the allocation of power. Justice White's *Shaw* dissent summarizes the point: "it is not mere suffering at the polls but discrimination in the polity with which the Constitution is concerned";[62] the majority's formalism "will unnecessarily hinder to some extent a State's voluntary effort to ensure a modicum of minority representation."[63] Justice Ginsburg began her dissent in *Miller v. Johnson* by describing the legacy of discrimination against Black voters and declaring that the purpose of judicial review was "to secure to members of racial minorities equal voting rights" historically denied them.[64] In *Shaw v. Hunt*, Justice Stevens critiqued the Court's conclusion that finding an (oddly shaped) majority–minority district unconstitutional undermines "state action designed to accommodate the political concerns of historically disadvantaged minority groups."[65] While the progressives have now accepted the precedential status of the formalist test of equality and pushed back primarily by limiting its application,[66] their foundational disagreement remains unequivocal.

Advocates of minimalist race-blind formalism have a convenient reply. For the judiciary to substantively conclude what conditions of racial equity are required for democratic fairness is profoundly counterpopular, and, by ossifying racialized political dynamics through external fiat, potentially pathological. According to this argument, where the judiciary assesses legislation on the basis of whether such racial categorization is beneficial for minorities, the judiciary risks exacerbating racial essentialism and polarization.

The conservative view disregards the unique role of electoral procedure, where discriminatory effects operate at two different levels. First, even absent deliberate efforts to deny minorities ballot access, historical patterns of discrimination and subordination will result in inferior electoral outcomes. This in turn will result in less representative power, with a knock-on effect of less allocation of state resources to minority interests, and a worsening of their original subordination. If such subordination was limited to typical resource allocation policy, minority voters could work together as an interested wedge group to exploit the typical practices of democratic contestation and coalition building to assert their power.[67] Second, however, legislation that effects electoral subordination diminishes minority groups' capacity to undertake such political maneuvering. Such patterns of power-depriving discrimination were precisely the evil that occurred prior to the Civil Rights era.

These two effects comprise a vicious spiral of racial discriminatory effects. Where discriminatory electoral procedure takes hold – whether or not it is intentional – there is no way to "correct" the discrimination absent an exogenous shock such as a constitutional intervention. Arguing for the desirability of such shocks lies

---

[62] *Shaw v. Reno*, 509 US at 661.
[63] Ibid., at 673.
[64] *Miller v. Johnson*, 515 US at 936.
[65] *Shaw v. Hunt*, 517 US at 918.
[66] See *Easly v. Cromartie*, 532 US at 258.
[67] Kang, "Race and Democratic Contestation."

precisely behind the anti-lockup view advocated by, most prominently, Issacharoff and Pildes.[68] However, such a claim regarding such shocks cannot be made in a moral vacuum. The broader claim of this chapter, and this book more broadly, is that any structural assertion about the desirability of shocks is itself, or must stand atop a foundation of, a normative claim about self-rule and the appropriate judicial role in defining it.

Disagreement over how the judiciary should enforce the EPC's mandate for equality with regard to districting epitomizes the two overarching levels of the jurisprudence on race and elections. The first can be understood as a thorny question of constitutional interpretation internal to the judicial role. Do the Reconstruction Amendments dictate race blindness in electoral process, or do they permit (or demand) the Court evaluate if legislation holistically jeopardizes or advances the political power of racial minorities? This struggle between formalism and substantive racial equity has been the subject of open judicial contestation. Yet underlying it is a second, deeper struggle: the appropriate judicial posture toward crafting democratic procedure. Both formalism and substantive racial equity can significantly constrain legislative design of electoral process, so the question is not one of first-order counterpopularism. Rather, the question is if the judiciary should accommodate racial power realities in its assessment of electoral process (and perhaps impose upon the polity a particular vision of racial equity in representation) or whether it should only narrowly assess the presence of racial categories (leaving the resolution of racial inequities to political struggle – including continued oppression, if that is the outcome of such contestation). These are two visions of constitutional freedom in electoral design: one that only identifies freedom where racial equity exists in power allocation, and another that only identifies freedom where the electorate as a whole has the authority to set its terms of electoral process, within minimal, formalistically interpreted constitutional bounds.

7.3 THE VOTING RIGHTS ACT: BACKGROUND AND CONTEXT

When the early Civil Rights era Court struck down obvious first-generation barriers, Southern states resorted to opaque and circuitous discriminatory legislation. Local officials used "vague and subjective" tests, such as good morals requirements and literacy tests, to deprive minorities of ballot access.[69] Combatting these racist policies through reactive litigation faced multiple obstacles. After one such piece of legislation was struck down, a state could then pass another ostensibly distinct piece of legislation with the same ballot-depriving effect (for example, swapping out an arbitrarily enforced good-morals requirement for an arbitrarily enforced literacy test,

---

[68] Samuel Issacharoff and Richard H. Pildes, "Politics as Markets: Partisan Lockups of the Democratic Process" (1998) 50 *Stanford Law Review* 643. They discuss *Terry v. Adams*, and its limits, as an attempt to bring about such a shock, at 656–68.
[69] *Katzenbach*, 383 US at 312–13.

both deployed against Black voters). The litigation to strike down such measures was costly and time consuming – and in the meantime, Black enfranchisement would remain impaired. As Guy-Uriel Charles and Luis Fuentes-Rohwer recount, the Court was hesitant to proactively prohibit disenfranchisement with the same adaptive fluidity with which the Southern states effected it, a gap illustrated most vividly in the Court's decision to absolve literacy tests in *Lassiter*.[70]

This inspired Congress to pass the VRA in 1965. Charles and Fuentes-Rohwer describe the VRA as "a significant historical intervention in the life of the country"[71] that has transformed the practices and development of American democracy through robust oversight of state voting law. They call it an archetypal superstatute that has transformed the American constitutional order and elicited novel modes of cooperation among branches. The VRA relied upon the text of provisions of the Reconstruction Amendments: Section 5 of the Fourteenth Amendment and Section 2 of the Fifteenth granted Congress the authority to advance the amendments through appropriate legislation. Of course, the interpretation of this grant ultimately falls to the judiciary, but as Charles and Fuentes-Rohwer note, the Court initially "interpreted the VRA pragmatically, often expansively, and in a manner consistent with what it views as the Act's ideals."[72]

The VRA and the initial realization of its promise represents a unique synthesis of the wellsprings of electoral procedure. The legislature drew off an explicit grant of authority from the normatively supreme commitments of the Constitution to advance the constitutional command of equality, and the Court interpreted this synthesis of "normal" legislative action and higher law to advance the constitutional values in a practically meaningful way. The circumstances of the 1960s and the struggle against Black disenfranchisement made judicial approbation of the VRA (plainest in *Katzenbach*)[73] easy in political and first-order moral terms. Some of the principles – particularly the general authority of Congress to combat racial discrimination – have been durably decontested.[74] In its genesis, the VRA unified, rather

---

[70] Charles and Fuentes-Rohwer, "The Voting Rights Act in Winter," 1401. They trace this back to the Court's suggestion in *Guinn* that literacy tests are constitutional, a point that the *Lassiter* Court itself invokes. The *Lassiter* Court, however, could have circumvented *Guinn* much as later Courts circumvented *Lassiter*. While *Guinn* itself is unequivocal that a race-neutral literacy test would be legal, it is noteworthy that the federal government itself did not challenge their validity in the *Guinn* litigation, 238 US at 347, 366; and that changed social understanding of the racially pretextual use of literacy tests during the early Civil Rights era would provide the Court an easy interpretive context to, in light of changed norms, adapt a new treatment of them in *Lassiter*.
[71] Charles and Fuentes-Rohwer, "The Voting Rights Act in Winter," 1394.
[72] Ibid., 1389.
[73] *Katzenbach*, 383 US at 308–10. The sole dissenter in *Katzenbach*, Justice Black, challenged on federalism grounds the capacity of Congress to limit states' revision of their own constitutions, 383 US at 356–58, anticipating the arguments in *Shelby County* that would later hamstring the VRA.
[74] *Katzenbach v. Morgan*, 384 US 641 (1966), for example, established the general authority of Congress to advance racial equality under the Fifteenth Amendment in rejecting a challenge prohibiting

than elicited tension between, the three great national sources of American election law – the legislature, the Constitution, and the judiciary.

As the law has turned to second-generation barriers to minority representation, the judicial consensus that surrounded the illegality of first-generation barriers (and the unacceptable condition of American democracy at the time of the VRA's passage) deteriorated. The continued cogence of the VRA has faced particular judicial hurdles in the past decade. A sharply split partisan bench declared in *Shelby County v. Holder* that the preclearance formula was unconstitutional. Beginning with *Mobile v. Bolden* and most recently exemplified by *Brnovich v. Democratic National Committee*, VRA Section 2 has become a locus for debates regarding the remit to advance racial equity under the Fifteenth Amendment, with the minimalist conservative position ascendant.

On the surface, these debates reflect the content of the constitutional mandate for racial equity in voting procedure (particularly in Section 2, following the 1982 congressional reauthorization) and how the constitutional mandate for racial equity that legitimizes the VRA should be balanced against other constitutional concerns (specifically the tension between federalism and the preclearance requirement). These evoke familiar first-order contestation of whether racial equity is better served by formalist equality or a representative-outcome view of racial justice. Yet lurking beneath is a deeper normative question. The Court is inevitably contesting if its constitutional remit entails a substantive view of just democratic procedure in a racially unequal society. While the progressives have continued to struggle for a rich vision of what the Constitution demands of a racial equitable democracy, the conservatives have sought to diminish the judicial accommodation of minority representation.

7.4 VRA SECTION 2: CONTESTING THE DISTINCTIVE PROTECTION OF MINORITY VOICE

As originally drafted, Section 2 of the VRA declared, "No voting qualification or prerequisite to voting, or standard, practice, or procedure shall be imposed or applied by any State or political subdivision to deny or abridge the right of any citizen of the United States to vote on account of race or color."[75] Such a provision clearly renders illegal explicit "first generation" ballot access denial (such as grandfather clauses).[76] As Kathryn Abrams notes, such blunt use of Section 2 seems redundant with the

---

language tests for poll access. While contested at the time – Harlan's dissent suggests that the costs to separation of powers (particularly Congress advancing an interpretation of constitutional law typically left to the judiciary) and federalism entail "sacrifice of fundamentals in the American constitutional system," 384 US at 659, evoking the same normative critique as Black's dissent in *SC v. Katzenbach* – the general power of Congress has not been challenged, unless some other constitutional principle is contravened.

[75] *Mobile*, 446 US at 60, quoting 79 Stat. 437, as amended, 42 U.S.C. § 1973.
[76] See Issacharoff, "Polarized Voting and the Political Process," 1838 n.25.

application of the Fourteenth and Fifteenth Amendments.[77] The question is what else Section 2 might require of racially equitable electoral procedure.

7.4.1 Mobile v. Bolden and the Struggle over the Meaning of the Fifteenth Amendment

As with modern EPC jurisprudence, the legality of districting has dominated Section 2 jurisprudence (at least until recently).[78] In 1980, *Mobile v. Bolden* addressed the first question squarely brought under Section 2: the legality of multimember districts that were adopted for race-neutral reasons, but which had a disparate impact on minority representation. Justice Stewart's leading plurality opinion concluded: (1) the substance of VRA Section 2, as initially passed, "no more than elaborates upon that of the Fifteenth Amendment,"[79] and renders no additional conduct illegal and (2) in line with established constitutional standards, such conduct would only be illegal if there were "purposeful discrimination."[80]

Mobile's reasoning exemplifies the conservatism typical of the contemporary treatment of race in elections. The plurality's conclusion that only purposeful discrimination is illegal epitomizes the (now-ascendant) commitment to a minimalist–formalist understanding of racial equity. Stewart suggests that *Guinn*, *Terry v. Adams*, and *Gomillion* all stand for the same proposition: discriminatory intent is the sole grounds for the illegality of electoral procedure. This lumps together cases addressing vastly different degrees of discrimination and disregards the Court's rising perceptiveness in identifying discrimination at the beginning of the Civil Rights era. The *Mobile* Court also declined to use the opportunity presented by the statutory context. By declaring that Section 2 only prohibits *intentional* discrimination, the plurality squarely aligned it with *Washington v. Davis*. The statutory command, while underspecified, created a plausible opportunity for the Court to advance a broader conception of racial equity; indeed, doing so would have been consonant with *Duke v. Griggs Power Company*. Paralleling the development of the Court's EPC jurisprudence, the reticence to do so suggests judicial discomfort in confronting the inequities in the fundamental power structure.

Mobile's other opinions hotly contested this reasoning. Justice Blackmun and Justice Stevens both concurred with the decision that the multimember districts were not unconstitutional, but for fundamentally different reasons. Blackmun

---

[77] Kathryn Abrams, "Raising Politics Up: Minority Political Participation and Section 2 of the Voting Rights Act" (1988) 63 *New York University Law Review* 449, 454 n. 26.

[78] The first step regarding how robustly Section 2 will be applied is its applicability to given state action at all, a question that drove *Brnovich v. Democratic National Committee*, 141 S.Ct. 2321 (2021) discussed below.

[79] *Mobile*, 446 US at 60.

[80] Ibid., at 63.

accepted the lower court's conclusion that the standard of discriminatory intent was satisfied (an approach compatible with *White v. Regester* in widening the concept of intentional discrimination), but found mandating a new form of city government an unacceptable intrusion into local governance. Stevens advanced a unique typology of voting rights and concluded that while impact harmful to group access ("objective effects") could render an electoral procedure unconstitutional, that standard was not met here.[81] Neither Blackmun nor Stevens – necessary for the plurality's victory – agreed with Stewart's formulation of a bright-line intent rule, but neither believed that the multimember districts at issue justified constitutional nullification. Justice White, conversely, dissented precisely because he interpreted *White v. Regester*'s holistic test for vote dilution as supporting the identification of purposeful discrimination in the situation at hand. Justice Marshall (joined by Justice Brennan) advanced a far more full-throated basis for dissent. He unequivocally rejected an intent requirement for finding a Fifteenth Amendment violation and found support in both precedent and constitutional text for the proposition that a practice diminishes equal voter power is illegal.[82]

The fractured bench in *Mobile* represents the full spectrum of understandings of what racial equity requires in electoral design. Each opinion takes a position on two theoretically substantive issues: (1) the constitutional mandate for racial equity in electoral process and (2) the underlying allocation of authority between state legislatures, the Constitution, and the courts. The conservative plurality restricted the judicial–constitutional role to its plausible minimum of prohibiting intentional discrimination. It therefore rejected the notion that democratic power outcomes could be used to inform the arrangement of democratic practices. Embedded within this was a view of the judiciary's role as only the guardian of an abstract (and abstracted from) circumstance – the conception of democratic racial equity. The Court denied it should participate in the substantive struggle over racial power. The concurrences and dissents, however, each asserted (either by expanding the concept of intentionality or acknowledging illegality based on effects) that electoral practices with outcome-based (i.e., dilutive) effects are illegal even where they are not intentionally oppressive.[83] Underlying this is the conclusion that democratic legitimacy may require guaranteeing minority groups some baseline of political power as a pre-emptive constitutional matter. However, such a baseline of minoritarian power constrains legislatures (whose own legitimacy may be suspect due to a legacy of discrimination) through the intervention of the judiciary as the arbiter of this constitutional commitment.

---

[81] *Ibid.*, at 90.
[82] *Ibid.*, at 125 et. seq.
[83] Notably, a sub-issue in dispute – the degree to which minority groups can claim any margin of a right to proportional representation, or, negatively stated, to not endure wholly disproportionate numbers of representatives – emerged as a major issue in the post-1982 Section 2 litigation.

7.4.2 VRA Section 2, post-1982: Parsing the Margins of Non-discriminatory Impact

Congress quickly countermanded the *Mobile* plurality's narrow conception of discrimination as intent. The revised statute declares a Section 2 violation when a voting procedure "results in a denial or abridgement" of the right to vote based on race, and elaborates that such a denial occurs:

> if, based on the totality of circumstances, it is shown that the political processes leading to nomination or election in the State or political subdivision are not equally open to participation by [racial minorities] in that [such minorities] have less opportunity than other members of the electorate to participate in the political process and to elect representatives of their choice. The extent to which members of a protected class have been elected to office in the State or political subdivision is one circumstance which may be considered: *Provided*, That nothing in this section establishes a right to have members of a protected class elected in numbers equal to their proportion in the population.[84]

The heart of the provision is that "proof of discriminatory intent is not required to establish a violation of Section 2."[85] The legislative record framed this shift as a return to *White v. Regester*, which, contra the *Mobile* plurality, the Senate Judiciary Committee read to require no consideration of legislative intent. The Senate Judiciary Committee further clarified the factors that should inform the full circumstances analysis, emphasizing any legacy of discrimination, established minority electoral success, and whether the socio-political dynamics suggest oppression, including the presence of racial polarization.[86]

The 1982 amendment is a remarkable moment of institutional dialogue. Congress relied on a constitutional grant of authority to interpret a Court decision to dictate to the Court how it should advance racial equity by prohibiting discriminatory results in electoral procedure. This calls into question who has the authority to interpret the Constitution, since Congress, of course, may not dictate to the judiciary how to interpret higher legislation binding law[87] – though this question of constitutional competence has not yet bubbled to the surface of the jurisprudence. Rather, the Court has ostensibly obeyed the Congressional instruction to prohibit discriminatory results in electoral procedure. The pivotal question may be if Section 2 of the Fifteenth Amendment gives Congress a unique degree of power to prevent the denial or abridgement of racial discrimination.

---

[84] 42 USC 1973 (June 29, 1982) (emphasis added).
[85] S Rep 97–417 (1982) at 2.
[86] *Ibid.*, at 28–9.
[87] Luis Fuentes-Rohwer, "The Future of Section 2 of the Voting Rights Act in the Hands of a Conservative Court" (2010) 5 *Duke Journal of Constitutional Law and Public Policy* 125, 131, 134 ("it may be argued that the 1982 Amendments to section 2 of the Act were a direct rebuke to the Court and its power – a moment in time when Congress asserted its power to interpret the Constitution alongside the Court").

Since it has accepted the authority of the 1982 amendment of Section 2, the challenge for the Court has been determining what attributes condemn electoral procedures for their discriminatory effects. The Senate Judiciary Committee instructed the Court to identify discriminatory effect by weighing a variety of non-exhaustive factors.[88] This required the Court to differentiate discrimination from the normal defeats that a minority wedge bloc group may face in a political struggle. In a first-past-the-post democracy, minority groups (racial and otherwise) will often have their political will thwarted, or be forced to strike compromises to advance their agenda. Identifying discrimination entails a normative judgment regarding what degree of power should be reserved for racial minorities. Thus, the counterpopular dilemma is elicited with an added layer of complexity. The Court must balance the legitimacy of the normal processes of majoritarian politics to set electoral procedure at the state level[89] against a constitutionally empowered legislative instruction to advance its own judicially crafted conception of racial equity.

Thornburg v. Gingles articulated the solution as well as provided the main critique of it. The case queried whether a multimember districting plan diluted racial minority voting power. Writing for a bare progressive majority of five justices, Brennan described the still-controlling three-factor test for a Section 2 violation based on districting:[90]

> First, the minority group must be able to demonstrate that it is sufficiently large and geographically compact to constitute a majority in a single-member district... Second, the minority group must be able to show that it is politically cohesive... Third, the minority must be able to demonstrate that the white majority votes sufficiently as a bloc to enable it...usually to defeat the minority's preferred candidate.[91]

In subsequent cases, the Court has declined to articulate bright-line circumstances that can be "applied mechanically"[92] to determine non-compliance (or safe-harbor compliance) with the *Gingles* test. The most dramatic illustration is in *Johnson v. De Grandy*. A mixed bench concluded that a particular instance of proportionality

---

[88] Justice O'Connor's concurrence in *Thornburg v. Gingles*, 478 US 30, 85 (1986) captures the political and analytic knife-edge the Court is forced to walk upon. She noted the "inherent tension between what Congress wished to do and what it wished to avoid, because any theory of vote dilution must necessarily rely to some extent on a measure of minority voting strength that makes some reference to the proportion between the minority group and the electorate at large", yet the legislation explicitly disclaimed any pursuit of proportional representation.

[89] *Growe v. Emison*, 507 US 25, 34 (1993) and *Voinovich v. Quilter*, 507 US 146, 156 (1993) make explicit that the power of state authorities to set terms of elections is general, and the ability of the judiciary to deny or dictate terms of elections is special, activated only by constitutional violations.

[90] While *Gingles* referred to multimember districts, *Growe v. Emison*, 507 US 25 and *Voinovich v. Quilter*, 507 US at 157–8 established that the same test applies to single-member districting.

[91] *Gingles*, 478 US at 50–1.

[92] *Quilter*, 507 US at 158.

could weigh against a claim of vote dilution, but refused to make proportionality a safe harbor against a Section 2 claim.[93] The Court tends to make holistic, cumulative assessments of whether a given practice impairs minority voting power, which inevitably requires contesting the basic terms of fair democratic self-rule.

In a rare post-Warren Court victory for the substantive–outcome view of racial equity, *Gingles* requires that electoral procedure allocate power to racial minorities. It exemplifies the progressive view that the Constitution imposes requirements regarding the *outcomes* of elections, rather than merely formal equality of access. Yet this feature resulted in fierce challenges from justices who prefer the formalist position that the Constitution commands neutral process rather than any guarantee of the distribution of power.

The bluntest form of this challenge has been the critique that the *Gingles* test contravenes Congress's instruction that the revised Section 2 does not mandate proportionality.[94] In her *Gingles* concurrence, O'Connor disavowed Brennan's test for this reason. She described the test as concluding that "undiluted minority strength means the maximum feasible minority voting strength," and characterized this as "a right to *usual, roughly* proportional representation."[95] She would have instead advanced an assessment of "the minority group's access to the political process generally, not solely consideration of the chances that its preferred candidates will actually be elected."[96] Thomas later even more radically construed this argument by interpreting the application of Section 2 to *any* districting practice as a functional advancement of proportionality, and an exercise in "political theory" beyond the judicial remit.[97]

This struggle between the substantive–output and formalist–access view of Section 2 has continued.[98] The characteristic question has been whether Section 2

---

[93] *Johnson v. De Grandy*, 512 US 997, 1017–8 (1994).
[94] Progressive, conversely, have embraced the role of proportionality as a baseline that indicates if minorities suffer discrimination. *Bartlett v. Strickland*, 566 US 1, 29 (2009) (Souter, dissenting).
[95] *Gingles*, 478 US at 90–1.
[96] Ibid., at 105. O'Connor reiterated this position in her concurrence in *Johnson v. De Grandy*, 512 US at 1025.
[97] *Holder v. Hall*, 512 US 874, 901–2 (1994).
[98] Topics that related to this debate include the questions: 1) if there is a legal requirement that districts be compact, cf. Kennedy, *League of United Latin American Citizens* (*LULAC*) v. *Perry*, 548 US 399, 435 (2006) (compactness must be taken into account to ensure cohesion of minorities communities) with Roberts, *LULAC*, 548 US at 494 (compactness should not be grounds for a state failing to satisfying Section 2), essentially a debate that parallels the coalition district question of what political circumstances the judiciary should protect to ensure a minority's capacity to ensure equal self-rule; 2) the "benchmark" question of how widely courts may range conceptually in comparing different types of electoral arrangements to determine minority voting power, cf. Kennedy, *Hall*, 512 U.S. at 883 (limiting the dilution enquiry to comparisons to the existing form of practice) with Blackmun, *Hall*, 512 US at 950 (dissenting) (arguing that the remit of Section 2 is to protect any impairment of ability of minorities to elect preferred representatives and benchmarking comparisons do not exclude Section 2 claims). Both issues reflect the divide over how much institutional authority and sweep the judiciary should deploy in championing the political power of minorities, and parallel the proportionality and coalition district questions.

protects majority–minority districts as well as those that give minority groups meaningful, if not decisive, influence over electoral outcomes. Souter's *De Grandy* opinion, in rejecting a proportionality safe harbor, observed that minority voters can form coalitions with other voters and groups to elect representatives who are satisfactorily responsive to minority interests.[99] While some political communities – such as those beset by extreme racial polarization and a history of hostile discrimination against racial minorities – might require majority–minority districts to avoid dilution, in others "minority citizens are able to form coalitions with voters from other racial and ethnic groups."[100] The representatives advanced as a result of such coalitions "may not represent perfection to every minority voter, but minority voters are not immune from the obligation to pull, haul, and trade to find common political ground."[101] Yet writing for a three-justice plurality of moderate conservatives who accepted that Section 2 addresses districting, but wished to limit its scope, Kennedy concluded in *LULAC* and *Bartlett v. Strickland* that Section 2 does not protect influence or crossover[102] districts.

Kennedy's primary concern was institutional competence – the need for "workable standards and sound judicial and legislative administration."[103] He suggested that protecting such a wide array of districting types might entangle the judiciary even more extensively in a state process that should be as autonomous as possible (within constitutional bounds). The progressives, led by Souter, have argued that since influence and crossover districts allow minorities to elect representatives of their choice, they should be protected under Section 2. The logic of their claim is that there are districts in which minorities comprise less than 50 percent of the franchise, but due to the broader political circumstances surrounding elections of the type evaluated by the *Gingles* test, have the opportunity to elect their preferred representatives. Nothing in Section 2 or political logic suggests such "opportunity" districts should not receive the same consideration the same as majority–minority districts where they yield the same outcomes.[104] The underlying question is

---

[99] As Kennedy notes in *Bartlett*, 556 US at 12, the initial revised Section 2 opinions reserved the question of if influence districts were protected.

[100] *De Grandy*, 512 US at 1020.

[101] *Hall*, 512 US at 1020.

[102] Kennedy differentiates between "influence" (minority voters can impact the ultimate representative selection, even if their preferred candidate is not elected) and "crossover" (minority group can do so through appealing to a number of white voters for support) districts, *Bartlett*, 566 US at 12, though the distinction appears to reflect a spectrum rather than clearly differentiated types. In both types the defining feature is that minorities, rather than comprising a majority of voters who can ensure the victory of a preferred candidate, must form coalitions with white voters in the district.

[103] Ibid., at 17. The same justification is given in *LULAC*, 548 US at 447. See Jowei Chen and Nicholas O. Stephanopoulos, "The Race-Blind Future of Voting Rights" (2021) 130 *Yale Law Journal* 778, 876 for the question of whether this will remain stable given the conservative court.

[104] *Bartlett*, 566 US at 31; *LULAC*, 548 US at 485–6 (suggesting a specific test that if a minority group makes up more than 50 percent of the party that tends to win the primary in a district, it should enjoy Section 2 protection).

balancing the value of advancing equitable minority representation against concerns that the judiciary will excessively interfere in popular choices regarding democratic process – a concern that exemplifies the counterpopular dilemma.

7.4.3 The Future of Section 2: Hopes for Empowerment, Realities of Conservatives Bench

Shelby County's defanging of the preclearance regime has led to renewed interest in Section 2 as a tool against a broader array of state-implemented discriminatory voting practices. Some have suggested that Section 2 might be adapted to address a wider array of harms, particularly the types of more aggressive ballot deprivation that Section 5 usually interdicted.[105] Others have anticipated that the *Gingles* test (as noted above, a liberal anomaly in a general conservative drift) faces an uncertain future before a conservative bench,[106] particularly given the difficulty of applying a disparate impact test (as revealed by struggles in the lower federal courts).[107]

While the Court has not yet settled the fate of *Gingles*, there have been some signals regarding how forcefully it will apply Section 2. *Brnovich v. Democratic National Committee* explored whether a 2016 (i.e., post-*Shelby County*) Arizona law that imposed relatively marginal constraints on voting (discarding ballots cast in the wrong precinct and criminalizing anyone other than specific classes of agents acting as intermediaries to deliver mail-in ballots) violated Section 2. The evidence showed that one of the measures was significantly more likely to result in ballots by racial minorities being discarded, though this affected only a small percentage of voters; yet Justice Kagan's dissent observed that elections are often "fought and won on the margins."[108] The Court did not debate the presence of intent, which is difficult to infer in an electoral system in which race and partisanship are conjoined.[109] It is plausible to speculate that the law in question in *Brnovich* was ultimately a measure taken by a Republican legislature to entrench itself, even if the vehicle of that entrenchment was exacerbating systemic racial differences in the opportunity to participate in elections.

---

[105] Daniel P. Tokaji, "Applying Section 2 to the New Vote Denial" (2015) 50 *Harvard Civil Rights-Civil Liberties Law Review* 439; Fuentes-Rohwer and Charles, "The Voting Rights Act in Winter," 1391 n. 7.

[106] Fuentes-Rohwer, "The Future of Section 2," 131, 157; See Chen and Stephanopoulos, "The Race-Blind Future of Voting Rights"; Guy-Uriel Charles and Luis Fuentes-Rohwer, "Race and Representation Revisited: The New Racial Gerrymandering Cases and Section 2 of the VRA" (2018) 59 *William and Mary Law Review* 1559, 1593.

[107] Nicholas O. Stephanopoulos, "Disparate Impact, Unified Law" (2019) 128 *Yale Law Journal* 1478, 1582.

[108] *Brnovich*, 141 S. Ct. at 2367.

[109] Nicholas O. Stephanopoulos, "Elections and Alignment" (2014) 114 *Columbia Law Review* 283; Bruce E. Cain and Emily Rong Zhang, "Blurred Lines: Conjoined Polarization and Voting Rights" (2016) 77 *Ohio State Law Journal* 868; Richard L. Hasen, "Race or Party, Race as Party, or Party All the Time: Three Uneasy Approaches to Conjoined Polarization in Redistricting and Voting Cases" (2018) 59 *William and Mary Law Review* 1837.

The response to *Brnovich* was fiercely partisan. As discussed through the frame of *Bush v. Gore* in the book's conclusion, the opinions reflect a strident rising partisanship that afflicts the clarity and neutrality of the reasoning. The majority's treatment of the quantitative impact on racial voting in *Brnovich* is analytically untenable, and the dissent distorts the statutory record, interpolating questionable language (such as "all") to artificially enhance its argument.[110] Analytically, however, two opinions fit perfectly with the two-tiered contestation over what racial equity requires for racial procedure. Concluding that the *Gingles* test is appropriate only for vote dilution, Alito's conservative opinion fabricates a new test for vote ballot access voting rules.[111]

The five-factor test – much like the *Gingles* test – is atmospheric and granular, placing heavy weight on the revised Section 2's instruction to consider the "totality of the circumstances"[112] to justify a holistic balancing. The test gives the Court enormous discretion: it compares the weight of the burden (as atmospherically evaluated by the Court); the deviation from the standard in 1982 (same, and particularly uninformative given the changing voting standards); the magnitude of the impact (which, with its peculiar preference for absolutes, is nigh untenable as an analytical matter); the totality of the voting system; and any countervailing state interest (here, anti-fraud). Perhaps unsurprisingly, the Court concluded that the measure does not violate Section 2.

Yet the underlying justification for the decision seems only to come in closing dicta that justifies the test against the dicta's plaintive invocations of continual racial discrimination: "§ 2 does not deprive the States of their authority to establish non-discriminatory voting rules…there is nothing democratic…about a wholesale transfer of the authority to set voting rules from the States to the federal courts."[113] This statement encapsulates both features of the approach to race in electoral procedure that conservatives now advance. It articulates a minimalist–formalist conception of what comprises "discrimination" that looks only at the superficial neutrality of measures, rather than their impact on systemic racial inequity (recounted in detail in Kagan's dissent),[114] and justifies it by invoking the autonomy of the electorate to set their own terms of self-rule (as allocated by the broader constitutional structure) in the face of the counterpopular dilemma.

The progressive dissent, conversely, is dominated by concerns about the legacy and continued presence of racial discrimination in American democracy. It applies Section 2 whenever, due to any intersection of legal instruction and social context,

---

[110] *Brnovich*, 141 S. Ct. at 2357.
[111] Given the centrality of *White v. Regester* to instruction in the Section 2 revision, a critical question is if *White* can be taken as a guide for addressing discriminatory process generally, or if it is only appropriate for guiding analysis of discriminatory effect in districting. If the former, fabricating a new test may have been gratuitous.
[112] *Brnovich*, 141 S. Ct. at 2338.
[113] Ibid., at 2343.
[114] Ibid., at 2366–9.

"political participation [is] less favorable (or advantageous for one racial group than for another."[115] This approach exemplifies the concern for a substantive, outcome-regarding racial equity perspective in the scholarship. The test advanced by the dissent would, however, prospectively transform electoral practice by mandating the equality of impact of *all* voting procedures by race, regardless of animus – a test that would declare a voting practice illegal whenever there was unequal impact, making Section 2 potentially far more wide-reaching than any constitutional or statutory provision in history. Other than the ambiguous gesture toward effect in *White v. Regester*, the EPC has only applied to provisions that reflect discriminatory intent. As *Reno v. Bossier Parish* established, Section 5 only challenged retrogression (i.e., worsening of position); and Section 2 only challenged the minimization of *minority* groups' voting strength, not racial equity more broadly.[116]

By prospectively touching *any* measure that generates racially unequal *effects*, the effects of dissent's proposed Section 2 test are potentially as wide-ranging as the one person, one vote rule, but much more complex and discretionary in application. It would require the Court to assess what comprises equal electoral opportunity for racial groups. While laudable in principle, if consistently applied, such a project would involve extensive judicial oversight of state-level authority over electoral procedure, particularly given that the concept of equality is descriptively as well as normatively contestable. This project could only be undertaken if the Court were willing not only to serve as the arbiter of evidence, but of the broader terms by which racial equity should precondition popular self-rule. It would remake Section 2 as a tool with radical implications not only for racial equity but also for the judicial role in shaping electoral process in the constitutional order.

7.4.4 *Evaluating the Section 2 Jurisprudence: Institutional Competence and Racial Equity*

While *Brnovich* hardens the partisan battle lines over the appropriate application of Section 2, it also highlights the characteristic contestation in the Section 2 jurisprudence – what conception of racial equity is required of a racialized democracy and which institution should advance it. Because Section 2 includes an explicit congressional instruction that the judiciary should identify discrimination based on effects, it brings the competing bases of institutional authority to the forefront of judicial decision-making.

The Court is thus faced with parallel bases of authority at each level.[117] It must weigh the legislative force of the congressional instruction against the authority

---

[115] Ibid., at 2358.
[116] *Reno v. Bossier Parish School Board*, 520 US 471, 477–9 (1997).
[117] Franita Tolson, "The Elections Clause and the Underenforcement of Federal Law" (2019) 129 *Yale Law Journal Forum* 171 has argued that the Elections Clause could vindicate broad extension of federal oversight of electoral procedure, looking in particular to reforms currently under consideration.

allocated to the state legislatures to set their own electoral procedures. Above these in the hierarchy of interpretation, the Court must weigh the explicit textual grants to Congress to advance the Reconstruction Amendments against the structural allocation of electoral procedure to the states. Balancing these competing pressures gives the Court the interpretive discretion to favor either constitutional instruction, but this in turn forces it to make a purely normative decision about the judiciary's appropriate institutional role.

Therefore, in resolving cases, the Court has had to generate policy-like tests to determine how racial minorities should be protected from discriminatory electoral procedure. The *Gingles* test and the debates it engendered (such as over the status of coalition districts), and the tests proposed by both the majority and dissenting opinions in *Brnovich*, instantiate this policy-like contestation. Reflecting the overarching theme of judicial involvement in electoral procedure, this debate has not consisted of a pure theory of racial equity in a democracy, but rather weighing the benefits of advancing racial equity against the counterpopular effects of the judiciary asserting the authority to do so.

The question is not the ideal role of race in elections; it is unequivocal that eliminating racial discrimination and establishing a democracy without racial animus would be desirable. Rather, it is how muscular a role the Court should play in effecting such circumstances. In this regard, *Brnovich* crystallizes the debates that have long characterized the post-1982 Section 2 doctrine. The justices have fought over if more extensive protections of minority voting power achieved through a proactive judiciary would benefit the political position of minorities as well as American democracy more generally. The conservative view is based on the idea that political contestation, even if racialized, is an appropriate means of the determining the structure of American democracy, so long as minorities have equal baseline access to political inputs. They view extensive judicial intervention as costly not only as a constitutionally suspect intrusion into a domain legitimately determined through state-level politics, but more importantly as undermining the "natural" self-determined resolution of American politics through political discourse. Conversely, the progressives identify a legacy of shameful racial discrimination – marked by the relatively recent presence of Jim Crow – and a responsibility to interdict it. According to this view, the counterpopular cost of robust, output-focused minoritarian protection is outweighed by the subjugation that minorities will continue to experience by the

---

Yet as Derek T. Muller, "Legislative Delegations and the Elections Clause" (2017) 43 *Florida State Law Review* 717, 718 notes, the Supreme Court has done little to interpret the Elections Clause. The jurisprudence is mixed, and gives few indications that it is likely to become a central pillar in justifying extensive federal intervention in state law, in no small part because the Clause only applies to the election of federal officeholders. Cf. *Arizona State Legislature v. Arizona Independent Redistricting Comm'n*, 135 S.Ct. 2652 (2015) (declining a broad definition of "legislature" and allowing popular referenda to select an independent redistricting commission) with *Arizona v. Inter Tribal Council of Arizona*, 570 US 1 (2013) (mandating that a state use forms for Congressional elections that conform to Congressionally mandated standards).

continued manipulation of electoral procedure. The progressives identify a clear benefit to self-rule through minoritarian protection. Otherwise, groups that have already been disadvantaged by history will suffer continued oppression, an unacceptable outcome in a liberal democracy.

The normative underpinnings of the Section 2 jurisprudence parallel the debate over the EPC. The interpretive contexts are distinct. The EPC debate has centered on the internal interpretation of a constitutional clause, while the Section 2 jurisprudence has balanced differing institutional claims to authority based on competing constitutional commitments. And while the EPC addresses race blindness, in light of the post-1982 legislative revisions, Section 2 queries what effects justify intervention. But the basic underlying disputes are identical. Should the judiciary protect only the equity of input participation (i.e., equality of formal access), indicating that the bulk of the struggle over racial equity should occur through directly democratic processes?[118] Or should the judiciary consider the outputs of such process in setting a minimum of what racial equity requires, overdetermining elections at some level but ensuring that racial equity includes some modicum of influence over policy? Underlying this are two different conceptions of what it means for a racially polarized majoritarian franchise to be truly autonomous.

7.5 THE VRA PRECLEARANCE REQUIREMENT AND ITS DEMISE

Congress's most radical and creative intervention into electoral design was the VRA preclearance of state voting procedure. It was the most effective mechanism for interdicting the passage of discriminatory voting procedures and required the most nuanced balancing of existing constitutional principles. In 1965 the preclearance requirement survived judicial review in *Katzenbach*; its legitimacy was vindicated without question by persistent and egregious racial discrimination. However, its constitutional costs came under increasing pressure over time with the amelioration of the ghastly discrimination that had occurred under Jim Crow. In *Shelby County*, a conservative majority functionally deactivated the preclearance requirement. This followed a debate that reflected the same struggle over the questions as Section 2 – how best to maintain racial equity in light of competing constitutional concerns, and the appropriate judicial role in a complex institutional context – but with heightened stakes, given the preclearance requirement's unique operation.

7.5.1 *The Genesis and Initial Success of the Preclearance Requirement*

The preclearance requirement operated through two provisions of the VRA. Section 4(b)'s "coverage formula" identifies states and subdivisions suspected of engaging in

---

[118] Kang, "Race and Democratic Contestation", notes that if the Court fails to protect terms of such contestation, it leaves them in a weakened position.

oppressive voting practices (using a test or device for voter ballot access, such as a literacy test, plus less than 50 percent voter registration); Section 4(a) banned such tests and devices.[119] Section 5 requires covered jurisdictions to seek preclearance (from either the attorney general or the DC federal district court) before implementing changes to their voting procedures.[120] States and subdivisions could also seek to use the bailout provision detailed in Section 4(a) to avoid treatment as a covered jurisdiction by seeking a declaratory judgment from a three-judge panel on the District of Columbia district court, though the requirements to receive bailout were stringent.[121] The Court later clarified that the test for preclearance under Section 5 was non-retrogression. Clearance to change voting procedure would only be granted to a covered jurisdiction if it does not worsen "the position of racial minorities with respect to their effective exercise of the electoral franchise."[122]

Many states and municipalities therefore lost independent authority over their own procedures of self-rule. This loss of autonomy was intended by the design of the legislation. Section 5 deliberately effected such deprivation because of the "variety and persistence" of the electoral practices adopted to deprive Black voters of ballot access.[123] Reactive case-by-case litigation was slow and gave states the opportunity to pass new, formally different but functionally similar discriminatory voting procedures, and placed the onus on civil rights litigants to continue the uphill battle for Black enfranchisement. *Katzenbach* noted that this coverage-and-preclearance approach "shift[ed] the advantage of time and inertia from the perpetrators of the evil to its victims."[124] On the heels of *Katzenbach*, the Court further vindicated the broad applicability of Section 5 to all changes to electoral procedure, further shifting power to the federal government over localities with indicators of racist voter suppression.[125]

Since the Court has remained steadfast that states have the primary authority and responsibility to set electoral procedures, this oversight comes at a cost to the typical federal allocation of power.[126] In *Katzenbach*, eight justices[127] found that the pervasive levels of persistent voter suppression justified a unique measure. "[E]xceptional conditions" vindicate this "uncommon exercise of congressional power," such that Section 5 did not "exceed the powers of Congress and encroach on an area reserved to the States by the Constitution."[128]

---

[119] 52 USCA § 10303, formerly 42 USCA § 1973b.
[120] 52 USCA § 10304, formerly 42 USCA § 1973c.
[121] *Northwest Austin Municipal Utility District No. One* (NAMUNDO), 557 US 193, 198 (2009). For a list of bailed-out jurisdictions, see www.justice.gov/crt/section-4-voting-rights-act.
[122] *Beer v. U.S.*, 425 US 130, 141 (1976).
[123] *Katzenbach*, 383 US at 311–3.
[124] *Katzenbach*, 383 US at 328.
[125] *Allen v. State Board of Elections*, 393 US 544 (1969).
[126] *Katzenbach v. Morgan*, 384 US at 647; *Quilter*, 507 US at 156–7.
[127] Only Justice Black dissented, and remained adamant that Section 5 was overreach; see *Allen* 393 US at 597.
[128] *Katzenbach*, 383 US at 328, 323, 334.

Katzenbach's vindication of preclearance presents at three levels. First, its surface-level analytic character is a cursory review of the constitutional issues at hand (framed by an expansive interpretation of the power granted to Congress under the Fifteenth Amendment). Yet the opinion's rhetoric demonstrates that the truly dispositive fact was not abstract reasoning, but the reality of racial discrimination. However, to simply deem the Court's approval of the preclearance mechanism a policy decision disregards the institutional complexity and social context of the provision. The mechanism was not a judicially crafted remedy, but rather the result of congressional action, and the social reality of gross discrimination and the inefficacy of standard modes of litigation were not disputed.[129]

The Court's reasoning hangs on normative priorities of democratic procedure. Protecting racial equality is a higher-order norm than safeguarding the default locus of authority. Both of these principles manifest constitutionally, in the Fifteenth Amendment and federalism, respectively. Weighing them, however, is a normative question of what conditions are most essential for a franchise to legitimately rule itself. The majority's concession that Section 5 comprises an "uncommon exercise of congressional power" is an analytically equivalent characterization to Justice Black's assertion that preclearance "distorts our constitutional structure of government." The difference is that the majority justifies the unorthodox use of congressional power by need to combat intractable racial discrimination. Whether preclearance is innovation or distortion depends on what norms are prioritized to make liberal constitutional democracy legitimate.[130] The baldest demonstration is that the majority opinion and Black's dissent both cite for support the same Justice Marshall quote regarding the constitutionality of any measure that satisfies legitimate ends, constitutional scope, and appropriate means.[131]

The preclearance analysis reveals that judicial review of election law opines on the legitimate arrangement of constitutional democracy, and cannot be adequately described as a technical analysis. In this sense the struggle over preclearance vividly illustrates Dworkin's point that a court must take community norms into account to resolve hard cases.[132] The norms of self-rule speak to the very bedrock of democratic legitimacy and personal freedom, evoking community values. The preclearance requirement unequivocally contravenes the allocation of power over electoral procedure to state-level constituencies. The question is whether the competing

---

[129] Justice Black's lone dissent did not dispute the reality of racial discrimination, agreeing they were a "notorious means to deny and abridge voting rights on racial grounds." His objection was that a more constitutionally palatable option, in the form of vesting discretionary power in the executive (the Attorney General) was available. *Katzenbach*, 383 US at 356. Indeed, the social reality of vote suppression has seemingly not be disputed by the Court even in cases where the Court was notoriously delinquent in preventing suppression, such as *Giles*.

[130] It is the normative and practical transformation of such constitutional relations that lead Charles and Fuentes-Rohwer, "The Voting Rights Act in Winter," to deem the VRA a transformative superstatute.

[131] *Katzenbach*, 383 US at 326, 358 (Black, dissenting).

[132] Ronald Dworkin, *Law's Empire* (Cambridge: Harvard University Press, 1986), p. 226.

constitutional value of racial justice in electoral procedure (which these state-level constituencies refused to respect) is a higher priority for ensuring the legitimacy of democratic self-rule. The answer in *Katzenbach* was a resounding "yes".

Preclearance raises a unique dilemma because legislative power lies on both sides of it. State legislatures are the institution can declare, by the power allocated to them by constitutional federalism, authority over electoral process. Yet Congress, empowered by the Fifteenth Amendment, can assert that it has constitutional authority to prevent racial discrimination. Because there is legitimate legislative authority on both sides of the dilemma, the question is not one of direct counterpopular action by the Court. The counterpopular aspect emerges because the Court must make a directly substantive normative judgment regarding the higher priority of popular self-rule. Should the Court favor typical devolved allocation of power to state constituencies or nationally enforced norms of racial equity? *Katzenbach* unequivocally signaled that racial equality, rather than the default subnational allocation of power, is the higher-priority feature of legitimate democracy.

7.5.2 *Rising Skepticism and the End of the Consensus: The Path to* Shelby County

How the Court should apply *Katzenbach* yielded fierce contestation over technical questions.[133] However, such debates took place in the shadow of the existential struggle over whether preclearance was constitutional – a question that returned to the competing norms of federalism and racial equity. Fifteen years after *Katzenbach*, the Court again jousted over if the preclearance requirement was constitutional in *City of Rome* – but with less consensus regarding its validity. The city of Rome, Georgia sought to have changes to its municipal voting practices precleared, and brought suit when it was denied – including a challenge to the validity of the provisions generally. The majority opinion largely reiterated *Katzenbach* and acknowledged that the circumstances of minority voters had improved, but that such gains had been "modest and spotty" (citing Congress's own wording) – and that the VRA battled against deeply ingrained discriminatory practices, the damage of which could not be rapidly undone.[134] Supported by this assessment, the Court

---

[133] Prominent among such questions were does Section 5 prohibit discriminatory plans, or merely those that are retrogressive, *Beer and Bossier Parish*; should coalition districts receive weight under a retrogression analysis, *Georgia v. Ashcroft*, 539 US 461 (2003); and when local political subdivisions would be required to seek preclearance, *United States v. Board of Commissioners of Sheffield*, 435 US 110 (1978); *City of Pleasant Grove v. United States*, 479 US 462 (1987); and *Lopez v. Monterey County*, 525 US 266 (1999). Such jurisprudence often elicited congressional reaction in VRA reauthorizations. Nathaniel Persily, "The Promise and Pitfalls of the New Voting Rights Act" (2007) 117 *Yale Law Journal* 174; Charles and Fuentes-Rohwer, "The Voting Rights Act in Winter," 1430. For an overview of congressional reauthorizations, see *Shelby County v. Holder*, 570 US 529, 538 (2013).

[134] *City of Rome v. U.S.*, 446 US 156, 181 (1980). The technical question in *City of Rome* was if 4(a) was meant to permit subdivisions of states to bail out of preclearance when the entire state had not bailed out; the majority answered clearly in the negative.

reaffirmed that the Fifteenth Amendment grants Congress wide-ranging powers to prohibit conduct with discriminatory effects as well as discriminatory intent, and thereby declined the implicit suggestion by the appellants to "do nothing less than overrule…*Katzenbach*."[135]

Three justices in *City of Rome* now found the federalism costs too great to bear. Powell, focused on the fact that Rome had engaged in no intentional discrimination, was offended that it was denied the possibility of a bailout on technical grounds.[136] Generalizing from this refusal of a piecemeal bailout for non-intentional discrimination, Powell found the preclearance requirement to "intrude[] on the prerogatives of state and local governments and abridge[] the voting rights of all citizens in [covered] States"[137] untenable. Powell's weighting of the competing constitutional interests of anti-discrimination and devolved autonomy thus emphasized the circumstances of a particular subdivision and downplayed the systemic effects of discrimination.

Rehnquist's dissent launched a more foundational attack on preclearance. He suggested that the Reconstruction Amendments could not support the constitutionality of preclearance for "second-generation" retrogression (i.e., dilutive districting) that lacked discriminatory animus, because any retrogressive effect can be traced to bloc voting and ultimately to voters' private preferences.[138] Rehnquist drew a contrast with literacy tests, the suppressive effect of which could be attributed to the inferior state of Black education, which was itself a function of state policy. Rehnquist saw demanding preclearance as forged in a racially essentialist view that race is the prevalent factor in representation.[139] Compared to Powell's disagreement with the majority's weighting of anti-discrimination and subdivision autonomy, Rehnquist's position is a far more foundational attack on the scope of anti-discriminatory lawmaking.

20 years later, *Lopez v. Montgomery County* illustrated the bench's continued struggle to balance the anti-discriminatory benefits of preclearance and the cost to federalist autonomy. The case established that even where a covered subdivision in a state that is not covered is required by statewide legislation to change

---

[135] *Ibid.* at 173.

[136] The Court's interpretation meant that Rome could not bail out independently of the state of Georgia, even though the city had not purportedly engaged in purposeful racial discrimination). Notably, two years later, the 1982 reauthorization of the VRA authorized piecemeal bailouts. See *NAMUNDO*, 557 US at 207.

[137] *City of Rome*, 446 US at 202.

[138] *Ibid.*, at 216–17. One aspect of Rehnquist's argument – that preclearance is unsuitable for handling new types of voter suppression – anticipates Issacharoff's view that the preclearance mechanism is no longer contextually appropriate in light of the current dynamics of racial suppression. Samuel Issacharoff, "Is Section 5 of the Voting Rights Act a Victim of Its Own Success?" (2004) 104 *Columbia Law Review* 1710; Issacharoff, "Discrimination Model."

[139] *Ibid.*, 446 US at 216–8. Of course, Rehnquist's view can be critiqued as overly cabined. For example, the *Brnovich* dissent notes that the legacy of discrimination continues to depress Black voting participation.

its electoral procedures, the subdivision must comply with Section 5 (i.e., seek preclearance or bailout). Even as the majority opinion confirmed the broad practical sweep of the preclearance requirement,[140] *Lopez* acknowledged, in strikingly concessionary language, that the VRA "authorizes federal intrusion into sensitive areas of state and local policymaking, impos[ing] substantial federalism costs."[141] The Court thus concluded that the effective application of the preclearance policy effect to advance electoral racial equity requires infringing upon other principles of self-governance.

That the *Lopez* bench (including all progressives) so conceded the burden facing preclearance may have signaled its shifting fortunes. A decade later, in *Northwest Austin Municipal Utility District Number One v. Holder* (NAMUDNO) a near-unanimous bench articulated far more serious doubts about the continued viability of preclearance (Thomas again took a more extreme position in suggesting Section 5 was unconstitutional, anticipating *Shelby County*). The Court not only reviewed the exceptional nature of the provision and how much progress had been made since the initial passage of the VRA in 1964, but also recognized the need to defer to Congress, and dodged evaluating the provision's constitutionality by resolving the case through technical statutory interpretation.

7.5.3 *The Nullification of Preclearance*

NAMUDNO's skepticism regarding Section 5's viability "herald[ed]"[142] its subsequent demise four years later in *Shelby County*. The covered jurisdiction that brought the suit sought a declaratory judgment that VRA Sections 4(b) and 5 were facially unconstitutional, forcing the Court to consider the constitutionality question it had evaded in *NAMUDNO*. The bench split along predictable conservative–progressive lines, and reiterated familiar themes. Justice Roberts's opinion emphasized two political realities: (1) the coverage formula creates vastly different burdens for states and (2) the racially discriminatory conditions of the original coverage formula had been significantly ameliorated. Roberts also invoked two constitutional principles – the equality of the states, and the need for congressional remediation to satisfy a means–ends requirement. Issacharoff describes the granular doctrinal analysis in *Shelby* as "a little odd,"[143] particularly the novel suggestion that states have a right to equal legislative treatment. Yet the ruling's underlying impetus is a norm of devolved popular autonomy that places the onus on federal oversight. Roberts invokes *Katzenbach* to signal

---

[140] Justice Thomas, echoing Rehnquist's broader skepticism due to the federalism costs, dissented, and would only find preclearance acceptable where there were "direct product of a covered jurisdiction's policy choices", 525 US at 290.
[141] *Ibid.*, at 703 (quoting *Miller v. Johnson*, 515 US at 926) (quotation marks removed).
[142] Charles and Fuentes-Rohwer, "The Voting Rights Act in Winter," 1391.
[143] Issacharoff, "Discrimination Model on Voting," 100.

judicial awareness of this onus,[144] suggesting that the unique burden facing the preclearance requirement had been present since its inception. By pointing to the purported improved circumstances of minority voters (a decision buttressed by the holding taking effect by nullifying the Section 4(b) coverage formula rather than Section 5 itself), Roberts argues that this onus no longer applies. He thus characterizes the *Shelby County* decision as a culmination of the Court's ongoing contestation over the validity of preclearance.

Ginsburg's dissent for the progressives assailed almost every legal and factual basis of the majority's holding (including the novel use of the equal sovereignty principle). The progressives simply rejected both the premises and perception of the conservative opinion. Ginsburg asserted that the Reconstruction Amendments allocated significant power to Congress and thereby deserved greater judicial deference. She invoked the significant evidentiary record gathered in the process of passing the 2006 VRA; unlike the conservatives, the progressives interpreted this evidence as indicating a looming systemic peril from electoral discrimination that justifies the preclearance measure.[145]

Shelby County epitomizes continual contestation over the terms of free self-rule that characterizes election law. *Katzenbach* recognized that approbation of preclearance required weighing competing claims to shape democratic procedure, but the glaring racial injustices of the time made the conclusion easy. As the worst injustices of Jim Crow were at least superficially ameliorated and the bench grew more conservative, the issue of whether this constitutional cost remained satisfied increasingly came under question. Although the outcome (though not, as discussed in the next chapter, the suspect reasoning) of *Shelby County* is historically unsettling, it is neither unexpected nor anomalous as a matter of legal analysis.

7.5.4 *The Preclearance Debate as a Struggle over Formalist Inputs and Outputs of Racial Justice*

Shelby County's charged partisan resolution obscures the normative debate at the root of preclearance. At first glance, the debate appears to be a struggle over how badly off racial minorities are in contemporary democracy, and if this disadvantaged condition supports intruding on principles of federalism. Taken at face value, the opinions differ little regarding the underlying descriptive questions. The conservatives recognized the continued impact of racial discrimination (and in *Shelby* repeatedly pointed to the availability of Section 2, and the possibility of a new coverage formula, to ameliorate their decision). The costs of preclearance to federalism were conceded as early as *Katzenbach*, which the progressives recognized

---

[144] *Shelby*, 570 US at 545.
[145] Ibid., at 573.

(to Roberts' "obvious glee") by association by joining the opinion in NAMUDNO.[146] The ongoing judicial debate, while clearly influenced by weighting social facts differently, cannot be one of differing conclusions regarding social fact or simple policy – at least not if the sincerity and integrity of the judiciary's articulated reasoning, and its performance of legitimate constitutional analysis, are accepted. Yet some of the shoddy reasoning in both *Shelby* opinions suggests the erosion of this legitimacy, which I discuss in the conclusion.

The most familiar understanding of the preclearance debate is one of competing constitutional commitments. This at first appears to be the legitimate approach to judicial review. The franchise has, through constitutional process, authorized the principles of federalism and racial equity. However, these authorizations do not signal a clear prioritization, particularly given their different characters. The Reconstruction Amendments are an explicit and robust intercession into a pathology of American politics. Conversely, federalism is a "nontextual [and] free-floating"[147] general principle of political organization. The most normatively convenient approach – the Court should simply give effect to the will of the electorate as expressed by constitutional commitments – fails to offer satisfactory guidance.

Resolving such a balancing act through internal constitutional analysis is further complicated by the fact that anti-discrimination amendments and federalism serve the same value, protecting liberty, and because expressing each value in preclearance lawmaking empowers a legislative branch with some legitimate claim to authority over terms of self-rule. The importance of preventing racial discrimination to ensure legitimate democratic rule is self-evident, but as Franita Tolson has observed, federalism also advances the freedom of the polity by distributing power among multiple entities[148] (in context of elections, this has a long legacy of allocating power to the states).[149] The judiciary is left to balance two competing contributors to free self-rule: (1) a principle of anti-discrimination, which some states have long transgressed and (2) a principle of devolving the power to determine electoral procedure to lower-order polities to prevent high-level, self-dealing domination by a centralized entity (a variation of the lockup concern that has dominated contemporary election law scholarship). Neither possible outcome is typically counterpopular. The Court will allocate authority over electoral process advanced to one legislature or another. It does not, as it does in other areas of race and election law, directly introduce its own conception of electoral fairness.

---

[146] Issacharoff, "Discrimination Model on Voting," 101.
[147] Franita Tolson, "Reinventing Sovereignty? Federalism as a Constraint on the Voting Rights Act" (2012) 65 *Vanderbilt Law Review* 1195, 1200.
[148] Tolson, "Reinventing Sovereignty," 1219.
[149] *Katzenbach v. Morgan*, 384 US at 647; *Quilter*, 507 US at 156–7; *Chapman v. Meier*, 420 US 1 (1975); *Growe*.

The struggle over preclearance is best described as a purely normative debate over what conditions are most essential for legitimate democratic self-rule. This manifests at one level in granular and often familiar specific arguments of the justices. For example, Rehnquist's attack on preclearance in *City of Rome* was ultimately premised on racial essentialism in representation, which, by vindicating the preclearance requirement, led to the expansion of congressional power at the cost of "local democratic process." While he attacks the Court's continued approval of preclearance as "political theory," Rehnquist's own reasoning is premised on a political theory of how minority protections should be balanced against localized authority.[150] These claims are familiar to the anti-essentialist analysis advanced by Kennedy regarding the EPC and against Thomas's political theorizing on Section 2. Likewise, the debate over how coalition districts should be assessed for the purposes of retrogression in *Georgia v. Ashcroft* is resonates with the debate over Section 2 regarding the terms by which cooperation with other voters empowers a racial minority.[151]

Yet the crux of the normative debate over preclearance reflects the broader struggle over whether the judiciary should focus on protecting inputs when advancing self-rule as the highest value. For the preclearance question, this becomes a struggle between realization of the federal structure and ensuring that minorities can achieve fair outcomes in the light of pervasive yet often subtle discrimination. Conservatives who have challenged the preclearance mechanism since the 1980s have emphasized how preclearance deprives constituents of the typical authority to set their own electoral procedures.[152] The normative interest is clear. Absent glaring racial discrimination, constituents should be free to set their own terms of governance under the basic structural commitments of the Constitution. This allocation is not ostensibly justified by distrust of the federal government, but by the desirability of achieving default constitutional power allocations as a matter of constituent autonomy expressed in higher constitutional law. Powell's declaration in *City of Rome* that excessive congressional oversight "abridges the voting rights of *all* citizens"[153] in covered jurisdictions exemplifies this commitment. Universal adherence to the terms of the constitutional arrangements ensures all constituents participate in the political process as equals, and is one of the strongest guarantors of political

---

[150] *City of Rome*, 446 US at 220–1.
[151] Cf. *Georgia v. Ashcroft*, 539 US at 487 (only considering population numbers) with 539 US at 492 (Souter, dissenting) (asserting that showing non-retrogression requires a more nuanced analysis of prospective political behavior).
[152] *City of Rome* 446 US at 200–1 ("abridges the voting rights of all citizens in States covered under the act...[and] destroy local control of the means of self-government, one of the central values of our polity") (Powell, dissenting); 446 US at 209 ("significant intrusion on local autonomy"); *Lopez*, 525 US at 594 (quoting Powell in *City of Rome*) (Thomas, dissenting); *Shelby County*, 570 US at 542–5 (summarizing bases and extent of state authority, observing costs to federalism, and observing the Court's tentativeness in approving it).
[153] *City of Rome*, 446 US at 200 (emphasis added).

autonomy. Deviation from the constitutional setup impairs all constituents who are both bound and guided by the Constitution, because it intrudes upon the baseline of equality they all should enjoy. *Shelby County*'s invocation of the principle of the equality of the states champions precisely this value, even if its analysis is awkward.

The progressive position has staunchly emphasized the need for racial equity in electoral outcomes as the driving feature of the free self-rule of the *entire franchise*. This is clearest in cases where the normative priority of racial equity was either established or dismissed. *Katzenbach* forged its approval of the VRA in the need to prevent "widespread resistance to the Fifteenth Amendment," exemplified by the "extraordinary stratagem of contriving new [discriminatory] rules" the preclearance requirement was meant to prevent,[154] and the subsequent denial of voting opportunities to a large, politically engaged bloc of the population.[155] Underlying *Katzenbach* is the claim that a polity that systematically denies the franchise to a disadvantaged subgroup is not a legitimate democracy – a compelling claim according to the terms of liberal constitutionalism in which constituents' equality and liberty are the bedrock values.[156] The progressive dissent in *Shelby County* makes essentially the same point. It observed that the "grand aim of the Act is to secure to all our polity equal citizenship stature, a voice in our democracy undiluted by race," and pointed to second-generation vote dilution as a grave threat to this aim.[157] At the critical moments for preclearance, its advocates pointed to a concrete property possessed by, rather than an abstract process of, legitimate democracy – its achievement of racial equity for all participants in the polity. Yet this racial advancement is achieved by imposing it externally upon otherwise autonomous local polities, contra the formalist valuation of federalist power allocation as interested in an output of political process rather than an input.

The technical question at issue – whether congressional legislation will be permitted to constrain the terms of state legislative decision-making – alters the terms of this framing of contestation over preclearance. The debate occurs at a higher level of abstraction than in the other law that addresses racial discrimination (i.e., EPC and Section 2). These areas directly query if racial equity in elections only requires formal opportunity for participation or actually demands that minorities achieve substantive equity in power. In the context of preclearance, the question becomes one of differing constitutional priorities. Is the higher normative priority formal equivalence in the constitutional structure (i.e., federalism being applied consistently despite circumstances of discrimination), or is the higher priority providing additional safeguards against racial discrimination? Prioritizing formal constitutional equivalence will identify deviation from integrity of self-rule when the

---

[154] *Katzenbach*, 383 US at 334–7.
[155] *Ibid.*, at 314–15.
[156] See the discussion of John Rawls, *Political Liberalism* in Chapter 1.
[157] *Shelby County*, 570 US at 593.

universal structural features of the Constitution are disregarded, even in the pursuit of racial equity. Conversely prioritizing racial equity will accept such divergences from typical constitutional commitments if the end result is to create electoral processes that yield greater racial justice.

7.6 SYNTHESIZING THE DOCTRINE: A NOVEL PHILOSOPHICAL ANALOGUE, AND ITS IMPLICATIONS

The axis of contestation over racial equity described in this chapter – formalism–minimalism that only protects access to political process, and substantive advancement of minority political power – is certainly not exotic or unfamiliar. The most obvious parallel is in the Court's differing treatment of discriminatory intent and discriminatory impact in racial classifications generally. While it would be tempting to fit the contestation into this framework, or simply declare it a straightforward parallel, this would be inaccurate for two reasons: (1) the unique and diverse constitutional and legislative forms that efforts to combat racial discrimination in election law have taken, and the corresponding diversity of judicial interpretation; and more importantly (2) election law is qualitatively distinct because it addresses the fundamental allocation of political power. Election law deserves a novel framing.

This section offers an unconventional parallel that captures the spirit of the doctrinal contestation: the famous Nozick–Rawls dispute over whether property is justly allocated by original personal endowments, or to benefit the least well off. This analogy illuminates the core of the protection of access/protection of power dispute in race and elections. Does constitutional justice demand only protecting minorities' ability to participate in politics (otherwise leaving racial equity to political struggle), or does the Constitution allow for directly redistributing political power to disadvantaged minorities?

7.6.1 Existing Approaches and Their Limitations

The competition on the bench between electoral racial justice as formally equivalent access and as substantive outcomes evokes a prominent and widely analyzed constitutional analog: the distinct legal status of legislation with discriminatory *purpose* versus discriminatory *impact*. This distinction undergirds much of the Supreme Court doctrine[158] as well as leading scholarly analyses (which often treat election law as a

---

[158] Cf. *Washington v. Davis*, 426 US 299 (1976), *Griggs v. Duke Power Co.*, 401 US 424 (1971) and *Ricci v. DeStefano*, 557 US 557 (2009) with *Adarand Constructors, Inc. v. Pena*, 515 US 200 (1995) and *City of Richmond v. J. A. Croson Co.*, 488 US 469 (1989). For an extended analysis of this pattern of case law, see Samuel R. Bagenstos, "Disparate Impact and the Role of Classification and Motivation in Equal Protection Law after Inclusive Communities" (2016) 101 *Cornell Law Review* 1115; Primus, "Equal Protection and Disparate Impact," 496.

7.6 Synthesizing the Doctrine: A Novel Philosophical Analogue 283

leading example of general trends in anti-discrimination law).[159] It might be possible to map the inputs/outcomes divide this chapter adopts onto this distinction. However, I propose a novel framing rather than adopt the prevalent scholarly approach that incorporates election law as a subcategory of constitutional law for two reasons.

The first reason is simple doctrinal accuracy. If – as my project assumes – justices' writings are treated as earnest rather than pretexts for political agendas, the legal issues raised by race and election law do not coherently fit the standard anti-discrimination doctrinal categories. Certainly, the development of the EPC (particularly in the retreat from *White v. Regester* and the main thrust of *Shaw*) exemplifies the adoption of colorblindness rather than substantive justice for disadvantaged groups. But, as described above, the Court's analysis of Section 2 of the VRA (particularly following the 1982 amendment), and especially the preclearance requirement, cannot be fit into these narratives without significantly distorting their facial legal analysis. Some scholars are willing to do so. Reva Siegel, for example, has critiqued *Shelby County* as a core example of the Court's erosion of substantive anti-discrimination, rather than treated it as a struggle between two constitutional commitments. Yet this comes at some cost to the accuracy of her analysis. *Shelby County* would in the first instance advance the will of some legislature, whether at the state level or Congress, and thus favor some powerful, constitutionally empowered actor.

The second reason to doubt this mainstream framing, especially in the scholarship, is that it neglects the unique nature of elections which inspires this book. Election law is not only about *what* policy is effected, but how a people should implement it in the first place. As Pamela Karlan and Daryl Levinson note, electoral policy "ration[s] and apportion[s] the power to govern" including by minority groups.[160] It speaks directly to the distribution of political power as a "gatekeeper" of other domains of state action. This unique role of election law in the democratic order has further implications for integrating it into a standard anti-discrimination narrative. Election law does not seek particular outcomes, because desirable

---

[159] For examples from a leading scholar, see Siegel, "Equality Divided," 67 (using the paradox that the Court will now identify illegal disparate purpose in laws that are meant to achieve racial equity, thus protecting White majorities, yet laws with disparate impact, even where it harms disadvantaged minorities, will often survive, and using this trend to critique *Shelby County* as majority protective. See also Primus, "Equal Protection and Disparate Impact"); Reva B. Siegel, From Colorblindness to Antibalkanization, 120 *Yale Law Journal* 1278, 1295 (2011) (describing the EPC districting jurisprudence as reflecting a desire by "moderate" justices to use anti-discrimination law to prevent racial balkanization). For other examples see, e.g., Deborah Hellman, The Expressive Dimension of Equal Protection, 85 *Minnesota Law Review* 1, 17 (drawing off Pildes and Niemi specifically); Selmi "Proving Intentional Discrimination," 309 (treating voting rights as one example along with criminal and employment discrimination).

[160] Pamela S. Karlan and Daryl J. Levinson, "Why Voting is Different" (1996) 84 *California Law Review* 1201, 1202. Richard H. Pildes, "Principled Limitations on Racial and Partisan Redistricting" (1997) 106 *Yale Law Journal* 2505 makes a similar point regarding the inappositeness of treating districting as a normal equal protection matter.

election outcomes cannot be predetermined; it can only seek to facilitate legitimate self-rule by the franchise. This property underlies Michael Kang's broadening of the aim of election law to include the terms of fair contestation in political life, instead of merely looking to set expectations for outcomes.[161] Unlike resource-distributing legislation, which is the result of democratic process, electoral legislation is part of the political process that comprises franchise self-rule. A further ramification is that any law that shapes electoral procedure is *internal* to the polity's political struggle that manifests this freedom (a feature most familiar in some accounts of partisan gerrymandering). As such, judicial review of election law has the additional onus that it directly shapes a franchise's ongoing exercise of self-rule – a process that must reflect popular autonomy to be legitimate – rather than only speaking to a fair distribution of state resources. This explains why, for example, the approach of *Shaw* may not become typical for addressing discrimination claims even before a conservative Court, as Samuel Bagenstos predicts. *Shaw* speaks to the unique characteristics of neutrality demanded in electoral design, not general policymaking.[162]

Constitutional limits imposed on election law must be justified as contributing to the process of ongoing self-rule rather than merely boundaries to policymaking. The narratives that include election anti-discrimination law without recognizing its distinctive character do not appropriately recognize these implications of the counterpopular review of election law. This is a somewhat ironic development, given that the protection of discrete and insular minorities was a central part of Ely's account, arguably the most prominent of the 1980s (see Chapter 2). Insofar as his account continues to resonate, it has manifested as concern for the vulnerable status of minorities rather than constitutionalism's complex relationship with democratic majoritarianism.

Yet dedicated analyses of election law have generally adopted an instrumentalist understanding of race as it affects this type of law, focused on structures and patterns of discrimination. Some scholars concentrate on immediate social realities, such as the continued presence of racial discrimination, whether interwoven and systemic[163] or new oppressive policies in the context of an unsympathetic Court.[164] Others have offered proposals to combat racial discrimination, often based on social science empirics.[165] Finally, some have argued that changing

---

[161] Kang, "Race and Democratic Contestation."
[162] Bagenstos, "Equal Protection Law after Inclusive Communities," 1167.
[163] Joshua Sellers, "Election Law and White Identity Politics" (2019) 87 *Fordham Law Review* 1515 (arguing that all election law suffers from "racial blind spots" that taint the law's justice).
[164] Fuentes-Rohwer, "The Future of Section 2" (describing how a conservative bench may hamstring Section 2); Daniel P. Tokaji, "Responding to Shelby County: A Grand Election Bargain" (2014) 8 *Harvard Law & Policy Review* 71, 72 (describing the development of new oppressive practices).
[165] Christopher S. Elmendorf and Douglas M. Spencer, "Administering Section 2 of the Voting Rights Act after Shelby County" (2015) 115 *Columbia Law Review* 2143 (offering a revised approach to Section 2 based on new models); Stephanopoulos and Chen, "The Race-Blind Future of Voting Rights" (describing a new quantitative approach to election law).

conditions require new approaches, particularly regarding the propriety of the preclearance requirement (a point exemplified by Issacharoff both before and after *Shelby County*).[166]

These approaches all treat the role of race in elections as a matter of judicial policy. Such approaches have greatly contributed to the advancement of justice in analysis of racial discrimination in democracy, but the predominant trend does not focus on making sense of the doctrine on its own terms as addressing how a free people should rule itself. This tendency to treat racial discrimination as a policy problem, and disregard the ramifications of the judicial role, mirror the difficulty of directly implementing a theory of just representation discussed in this chapter's introduction.

7.6.2 Analogizing the Role of Race: Rawls and Nozick on Property

This chapter has shown that the basic struggle in the doctrine has been over how free self-rule should be understood in the context of America's history of racial injustice. Should minorities be guaranteed some degree of representative power to address this legacy, or merely be guaranteed equal participation in elections? While the unequivocal ultimate aim is the elimination of racial disparity from democratic life altogether, the question the Court faces is more specific. How should it serve this racial equity under the Reconstruction Amendments, given that (1) it has competing constitutional commitments and (2) judicial intervention can be intrinsically counterpopular? These questions are unified in the debate between the two visions of racial equity as guaranteeing non-discriminatory access only (and leaving the power outcomes to democratic politics), and as ensuring minorities are guaranteed actual power in governance.

Existing accounts, which focus on the persistence of unequal structures of power, have not fully captured the principled characters of this divide, and pure theories of representative justice do not take into account the unique nature of the judicial role. To further draw out the normative contest at issue in the doctrine, it is helpful to draw an analogy with another domain in which the appropriate treatment of inequality has been fiercely debated – inequality in property distribution. The seminal dispute between John Rawls and Robert Nozick over the just allocation of property tracks the input–output distinction regarding how the Courts should advance racial equity in elections. The analogy helpfully captures the basis of the judicial dispute, and maps onto the granular justifications for the input–output divide given in the doctrine.

---

[166] Issacharoff, "Is Section 5 of the Voting Rights Act a Victim of its Own Success?"; Issacharoff, "Discrimination Model." Another common theme has been the complex relationship between racialized and politicized voting and how this affects districting. See Cain and Zhang, "Conjoined Polarization and Voting"; Hasen, "Race or Party."

The contrasting theories of just property allocation by Rawls and Nozick are foundational in contemporary political theorizing on justice and have been the subject of extensive scholarly analysis. The basic distinction between them is straightforward. Rawls begins from the premise that existential and personal differences that create economic inequality are ontologically and morally arbitrary; thus, resources should be distributed to benefit the least well off. The most rigorous explanation of this principle is given as the second principle of justice – the priority of justice in resource distribution.[167] The analytical apparatus that supports this principle is cogent for two reasons. First, it is subordinate to the first principle, of equal basic liberties. Second, these principles are derived by applying a thought experiment regarding what an individual would consider to be a just society. Rawls's key tools in establishing these two principles as the foundations of a just structure are the original position and the veil of ignorance, which together should lead a reasonable person to conclude that inequality is a function of "lesser luck in the social and natural lotteries."[168] If individuals reflect upon this arbitrariness, they will accept the premise that the state should adopt redistributive policies that give resources to the least well off, because their reflection will lead to the conclusion that there is no moral reason why they are not in such a least well off position.

Conversely, Nozick begins from the premise of the integrity of individual starting endowments. Since individuals can assert a claim of right over their initial endowments, so long as transfers occur without infringing upon others' rights, the resulting distribution "can be fully legitimate…no matter how unequal the distribution of privately owned property."[169] Nozick observes that a just distribution of resources based on some value other than the tracing back to individual choices is "patterned," and can only be given effect by intruding upon liberty.[170] In Nozick's view, distributions of resources do not intrude upon individual liberty only if they are "historical" (i.e., traceable back to these transactions).[171] The state has no legitimate right to reallocate property to achieve a fairer outcome of distribution, because this infringes upon the legacy of individual free choices that yielded the existing allocation.

The Rawls/Nozick treatment of property serves as a useful lens with which to analyze the output–input conception of what racial equity demands in elections. The progressive (outcome-protecting) view of racial equity in elections can be analogized

---

[167] John Rawls, *A Theory of Justice* (Cambridge: Harvard University Press, 1999), p. 266.
[168] Andrew Williams, "Liberty, Equality, and Property," in John S. Dryzek, Bonnie Honig, and Anne Phillips (eds.), *The Oxford Handbook of Political Theory* (Oxford: Oxford University Press, 2008), p. 289. For a summary of Rawls's reasoning, see Barbara H. Fried, *Facing Up to Scarcity* (Oxford: Oxford University Press, 2020), p. 159.
[169] Richard J. Arneson, Justice After Rawls, in Robert E. Goodin (ed.), *The Oxford Handbook of Political Science* (Oxford: Oxford University Press, 2011), p. 120.
[170] Nozick, *Anarchy, State, and Utopia* (Malden, MA: Basic Books, 1974), p. 160.
[171] Ibid., p. 155.

7.6 Synthesizing the Doctrine: A Novel Philosophical Analogue 287

to Rawls's view of property redistribution. Once persons recognize their position in the system (including race, which would fall behind the veil of ignorance), they will accept the principle that electoral rules should be arranged to benefit the least well off. In other words, electoral rules should ensure that minorities have adequate power, not merely equal opportunity to participate in initial processes. Conversely, the conservative (input-protecting) approach can be analogized to the Nozickean understanding of property. Racial equity, at least in the contemporary era, only justifies protecting a baseline of fair access to participation rather than any guaranteed powerholding, a quality analogous to Nozick's claim that only a minimalist state is justified. The unifying question is "what does justice demand?" The answers that Rawls (outcomes that benefit the disadvantaged) and Nozick (only an equal playing field) give for property distribution mirror those adopted by the progressives and conservatives, respectively, regarding the judicial role in advancing racial equity.

This analogy can be further developed by evaluating the role of institutions. Rawls and Nozick debate what the appropriate role of the state is in shaping individual property holding. The bench has been riven by a parallel debate over what role the Court should have in dictating to the franchise and to state legislatures the appropriate terms of racial equity for legitimate elections. Nozick's claim that only a minimalist state is morally justified by the legitimacy of initial personal endowments followed by fair exchanges tracks the conservative reluctance to do more than mandate equivalent procedural access to elections for minorities. This parallel tracks to the justices' foundational views of legitimate democratic process. Rehnquist's and Thomas's concerns about racial essentialization among the electorate and the conservative justifications in *Shelby County* and *Brnovich* that voters and state legislatures need to retain authority are effectively arguments that stronger judicial demands for substantive equity in racial power illicitly shift electoral process and outcomes from what should be managed through pure political struggle. In the conservative view, even if such stronger intervention was necessary in the past to correct illicit pre-Civil Rights discrimination (as in *Katzenbach*), it is no longer justified. In this sense the conservatives condemn more extensive intervention as "patterned" by the judiciary rather than the natural result of politics, in the same way that Nozick condemns the redistribution of property as "patterned" rather than freely chosen. Conversely, Rawls's claim that reasonable reflection upon the just arrangement of society would include a certain allocation of property for the less well-off parallels the progressive claim that the Court should interpret the Constitution to require that just electoral arrangements advance the actual allocation of power to disadvantaged groups in politics. The universality that Rawls ascribes to his reflective practices takes the form of the universality of substantive racial equity from constitutional commitments, despite the fact that such reallocations impose, at a lower level of priority, some of the optionality (to hold property and to select electoral procedures, respectively) that would otherwise be present in social arrangements.

In this analogy, the appropriate role of the state in justly redistributing property mirrors the role of the Court in justly setting the terms of electoral procedure. In both cases, the relevant question is the just institutional intervention to influence an otherwise unconstrained party – the power of private individuals to dispose of property, and the power of state legislatures to set their own electoral procedures, respectively – in light of countervailing normative interests (social justice in distribution and racial equity). In each case, the extent of legitimate institutional intervention is determined by the broader normative onus of social intervention. As such, this analogy helpfully informs conservative and progressive views of how much the counterpopular dilemma constrains the Court from advancing the power realities of racial equity. Just as Rawls sees in the basic terms of social organization an obligation to achieve a certain distribution of property, the progressives see in the obligations of racial justice, formalized by the Reconstruction Amendments, an obligation to ensure minorities enjoy some degree of real political power. Likewise, just as Nozick perceives the state as acting illegitimately when it redistributes property, conservatives see the Court as acting illegitimately when it sets electoral process to enhance minorities' substantive representative power.

However, this analogy to the Rawls/Nozick view of property is evoked as a lens, rather than a congruent mapping, in two ways. First, the divide between Rawls and Nozick over property allocation runs far deeper than the division over racial equity on the bench. It is unequivocal that the elimination of racial inequity would be good. The controversy relates to determining the appropriate role of one branch of the state – the judiciary. Conversely, Rawls and Nozick speak to the power of the state as a whole to redistribute property *at all*. Second, the property analogy does not accurately map significant qualities of race and elections. Nozick would certainly recognize in the history of slavery an unjust transference that might in fact justify the continued correction of racial outcomes. And Rawls's own views on elections would be informed by the lexically prior principle of equal liberty rather than the distributional principle. Third, and most fundamentally, the analogy speaks to different types of social goods. Rawls and Nozick discuss property distribution, while the Court's analysis of electoral procedure relates to the allocation of political power in a context of racial inequity. Most importantly, property distribution and property inequality are "singular" features of social design, whereas inequities of political quality distributed by race cut across two different features of social reality.

7.6.3 Should the Legacy of Race be Contested in Politics, or by Constitutional Commitment? A Path Forward under a Conservative Court

Despite these differences, the Rawls/Nozick analogy is helpful because it captures the fundamental question of the judiciary's role in shaping electoral design in a context of racial inequity. Should the legacy of racial inequity be addressed by outcome-shifting rules that reallocate, by electoral design, some degree of power to minorities, or should the Court only serve as a minimalist umpire who ensures terms of equal access, and otherwise leaves addressing racial inequity to the political process? Underlying this – and paralleling the role of the state in allocating property in the Rawls/Nozick debate – is the question of what foundational role the judiciary should play in shaping electoral justice. The purpose of electoral procedure is to advance free self-rule among the electorate. Judicial interventions to alleviate racial inequity in politics seek to determine what would most effectively alleviate this inequity to generate the conditions of legitimate democratic self-governance.

Given the Court's constitutionally defined remit, and the validity of the Constitution as expressing the will of the franchise, the ultimate question is what approach to racial equity should be attributed to a free polity that has assigned power to the judiciary. This again parallels the final return to political legitimacy that defines Rawls and Nozick. Much as they inform their theories of just property allocation by considering individuals' moral standing, establishing what constitutional commitments demand of electoral process for subgroups requires re-examining how individual political freedom (including that of oppressed persons) legitimates state power.

Such an examination creates a new approach that resonates with the case law – contestation over freedom – that addresses new questions. For instance, how would free persons in a democracy with a legacy of racial oppression instruct the judiciary to legitimately address this legacy? Would these free persons recognize the moral arbitrariness and unjustifiability of the oppression, and interpret the Reconstruction Amendments as meaningfully reallocating power to ameliorate the condition of oppressed minorities? Or would they limit such a baseline instruction to narrow equality of access, presuming that political struggle can legitimately resolve racial inequity? The latter view seems increasingly unrealistic given the continued racialization of American politics, and evidence that a new wave of suppressive voter practices was implemented after *Shelby County*.[172] But the roots of the conservative view are resistant to claims that these practices are unconstitutional as long as they do not deliberately deprive minorities of the vote, because their view is based on a vision of what underlying conditions make a polity free. This affirms that the conservative view treats racial inequity in a fundamentally Nozickean matter – as a historical fact that, as long as minimal requirements of non-coercion are met, falls outside the remit of the judiciary.

This chapter uses this analogy as a capstone to suggest a way forward for the Court to address racial inequity. To date, the scholarship and doctrine have deferred to structural dynamics and collective interest to inform the appropriate judicial

---

[172] See Tokaji, "Applying Section 2 to the New Vote Denial"; Stephanopoulos, "Disparate Impact, Unified Law," n. 1 for initial accounting of these practices. For an even broader view, see Lisa Marshall Manheim and Elizabeth G. Porter, "The Elephant in the Room: Intentional Voter Suppression" (2018) 2018 *Supreme Court Review* 213.

intervention in race and elections. Yet the contestation has grown increasingly fractious. In *Shelby County* and *Brnovich* in particular, the progressives and conservatives have failed to offer arguments that reasonably engage each another.

Outcome-oriented claims of structurally unjust results of voting laws are unlikely to convince the durable conservative majority, given its commitment to a minimalist vision of racial equity in electoral procedure. I propose a new approach – contestation over freedom – in which the Court's constitutional remit is informed by considering what free members of the polity (including those with legitimate grievances of denial of political process) would commit to as principles of self-rule. This approach offers the best way to connect individuals' bedrock commitment to the judicial–constitutional principles regarding injustice.

Conclusion

The Battle over Liberalism, the Trap of Partisanship, and the Future of Election Law

This review of the doctrine and the underlying theoretical struggles illuminates a grander pattern in election law doctrine: the bench has struggled over what approach to liberalism best serves constituent autonomy. Is this autonomy best served by constitutional protection of individuals' pre-electoral[1] endowments – including privileges of wealth, race, or social status that allow for disproportionate electoral influence – from state interference? Or should the Supreme Court allow – or require – the state to treat constituents as meaningful co-participants in self-governance, and demand material equity of electoral authority for each person? This debate balances the role of persons as participants in collective self-rule against the insulation of persons from state intrusion. Since elections are the mechanism by which personal power is transformed into state power, this question takes on an added layer of complexity. Inequitable freedom from the state can become inequitable power over the state; state intrusion into personal freedom distorts the legitimacy of any state action. How to balance legitimate terms of constituent participation with appropriate insulation from state power in the context of elections is the unifying question in the Supreme Court doctrine. Both sides of this debate fall within a liberal tradition. This suggests a comforting quality in the arc of election law. The well-developed areas of the law I explore in this book can be understood as contestation within an established philosophical tradition of free democratic self-rule.

However, recent developments highlight problems associated with reconciling the Supreme Court's election law doctrine with the values of liberal democracy. The most salient threat is that partisanship on the bench could become the sole determinant of election law rulings, a particularly ominous threat as such cases become increasingly urgent and decisive for specific electoral outcomes. The most

---

[1] I use the term pre-*electoral*, instead of pre-*political*, because the endowments at issue – e.g. disparities of wealth and racial power – are at least partly (and, for some, wholly) functions of political society. For example, disparities in wealth depend on state intervention to maintain them by enforcing property rights, which creates a paradox for normative foundations of the conservative endowment-protecting view of election law.

notorious election law case in history, *Bush v. Gore*, illustrates this partisan overdetermination. It is difficult to make sense of as a reasoned opinion, and thankfully remains an exceptional case – including in failing to be tractable as an exercise in judicial contestation over popular self-determination.

The looming threat of partisan overdetermination is exacerbated by another trend – an increased reliance on abbreviated modes of resolving election law questions, which came to prominence with cases such as *Purcell v. Gonzalez*. The use of unsigned orders, brief *per curiam* opinions, and other tools of the "shadow docket" to resolve exigent election law questions threatens to rob judicial decision-making of the normative contestation that reconciles judicial review of election law and democratic self-rule. The use of abbreviated decision-making is especially problematic when combined with partisan overdetermination. Such a pattern gives the Court the authority to shape electoral process and outcomes without illuminating the underlying norms, or the need to discipline and justify its intervention on the terms of popular self-rule.

Examining these two threats to the legitimacy of election law not only serves as a warning for the future but also highlights the virtue of the long-established lineages of law. While these lineages have reflected partisan cleavages, these cleavages have incubated the dispute over liberalism. While the Court has become increasingly partisan, that partisanship is often reconcilable to self-governance by working within, and serving to frame, liberal debates regarding constituent freedom in democratic process. The longer legacy of the Supreme Court suggests the possibility – albeit increasingly fragile – of reconciling popular self-rule and judicial intervention in democratic process.

This conclusion ends by directing the book's argument toward a broader understanding and legitimation of judicial review in a liberal society. Judicial review must ultimately be made tractable to the touchstone of morally legitimate governance – constituents' autonomy. No other basis can legitimize it, because such a basis becomes the hierarchical imposition of values contrary to moral self-determination. This suggests that the judiciary's reasoning should always be vindicated by a return to personal autonomy, and that contestation over autonomy may offer a unifying lens to evaluate and legitimize judicial review generally.

UNIFYING THEORY AND LAW: THE MANIFESTATION OF CONTESTATION OVER AUTONOMY IN THE DOCTRINE

Two prevalent contemporary understandings of liberalism offer the most cogent frames for doctrinal contestation over constituent autonomy in election law – Rawlsian egalitarianism and Nozickean libertarianism. Recognizing the conflict between them enriches normative contestation as ameliorating the counterpopular dilemma.

John Rawls advances the view that liberalism should advance the freedom (and thus the equality) of members of the political community.[2] In response to instrumentalist utilitarian understandings of state organization, Rawls famously sought to justify and describe the legitimate organization of the state from a perspective that freely reasoning individuals would choose to commit to. As such, his view is deontological, forged in respect for individuals' moral freedom. His conceptual apparatus has three pillars: the original position, the veil of ignorance, and public reason. The original position is the ontological posture from which individuals are posited to engage in the process of reasoning to agree on political structures. The seminal feature of the original position is the veil of ignorance. Rawls posits that just reasoning about social structures requires individuals to abstract themselves from their personal characteristics. The character of the analysis that individuals undertake from the original position to construct social structures (under the veil of ignorance) is public reason. The subsequent construction of the state is justified by individual freedom, but from a position that does not serve personal interest or individual attachments. Consequently, Rawls argues that individuals reasoning under such constraints would agree to political structures that protect personal liberty as well as political and social equality, since each individual would recognize that they cannot be assured a privileged position in society. The subsequent social organization thereby advances a view of liberty (both in its thought-experiment methodology and substantive argument for social structures) that conceives of individuals first and foremost as shared participants in a mutual project of governance. Rawls's profound innovation is that he advances such a mutualistic commitment without imposing an altruistic moral assumption. Rather, he shows that individuals reasoning soundly (which he argues requires reasoning from a position abstracted from personal circumstance) would freely advance egalitarian social structures to advocate for their own interest in political and personal liberty.

The most influential critic of Rawls's view, Robert Nozick, firmly rejects the idea that freely reasoning persons would construct an ideal legitimate political order that aspires to negate personal endowments.[3] He describes the Rawlsian approach as "patterned" rather than "historical" in its commitments, imposing a set of values upon the members of a society. Nozick argues that free individuals have the right to retain their private endowments in political organization, and to protect, rather than alienate themselves from, their pre-political commitments. The resulting freely entered (and thus legitimate) society that Nozick describes looks vastly different from Rawls's, because individuals have the right to advance their private

---

[2] The account given below is synthesized from Rawls's two most authoritative and comprehensive accounts of democracy, John Rawls, *A Theory of Justice* (Cambridge: Harvard University Press, 1999) and John Rawls, *Political Liberalism* (New York: Columbia University Press, 1996).

[3] This account is synthesized from Nozick's most seminal account of his theory, Robert Nozick, *Anarchy State and Utopia* (Malden, MA: Basic Books, 1974), p. 156.

interests – and minimize state intrusion. The libertarianism he describes yields a minimalist political order that contrasts with Rawls's redistributive focus on advancing the well-being of the least well-off. Yet Nozick's position still derives from a claim regarding the institutional choices that freely reasoning individuals would make. The focus on free reason as the basis of legitimacy demonstrates that both Rawlsian egalitarianism and Nozickian libertarianism operate squarely within the liberal tradition. Even as Rawls and Nozick disagree on the correct substance of the reasoning process, and what a just state would look like, they share a foundational starting commitment: that a legitimate state has power because its design derives from the ideal free reasoning of its constituents.

At the highest level, this dispute echoes through the two competing priorities of constitutional democracy – enhancing constituent freedom either via (1) democratic participation (recognizing individuals as members of the public undertaking a shared project of self-governance) or (2) rights-based state restraint (recognizing individuals as having private endowments beyond legitimate state reach). The debate between these two understandings of liberalism has yielded a scholarship as rich as it is fiercely riven.[4] It is widely accepted that the egalitarian–libertarian divide comprises a central debate over the terms of legitimate democratic social ordering, including the design of just institutions.[5]

THE EGALITARIAN–LIBERTARIAN DIVIDE IN THE DOCTRINE

Modern election case law, while superficially a raw partisan battle between progressives and conservatives, can be most insightfully synthesized through the egalitarian–libertarian debate. The egalitarian view identifies electoral process specifically and democratic self-rule generally as collective practice undertaken by mutually regarding equals. According to the libertarian view, electoral process is a conduit for private identities and interests, which serves as a venue for self-interested competition

---

[4] David Schmidtz, "History and Pattern," in Ellen Frankel Paul, Fred Dycus Miller; Jeffrey Paul (eds.), *Natural Rights Liberalism from Locke to Nozick* (Cambridge: Cambridge University Press, 2004), p. 148, observes that much of Rawls's subsequent intellectual agenda was a response to Nozick, as well as shaping the discipline.

[5] See, e.g., Samuel Freeman, "Illiberal Libertarians: Why Libertarianism is Not a Liberal View" (2001) 30 *Philosophy & Public Affairs* 105, 106–7. (classifying 'high liberalism' (eg, egalitarianism) and libertarianism as two categories of contemporary liberalism, and Rawls and Nozick as their exemplary champions; Freeman's attack on libertarianism as quasi-feudal in its normative commitments is, in effect a demonstration of the contestation over liberalism that the debate reflects); Gerald Gaus, 'Coercion, Ownership, and the Redistributive State: Justificatory Liberalism's Classical Tilt' (2010) 27 *Social Philosophy and Policy* 233, 234–6 (observing the derivation of egalitarianism and libertarianism from Kantian deontology, and the first dispute between the two schools); Peter J. Boettke and Rosolino A. Candela, 'Liberal Libertarians: Why Libertarianism is a Liberal View', in Jason Brennan, David Schmidtz, and Bas van der Vossen (eds.), *Routledge Handbook on Libertarianism* (New York: Routledge, 2017), pp. 92–107 (defending libertarianism as a liberal view against egalitarian critiques).

over scarce government resources. Applying these frames to the domain-by-domain account of the case law and associated academic criticism from Chapters 4–7 establishes this most decisively.

LIVE DOCTRINAL CONTESTATION

The campaign finance jurisprudence expresses the egalitarian–libertarian divide mostly plainly. As Chapter 5 established, progressives and conservatives are both concerned about how an external source (private wealth and the state, respectively) affects voter cognition. The source of this distortion is attributed either to public or private power. The egalitarian view is that since constituents engage as equals to guide mutual self-governance, mitigating the impact of private sources of inequality on how citizens reason about their public commitments poses little normative difficulty (so long as they retain the power to freely reason generally, as protected by viewpoint neutrality).[6] This view exemplifies the Rawlsian ideal that while liberty is the highest value, public reasoning should reflect the collective nature of governance and individuals' equal standing in political engagement. Measures that retain and express this liberty while advancing such equal standing – such as limiting the political influence of economic inequality – in political reasoning are legitimate.

The converse libertarian view assigns no such public character to political life or reasoning. According to this view, governance expresses private interests, and restricting the influence of private interests comprises state domination and distorts constituents' reasoning. In the libertarian view, the presence of private power in political discourse does not pose a normative problem, it merely expresses the substance of governance. Campaign finance regulation threatens to intrude upon this legitimate exercise of private power, and thereby strip individuals of their personal liberty.

The debate over parties calls into question whether actors' capacity to coordinate (and exploit that coordination) should be policed to ensure the equal procedural status of all actors. While this manifests across the doctrine,[7] the partisan

---

[6] This view may be most plainly evident in the very legislation that sought to put into effect extensive campaign finance regulation pre-*Buckley*: elections are "not a private affair." S. REP. NO. 93–689, at 5. The clearest expressions of this sentiment in the scholarship that describe democracy as a 'partnership' (Ronald Dworkin, *Sovereign Virtue: The Theory and Practice of Equality* (Cambridge: Havard University Press, 2002), and that legitimate self-rule will "democratize the influence that money can bring to bear upon the electoral process" (Stephen Breyer, *Active Liberty: Intrepreting a Democratic Constitution* (Oxford: Oxford University Press, 2008), p. 27) – a view paralleled in the case law somewhat more obliquely by the incorporation of the corruption interest into the First Amendment interest. *McCutcheon v. Federal Election Commission*, 572 US 185, 235 (2014) (Breyer, dissenting).

[7] For example, Powell's dissent in *Democratic Party v. Wisconsin ex rel. La Follette*, 450 US 107, 137 (1981) and Stevens dissent in *California Democratic Party v. Jones*, 530 US 567, 590 (2000) both hang on the premise that the balance of the interests of the state and constituents can legitimately dominate the organizational preferences of parties, an incrementally egalitarian assertion that public norms dominate private ones.

gerrymandering dispute epitomizes the egalitarian–libertarian struggle. The partisan gerrymandering question is constitutionally framed through justiciability, but as Chapter 6 demonstrates, the underlying judicial debate is whether party organization contributes to or threatens constituent self-rule.

The progressive view that party organization can dominate the franchise, and that constitutional principle limits its impact, is an egalitarian position.[8] The progressive view posits that the power political actors can attain by acting through parties (within and outside of the state) should be disciplined and subordinated to the equal position of constituents as participants in a shared public project. Conversely, the conservative invocation of justiciability is a shroud for the claim that any distortions of power distribution due to the organizational effects of partisanship lie beyond the constitutional remit. According to the libertarian view, it is legitimate to deploy private power, even the organizational power of disproportionately powerful cliques and wedge groups, including where that power is deployed through the intermediary of parties.

The dispute over race in elections queries whether (1) just collective self-rule should ameliorate the substantive inequities from America's racist past and aspire toward an egalitarian present or if (2) equal protection demands formal race blindness, *preventing* electoral process from correcting power distributions that flow from such a racist past. The egalitarian position aspires to govern from a standpoint of substantive constituent equity. In a society with a racist malapportionment of political power, this requires correcting vast racial inequities, even if doing so entails adjusting electoral process to shift the substantive allocation of power. Such a requirement vindicates buttressing minority representation by legislatures (e.g., Congress's promulgation of Section 5 of the Voting Rights Act preclearance requirement, and drawing districting lines that benefit minority power) and courts (e.g. by developing a jurisprudence of Section 2 of the Voting Rights Act and a general interpretation of the equal protection clause). The libertarian position, however, sees no role for the state or the courts in advancing substantive, rather than minimally formal, racial equality. For libertarians, historical echoes of racial inequity are aspects of pre-electoral identity, and should not be rectified by political (i.e. legislative) or judicial alterations to democratic process. For example, equal protection clause enforcement will strictly scrutinize racial categories even where it benefits minorities, and legislation, such as the preclearance requirement, will be treated with skepticism.

---

[8] This may seem initially surprising in that some recent apologists for parties – Nancy Rosenblum and Russell Muirhead in particular – argue for the oft-neglected benefits of partisanship. But as discussed in Chapter 6, this view typically takes a 'balanced' view of partisanship, as epitomized by the critique of low partisanship in Russell Muirhead, *Promise of Party in a Polarized Age* (Cambridge, MA: Harvard University Press, 2014), p. 249. The libertarian view is that the state – or at least the Court advancing the Constitution – is not appropriately positioned to identify when illicit low partisanship is a misuse of private organizational power.

The Decontestation of One-Person, One-Vote

Given the fundamental divergence between the egalitarian and libertarian perspectives, why has the one person, one vote rule remained a bastion of consensus? The doctrine seems eminently egalitarian because it advances equal voting power. Given the conservative–libertarian tolerance for other forms of inequity, particularly the close analog of partisan gerrymandering, why should a libertarian view accept an equalizing doctrine with an ostensibly thin constitutional basis? The effect of malapportionment might be characterized, from a libertarian perspective, as reflecting pre-electoral victories (such as those of rural voters[9] who subsequently enshrined them in legislation) – and thus as advancement of their private interests.

The decontestation of one person, one vote exposes subtle consensus of modern election law. In each of the still-contested domains of election law, the attribute in question could be plausibly framed as having private as well as public aspects. Wealth is private power, parties are private as well as public coalitions, and race is a private feature. Libertarians claim that the private aspect of these characteristics should be excluded from the legal consideration of electoral process.

By contrast, malapportionment has no foundation in a private attribute. It is the pure distortion of public constituent power on the basis of legislative action. Even in libertarian terms, malapportionment can only be understood as the arbitrary application of public power in a manner that contravenes individual liberty. This is because malapportionment arbitrarily differentiates between persons as citizens, such that there is no "private" attribute that malapportionment protects. It is therefore a distortion of even the minimal "umpiring" that libertarians concede as the legitimate exertion of state power. Its correction through the one person, one vote rule is best framed as minimal procedural egalitarianism, and the only way of excluding it from a prerequisite of just electoral design is to declare elections wholly beyond judicial cognizance – which was the precise issue in the political question doctrine.

Thus, one person, one vote was decontested because it rests on the statement that wholly public power cannot be used to distort constituent self-rule. It is therefore the foundational gateway premise to modern election law: that electoral process is a legitimate subject matter for judicial review. Its decontestation reflects only the shared principle that elections are a public matter, and subject to some degree of judicial oversight.

Elections at the Public–Private Boundary

It is telling that one person, one vote is the consensual touchstone as well as the gateway to modern election law. Cutting across the arenas of "live" doctrinal contestation over liberalism is a unifying question: should self-governance, and the

---

[9] Samuel Issacharoff, "Political Judgments" (2001) 68 *University of Chicago Law Review* 637, 655.

commitments of constituents when they undertake it, be conceived as a public endeavor – that is to say, other-regarding, collectivizing, and beholden to the public good – or as a private endeavor – an arena in which individuals protect their private self-interest? Each of the progressive–egalitarian positions in the doctrine seeks to advance a mutualist, collective-regarding interests in elections, diminishing inequities of wealth, race, and organizational capacity in favor of citizens' shared attributes and synthesizing their interests as cooperative participants in governance. The libertarians, conversely, wish to ensure that the state does not infringe upon individuals' capacity to consider (and leverage) such private features in the conflictual, zero-sum game of fighting for government resources.

Election law doctrine thereby reflects two well-established but fundamentally different visions of democracy, a framing that further illuminates the struggle between the progressive–egalitarian and conservative–libertarian approaches. The egalitarian approach is ultimately premised on governance forged in interdependent, mutual regard for other constituents. Rawls embeds this quality abstractly in his methodology, with procedural detachment from personal circumstances and advocating public reason. This has taken an applied, prescriptive form in theories of deliberative democracy, which claim that democracy should be mutually engaged and other regarding. Scholars have offered both normative accounts of why democracy should have this character[10] as well as mechanisms for implementing deliberative, other-regarding democratic practice.[11]

The libertarian approach is characterized by agonistic understandings of democracy. Methodologically, these theories correlate less closely with a Nozickean libertarian understanding of morality. Rather, they reflect what might be called realist accounts of democracy, describing it as a mechanism for ruthless bargaining and conflict resolution.[12] According to these accounts, a power-based understanding of democracy is descriptively accurate and helps preserve constituent liberty.[13] Since democracy is inevitably a process that allocates scarce, unique government resources and has coercive implications, failing to recognize that it is about individual self-interest in power outcomes obscures its real nature as well as its oppressive

---

[10] E.g., Amy Gutmann and Dennis F, Thompson, *Why Deliberative Democracy?* (Princeton: Princeton University Press, 2004); Russell Muirhead and Nancy L. Rosenblum, "The Political Theory of Parties and Partisanship: Catching Up" (2020) 23 *Annual Review of Political Science* 95.

[11] See, e.g., K. Sabeel Rahman and Hollie Russon Gilman, *Civic Power: Rebuilding American Democracy in an Era of Crisis* (Cambridge: Cambridge University Press, 2019); John Gastil and Peter Levine (eds.), *The Deliberative Democracy Handbook: Strategies for Effective Civic Engagement in the Twenty-First Century* (San Francisco: Jossey-Bass, 2005).

[12] This has a long tradition in American political thought. See, e.g., Joseph Schumpeter, *Capitalism and Democracy* (Oxford: Routledge, 2010); Anthony Downs, "An Economic Theory of Political Action in a Democracy" (1957) 65 *Journal of Political Economy* 135; Robert Dahl, *A Preface to Democratic Theory* (Chicago: University of Chicago Press, 1964).

[13] Adam Prezworski, "Minimalist Conception of Democracy: A Defense," in Ian Shapiro and Casiano Hacker-Cordon (eds.), *Democracy's Value* (Cambridge: Cambridge University Press, 1999); Ian Shapiro, *The State of Democratic Theory* (Princeton: Princeton University Press, 2009).

potential. These agonistic accounts have kinship with libertarian normative theory. Democracy reflects private reasoning and private interests and should be legitimated by the protection of private rights.

Debating these broad democratic theories and corresponding policy proposals lies beyond the remit of judicial decision-making on specific electoral practices. The Court resolves individual legal disputes, even if the pattern of such case resolution resonates with theories of democracy. The correlation is useful because it illuminates the underlying debate of which this pattern is a part. The pattern involves whether democratic politics should be conceived as a public or private matter. The spirit cutting through the progressive decisions on election law is that democracy should be axially conceived as public in nature. While some aspects necessarily retain private components – such as the right to speech that is not subject to content regulation – the structures of politics should emphasize that constituents are first and foremost members of a united polity. This spirit guides progressives' doctrinal outcomes. Free self-rule, and electoral practices that serve this, seeks to nurture and facilitate such collective reasoning among constituents.

Conservatives, conversely, emphasize that democracy is a domain that seeks to serve and safeguard the private aspects of individual identity. They are fundamentally hostile to efforts by legislatures or the bench to advance a public conceptualization of political engagement. Conservatives are therefore left with a sparsely minimalist conceptualization of politics. It is merely a domain for handling the private power allocation that results from state action. Free self-rule seeks to insulate the private nature of democracy from prospective state domination. The conservative view has long been critiqued for displaying a type of structural as well as conceptual myopia. This is best encapsulated by the progressive rallying cry that "the personal is political" – and that, transitively, the personal is also public. I do not revisit this debate here, but only note that it remains at the foundations of contemporary election law.

RETURNING TO THE COUNTERPOPULAR DILEMMA

This book began with a puzzle: how can the primacy of constituent autonomy be reconciled with judicial review that substantively curates electoral procedure? In Chapter 3, I argued that the best reconciliation was for the Court to contest norms of constituent autonomy. This approach permits substantive intervention without decisively imposing a conception of democracy and thereby intruding upon the very autonomy that vindicates democracy. That American election law doctrine can be framed as a struggle between egalitarian and libertarian conceptions confirms that normative contestation is not merely a theoretically plausible account. It is also descriptively accurate in a polity where the Supreme Court has had a uniquely transformative effect on democracy.

Furthermore, the election law doctrine itself demonstrates that normative struggle ameliorates the counterpopular dilemma. The Court's debate over the practical meaning of free self-rule by the constituency crystallizes the questions that constituents must ask about the terms of their own self-rule. How extensively should engagement with governance be a matter of mutual respect and collaborative engagement, as opposed to the competitive pursuit of private ends? To what extent should those who hold political power be able to leverage that power to accumulate future self-interested gains, rather than be constrained by the norms of collective mutualism?

On the bench, the outcomes of these debates have transformed American democracy. This points to another feature that ameliorates the counterpopular dilemma and differentiates this account of judicial review from deliberativism–interpretivism. The continuously unsettled nature of the debate and the lack of unique moral authority (as opposed to merely exemplifying contestation) means that the Court cannot claim the authority asserted by many other justifications for judicial review. Rawls's lionization of the Supreme Court as an "exemplar of public reason"[14] to justify its authority over governance exemplifies this position. Yet describing the struggle over election law as normative contestation does not idealize the Court's capacity in this way. This does not deny the insights of approaches that grant the Court moral authority, such as deliberativism or interpretivism. However, the debate over which of these approaches is the best way to make judicial decisions about election law is part of this very normative contestation.

This indicates a further feature of contestation: It explains the debate over the legitimate approach to judicial interpretation as well as the substantive resolution of constitutional questions and particular disputes. The normative contestation includes questions such as the appropriate remit of the Court in shaping the will of a free people (a question with Waldronian and originalist overtones, which has manifested most clearly in the conservative refusal to police partisan gerrymandering). This contestation also covers the extent of constitutional values such as freedom, which egalitarians have sought to interpret more holistically, for example in the campaign finance context by advocating a wider conceptualization of the anti-corruption rationale. The contestation therefore includes basic debates over methodology and the judicial role – which are the very types of debates that animate voters (perhaps in a less abstract fashion) in selecting judges or the representatives who will select judges.

THE OMINOUS ALTERNATIVE: *BUSH V. GORE* AND JUDICIAL REVIEW AS PURE PARTISANSHIP

The most notorious election law case in recent memory does not reflect contestation over constituent autonomy, but rather the most visible threat to the legitimacy of judicial review. *Bush v. Gore* functionally resolved the 2000 presidential

---

[14] Rawls, "Political Liberalism," 235. Similarly, Habermas identifies a mode of reasoning about rights that serves a parallel function. Jürgen Habermas, *Between Facts and Norms: Contributions to a Discourse Theory of Law and Democracy*, William Rehg (trans.), (Malden, MA: Polity Press, 1996), pp. 103–4, 128.

election, thereby usurping popular authority over selecting the president. As a decision, it is widely understood to be devoid of internal moral or constitutional logic and instead to be overdetermined by the justices' partisan allegiances. Along with the nation as a whole, the Supreme Court has become increasingly polarized in the past few decades, especially in election law. In *Bush v. Gore*, partisanship was not merely used to frame normative contestation; it was the sole determinant. Doubly damning is that the ruling did not produce a general rule, but rather resolved a particular election via a *sui generis* holding. Combining partisan overdetermination of the judicial resolution of election law disputes with decisions on particular elections is antithetical to normative contestation and fatal to the moral legitimacy of judicial review of election law. Because the Court resolved such an urgent decision *not* by any normatively defensible method of legal analysis but rather by tribal partisan affiliation, *Bush v. Gore* "sh[ook] the faith of many legal academics in the Supreme Court and in the system of judicial review."[15]

The granular facts make clear the unique urgency of the case. The Court was forced to determine the legality of the Florida Supreme Court's order to undertake a recount of votes cast in the state during the 2000 presidential election. The determinative question was whether requiring manual recounts of ballots in some counties contravened the allocation of responsibility to select electors to the state legislature under Article 2 of the federal Constitution. The bench split along so fiercely partisan lines that Laurence Tribe declared *Bush v. Gore* the orphan resolution of a momentary political crisis that "belong[ed] to *no* constitutional tradition,"[16] while Balkin excoriated the 5–4 majority opinion as a rank act of partisan bias.[17] The case was ostensibly decided as an equal protection issue.[18] The five-justice conservative majority ruled that the Florida Supreme Court was not permitted to order a recount because its failure to order a remedy that treated *all* voters in the state equally violated the equal protection clause.[19] Two of the liberal dissenters suggested that an equal protection violation might be present, but that an appropriate solution was to fairly recount *all* the votes,[20] whereas two rejected the propriety of constitutional intervention on federalism grounds.[21]

---

[15] Jack M. Balkin, "*Bush v. Gore* and the Boundary Between Law and Politics" (2001) 110 *Yale Law Journal* 1407, 1407.
[16] Laurence H. Tribe, "*Bush v. Gore* and Its Disguises: Freeing *Bush v. Gore* from Its Hall of Mirrors" (2001) 115 *Harvard Law Review* 170 at 269.
[17] See, e.g., Balkin, "*Bush v. Gore* and the Boundary Between Law and Politics." For a roundup, see Sanford Levinson, "*Bush v. Gore* and the French Revolution: A Tentative List of Some Early Lessons" (2002) 65 *Law & Contemporary Problems* 7, 10.
[18] For a more extended analysis of the equal protection problems, see Richard Briffault, "*Bush v. Gore* as an Equal Protection Case" (2001) 29 *Florida State Law Review* 325.
[19] *Bush v. Gore*, 531 US 98, 109 (2000).
[20] *Ibid.*, at 134–5 (Souter); at 146 (Breyer).
[21] *Ibid.*, at 123 (Stevens); at 136 (Ginsburg).

Regardless of the frame deployed – familiar constitutional tradition or contestation over democratic autonomy – trying to make sense of the majority decision in *Bush v. Gore* affirms its status as an orphan in legal analysis. This can be deduced by considering the practical ramification of the majority's logic. The conservative majority concluded that the Florida Supreme Court's decision to recount ballots violated equal protection simply because the order did not apply consistently across the state. The recounts as initially ordered presumably increased the accuracy of the vote tabulation in the districts where they were ordered. It is difficult to identify any intrinsic wrong as a matter of self-rule that such an accuracy-increasing recount would generate, so the unfairness must be assumed to come from the application of different electoral procedures (in a context of exigency) itself. The conservative view must devolve upon a principle that constituents must enjoy uniform procedure, at least with regard to the recounting of ballots (though it is hard to conceive of why such a requirement would be logically constrained to ballot counting). Such a broad norm of electoral fairness has dramatic ramifications regardless of whether the remedy was interdicting the Florida Supreme Court's order or requiring a universal consistent recount. This suggests a principle of equivalent procedural treatment of all voters that is far more drastic than the minimal requirement of equipopulous districting established in one person, one vote.[22]

Yet the Court's articulation of the one person, one vote principle is unequivocally a substantively thin principle. The contrast is clearest if one compares the extensive norm of fairness advanced by *Bush v. Gore* with the pure procedural justice (described and contrasted with imperfect procedural justice) discussed in Chapter 3. Extrapolating a norm from *Bush v. Gore*'s requirement of equal treatment suggests thoroughly substantive requirements of (imperfect) procedural justice. Fair electoral procedures must not merely provide fair background conditions; they must also aim to satisfy some known outcome criterion of fairness. It is not merely conditions that yield fair starting conditions that indicate the presence of fairness, but the outputs of that fairness. In *Bush v. Gore*, the desired output was the consistent application of ballot recounting procedures across counties. That output was violated even if the alternate procedure (the recount ordered by the Florida Supreme Court) created a more accurate ballot tally. Here, that known criterion of outcome fairness is a particular condition of homogeneity in electoral process. The norm-derived process advanced by the majority does not merely impose a background principle related to whether elections are to be *fair*, it instead seeks to achieve a particular outcome regarding what electoral framework will be used in the election. In practice, such a requirement of (im)perfect procedural justice would likely constrain the state to a much narrower range of political structures. By contrast, the minimalist requirement of the one person, one vote principle only requires satisfying one condition of districting.

[22] This quality of thinness is most clearly articulated in *Weiser v. White*, 412 US 783 (1973). See Chapter 4, Section 4.3.2.1.

Of course, the Court (or more precisely, the conservatives on the Court) has done nothing to suggest that there is such a general principle of equivalent procedural treatment necessary for free self-rule. As Lawrence Tribe correctly anticipated, the doctrinal principles ostensibly advanced in *Bush v. Gore* have not become a general touchstone in electoral fairness. Indeed, recent decisions such as *Brnovich* and Scalia's concurrence in *Crawford v. Marion County* indicate that conservatives are *less* likely than progressives to advance such procedural fairness. This reinforces the prevalent conclusion that *Bush v. Gore* is a *sui generis* decision – politically motivated and resistant to consistent integration into the law or constitutional–normative analysis. Since the majority opinion was advanced to reach a desired outcome, any attempt to reverse engineer a norm from it that would have later applications in electoral justice would mistake the character of the decision.

The particularly perverse feature of *Bush v. Gore* is that given its lack of legitimate legal basis, its highly partisan nature, and the absence of any lasting common law resonance, it was achieved by reverse engineering a norm of free self-rule that supported the desired conclusion, but without any meaningful philosophical content either as a legacy or in relation to past common law decision-making (the chain novel-like character of the philosophizing in election law that has led this book to treat Dworkin's account of common law as a touchstone). With no clear constitutional basis for a decision, the Court had to advance the logic of *Bush v. Gore* as a norm. Yet as a highly partisan decision motivated to reach a specific outcome, this norm had to entail a great deal of specific substantive content. In Rawlsian terms, *Bush v. Gore* required (im)perfect procedural justice – knowledge of what the right outcome would be and then designing the procedure to attain it. These qualities are linked by a specific logical chain. Reaching a specific substantive decision with no constitutional basis requires advancing a norm where the desired outcome is known, and the procedures are arranged to ensure that desired outcome is reached. The Court did not, of course, articulate the desired outcome of George W. Bush's victory. Rather, it stated the desired outcome of finding the Florida Supreme Court's recount process illegal. But to even reason its way to this façade, it had to advance a norm that targeted a rich substantive outcome (and trampled the principle of federalism).

Bush v. Gore incarnates judge-made election law gone wrong: judges deciding the outcomes of democratic process by applying their own partisan preferences and thereby displacing constituent will, rather than engaging in normative reflection on how constituent freedom can best be realized. As such, it exemplifies how polarized decision-making erodes the legitimacy of judicial intervention in the political process. It has characteristics of illegitimate partisan overdetermination of outcomes: (1) the Court imposes political realities (structures, or, in this case, electoral outcomes) without the characteristic (and redeeming) feature of election law jurisprudence, normative contestation over the nature of self-governance and (2) this imposition is decided by tribal partisanship on the bench, such that the judiciary in effect becomes an undemocratic organ of politics.

The relationship between the imposition of political results and the unvarnished partisanship of *Bush v. Gore* is not incidental, invoking the hazards and demands of the counterpopular dilemma. If judges do not engage in normative contestation over self-rule when they resolve election law cases, they necessarily impose an ideological position regarding "legitimate" or "right" democratic process through institutional fiat – a contravention of democratic self-determination as described in Chapter 1. To those who adhere so strongly to an ideological view that they believe it to be true as a moral fact, this imposition will appear to be legitimate. But to those who disagree with the democratic ideology that is so advanced, putting it forward as an incontrovertible moral fact is an illicit imposition by an unaccountable actor. Disagreement over such an imposition presented as moral fact will be fractured and intractable, with no shared ground for reasoned negotiation – of which a familiar form is tribal partisanship. The tribal partisanship that overdetermined *Bush v. Gore* and is generally prevalent on the bench aligns along conservative–progressive lines and by Republican–Democratic appointees, but in one sense this is just an example of what occurs if decision-making loses its quality of reasoned normative contestation. Imposing democratic procedures without justifying them in terms of popular autonomy not only contravenes democratic values, it also necessarily lends itself to pure judicial exertion of power. The absence of normative contestation that simply leads to the imposition of a democratic procedure will lend itself to partisan conflict because it depends on partiality, of which partisanship is a subtype.

ELECTION LAW ON A KNIFE EDGE: URGENT DISPUTES, VOTER SUPPRESSION, AND ABRUPT CASE DISPOSITIONS

One aspect of *Bush v. Gore*'s failure to manifest normative contestation seems attributable to circumstance. The Court was placed in a difficult position since it was obliged to opine on an exigent, highly granular question that could decide an election. Only the most scrupulously abstracted philosophical engagement would retain the character of contestation.[23]

The COVID-19 disruptions and the litigious chaos of the Trump administration have accelerated the Court's engagement with urgent election law questions that have the potential to tilt specific electoral outcomes. The result is multiply disruptive for reconciling judicial review of election law with free constituent self-rule. The short-time frame and urgency of the questions discourage sustained and reflective engagement on norms of democratic self-rule;[24] the procedural context in which the

---

[23] One might wonder if relying on the 'passive virtues', Alexander Bickel, "'The Passive Virtues'" (1961) 75 *Harvard Law Review* 40, to avoid such issues would be beneficial, though this encounters the horn of implicitly resolving cases in a way that does not lend itself to transparent, reasoned contestation – the same difficulty that faces a minimalist approach to election law. See Chapter 2, Section 2.3.2.

[24] For doctrinal background, see Richard L. Hasen, "Reining in the Purcell Principle" (2017) 43 *Florida State University Law Review* 427.

questions are often decided (the "shadow docket")[25] tends to encourage instrumentalized and conceptually minimalist justifications for outcomes; and the fact that decisions often have the potential to influence specific electoral outcomes or face down crude and immediate allocations of power highlights the partisan stakes at issue.

One might therefore expect the type of vapid reasoning and politicized fractures that decided *Bush v. Gore* to become more common. The reality is more complex and less damning of the bench. Election law jurisprudence has without a doubt become increasingly polarized. Yet, the clearest examples of this are in the mainline domains of election law, such as *Citizens United* and *McCutcheon* in the campaign finance domain, *Vieth* and *Rucho* with regard to partisanship, and *Shelby County* and *Brnovich* in race and elections. Although the moral validity of the conclusions reached by the conservative majority in these cases can be assailed, their lawmaking character can be readily distinguished from the absence of recognizable legal analysis in *Bush v. Gore*. Judicial reasoning in the established lineages can be framed as ongoing contestation regarding the legitimate terms of democratic self-rule, as Chapters 5–7 have established. As I detailed at the beginning of this chapter, the partisan cleavage reflects a broader contest over what aspect of liberal self-determination (ensuring shared baselines of political access versus protecting pre-political endowments) democratic process should prioritize. Unlike *Bush v. Gore*, these decisions did not comprise direct judicial intervention regarding a specific electoral outcome. Even if the conservative holdings – which have been roundly criticized in progressive circles as undermining democratic fairness[26] – are rejected, I have established in this book that this hostility to the conservative approach is in effect a rejection of applying right–libertarian philosophy to the design of democratic process.

Bush v. Gore exemplifies a more particular threat than mere partisanship. Judicial decisions made under time pressure that shape specifically identifiable electoral outcomes, and which lack normatively meaningful reasoning, directly threaten the practice of constituent self-determination. The recent crises have generated circumstances that lend themselves to such decision-making, in that they demand the rapid resolution of granular issues, occur through abbreviated modes of judicial review, and could readily be overdetermined by partisan affiliation.

An emerging area of election law has predominated these questions and does not fit neatly into an existing lineage of election law (most saliently characterized by *Brnovich*, as discussed in Chapter 6) – the new forms of voter suppression,[27] often

---

[25] William Baude, "The Supreme Court's Shadow Docket" (2015) 9 *New York University Journal of Law & Liberty* 1.

[26] For a salient example, see Lynn Adelman, "The Roberts Court's Assault on Democracy"(2019) 14 *Harvard Law & Policy Review* 131.

[27] For a description of these new modes of voter suppression, and how they reflect pre-Jim Crow patterns as well as novel features, see Bertrall L. Ross II and Douglas M. Spencer, "Passive Voter Suppression: Campaign Mobilization and the Effective Disfranchisement of the Poor" (2019) 114 *Northwestern University Law Review* 633.

purportedly undertaken to prevent voter fraud.[28] The case law reveals that while some problematic characteristics portended by *Bush v. Gore* have become increasingly common, the most menacing feature – partisan overdetermination of election disputes, which effectively enables the bench to hijack democratic governance – has not yet come to pass. Indeed, some novel cases (such as the independence of presidential electors) have proven to be unusually pacific points of consensus.[29] Yet an increasing reliance on the rapid, informal resolution of cases without an opportunity to reflect on democratic norms creates an unsettling trend that could disrupt the legitimation of judicial intervention in democratic process.

This pattern is exemplified by an early case that has become a controversial touchstone for the Court, *Purcell v. Gonzalez*.[30] A federal appellate court, operating with a thin lower court record and shortly before an election, had enjoined enforcement of a law requiring proof of citizenship to vote. In *Purcell*, a unanimous Supreme Court issued terse, unanimous *per curiam* opinion that vacated the appellate injunction on the grounds that last-minute changes to electoral procedure might generate "voter confusion and consequent incentive to remain away from the polls."[31] It also emphasized that the opinion took no position on the measure's legality following fuller litigation.

Purcell has become guiding precedent for exigent election law disputes. Unfortunately,[32] it has therefore become a cloak for the abbreviated resolution of issues that deserve full constitutional and normative elaboration. For example, in *Democratic National Committee v. Wisconsin State Legislature* a conservative majority invoked the *Purcell* principle by name or theme to deny vacating an appellate stay of a district court decision to extend a mail-in ballot deadline to allow more citizens to vote safely during the COVID-19 pandemic. Kagan's dissent for the progressives invoked *Purcell*, but to differentiate on the facts, arguing that extending a mail-in deadline was unlikely to cause the voter the type of confusion that the *Purcell* principle was meant to stem. The result was a battle not of normative principles, but of fact-based policy interpretations. This tendency to pursue accelerated resolution to avoid deep and consistent reasoning has manifested in other cases as well,[33] such as *Trump v.*

---

[28] See Lisa Marshall Manheim and Elizabeth G. Porter, "The Elephant in the Room: Intentional Voter Suppression" (2018) *Supreme Court Review* 213.

[29] See, e.g., *Chiafalo v. Washington*, 140 S.Ct. 2316 (2020) (establishing states' authority to penalize faithless electors). The case that most extensively reflects on the status of voter ID measures, *Crawford v. Marion County Election Board*, 553 US 181 (2008), reflects a 3–3–3 moderate–conservative–progressive split (with the moderates and conservatives forming the decisive bloc) rather than the more familiar 5–4 split, though this pattern is present in some instances (*Husted v. Randolph Institute*, 138 S. Ct. 1833 (2018)).

[30] *Purcell v. Gonzalez*, 549 US 1 (2006).

[31] Ibid., at 4–5.

[32] See Wilfred U. Codrington II, "*Purcell* in Pandemic" (2021) 96 *New York University Law Review* 941, 945 (collecting criticism).

[33] The brief *per curiam* (against a fully elaborated three-justice progressive dissent) of *Trump v. New York*, 592 US __ (2020) on the grounds that the speculativeness of the injury raised standing and ripeness difficulties, which reflects such a pattern with a partisan edge.

New York, and includes cases where the fracturing of the bench does not track with traditional partisan battle lines.[34]

Purcell lends itself to judicial intervention that is fact-intensive and policy-like, rather than philosophical reflection over self-rule. Such decisions also often have the potential to influence the outcome of particular elections. Yet the problem of deterioration of reasoning is more general: this quality of granular, fact-intensive reasoning has become characteristic of the resolution of novel election law problems even where the decisions themselves are fully fleshed out.

Two recent prominent cases related to voter suppression demonstrate these risks. *Crawford v. Marion County* queried if a voter ID law imposed so much of a burden on the right to vote that it violated the permissiveness of "reasonable, nondiscriminatory restrictions" articulated in *Burdick v. Takushi*.[35] Stevens's centrist plurality opinion, however, does little to develop a normative theory of voter access. It instead speculates, via what might be called folk social science, on the extent to which the law at issue might burden voters to uphold it. By contrast, Scalia's conservative concurrence (identifying the burden as a morally trivial and thus legitimate exercise of state power) and the progressive dissents (seeing the potential for the suppression of vulnerable voters in particular) go into far more detail on the conditions under which laws crafting vote access are morally legitimate. Moreover, these could develop into contrasting traditions that would contest what understanding of voting access best serves the ultimate aim of self-rule. Yet the controlling plurality opinion lacks such philosophical potential. *Crawford* reinforces the notion that partisan dispute can serve as a structuring mechanism for robust, normatively rich debate over democratic process.

The more familiar 5–4 conservative–progressive split of *Husted v. Randolph Institute* shows that fierce partisan disagreement does not necessarily lead to philosophical contestation. *Husted* queried whether an Ohio procedure for removing inactive voters violated the federal statutory prohibition on failure-to-vote penalties. The case involved the complex interplay between congressional and state authority to set the terms of elections, and should have been resolved by querying what approach to statutory interpretation and federalism would best advance popular self-rule. Instead, it debated granular factual speculation on what circumstances are most likely to be indicative of voters changing residences and sought to differentiate (or correlate) these conditions with the prohibition of the failure-to-vote penalty. *Husted* demonstrates the infiltration of the granular factual speculation that deprives judicial reasoning of its moral content.

The deeper and more persistent pathology of *Purcell*, beyond the brevity of the resolution, is that the bench has drifted away from normative contestation. Where the

---

[34] See, for example, *Republican Party of Pennsylvania v. Boockvar*, 592 US __ (2020) (motion to expedite the review of a state supreme court decision that altered a mail-in ballot deadline during the pandemic denied); *Moore v. Harper*, 595 US __ (2022) (an application for stay of review of a state supreme court decision finding a state legislative map unconstitutional was denied, with three conservative justices dissenting).

[35] *Crawford*, 553 US at 190.

Court makes granular policy-like decisions, whether in the context of summary resolutions that fail to allow full debate, or because policy-emulating analysis is accepted as appropriate, it ceases to reconcile judicial review to democratic self-rule. The Court becomes less a venue for debating norms of democratic self-determination and more an arbiter of specific policy determinations or even electoral outcomes. This problematic displacement, which is the defining defect of Bush v. Gore, can occur in manners that both manifest in (*Husted*) and deviate from (*Crawford*) the partisanship that has riven the Court. The increasing exigency of certain election law crises may make it tempting for the Court to take on the role of an enforcer of outcomes, rather than a locus of normative reflection. This would pose a grave threat to judicial legitimacy in the democratic order and could undermine faith in the primacy of democratic self-rule generally.

Bush v. Gore and *Purcell* each show how legitimate judicial oversight of democratic process can go awry. The pathology of Bush v. Gore is straightforward: where partisanship alone dictates electoral outcomes, judges exert direct authority over such outcomes. This directly contravenes the principle of constituent self-determination that legitimizes democracy. The pathology of *Purcell*-like decisions more subtly relates to the absence of robust engagement with norms of self-rule in judicial decision-making. Where judges make decisions through abbreviated processes, this curtails any opportunity for the philosophical struggle that redeems judicial oversight of democracy. If the shadow docket becomes the primary mechanism for resolving electoral disputes and the Supreme Court continues to significantly shape democratic structure, this erodes the possibility of reconciling judicial review and democratic self-determination.

PARTISAN STRUGGLE AS A LABORATORY OF LIBERALISM

Thankfully, the established lineages of election jurisprudence have avoided these traps. Contestation has remained generally characteristic of election law despite the fact that disagreements now typically occur along partisan lines. As the beginning of this chapter demonstrates, a sufficiently capacious and synthetic view of the partisan contestation reveals that election law can be best understood as a contribution to a long-running and foundational debate over what participants in a liberal democratic society can demand as a function of their participation – substantive treatment as procedural equals or the preservation of their original endowments.

That partisan conflict has become a context for such a foundational normative dispute should inspire revisiting the partisan cleavage on the bench. While there has been something of a renaissance in the social science scholarship regarding the possible benefits of partisanship in representative governance,[36] partisanship in

---

[36] See the discussion of Rosenblum and Muirhead in Chapter 6. See also Muirhead and Rosenblum, "The Political Theory of Parties and Partisanship."

judicial decision-making is still widely condemned as corroding the rule of law, just adjudication, and the moral authority of the courts.[37] Legal scholars have expressed particular pessimism regarding conservatives' commitment to democratic values. Nicholas Stephanopoulos advances a "legal realist thesis" that the current Court's "anti-*Carolene* [*Products*]" bent (i.e. *Citizens United*, *Shelby County*, and *Rucho*) is "consistent with the recommendations of conservative elites."[38] Richard Hasen has likewise indicated that the "Supreme Court's conservative majority has taken the Court's election jurisprudence on a pro-partisanship turn," which can be explained as "a self-interested reality of Republican-appointed Justices doing the bidding of the Republican party."[39] These accounts mourn the rise of conservative partisanship as multiply pathological – undermining principled lawmaking in favor of unadulterated partiality for the justices' patrons, and advancing an election law regime that benefits plutocrats, entrenched elites, and racists.

While a close analysis of the doctrine does not redeem the conservative bench to its critics or forgive the destructive effects of its particular holdings, it shows that the partisan cleavage is part of the narrative that reconciles judicial review of election law with constituent autonomy. The grand struggle between conservatives and progressives involves a confrontation between two understandings of liberal self-rule – protecting the shared baseline of public membership as opposed to protecting the private individual against state (i.e. collective) oppression. It is a version of contestation over norms of liberal freedom that can justify judicial intervention in democratic process.

Partisanship can thus be described as structuring the normative contestation that redeems election law with liberal autonomy of the people. Partisanship has created consistent conflicts regarding contestation over freedom, but both conservatives and progressives advance views of partisanship that are plausible within the liberal tradition. This does not mean that the granular resolution of the cases is equally valid. Rather, it means normative struggle structured along a partisan axis is not only compatible with reconciling judicial review of election law and constituent autonomy by characterizing judicial review as contestation over freedom, but also that partisan struggle may in fact contribute to this reconciliation.

TOWARD LAW AS EXPRESSIVE OF CONSTITUENT FREEDOM

This partisan debate over liberalism exposes the foundational dilemma for individuals in a democratic state. What does collective self-governance prize more highly: opportunities to direct the joint project of governance, or the personal powers and

---

[37] See Muirhead, "The Promise of Party," pp. 204, 239–41. Muirhead observes that, in a claim sympathetic to that of this section, that it is critical that any partisan dispute ought to occur within the shared values of the community.

[38] Nicholas Stephanopoulos, "The Anti-Carolene Court" (2019) *Supreme Court Review* 111, 177–80.

[39] Richard L. Hasen, "The Supreme Court's Pro-Partisanship Turn" (2020) 109 *Georgetown Law Journal* 50, 50.

privileges that remain beyond state power? When individuals join a polity, they relinquish their individual power to the sovereign authority.[40] Democracy – and this is the source of its unique legitimacy – compensates for that relinquishment by giving individuals the opportunity to shape the governance of the entire polity. The freedom of the state of nature that individuals relinquish in a democracy is *transformed* rather than surrendered. Participation in, and partial authority over, collective power takes the place of the total but isolated freedom of pre-political life. This account has clear contractarian overtones, but need not be understood as obedient to any particular understanding of contractarianism. Indeed, debates over the best understanding of contractarianism would comprise part of the deliberation over the nature of self-rule and what is required to preserve it in collective democratic self-governance.

The debate between the conservatives and progressives relates to the just terms and legitimate extent of this empowerment of collective self-rule. Democracy is only legitimate if individuals transfer their private power on appropriate terms, and if the subsequent gain of constituent democratic authority sufficiently offsets this transfer. The priority of conservative jurists is aggressively constraining the legitimate extent of this transfer; the priority of progressives is establishing that the compensatory authority is sufficient only if all constituents participate on substantively equal terms. Both factions recognize the primacy of self-rule,[41] even if they vociferously disagree over its appropriate realization in a society riven by complex inequities.

The primacy and continuity of self-rule, however, echo the tension that has inspired and animated this project – the power that the judiciary exercises over governance. This tension deepens the counterpopular dilemma. The defining property of democracy is that the practical power of personal self-rule is transformed, rather than sacrificed or suppressed, by entering into the political world. This explains why neutral (i.e. non-accountable) judicial authority is problematic. If judges are not accountable representatives but their decisions nonetheless exert power over constituent members of a democracy, judicial review suppresses the autonomy of members of the polity to some extent. Traditionally, this problem would have been resolved by adverting to the neutrality entailed in the rule of law that guides judicial decision-making. However, as discussed in Chapters 1 and 2, this amounts to an answer that judges' own moral impulses should be trusted (in effect, a claim of pure moral authority that is incompatible with the primacy of self-rule). Yet liberal constitutional democracies – the type of regimes that prize the freedom of persons both as individuals (through rights) and through their participation in the community (through popular autonomy) – inevitably afford a role for judicial review, and the loss of the judiciary's independence and integrity is a key marker of democratic backsliding.

---

[40] Indeed, this is the defining feature of contractarianism, a feature that can be traced back to Hobbes and Rousseau. See the discussion of Richard Tuck in Chapter 2.
[41] This vindicates, by Muirhead's terms, the judiciary's engagement, because the relevant norm itself is shared and becomes the grounds for contestation. Muirhead, "'The Promise of Party'," p. 241.

In this book I have investigated how this tension manifests in the domain where it is most explicit, and where its failure most jeopardizes constituents' freedom – authority over democratic process. I propose a solution that prizes the bedrock value of democracy, constituent autonomy, through continual judicial normative contestation over this very value of constituent autonomy. The close examination of the case law in Chapters 4–7 reveals that the Court has long debated how best to realize this autonomy. As the conservatives argue, is this autonomy best realized by protecting or clawing back as much individual pre-collectivized power as possible (even if this entrenches social inequalities and perpetuates pathologies)? Or, as the progressives argue, does democratic autonomy require as much post-collectivized equality as possible, given that the process of collectivization involves mutual self-rule, and subordinates each individual to the will of others (a subordination that can entrench pre-political inequities if not carefully managed)?

Answering the more general form of this question – how can judicial review be vindicated in a society founded on the principle of self-rule? –requires adverting to the same value, and evokes parallel debates. If the judiciary's authority is to be vindicated, it must be on terms that can be reconciled with, and are in the service of and answerable to, those who have committed their liberty to the polity – regardless of the area of law.[42] Democracy is uniquely legitimate because, by transmuting the power of self-rule into the opportunity to participate in collective self-governance, it preserves individual freedom in a direct and tangible way. When the judiciary shapes the terms of self-rule, it intervenes in this freedom in a way that constitutes a less direct and less tangible transformation of this personal power. To reconcile judicial review, and the essential benefits it confers for individual fairness and systemic integrity through rule-of-law neutrality, the judiciary must remain focused on preserving the constituent freedom that vindicates democracy.

Judicial review must universally be vindicated by looking to constituent freedom (often by explaining how judicial intervention serves or benefits the mutual and collective self-rule that democracy trades for pre-political liberty). Without linking the authority of judicial review back to constituent freedom, the unique and ineluctable moral force of freedom as autonomy cannot be satisfied. This points to a greater project – explaining *all* judicial intervention as serving the freedom of the constituent members of a polity.

This project is demanding, ambitious, and diverse. Yet it is far from unfamiliar. Many areas of law have already been subject to sympathetic analysis. The areas most obviously tractable to such analysis are those integral to self-governance. For example, Antonin Scalia explained how standing, as an aspect of the separation of powers,

---

[42] This suggests that Waldron's limitation of his analysis to 'strong' judicial review, Jeremy Waldron, "The Core of the Case against Judicial Review" (2006) 115 *Yale Law Journal* 1346, 1353, is unnecessary, and that freedom should be a universal touchstone for evaluating judicial legitimacy.

is an essential defense of democratic liberty.[43] Heather Gerken has more recently led a comprehensive movement to make sense of federalism as a comprehensive doctrine of the distribution of government authority[44] – which must be linked all the way down to individual autonomy and the terms of transfer to government authority to be complete.[45] Further afield, others have argued that diverse areas of law must be conceived on the basis of individual freedom. Ernest Weinrib, for example, has transformed the analysis of private law by arguing that it can be fundamentally understood in Kantian terms as an expression of personal moral autonomy[46] (an idea that resonates with Charles Fried's claims that contracts must be understood as promise).[47]

The most transformational ramification of this project is that all law – and particularly judge-made law – must be concretely linked to the transfer of freedom from the individual to the collective democratic state. Furthermore, the principles that explain this link must have shared universal premises. This broader project will inevitably engender new debates. In particular, the mid-level framing of liberalism as political equity rather than as preserving the pre-political may be more suitable to some areas of law, such as race and gender equal protection in education, employment, and health, and, more subtly, to areas such as antitrust and property law that elicit competition between unequal economic power and personal ownership rights. This framing will be less applicable to other areas of law (e.g. federalism and the separation of powers), which should be conceived as a problem of linking political authority to preserving individual freedom as a direct analytic problem.

An unequivocal and fixed point of moral certainty, however, is that only human autonomy, and its capacity to generate moral meaning, can be the vindicating touchstone of each of these areas of law. This relationship is especially important where an independent judiciary intervenes in the deployment of individual freedom of constituents of the democratic polity. This book investigates judicial oversight of democratic governance as a step toward addressing this problem. Its exploration of the universal demand for human freedom and moral meaning will hopefully inspire reformers, thinkers, and jurists in the scholarship and legal transformations that the future will inevitably demand.

---

[43] Antonin G. Scalia, "The Doctrine of Standing as an Essential Element of the Separation of Powers" (1983) 17 *Suffolk University Law Review* 881.
[44] Heather K. Gerken, "Federalism 3.0" (2017) 105 *California Law Review* 1695; Jessica Bulman-Pozen, "Federalism All the Way Up: State Standing and 'The New Process Federalism'" (2017) 105 *California Law Review* 1739.
[45] For a discussion of the complexities of linking federalism and freedom, see Seth F. Kreimer, "Federalism and Freedom" (2001) 574 *The Annals of the American Academy of Political and Social Science* 66.
[46] Ernest J. Weinrib, *The Idea of Private Law* (Oxford: Oxford University Press, 2012).
[47] Charles Fried, *Contract as Promise: A Theory of Contractual Obligation* (Oxford: Oxford University Press, 2015).

Selected Bibliography

This selected bibliography is a sample of sources on, or especially useful for the study of, election law, judicial review, and democracy. It is not exhaustive of the sources cited in this book. It only reflects a reference source for those wishing to see a consolidated set of sources directly relevant to this book's central themes. As such, if a source is cited in the text, but not included here, is not a judgment regarding quality or standing in the scholarship more broadly.

Achen, C. H. and L. M. Bartels, *Democracy for Realists: Why Elections Do Not Produce Responsive Government* (Princeton University Press, 2017)

Ackerman, B. A., *We the People, Volume 1: Foundations* (Harvard University Press, 1993)

Aleinikoff, T. A. and S. Issacharoff, "Race and Redistricting: Drawing Constitutional Lines after Shaw v. Reno" (1993) 92 *Michigan Law Review* 588

Ansolabehere, S., "Arizona Free Enterprise v Bennett and the Problem of Campaign Finance" (2012) 2011 *The Supreme Court Review* 39

Ansolabehere, S. and J. M. Snyder Jr., "The Incumbency Advantage in U.S. Elections: An Analysis of State and Federal Offices, 1942–2000" (2004) 1 *Election Law Journal* 315

Bagenstos, S. R., "Disparate Impact and the Role of Classification and Motivation in Equal Protection Law after Inclusive Communities" (2016) 101 *Cornell Law Review* 1115

Baker, G. E., *The Reapportionment Revolution: Representation, Political Power, and the Supreme Court* (Random House, 1966)

Balkin, J. M., "Bush v. Gore and the Boundary between Law and Politics" (2001) 110 *Yale Law Journal* 1407

Balkin, J. M., *Living Originalism* (Harvard University Press, 2014)

Barkow, R. E., "More Supreme than Court? The Fall of the Political Question Doctrine and the Rise of Judicial Supremacy" (2002) 102 *Columbia Law Review* 237

Bartels, L. M., *Unequal Democracy: The Political Economy of the New Gilded Age – Second Edition* 2nd ed. (Princeton University Press, 2018)

Baude, W. and S. E. Sachs, "The Law of Interpretation" (2017) 130 *Harvard Law Review* 1079

Bellamy, R., *Political Constitutionalism: A Republican Defence of the Constitutionality of Democracy* (Cambridge University Press, 2007)

Berlin, I., *"Two Concepts of Liberty" Liberty* (Oxford University Press, 2002)

Bickel, A., "The Passive Virtues" (1961) 75 *Harvard Law Review* 40

Bickel, A. M., *The Least Dangerous Branch* (Yale University Press, 1986)

Black, C. L., "Inequities in Districting for Congress: Baker v. Carr and Colegrove v. Green" (1962) 72 *Yale Law Journal* 13

Breyer, S., *Active Liberty: Interpreting a Democratic Constitution* (Oxford University Press, 2008)
Briffault, R., "Bush v. Gore as an Equal Protection Case" (2002) 29 *Florida State University Law Review* 325
Briffault, R., "Reforming Campaign Finance Reform: A Review of Voting with Dollars" (2003) 91 *California Law Review* 643
Briffault, R., "McConnell v. FEC and the Transformation of Campaign Finance Law" (2004) 3 *Election Law Journal* 147
Briffault, R., "Defining the Constitutional Question in Partisan Gerrymandering" (2005) 14 *Cornell Journal of Law and Public Policy* 397
Brown, G. D., "Putting Watergate Behind Us: Salinas, Sun-Diamond, and Two Views of the Anticorruption Model" (2000) 74 *Tulane Law Review* 68
Bulman-Pozen, J., "Federalism All the Way Up: State Standing and 'The New Process Federalism'" (2017) 105 *California Law Review* 1739
Cain, B. E., *The Reapportionment Puzzle* (University of California Press, 1984)
Cain, B. E., "Moralism and Realism in Campaign Finance Reform" (1995) 1995 *University of Chicago Legal Forum* 111
Carpenter, R. V., "Wesberry v. Sanders: A Case of Oversimplification" (1964) 9 *Villanova Law Review* 415
Charles, G.-U. E., "Constitutional Pluralism and Democratic Politics: Reflections on the Interpretive Approach of Baker v. Carr" (2002) 80 *North Carolina Law Review* 1103
Charles, G.-U. E. and L. Fuentes-Rohwer, "Reynolds Reconsidered" (2015) 67 *Alabama Law Review* 485
Charles, G.-U. E. and L. E. Fuentes-Rohwer, "The Voting Rights Act in Winter: The Death of a Superstatute" (2015) 100 *Iowa Law Review* 1389
Charles, G.-U. E. and L. Fuentes-Rohwer, "Race and Representation Revisited: The New Racial Gerrymandering Cases and Section 2 of the VRA" (2018) 59 *William and Mary Law Review* 1559
Chen, J. and J. Rodden, "Cutting Through the Thicket: Redistricting Simulations and the Detection of Partisan Gerrymanders" (2015) 14 *Election Law Journal: Rules, Politics, and Policy* 331–45
Chen, J. and N. O. Stephanopoulos, "The Race-Blind Future of Voting Rights" (2021) 130 *Yale Law Journal* 778
Cox, A. B. and T. J. Miles, "Judicial Ideology and the Transformation of Voting Rights Jurisprudence" (2008) 75 *The University of Chicago Law Review* 1493
Cox, G. W. and J. N. Katz, *Elbridge Gerry's Salamander: The Electoral Consequences of the Reapportionment Revolution* (Cambridge University Press, 2002)
Crum, T., "Deregulated Redistricting" (2022) 107 *Cornell Law Review* 359
Dahl, R. A., *A Preface to Democratic Theory, Expanded Edition* (University of Chicago Press, 2006)
Dworkin, R., *Law's Empire* (Harvard University Press, 1986)
Dworkin, R., *Freedom's Law: The Moral Reading of the American Constitution* (Harvard University Press, 1997)
Dworkin, R., *Sovereign Virtue: The Theory and Practice of Equality* (Harvard University Press, 2002)
Eisgruber, C. L., *Constitutional Self-Government* (Harvard University Press, 2001)
Eisler, J., "The Deep Patterns of Campaign Finance Law" (2016) 49 *Connecticut Law Review* 57

Eisler, J., "Partisan Gerrymandering and the Illusion of Unfairness" (2018) 67 *Catholic University Law Review* 229

Eisler, J., "The Unspoken Institutional Battle over Anticorruption: Citizens United, Honest Services, and the Legislative-Judicial Divide" (2018) 9 *First Amendment Law Review* 363

Eisler, J., "Partisan Gerrymandering and the Constitutionalization of Statistics" (2019) 68 *Emory Law Journal* 979

Elmendorf, C. and D. Spencer, "Administering Section 2 of the Voting Rights Act After Shelby County" (2015) 115 *Columbia Law Review* 2143

Ely, J. H., *Democracy and Distrust: A Theory of Judicial Review* (Harvard University Press, 1980)

Eskridge, W. N. Jr., "Pluralism and Distrust: How Courts Can Support Democracy by Lowering the Stakes of Politics" (2004) 114 *Yale Law Journal* 1279

Fallon, R. H., "The Meaning of Legal 'Meaning' and Its Implications for Theories of Legal Interpretation" (2015) 82 *The University of Chicago Law Review* 1235

Fishkin, J. and W. E. Forbath, "The Anti-Oligarchy Constitution" (2014) 94 *Boston University Law Review* 671

Foley, E. B., "Philosophy, the Constitution, and Campaign Finance" (1998) 10 *Stanford Law & Policy Review* 23

Foley, E. B., "Due Process, Fair Play, and Excessive Partisanship: A New Principle for Judicial Review of Election Laws" (2017) 84 *The University of Chicago Law Review* 655

Fraga, B. L., *The Turnout Gap: Race, Ethnicity, and Political Inequality in a Diversifying America* (Cambridge University Press, 2018)

Fuentes-Rohwer, L., "Doing Our Politics in Court: Gerrymandering, Fair Representation and an Exegesis into the Judicial Role" (2003) 78 *Notre Dame Law Review* 527

Fuentes-Rohwer, L., "The Future of Section 2 of the Voting Rights Act in the Hands of a Conservative Court" (2010) 5 *Duke Journal of Constitutional Law & Public Policy* 125

Gardner, J. A., "Madison's Hope: Virtue, Self-Interest, and the Design of Electoral Systems" (2000) 86 *Iowa Law Review* 87

Gardner, J. A., *What Are Campaigns For? The Role of Persuasion in Electoral Law and Politics* (Oxford University Press, 2009).

Gerken, H. K., "Understanding the Right to an Undiluted Vote" (2001) 114 *Harvard Law Review* 1663

Gerken, H. K., "The Costs and Causes of Minimalism in Voting Cases: Baker v. Carr and Its Progeny" (2002) 80 *North Carolina Law Review* 1411

Gerken, H. K., "Lost in the Political Thicket: The Court, Election Law, and the Doctrinal Interregnum" (2004) 153 *University of Pennsylvania Law Review* 503

Gerken, H. K., "Federalism 3.0" (2017) 105 *California Law Review* 1695

Gilens, M., *Affluence and Influence: Economic Inequality and Political Power in America* (Princeton University Press, 2012)

Gilens, M. *Economic Inequality and Politics Power in American* (Princeton University Press, 2012)

Grofman, B. and G. King, "The Future of Partisan Symmetry as a Judicial Test for Partisan Gerrymandering after LULAC v. Perry" (2007) 6 *Election Law Journal: Rules, Politics, and Policy* 2

Grove, T. L. "The Lost History of the Political Question Doctrine" (2015) 90 *New York University Law Review* 1908

Grumbach, J. M. and A. Sahn, "Race and Representation in Campaign Finance" (2020) 114 *American Political Science Review* 206

Habermas, J., *Between Facts and Norms: Contributions to a Discourse Theory of Law and Democracy* (Polity Press, 1996)

Hajnal, Z. L., *Dangerously Divided: How Race and Class Shape Winning and Losing in American Politics* (Cambridge University Press, 2020)

Hart, H. L. A., *The Concept of Law* (Oxford University Press, 2012)

Hasen, R. L., *The Supreme Court and Election Law: Judging Equality from Baker v. Carr to Bush v. Gore* (New York University Press, 2003)

Hasen, R. L., "Do the Parties or the People Own the Electoral Process?" (2000) 149 *University of Pennsylvania Law Review* 815

Hasen, R. L., "Buckley Is Dead, Long Live Buckley: The New Campaign Finance Incoherence of McConnell v. Federal Election Commission" (2004) 153 *University of Pennsylvania Law Review* 31

Hasen, R. L., "Reining in the Purcell Principle" (2017) 43 *Florida State University Law Review* 427

Hasen, R. L., "Race or Party, Race as Party, or Party All the Time: Three Uneasy Approaches to Conjoined Polarization in Redistricting and Voting Cases" (2018) 59 *William and Mary Law Review* 1837

Hasen, R. L. "The Supreme Court's Pro-Partisanship Turn" (2020) 109 *Georgetown Law Journal* 50

Hayden, G. M., "The False Promise of One Person, One Vote" (2003) 102 *Michigan Law Review* 213

Highton, B., "Voter Identification Laws and Turnout in the United States" (2017) 20 *Annual Review of Political Science* 149

Hirschl, R., *Towards Juristocracy: The Origins and Consequences of the New Constitutionalism* (Harvard University Press, 2009)

Issacharoff, S., "Judging Politics: The Elusive Quest for Judicial Review of Political Fairness" (1992) 71 *Texas Law Review* 1643

Issacharoff, S., "Private Parties with Public Purposes: Political Parties, Associational Freedoms, and Partisan Competition" (2001) 101 *Columbia Law Review* 274

Issacharoff, S., "Is Section 5 of the Voting Rights Act a Victim of Its Own Success?" (2004) 104 *Columbia Law Review* 1710

Issacharoff, S., "Beyond the Discrimination Model on Voting" (2013) 127 *Harvard Law Review* 95

Issacharoff, S., *Fragile Democracies: Contested Power in the Era of Constitutional Courts* (Cambridge University Press, 2015)

Issacharoff, S., "Outsourcing Politics: The Hostile Takeover of Our Hollowed-Out Political Parties" (2017) 54 *Houston Law Review* 845

Issacharoff, S. and P. S. Karlan, "Where to Draw the Line: Judicial Review of Political Gerrymanders" (2004) 153 *University of Pennsylvania Law Review* 541

Issacharoff, S. and P. S. Karlan, "The Hydraulics of Campaign Finance Reform" (1999) 77 *Texas Law Review* 1705

Issacharoff, S. and R. H. Pildes, "Politics as Markets: Partisan Lockups of the Democratic Process" (1998) 50 *Stanford Law Review* 643

Iyengar, S., Y. Lelkes, M. Levendusky, N. Malhotra, and S. J. Westwood, "The Origins and Consequences of Affective Polarization in the United States" (2019) 22 *Annual Review of Political Science* 129

Kang, M. S., "The Bright Side of Partisan Gerrymandering" (2005) 14 *Cornell Journal of Law and Public Policy* 443

Kang, M. S., "When Courts Won't Make Law: Partisan Gerrymandering and a Structural Approach to the Law of Democracy" (2007) 68 *Ohio State Law Journal* 1097

Kang, M. S., "Race and Democratic Contestation" (2008) 117 *Yale Law Journal* 734
Kang, M. S., "Sore Loser Laws and Democratic Contestation" (2010) 99 *Georgetown Law Journal* 1013
Kang, M. S., "The End of Campaign Finance Law" (2012) 98 *Virginia Law Review* 1
Kang, M. S., "Gerrymandering and the Constitutional Norm against Government Partisanship" (2017) 116 *Michigan Law Review* 351
Kang, M. S., "Hyperpartisan Gerrymandering" (2020) 61 *Boston College Law Review* 1379
Kang, M. S. and J. M. Shepherd, "The Long Shadow of Bush v. Gore: Judicial Partisanship in Election Cases" (2016) 68 *Stanford Law Review* 1411
Karlan, P. S. "Democracy and Disdain" (2012) 126 *Harvard Law Review* 1
Karlan, P. S. and D. J. Levinson, "Why Voting Is Different" (1996) 84 *California Law Review* 1201
Key, V. O. *Politics, Parties, and Pressure Groups* (Cromwell, 1958)
Keyssar, A. *The Right to Vote* (Basic Books, 2009)
Kim, Y. and J. Chen, "Gerrymandered by Definition: The Distortion of 'Traditional' Districting Criteria and a Proposal for Their Empirical Redefinition" (2021) 2021 *Wisconsin Law Review* 101
Klarman, M. J., "The Puzzling Resistance to Political Process Theory" (1991) 77 *Virginia Law Review* 747
Klarman, M. J., "Majoritarian Judicial Review: The Entrenchment Problem" (1996) 85 *Georgetown Law Journal* 491
Klarman, M. J., "The White Primary Rulings: A Case Study in the Consequences of Supreme Court Decisionmaking" (2001) 29 *Florida State University Law Review*
Klarman, M. J., *From Jim Crow to Civil Rights: The Supreme Court and the Struggle for Racial Equality* (Oxford University Press, 2004)
Kramer, L. D., *The People Themselves: Popular Constitutionalism and Judicial Review* (Oxford University Press, 2006)
Kuhner, T. K., *Capitalism v. Democracy: Money in Politics and the Free Market Constitution* (Stanford University Press, 2014)
Kuhner, T. K., *Tyranny of Greed: Trump, Corruption, and the Revolution to Come* (Stanford University Press, 2020)
Lafont, C., *Democracy without Shortcuts* (Oxford University Press, 2019)
Landau, D., H. J. Wiseman, and S. R. Wiseman, "Federalism for the Worst Case" (2020) 105 *Iowa Law Review* 1187
Lavine, H. G., C. D. Johnston, and M. R. Steenbergen, *The Ambivalent Partisan: How Critical Loyalty Promotes Democracy* (Oxford University Press, 2012)
Lessig, L., "What an Originalist Would Understand 'Corruption' to Mean" (2014) 102 *California Law Review* 1
Lessig, L., *Republic, Lost: How Money Corrupts Congress – and a Plan to Stop It* (Twelve, 2015)
Levinson, D, J., "Rights and Votes" (2012) 121 *Yale Law Journal* 1286
Levinson, D. and B. I. Sachs, "Political Entrenchment and Public Law" (2015) 125 *Yale Law Journal* 400
Levinson, S., "One Person, One Vote: A Mantra in Need of Meaning" (2002) 80 *North Carolina Law Review* 1269
Lowenstein, D. H. and J. Steinberg, "The Quest for Legislative Districting in the Public Interest: Elusive or Illusory" (1985) 33 *UCLA Law Review* 1
Lucas, J. D., "Legislative Apportionment and Representative Government: The Meaning of Baker v. Carr" (1963) 61 *Michigan Law Review* 711

Manheim, L. M. and E. G. Porter, "The Elephant in the Room: Intentional Voter Suppression" (2018) 2018 *Supreme Court Review* 213

Mansbridge, J., "Should Blacks Represent Blacks and Women Represent Women? A Contingent 'Yes'" (1999) 61 *The Journal of Politics* 628

McConnell, M. W., "The Redistricting Cases: Original Mistakes and Current Consequences Nineteenth Annual National Student Federalist Society" (2000) 24 *Harvard Journal of Law & Public Policy* 103

Muirhead, R., *The Promise of Party in a Polarized Age* (Harvard University Press, 2014)

Muirhead, R. and N. L. Rosenblum, "The Political Theory of Parties and Partisanship: Catching Up" (2020) 23 *Annual Review of Political Science* 95

Muller, D. T., "Perpetuating 'One Person, One Vote' Errors" (2016) 39 *Harvard Journal of Law and Public Policy* 371

Muller, D. T., "Legislative Delegations and the Elections Clause" (2017) 43 *Florida State University Law Review* 717

Norris, P., *Electoral Engineering: Voting Rules and Political Behavior* (Cambridge University Press, 2004)

Nozick, R., *Anarchy, State and Utopia* 1st ed. (Wiley-Blackwell, 2001)

Ortiz, D. R., "The Democratic Paradox of Campaign Finance Reform" (1998) 50 *Stanford Law Review* 893

Ortiz, D. R., "Duopoly versus Autonomy: How the Two-Party System Harms the Major Parties" (2000) 100 *Columbia Law Review* 753

Overton, S., "The Donor Class: Campaign Finance, Democracy, and Participation" (2004) 153 *University of Pennsylvania Law Review* 73

Overton, S., "Voter Identification" (2007) 105 *Michigan Law Review* 631

Parsons, G. M., "Gerrymandering & Justiciability: The Political Question Doctrine After Rucho v. Common Cause" (2020) 95 *Indiana Law Journal* 1295

Patel, A., "Purcell in Pandemic" (2021) 96 *New York University Law Review* 941

Perry, M. J., *The Constitution in the Courts: Law or Politics?* (Oxford University Press, 1994)

Persily, N. "Toward A Functional Defense of Political Autonomy" (2001) 76 *New York University Law Review* 750

Persily, N. "When Judges Carve Democracies: A Primer on Court-Drawn Redistricting Plans" (2006) 73 *George Washington University Law Review* 1131

Persily, N., "In Defense of Foxes Guarding Henhouses: The Case for Judicial Acquiescence to Incumbent-Protecting Gerrymanders" (2002) 116 *Harvard Law Review* 649

Persily, N. and B. E. Cain, "The Legal Status of Political Parties: A Reassessment of Competing Paradigms" (2000) 100 *Columbia Law Review* 775

Pettit, P., *Republicanism: A Theory of Freedom and Government* (Oxford University Press, 1997)

Pildes, R. H., "Principled Limitations on Racial and Partisan Redistricting" (1997) 106 *Yale Law Journal* 2505

Pildes, R. H., "Is Voting-Rights Law Now at War with Itself – Social Science and Voting Rights in the 2000s" (2002) 80 *North Carolina Law Review* 1517

Pildes, R. H., "The Constitutionalization of Democratic Politics" (2004) 118 *Harvard Law Review* 116

Pildes, R. H. and R. G. Niemi, "Expressive Harms, Bizarre Districts, and Voting Rights: Evaluating Election-District Appearances after Shaw v. Reno" (1993) 92 *Michigan Law Review* 483

Posner, R. A., *Law, Pragmatism, and Democracy* (Harvard University Press, 2005)

Primus, R. A., "Equal Protection and Disparate Impact: Round Three" (2003) 117 *Harvard Law Review* 494
Przeworski, A., "Minimalist Conception of Democracy: A Defense" in I. Shapiro and C. Hacker-Cordon (eds.), *Democracy's Value* (Cambridge University Press, 1999)
Rahman, K. S., *Democracy Against Domination* (Oxford University Press, 2017)
Raviv, A., "Unsafe Harbors: One Person, One Vote and Partisan Redistricting" (2005) 7 *University of Pennsylvania Journal of Constitutional Law* 1001
Rawls, J., *Political Liberalism* (Columbia University Press, 1996)
Rawls, J., *A Theory of Justice* (Harvard University Press, 1999)
Rosenblum, N. L., *On the Side of the Angels: An Appreciation of Parties and Partisanship* (Princeton University Press, 2010)
Ross, B. L., "Democracy and Renewed Distrust: Equal Protection and the Evolving Judicial Conception of Politics" (2013) 101 *California Law Review* 1565
Ross, Bertrall II. and D. M. Spencer, "Passive Voter Suppression: Campaign Mobilization and the Effective Disfranchisement of the Poor" (2019) 114 *Northwestern University Law Review* 73
Scalia, A., "Originalism: The Lesser Evil" (1989) 57 *University of Cincinnati Law Review* 849
Schattschneider, E. E., *American Government in Action Party Government (1942)* (Routledge, 2004)
Schlesinger, J. A., *Political Parties and the Winning of Office* (University of Michigan Press, 1994)
Schuck, P. H., "The Thickest Thicket: Partisan Gerrymandering and Judicial Regulation of Politics" (1987) 87 *Columbia Law Review* 1325
Schumpeter, J. A., *Capitalism, Socialism and Democracy* (Routledge, 2010)
Schweigert, B. J., "'Now for a Clean Sweep!': Smiley v. Holm, Partisan Gerrymandering, and At-Large Congressional Elections" (2008) 107 *Michigan Law Review* 133
Sellers, J. S., "Election Law and White Identity Politics" (2019) 87 *Fordham Law Review* 63
Selmi, M., "Proving Intentional Discrimination: The Reality of Supreme Court Rhetoric" (1997) 86 *Georgetown Law Journal* 279
Shapiro, I., *The State of Democratic Theory* (Princeton University Press, 2009)
Shaw, K., "'A Mystifying and Distorting Factor': The Electoral College and American Democracy" (2021) 120 *Michigan Law Review* 1285
Siegel, R., "Why Equal Protection No Longer Protects: The Evolving Forms of Status-Enforcing State Action" (1997) 49 *Stanford Law Review* 1111
Sitaraman, G., *The Crisis of the Middle-Class Constitution: Why Economic Inequality Threatens Our Republic* (Alfred A. Knopf, 2017)
Smith, B. A., "Faulty Assumptions and Undemocratic Consequences of Campaign Finance Reform" (1996) 105 *Yale Law Journal* 1049
Smith, J. D., *On Democracy's Doorstep: The Inside Story of How the Supreme Court Brought "One Person, One Vote" to the United States* (Hill and Wang, 2014)
Solum, L. B. "Originalism Versus Living Constitutionalism: The Conceptual Structure of the Great Debate" (2019) 113 *Northwestern University Law Review* 1243
Stephanopoulos, N., "The Anti-Carolene Court" (2019) *Supreme Court Review* 111
Stephanopoulos, N. and E. McGhee, "Partisan Gerrymandering and the Efficiency Gap" (2015) 82 *University of Chicago Law Review* 831
Stephanopoulos, N. O., "Spatial Diversity" (2012) 125 *Harvard Law Review* 1903
Stephanopoulos, N. O., "Elections and Alignment" (2014) 114 *Columbia Law Review* 283
Stephanopoulos, N. O., "Aligning Campaign Finance Law" (2015) 101 *Virginia Law Review* 1425
Stephanopoulos, N. O., "Disparate Impact, Unified Law" (2019) 128 *Yale Law Journal* 1478

Strauss, D. A., *The Living Constitution* (Oxford University Press, 2010)
Strauss, D. A., "Corruption, Equality, and Campaign Finance Reform" (1994) 94 *Columbia Law Review* 1370
Sullivan, K. M., "Two Concepts of Freedom of Speech" (2010) 124 *Harvard Law Review* 143
Sunstein, C. R., "Political Equality & Unintended Consequence" (1994) 94 *Columbia Law Review* 1390
Sunstein, C. R., *Democracy and the Problem of Free Speech* (Simon and Schuster, 1995)
Tang, A., "Reverse Political Process Theory" (2017) 70 *Vanderbilt Law Review* 1427
Teachout, Z., *Corruption in America: From Benjamin Franklin's Snuff Box to Citizens United* (Harvard University Press, 2014)
Tokaji, D. P., "Applying Section 2 to the New Vote Denial" (2015) 50 *Harvard Civil Rights-Civil Liberties Law Review* 439
Tokaji, D. P., "Voting Is Association" (2017) 43 *Florida State University Law Review* 763
Tolson, F., "Reinventing Sovereignty?: Federalism as a Constraint on the Voting Rights Act" (2012) 65 *Vanderbilt Law Review* 1195
Tolson, F., "The Elections Clause and the Underenforcement of Federal Law" (2019) *Yale Law Journal Forum* 171
Tolson, F., "Election Law 'Federalism' and the Limits of the Antidiscrimination Framework" (2018) 59 *William & Mary Law Review* 2211
Tribe, L. H., "The Puzzling Persistence of Process-Based Constitutional Theories" (1990) 89 *Yale Law Journal* 1063
Tribe, L. H., "Bush v. Gore and Its Disguises: Freeing Bush v. Gore from Its Hall of Mirrors" (2001) 115 *Harvard Law Review* 170
Tuck, R., *The Sleeping Sovereign: The Invention of Modern Democracy* (Cambridge University Press, 2016)
Tushnet, M., "Darkness on the Edge of Town: The Contributions of John Hart Ely to Constitutional Theory" (1980) 89 *Yale Law Journal* 1037
Tushnet, M. V., "Law and Prudence in the Law of Justiciability: The Transformation and Disappearance of the Political Question Doctrine" (2002) 80 *North Carolina Law Review* 1203
Waldron, J., *Law and Disagreement* (Oxford University Press, 1999)
Waldron, J., "The Core of the Case against Judicial Review" (2006) 115 *Yale Law Journal* 1346
Waldron, J., "The Rule of Law and the Role of Courts" (2021) 10 *Global Constitutionalism* 91
Weinstein-Tull, J., "Election Law Federalism" (2015) 114 *Michigan Law Review* 747
Whittington, K. E., "Originalism: A Critical Introduction" (2013) 82 *Fordham Law Review* 375
Wright, J. S., "Politics and the Constitution: Is Money Speech?" (1975) 85 *Yale Law Journal* 1001
Zhang, E. R. and B. E. Cain, "Blurred Lines: Conjoined Polarization and Voting Rights" (2016) 77 *Ohio State Law Journal* 868

Index

Achen, Christopher, 160, 161, 189
Ackerman, Bruce, 65, 66, 93
activist judicial review, 74
agonist democracy, 298, 299
Alabama v. Holder, 12
Aldrich, John H., 204
Alito, Samuel (Justice), 83, 168, 169, 268, 269
Allen, Anita, 52
Amar, Akhil, 54
anti-fusion laws, 78, 79
anti-lockup theory, 77, 82
   Baker v. Carr, 132
   in campaign finance case law, 80, 81
   decontestation and, 132
   election law and, 91, 94
   judicial review and, 91, 94
   in partisan gerrymandering cases, 81, 82
Arizona State Legislature v. Arizona Independent Redistricting Commission, 66, 67, 236, 237
attitudinal model, of partisanship, 84, 87
Austin v. Michigan Chamber of Commerce, 12, 105, 106, 165, 166
autonomy (philosophical concept). *See also* constituent autonomy
   Darwall on, 177
   as generally expressed in election law, 292, 294
   Kant on, 177, 178
Avery v. Midland County, 149

Bagenstos, Samuel, 284
Baker, Gordon, 118, 119
Baker v. Carr, 9, 10, 18, 32, 37, 109, 117, 121, 141
   decontestation under, 128, 131, 135, 141
      anti-lockup theory and, 132
      decisive living constitutionalism and, 132
      political question doctrine and, 139, 141
   malapportionment and, 125, 128, 129
   originalism and, 133
   political question doctrine and, 135, 141

   scholarly debate over, 135, 137
   separation of powers principle, 140
   popular will and, 122, 125
   rule-of-law neutrality and, 133
Balkin, Jack, 63–5, 67
ballot access, 222, 223
Barkow, Rachel, 92, 136
Barrett, Amy Coney (Justice), 83
Bartels, Lawrence, 160, 161, 189
BCRA. *See* Bipartisan Campaign Reform Act
Bellamy, Richard, 4, 8
   critique of judicial review, 38, 39
Berlin, Isaiah, 7, 39, 40
Bickel, Alexander, 7, 37
   countermajoritarian difficulty, 37, 40, 47, 48, 70
   on passive virtues, 96
Biden, Joe, 206
Bipartisan Campaign Reform Act (BCRA), 163, 164, 168
   Section 203, 169
Black, Hugo (Justice), 126, 138, 139, 274
Blackmun, Harry (Justice), 83
Borda counting, as electoral process, 23, 24
Brennan, William (Justice), 83, 130, 131
Breyer, Stephen (Justice), 83
   "active liberty," definition of, 115
Brnovich v. Democratic National Committee, 268, 269
Brown, Rebecca, 47, 48, 70
Brown v. Board of Education, 32, 44
Buckley v. Valeo, 18, 34, 60, 159, 161, 173
   flawed legal architecture of, 162–4
Burdick v. Takushi, 307
Bush, George W., 303
Bush v. Gore, 3, 67, 300, 306–8
   partisan overdetermination and, 301, 303
   partisanship in, 89

321

California v. Jones, 200, 226, 227
campaign finance, jurisprudence and case law for. *See also* corruption, *specific cases*
　Bipartisan Campaign Reform Act, 163, 164, 168
　　Section 203, 169
　conservative approach to, 168, 173, 176, 191, 193, 194
　under First Amendment, 161, 171, 172, 187, 188
　heteronomous electorate, 176, 188
　　progressive position in, 178, 185
　　state tyranny and, 185, 188
　Issacharoff and, 159
　Lochnerism and, 190
　moral autonomy and, 158, 161
　neoliberalism and, 189, 191
　progressive approach to, 173, 176, 178, 185, 189, 191, 193, 194
　soft money funding, 165, 166
　wealth inequality and, 182, 184, 189, 191
Charles, Guy-Uriel, 260
Chen, Jowei, 237, 238
Citizens United v. Federal Election Commission, 12, 94, 95, 105, 106, 158, 169, 170, 173, 174
　corruption definition in, 179, 180
City of Mobile v. Bolden, 254, 255, 262, 264
City of Rome, 275, 276, 280, 281
Colegrove v. Green, 120, 122, 125, 128–30, 135
　Equal Protection Clause and, 129, 130
　political question doctrine and, 137, 139
constituent autonomy, 2, 3, 5. *See also* contestation over freedom
　Baker v. Carr, 9, 10, 18, 32, 37, 109, 117
　counterpopular dilemma and, 96
　democracy and, 4, 5
　deprioritization of citizen autonomy, 48
　democratic integrity and, 8, 10
　election law and, 309, 312
　Ely on, 48, 49
　judicial review and, 51, 53
　philosophical struggle over, 96
　rule-of-law and, 5, 6
Constitution, U.S. *See also* contractarianism; living constitutionalism; originalism
　as contract, 51, 53, 62
　Elections Clause, 236, 237
　as expression of autonomy, 56, 57
　Fifteenth Amendment
　　Voting Rights Act, Section 2, 262, 264
　First Amendment, 161, 171, 172, 187, 188
　Fourteenth Amendment
　　Equal Protection Clause in, 113
　　racial equity under, 244, 245, 249, 259
　as resolution to counterpopular dilemma, 72

contestable concepts, 99. *See also* decontestation
contestation over freedom, citizen autonomy and, 95, 101. *See also* decontestation
　campaign finance and, 102
　debates over, 197, 199
　countermajoritarianism and, 104
　deliberative approach and, 104
　interpretivism and, 104
　living constitutionalism and, 101, 102
　non-domination and, 112
　one-person one-vote doctrine and, 102, 103
　originalism and, 102
　partisan gerrymandering and, 102, 103, 108, 109
　racial justice in elections, 102
　right to equality and, 111, 116
　in rule-of-law regimes, 115
　stare decisis principle and, 105, 106
　as transcendental, 98
contractarianism, 8, 9, 51–3
　deliberative democracy and, 13
　hypothetical accounts of, 54, 55
　living constitutionalism and, 62
contractualism, Rawls and, 13
corruption. *See also* campaign finance
　in *Buckley v. Valeo*, 162, 164
　in *Citizens United v. Federal Election Commission*, 179, 180
　dependence; conception of, 183
　First Amendment and, 188
　Lessing on, 179, 180
　Teachout on, 188
countermajoritarian difficulty, 37, 40, 47, 48, 70
counterpopular dilemma, 3, 5, 8, 50
　anti-lockup theory and, 79
　Baker v. Carr, 139
　campaign finance and, 161, 196, 197
　constituent autonomy and, 37, 40, 96
　contestation over freedom and, 104, 106, 113
　decisive living constitutionalism and, 69
　definition of, 2
　durability of, 47, 50
　electoral processes, judicial review of, 50
　freedom and, 10, 13
　instrumentalist institutionalism and, 74
　judicial review and, 7, 8, 79, 92
　　constituent autonomy and, 32, 43
　　of election law scholarship, 40, 43
　　skepticism of, 37, 40
　moral onus of, 43, 47
　moral power of democracy and, 7, 8
　one-person one-vote doctrine and, 119, 120, 146, 151, 154, 156
　　federalist flexibility, 148, 150
　　local districting, 148, 150

minimization of, 150, 151
safe harbor principle, 149, 150
originalism and, 55
partisanship and, 86
political parties and, 213, 215, 230, 242, 243
political question doctrine and, 139
process-based representation reinforcement argument and, 76
U.S. Constitution as resolution to, 72
Cox, Gary, 203, 204
Crawford v. Marion County, 307
Cross, Frank, 85

Dahl, Robert, 11
Darwall, Steven, 177, 177
Davis v. Bandemer, 12, 105, 106, 213, 214, 233, 236
Davis v. Hildebrant, 122, 123
"dead hand" problem, 55
decisive living constitutionalism, 63, 64, 68, 73
 Baker v. Carr, 132
 counterpopular dilemma and, 69
 decontestation and, 132
 Dworkin on, 68, 73
decontestation, 103
 Baker v. Carr, 128, 141
  anti-lockup theory and, 132
  decisive living constitutionalism and, 132
  as exemplar of, 131, 135
  as expression of consensus, 133, 134
  political question doctrine and, 139, 141
 election law and, 297
 one-person one-vote doctrine and, 119, 120, 150, 151
deliberative democracy, 8, 9, 12, 104, 300
 contractarianism and, 13
 Dworkin on, 12, 13
 Rawls on, 12, 13
democracy. *See also* deliberative democracy; representative democracy; *specific topics*
 agonist, 298, 299
 centrality of judiciary in, 6, 7
 constituent autonomy and, 4, 5
  deprioritization of, by some progressive scholars, 47, 48
 counterpopular dilemma and, 7, 8
 as cultural practice, 24
 elections as central element of, 31
 individual political freedoms and, 5, 6
 legal theories on, 4
 moral legitimacy of, 1, 2
 moral power of, 7, 8
 as right of rights, 38, 39
 self-rule in, 5, 48
 as social practice, 24

Democracy and Distrust (Ely), 1, 74
democratic politics, constitutionalization of, 6
deontology
 of campaign finance, 158, 161
 for contestation over freedom, 97, 99
dependence corruption, 183
discrimination. *See also* racial equity
 expressive harm and, 256
 in Voting Rights Act, 264, 268
districting. *See also Baker v. Carr*; equipopulous districting; gerrymandering; partisan gerrymandering
 local, 148, 150
 partisan, 15
  vote dilution, 20, 127, 231
 racial equity and, 252, 256
 racialized, 74, 76
Downs, Anthony, 30
Due Process Clause, in Second Amendment, 107, 108
Duverger's law, 209, 210
Dworkin, Ronald
 on decisive living constitutionalism, 68, 73
 on elections, 47, 48
 Freedom's Law, 68, 69, 92
 interpretivism and, 12, 13
  legal interpretation theory and, 68
 on judicial review, 70, 71
 Law's Empire, 68, 134
 on partnership democracy, 16
 on political liberty, 14, 15

Easterbrook, Frank, 53
egalitarian progressives, 95
 campaign finance and, 18, 175
egalitarianism, 2, 3
 campaign finance jurisprudence, 18
 election law and, 294, 295
 liberal self-governance and, 3
 liberalism and, 13
 libertarianism and, 3, 11
  in electoral procedures, 14, 17
  by legal domain, 17
Eisele, Thomas, 68, 69
Eisgruber, Christopher, 10, 11
 on decisive living constitutionalism, 68, 73
 on elections, 47, 48
 on judicial review, 70, 71
 on moral content of constitutionalism, 63
 on originalism and, 58
Elections Clause, 236, 237
 Voting Rights Act and, 270, 271
Electoral College, 21, 22, 111

electoral processes. *See also* elections
  Borda counting, 23, 24
  egalitarianism and, 14, 17
  libertarianism and, 14, 17
  ranked-choice voting, 23, 24
  role of judiciary in, 6
  victory bonus and, 15
Ely, John Hart, 1, 35, 40, 42, 74
  on constituent autonomy, 48, 49
  minoritarianism and, 77
  non-interpretivist approach and, 74–5
  process-based representation reinforcement argument, 74, 77
    counterpopular dilemma and, 76
    racial gerrymandering and, 76
entrenchment, 41, 79, 80, 82, 92, 131
  anti-entrenchment mandates, 66, 112
  justified, 235
  representative, 243
  rural, 45
Epstein, Leon, 204, 210
Equal Protection Clause. *See* Fourteenth Amendment; racial equity; *Reynolds v. Sims*
equipopulous districting, 119–21, 124, 125
  equal liberty and, 152, 154
  one-person one-vote doctrine and, 156, 157
    development of standard for, 141, 144
    doctrinal construction of, 141, 146
Eskridge, William, 76
Estlund, David, 154

Fallon, Richard, 21, 22
FEC v. Wisconsin Right to Life, 169
Federal Election Campaign Finance Act (FECA) (1974), 162
Federalist Papers (Madison), 202, 203
Fifteenth Amendment, U.S. Constitution
  racial equity under, 19, 42, 43, 87, 245, 249, 259, 262, 264
  Voting Rights Act, Section 2, 262, 264
First Amendment, U.S. Constitution
  campaign finance under, 161, 171, 172, 187, 188
  corruption and, 188
  protections under, 171
First National Bank v. Bellotti, 165
Fishkin, Joseph, 180
Forbath, William, 180
Fourteenth Amendment, U.S. Constitution. *See also* partisan gerrymandering; racial equity; *Reynolds v. Sims*; *White Primary* cases
  Equal Protection Clause in, 113
  racial equity under, 244, 245, 249, 259
Frankfurter, Felix (Justice), 125, 127, 128, 137, 138

Freeden, Michael, 103
Freedom's Law (Dworkin), 68, 69, 92
Fried, Barbara H., 4, 5
Fried, Charles, 312
Fuentes-Rohwer, Luis, 148, 260
Fuller, Lon, 5, 6

Gaffney v. Cummings, 73, 232, 233
Gallie, W. B., 99, 103
Gardner, Jim, 175, 202, 203
Gellner, Ernest, 24
Gerken, Heather, 34, 92, 311, 312
  anti-lockup theory and, 77, 82
  on election law scholarship, 41, 43
  on one-person one-vote doctrine, 147
  on pure procedural justice, 156
  structuralism and, 112
  on vote dilution, 256, 257
gerrymandering. *See also* partisan gerrymandering
  bipartisan, 73
  racial, 74
    process-based representation reinforcement argument and, 76
  Stephanopoulos on, 231, 237
Gilens, Martin, 160, 161, 189
Giles v. Harris, 9, 10, 250, 251
Gill v. Whitford, 108, 109
Ginsberg, Tom, 5, 6
Ginsburg, Ruth Bader (Justice), 83
Gomillion v. Lightfoot, 9, 10, 19, 74, 96, 129, 252, 253, 256
Gorsuch, Neil (Justice), 83
Gray v. Sanders, 121, 141, 142
Grove, Tara Leigh, 128
Grovey v. Townsend, 216, 217
Guaranty Clause, 129, 130

Habermas, Jürgen, 68, 175
Harlan, John Marshall (Justice), 117
Hart, H. L. A., 5, 6, 105
Hasen, Richard, 112, 114, 115, 309
  on equal protection for black voters, 250, 251
  on one-person one-vote doctrine, 147
Hayek, F. A., 100
Hine, Darlene Clark, 217, 218
Hirschl, Ran, 9
Hobbes, Thomas, 13, 176
Huq, Aziz, 5, 6
Husted v. Randolph Institute, 307
hyperpolarization, 205, 207

instrumentalist institutionalism, 73, 82
  anti-lockup theory, 77, 82
  in campaign finance case law, 80, 81

counterpopular dilemma, 79
  in partisan gerrymandering cases, 81, 82
  bipartisan gerrymandering and, 73
  process-based representation reinforcement argument, 74, 77
    counterpopular dilemma and, 76
    racial gerrymandering and, 76
interpretivism, 8, 9, 12, 51
  contestation over freedom and, 104
  Dworkin and, 12, 13
    legal interpretation theory and, 68
  election law and, 300
  living constitutionalism and, 62, 73
Issacharoff, Samuel, 5, 8, 33, 34, 77. *See also* anti-lockup theory
  anti-lockup theory and, 77, 82
  campaign finance and, 159
  on election law scholarship, 41, 42
  on political parties, 211, 213
  on racial equity, 248

Jackson, Kenji Brown (Justice), 83
Jim Crow laws, 19, 272, 276
judges
  accountability of, 49, 50
    as actors in political order, 11
  active liberty and, 115
  contestation over freedom and, 104, 106
  grant of authority for, 53, 57, 62
  moral order through, 68, 73
  in originalist arguments, 53, 57, 62
judicial authority
  constitutional limits of, 110, 111
  living constitutionalism and, 64, 67
judicial minimalism, 100, 101
judicial pragmatism, 63, 67
judicial review. *See also* counterpopular dilemma; election law; instrumentalist institutionalism
  activist, 74
  Bellamy critique of, 38, 39
  conceptual approach to, 90
  constituent autonomy and, 51, 53
  of constitution, 51, 62
  constitution as contract and, 51, 53
  contestatory approach to, 12
  critiques of, 5, 8, 41
  Dworkin on, 70, 71
  Eisgruber on, 70, 71
  methodological approach to, 2, 3, 20, 28
  originalism and, 51, 53, 59, 61
  of racial equity, 245, 249
  skepticism of, 9, 8, 10

Waldron critique of, 38, 39
judiciary. *See also* judicial review
  democracy influenced by, 6, 7
  as guardians of legal process, 5, 8
  role in electoral processes, 6

Kagan, Elena (Justice), 83, 200
Kang, Michael, 8, 89, 236, 284
Kant, Immanuel, 4, 160
  on autonomy, 177, 178
  on free will, 4
  on freedom, 4
  on heteronomy, 177, 178
  on political justice, 4
Karlan, Pamela, 8, 34
  anti-lockup theory and, 77, 82
Kavanagh, Brett (Justice), 83
Kennedy, Anthony (Justice), 83, 267
King, Gary, 236
Klarman, Michael, 48, 49, 216, 218
Kramer, Lawrence, 12, 65, 66, 93
Kuhner, Timothy, 81, 94, 95, 181

Lafont, Christine, 12
Lassiter v. Northampton County, 9, 10, 250, 251, 260
Law's Empire (Dworkin), 68, 134
Lessig, Larry, 81, 94, 95, 174, 179, 180
  on dependence corruption, 183
  on wealth inequality, 182, 184
Leviathan (Hobbes), 176, 196
Levinson, Daryl, 114
Levinson, Sanford, 154
liberalism
  election law and, 13, 14, 308, 309
    synthesis of, 17, 20
  neoliberalism, 189, 191
  Rawls on, egalitarian view of, 13
  "thick" and "thin" concepts of, 40
libertarianism
  campaign finance jurisprudence and, 18, 175
  egalitarianism and, 3, 11
    in electoral procedures, 14, 17
    by legal domain, 17
  election law and, 294–6
living constitutionalism, 62, 63, 73
  as contractualist endeavor, 62
  Dworkin on, 68, 73
  election law and, 94
  judicial discretion and, 64, 67
  judicial pragmatism and, 63, 67
  living originalism as variant of, 64, 65
  moderate, 63, 67

lock-ups. *See also* anti-lockup theory
  anti-fusion laws and, 78, 79
  destabilization of, 78, 80, 81
  representative democracy and, 78, 79
Lomasky, Loren, 4, 5
Luther v. Borden, 127, 135

MacDougall v. Green, 127
Madison, James, 202, 203
majority tyranny, 23, 24, 35
malapportionment, in districting. *See also Baker v. Carr*
  Colegrove v. Green, 120, 122, 125, 128–30, 135
    Equal Protection Clause and, 129, 130
    political question doctrine and, 137, 139
    one-person one-vote doctrine and, 118, 121
Mansbridge, Jane, 245
Marshall, Thurgood (Justice), 83
McConnell, Michael, 22, 68, 69
  on originalism, 56, 57, 61
McConnell v. Federal Election Commission, 87, 94, 95, 158, 166–9
McCubbins, Matthew, 203, 204
McCutcheon v. FEC, 170, 172
McGhee, Eric, 231, 237
minoritarian protection generally. *See also* racial equity
  in election law, 35
  Ely and, 77
Moyn, Samuel, 8
Muirhead, Ross, 204, 205, 207, 296
Muller, Derek, 148, 248

natural law, 97
neoliberalism, 189, 191
Nixon, Richard, 162
Nixon v. Herndon, 126, 129, 216
non-domination, 112
  one-person one-vote doctrine and, 153, 154
Norris, Pippa, 24
Nozick, Robert, 11, 77, 247
  on election law, 292, 294
  on property rights (as analogy to racial equity), 285, 290

Obergefell v. Hodges, 65
O'Connor, Sandra Day (Justice), 265, 266
one-person one-vote doctrine. *See also Baker v. Carr; Gray v. Sanders; Reynolds v. Sims; Wesberry v. Sanders*
  contestation over freedom and, 102, 103
  diversity of, 107, 111
  counterpopular dilemma and, 119, 120, 146, 151, 154, 156
  safe harbor principle, 149, 150
  doctrinal construction of, 141, 146
  election law and, 297
  equipopulous districting, 156, 157
    development of standard for, 141, 144
    doctrinal construction of, 141, 146
    Gerken on, 147
    Hasen on, 147
    normative character of, 151, 156
      equal liberty, 152, 154
      minimal equality, 154, 156
      pure procedural justice, 154, 156
    origins of, 117, 118
      malapportionment and, 118, 121
    political parties and, 213, 214
    Rawls on, 154
originalism, 8, 9, 51
  Baker v. Carr and, 133
  of constitutional clauses, 21
  contestation over freedom and, 102
  counterpopular dilemma and, 55
  critics of, 58, 59
  "dead hand" problem and, 55
  doctrinal foundations of, 60, 61
  Dworkin on, 60
  grant of authority for judges and, 53, 57, 62
  interpretive fidelity and, 22, 61
  judicial review and, 51, 53, 59, 61
  linguistic interpretation of, 57, 62
  McConnell on, 56, 57, 61
  normative interpretation of, 57, 62
  normative theory of, 56
  Rawls and, 59
  Scalia and, 53, 59
Ortiz, Daniel, 35, 164

parties. *See* political parties
partisan gerrymandering, 34, 102, 103, 108, 109, 229–32, 236, 239, 242
  anti-lockup theory and, 81, 82
  victory bonus and, 81
  vote dilution, 20, 127, 231
partisanship
  counterpopular dilemma and, 86
  election law and, 88, 89, 308, 309
  representative democracy and, 87
  on Supreme Court, 83, 89, 291, 292
    attitudinal model for, 84, 87
    in *Bush v. Gore*, 89, 301, 303
    conservative ideologies, 83, 84
    progressive ideologies, 83, 84
    stare decisis principle and, 87, 88
partnership democracy (Dworkin concept), 16
Party Government (Schattschneider), 203

party primaries
  design of, 224, 225
  White Primary cases, 45, 209, 216, 221
Perry, Michael, 21, 133
Persily, Nathaniel, 211, 213
Pettit, Philip, 112, 153, 154
Pildes, Richard, 6, 8, 11, 250, 251
  anti-lockup theory and, 77, 82
  on election law scholarship, 33, 34, 41, 42
Plato, 177
polarization. *See also* hyperpolarization; partisanship
  judicial, 3
Political Liberalism (Rawls), 62
political parties. *See also* partisan gerrymandering; partisanship; party primaries
  anti-factionalism and, 202, 203
  constitutionalization of, 228, 229
  counterpopular dilemma and, 213, 215, 230, 242, 243
  elite capture and, 205, 207
    misappropriation of party power, 206, 207
  extra-constitutional party governance, 200, 202
    during mid-twentieth-century, 203, 205
  Issacharoff on, 211, 213
  Madison on, 202, 203
  one-person one-vote principle and, 213, 214
  Persily on, 211, 213
  as public utilities, 210
  regulation of, 221, 229
    ballot access, 222, 223
    doctrine on, 222, 225
    judicial oversight of, 225, 228
    for party affiliation by voters, 223, 224
political question doctrine, 135, 141
  counterpopular dilemma and, 139
  decontestation under, 139, 141
  separation of powers principle and, 140
Posner, Richard, 63, 67, 175
Powell, Lewis F. (Justice), 244
primaries. *See* party primaries
procedural justice
  Gerken on, 156
  one-person one-vote doctrine and, 154, 156
  Rawls on, 155
progressive ideologies
  autonomous social organization and, 173, 176
  campaign finance and, 173, 176, 178, 185, 189, 191
    political autonomy in, 193, 194
  egalitarian, 95
  on Supreme Court, 83, 84

public reason (Rawls concept), 16, 111, 116, 196, 293
Purcell v. Gonzalez, 306–8

racial equity, in election case law, 19. *See also* Voting Rights Act, *specific cases*
  as concept, 245
  in districting, 252, 256
  expressive harm and, 256
  with conservative Supreme Court, 288, 290
  Fifteenth Amendment and, 19, 42, 43, 245, 249, 259, 262, 264
  Fourteenth Amendment and, 244, 245, 249, 259
  Hasen on, 250, 251
  Issacharoff on, 248
  Jim Crow laws and, 19
  judicial delineation of democratic outcomes, 256, 259
  Nozick on, 285, 290
  philosophical approach to, 282, 290
  racialized gerrymandering and, 74, 76, 248
  Rawls on, 285, 290
  Reconstruction Amendments, 257, 276
  vote dilution and, 251, 256, 257
racial essentialization, 247
Rahman, Sabeel, 81, 180
ranked-choice voting, 23, 24
rational choice institutionalism (Norris concept), 24
Raviv, Adam, 149
Rawls, John, 62, 247, 293
  contractualism and, 13
  on deliberative democracy, 12, 13
  on election law, 292, 294
  interpretivism and, 12, 13
  on liberal democracy, 30
  on liberalism, egalitarian view of, 13
  on liberty, ordering of, 4
  on one-person one-vote doctrine, 154
  originalism and, 59
  on perfect procedural justice, 155
  on property rights (as analogy to racial equity), 285, 290
  on public reason, 16
Raz, Joseph, 5, 6
Reconstruction Amendments, 257, 276
representation reinforcement, 35, 74, 77. *See also* Ely, John Hart
  counterpopular dilemma, 76
  racial gerrymandering, 76
Reynolds v. Sims, 67, 117–19, 121, 141–4
  accommodation for margin of deviation, 144, 146
right of rights, democracy as, 38, 39

Ripstein, Arthur, 68, 69
Roberts, John (Chief Justice), 83
Rodden, Jonathan, 237, 238
Roe v. Wade, 44
Rosenblum, Nancy, 204, 205, 296
Ross, Bertrall, 8, 74–5
Rucho v. Common Cause, 12, 105, 106, 108–10, 134, 135, 200, 238
rule of law
  constituent autonomy and, 5, 6
  contestation over freedom and, 115
  neutral, 5, 6, 37
    Baker v. Carr and, 133
rural entrenchment, 45
Rutledge, Wiley (Justice), 126, 127

Sailors v. Board of Education, 149
Scalia, Antonin (Justice), 53, 59, 83, 108, 109, 158, 200, 311, 312
Schattschneider, E. E., 203, 204
Schumpeter, Joseph, 30
Second Amendment, U.S. Constitution, 107, 108
Segal, Jeffrey, 84, 87, 89
Shaw v. Reno, 255, 256
Shelby County v. Holder, 12, 268, 277–9, 282
Shelley v. Kraemer, 244
Shepherd, Joanna, 89
Sitaraman, Ganesh, 74–5, 180, 181
The Sleeping Sovereign (Tuck), 51, 52
Smiley v. Holm, 123, 124, 129
Smith, Bradley, 186
Smith v. Allwright, 74, 217
social contractarianism, 52
soft money funding, 165, 166
Solum, Lawrence, 62
Sorauf, Frank, 209, 210
Sotomayor, Sonia (Justice), 83
Souter, Steven (Justice), 83
South Carolina v. Katzenbach, 244, 260, 261, 272, 276–9, 282
Sovereign Virtue (Dworkin), 68
Spaeth, Harold, 84, 87, 89
spatial diversity, 240
Spencer, Douglas, 74–5
stare decisis principle, 87, 88
  contestation over freedom and, 105, 106
Stephanopoulos, Nicholas, 8, 24, 34, 43, 189, 211, 212, 309
  on gerrymandering process, 231, 237
  spatial diversity and, 240
Stevens, John Paul (Justice), 83, 158
Stoicism, 176
Strauss, David, 58, 63–5, 67, 94, 113, 114, 163, 164

Sunstein, Cass, 100, 101, 113, 114
The Supreme Court and Election Law (Hasen), 112, 114

Teachout, Zephyr, 94, 95, 170, 174, 179, 180
  on corruption, 188
Tennant v. Jefferson, 145
A Theory of Justice (Rawls), 293
Thomas, Clarence (Justice), 119
Thompson, Dennis, 174
Thornburgh v. Gingles, 265, 266, 269
Tolson, Franita, 279
traditionalism, 64
transcendental, freedom as, 98
Tribe, Laurence, 301
Trump, Donald, 206, 212, 304, 308
Tuck, Richard, 36, 51, 52
Tushnet, Mark, 136
Two Concepts of Liberty (Berlin), 7
tyranny. *See* majority tyranny

Universal Declaration of Human Rights, 30
U.S. v. Classic, 217

veil of ignorance, 293
Vieth v. Jubelirer, 235, 236
vote dilution, 20, 127, 231
  under Equal Protection Clause, 251, 256, 257
  Gerken on, 256, 257
  racial equity and, 251, 256, 257
voter ID laws, 31, 32
voter suppression, 304, 308. *See also Brnovich v. Democratic National Committee; Crawford v. Marion County; Husted v. Randolph Institute*
Voting Rights Act (VRA) (1965), race protections under, 19, 78, 79, 259, 282
  Elections Clause and, 270, 271
  historical context of, 259, 261
  judicial legacy of, 248, 249
  Katzenbach v. Morgan, 260, 272, 276–9, 282
  preclearance requirements, 272, 282
    early success of, 272, 275
    formalism and, 278, 282
    genesis of, 272, 275
    nullification of, 277, 278
  Section 2, 85, 245, 247, 261, 272
    electoral arrangements in, 266
    under Fifteenth Amendment, 262, 264
    future applications for, 268, 270
    institutional competence under, 270, 272
    narrow conception of discrimination in, 264, 268

Section 4, 245
Section 5, 245, 247
   as superstatute, 260

Waldron, Jeremy, 7, 8
   critique of judicial review, 38, 39
Warren, Earl (Chief Justice), 117, 119, 244
wealth inequality, campaign finance
       jurisprudence and, 182, 184, 189, 191

Weinrib, Ernest, 312
Wesberry v. Sanders, 118, 121, 141–3
Whitcomb v. Chavis, 253
White Primary cases, 45, 209, 216, 221
White v. Regester, 253–5, 262, 265
Whittington, Keith, 53
Williams v. Rhodes, 222, 223
Wood v. Broom, 124, 125
Wright, J. Skelly, 60

Ingram Content Group UK Ltd.
Milton Keynes UK
UKHW022016110723
424979UK00016B/137